Wingfield

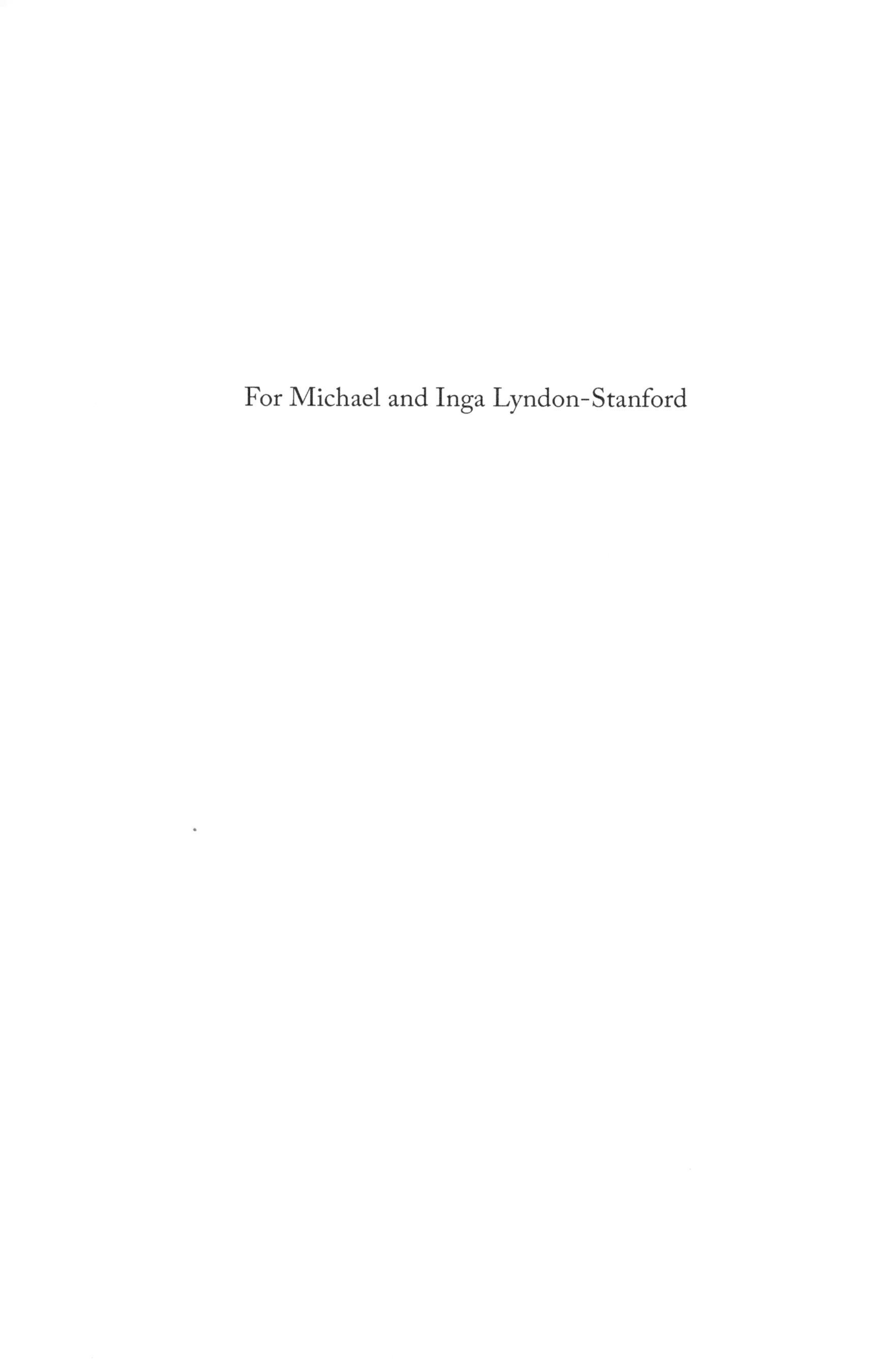

For Michael and Inga Lyndon-Stanford

Wingfield

Suffolk's Forgotten Castle

Elaine Murphy

First published 2021 by Poppyland Publishing, Lowestoft, NR32 3BB
www.poppyland.co.uk

ISBN 978 1 909796 88 1

Designed and typeset in 12 on 14 pt Caslon Pro.

Printed by Ashford Colour Press.

Also by Elaine Murphy

The Moated Grange
A history of south Norfolk through the story of one home, 1300–2000
2015
Book Publishers Guild, Hove.

Monks Hall
The History of a Waveney Valley Manor
2018
Poppyland Publishing, Lowestoft.

Suffolk Scene
A Book of Description and Adventure
(21st century commentary by author)
2019
Poppyland Publishing, Lowestoft.

front cover: Wingfield Castle Gatehouse, 2019, photographed by the author.

Contents

1. Map of Suffolk showing places in the book.

Contains Ordnance Survey data © Crown copyright and database right 2010-19

Acknowledgements

The willing support of Michael and Inga Lyndon-Stanford was invaluable to me in writing this book. They gave me wonderful access to the property and dug out from their own personal archives a wealth of material that made my task so much easier. Michael generously commented on early drafts and has been a source of endless well-informed encouragement. I thank them wholeheartedly and I hope they will not be disappointed in the result.

Thanks must go secondly to Professor Robert Liddiard, who surely should be called Professor in Castleography. He has been so liberal with his assistance and has written a foreword that adds helpfully to the text.

Much of the writing was done during the first waves of the pandemic of 2020, when the county archives and museums were closed. Nevertheless some archivists and librarians went above and beyond their remit to assist me and I want especially to thank Martin Taylor, the Hull City Archivist and Dr Tony Trowles of Westminster Abbey Library. Diana Spelman helped me with her palaeographic skills in deciphering some early accounts and archival material relating to the de la Pole family. I also owe gratitude to Ian Riley and Dennis Reeves of the Liverpool Scottish Regimental Museum Trust whose enthusiastic, detailed research enabled me to identify the Scottish regiment billeted at the castle during the Second World War. Philip Aitkens, a specialist architect in historic buildings, was exceptionally helpful in helping me explore the parts of the castle that are currently unlisted.

Thanks too to several local people, especially Gwyn Turrell and Charles Michell, who knew the castle during the tenure of Graham Baron Ash and had detailed memories of that interesting man. David Groom, whom I 'met' through the genealogy sites, was able to supply information about his father and grandfather's sojourn at the Castle.

My publisher Gareth Davies at Poppyland was, characteristically, a source of laid-back unflappable encouragement, reassuringly unfazed by the impact of the pandemic. Janet Davies painstakingly undertook the tedious task of copy editing the final manuscript, improving it substantially, for which I am indebted. My heartfelt thanks too to John Murphy for his generous and patient reading of a first draft. Finally, as always, my grateful appreciation to Mike Robb, constant source of expertise on fickle technology and patient travelling companion while I searched for long dead de la Poles.

Elaine Murphy, September 2021.

Foreword

I first visited Wingfield over fifteen years ago when I had a rare chance to spend a few hours at the castle. From even the briefest inspection of the fabric it was clear to me that the building's development was complicated and would repay further study. As it was my first time in the village I also took the opportunity to visit the church and the site of the adjacent medieval college and I vividly remember thinking that it would be a worthwhile undertaking to investigate the broader history of the place.

Little did I know then that some years later I would find myself involved in a university project charged with creating 3D computer reconstructions of both castle and college. Here was an opportunity to see if we could push our understanding of medieval Wingfield a little further. The 'Wingfield Project' as it came to be known, was not an academic research project *per se*; rather, the historical investigations it undertook were intended to help make the digital reconstructions as accurate as possible. But in the process new light was shed on the buildings and in turn on the lives and times of the principal figures associated with their history. The work undertaken by the project laid the foundations for a collection of essays on the college edited by Peter Bloore and Edward Martin, published by Boydell and Brewer in 2015.

But despite these successes, from my point of view the project was at times frustrating. As we found out time and again the documentation associated with medieval Wingfield was sparse, the archaeological and architectural remains of castle and college often raised more questions than answers and by concentrating on the Middle Ages we knew we were only looking at one small, albeit important, part of a longer history. During the project I often found myself wishing that someone had drawn together the various strands of the castle's history into a single narrative.

For this reason I was delighted to find out that Elaine Murphy was contemplating just such a project. Due warnings and caveats were given about the evidential perils, but with two books on the region's historic buildings already under her belt I was confident that I would learn a great deal. This proved to be the case almost on the first page as I discovered that Wingfield was the inspiration for the setting of Dodie Smith's *I Capture the Castle.* Not only had Wingfield sprung another surprise on me, but I could not help but think that the impression of the building given in the novel was one of which the builder, Michael de la Pole, 1st earl of Suffolk, would have approved.

As a monument Wingfield belongs to a clutch of late fourteenth-century castles that must be seen in the context of a society in turmoil. Climatic deterioration, foreign war, power struggles at the heart of government and popular revolt resulting from the longer-term effects of epidemic disease all made for a time sometimes labelled 'apocalypse then'. But periods of instability also bring opportunities, with the rise of the de la Pole family from Hull merchants to the English nobility a case in point. Wingfield castle is a monument to shrewd opportunism and skilful enterprise in a time of turbulence. In its architecture we undoubtedly see the hand of the patron. While contemporaries such as Edward Dallingridge in Sussex and John Cobham in Kent chose overtly militaristic designs for their castles at Bodiam and Cooling respectively, Wingfield is more subdued in its outward architectural appearance, with older forms for the window tracery and with decorative flushwork on the gatehouse more usually seen on ecclesiastical buildings. Here perhaps we see the de la Poles negotiating their way up the social ladder with a castle that is both assertive and demonstrative, but at the same time decorative and almost nostalgic. New authority cloaked in the mantle of chivalric longevity was conceivably what a new earl with mercantile origins wished to project to a regional society whose peasantry had attempted to violently overthrow the social order just a few years before.

As this meticulously researched book sets out, from the late fourteenth to the sixteenth centuries Wingfield castle was a building known to figures of national importance. Thereafter its importance waned. But while the medieval and Tudor history is what naturally draws attention, this book gives equal weight to later centuries. The post-medieval use as a minor residence, a farm and numerous periods of absenteeism might be somewhat unglamorous but are just as important to the story of the castle and crucial to our understanding of the surviving remains. We must also appreciate that much of the fabric as we see it today is the result of restoration in the post-war period, which here is given the most thorough treatment to date.

Alongside the remains of former monastic houses and our cathedrals and parish churches, castles are perhaps the most tangible material legacy of the Middle Ages. They continue to fascinate and captivate audiences of all ages. As a child castles were for Baroness Murphy grand mansions and dream homes. In my case, a boy brought up with tales of knights and siege engines, I tended to see only murder holes and arrow loops. Only much later did I discover that being a mansion was as much about the image as the battlements and some of these may not have been so utilitarian as I once imagined. Wingfield does not fit the picture of the grim fortress of some story books, but it is a castle nonetheless. And it is one that remains beguiling. Like many historic buildings it keeps some of its history and secrets to itself, but I wish this book had been available when the Wingfield project was ongoing as it would have proved invaluable.

Professor Robert Liddiard
School of History, University of East Anglia, 2021.

2. Illustration from *I Capture the Castle*, by Dodie Smith, drawing by Ruth Steed from a sketch by Dodie Smith, 1948.

Introduction

"And THIS is the famous sink". The chatelaine of Wingfield Castle pointed to an early twentieth century 'butler's' sink. I gazed at the one feature in the impressive Tudor kitchen of Wingfield Castle that I probably wouldn't have noticed, surrounded as I was by the compelling architecture of centuries long past. 'I write this sitting in the kitchen sink,' Dodie Smith's famous opening line of *I Capture the Castle*, is surely one of the most striking first lines in modern British fiction.[1]

The tale is of two young sisters living with their impoverished writer father and exotically fey stepmother in a house built into the side of a semi-ruined castle called Godsend. The description is unmistakably of Wingfield Castle.

> Then suddenly we drove out into the open and there it was - but not the lonely tower on a hill that we had been searching for; what we saw was quite a large castle built on level ground... How beautiful it looked in the late afternoon light! I can still recapture that first glimpse - see the sheer grey stone walls and towers against the pale yellow sky, the reflected castle stretching towards us on the brimming moat, the floating patches of emerald green water-weed. No breath of wind ruffled the looking glass water, no sound of any kind came to us. Our excited voices only made the castle seem more silent.
>
> How well I remember that run through the stillness, the smell of wet stone and wet weeds as we crossed the bridge, the moment of excitement before we stepped in at the little door. Once through we were in the cool dimness of the gatehouse passage. That was where I first *felt* the castle - it is the place where one is most conscious of the great weight of stone above and around one...we ran through to the daylight and stopped dead.
>
> On our left instead of grey walls and towers we had been expecting was a long house of whitewashed plaster and herringbone brick, veined by weather-bleached wood. It had all sorts of odd little latticed windows, bright gold from the sunset and the attic gable looked as if it might fall forward at any minute.

3. Gatehouse and south curtain wall, Wingfield Castle, etching by William Byrne, 1780 after a watercolour by Thomas Hearne (shown p. 277).

Wingfield gatehouse towers are not round. There is no herringbone brick in the Tudor house. But Smith has captured this bewitching castle's compelling charm and the delightful surprises that await the visitor as the hidden house emerges from behind the grey flint facade. Dodie Smith had visited Wingfield in the 1930s and been enchanted with 'the ramshackle Victorian interior' and then revisited in the late 1940s, disappointed to find that under the ownership of Graham Baron Ash 'it had become frighteningly grand'.[2] Of course she was writing a novel and even castles must bend to the imperative of plot. Other castles and grand Suffolk houses sneaked in to the description too but we can forgive that; after all, the high gable still looks as if it might tumble forward.

I first came across Wingfield Castle nearly fifty years ago, while hunting for the village pub that is now *The de la Pole Arms*. The gatehouse towers and south wall were then still clearly visible from the road running across Wingfield Green, giving a purposefully impressive view. Now sadly a privacy mound obscures the view and some recently arrived locals do not even know the castle is there. Back then, one could pause to enjoy a tantalising, evocative glimpse of beautifully restored fourteenth century walls and a solid westerly wall of cream render above a weedy moat, all keeping company on the Green with some nondescript cottages and a couple of rather mangy piebald Romany horses. The house was still occupied by Baron Ash (1889–1980), not a peer of the realm, his baptismal second name reflected his parents' prescient omen of his future grandeur.

4. Jerningham House, within Wingfield Castle, photo, c1950.

I will confess I hankered after this castle, and some years later when it came up for sale we seriously considered buying. The new owners had stayed for only a very short while and I wondered if they had succumbed to the realisation, as their predecessors had, that this grand old manor needed more than admiration, it needed solid on-going investment, a lifetime's commitment.

We first viewed the interior in mid-winter, when the north-easterlies blow directly across the Suffolk clay plateau keening the bones. The owners were huddled in the kitchen, admittedly the size of a bungalow, the only room that was heated. The young weekend Londoners were bundled up in multiple layers and gloves and we did not take ours off as we all drank coffee and they tried to convince us what a marvellous investment it would be. Even I, an incorrigible enthusiast for ancient houses, could see that was not going to be the case but like any enraptured suitor was prepared to overlook certain glaring disadvantages, such as that living there might be horribly uncomfortable while the necessary tens of thousands were spent on rehabilitation. The young couple were sleeping, eating, camping with an open fire big enough to roast an ox but sucking a fearsome draught under the doorways. Nowadays I go back to dine with good friends who have treasured this place for more than thirty years and I marvel at the transformation into comfortable family home.

We have often talked about the history of the castle. My friends complain, and rightly so, that no-one has ever written about the history of this castle that didn't stop when the de la Pole family left in the early sixteenth century. In fact they didn't so much leave as had the property prised off them. The de la Pole family that built and owned the fortified manor for over a hundred years played a central role in the great events that shaped England. Their story, from tradesmen to the highest offices of state over six generations between 1290 and 1525, is evidence of the dangers of impellent ambition in those violent times but also the curse of choosing the losing side. Not until the last of them was dead could Henry VIII rest easy that the last Yorkist pretender to the throne was gone. If Richard III had not been defeated at Bosworth Field, the story may have worked out differently. Ultimately the family failed, so they have been consigned to footnotes in most histories. History after all is written by the victors, rarely by the vanquished. Even so, many of the men and women associated with Wingfield would be remarkable people in any epoch. They deserve a narrative that links them to this Suffolk soil.

The story of Wingfield continued long after the last de la Pole was executed for treason. Wingfield Castle was home, or at least one home, to some of the most interesting characters of their generations; Charles Brandon, Henry VIII's best friend and his wife, Mary, the king's sister; Sir Henry Jerningham, whose swift intervention ensured Mary I's accession; the Royalist Catelyn family who almost lost everything in the Civil War; the wealthy Berners family and then the Adairs of Flixton, landlords to a social miscellany of farming tenants. Finally the devoted grandee who did so much to bring the spirit of chivalry and romanticism back to the castle, Baron Ash, was the first of a series of twentieth century owners who bought the castle for love, not for the farming estate that surrounds it.

The aim of this book is to show how the fortified manor house and estate of the late fourteenth century survived to take on new roles as each century dawned, to connect the fourteenth century builder Michael de la Pole through the ages to Dodie Smith's imagined Castle of Godsend. The story of a dwelling must include something about the bricks and mortar, or in this case flint, stone and rubble, and its development, that's the nuts and bolts of the narrative. Mostly though it is a story of the people who lived and worked here, owned or rented the house, farmed the land, were shaped by the terrain and the economic, political and religious context of their times. Above all, what we learn should inform local history and add to an understanding of the region we live in and how it fitted into the grander scheme of England's story.

Notes

1 Smith, D., 1949, *I Capture the Castle*, William Heinemann, London. The novel sold well over a million copies and is still in print. Dodie Smith is best known for her story *The One Hundred and One Dalmatians* made into a Disney film.

2 Grove, V. ,1996, *Dear Dodie, the life of Dodie Smith*, Chatto and Windus, London, pp. 224, 267.

A Castle Takes Shape, 1385

5. Wingfield Castle gatehouse, 2019.

A Licence to Crenellate. Michael de la Pole was riding high in 1385. He was about fifty-four years old, at the height of his political influence and in favour with the eighteen year old king, Richard II. He had been appointed Chancellor only two years earlier and was also the king's chief advisor, one of a handful of royal confidants. Michael had risen further and faster than any man in England. For this moment at least, he was one of the most powerful men in the land.

Yet, if Michael was sensitive to the nuances of other men's attitude towards him, he would have realised he was not the most popular of men with many of the nobility or with parliament. Resentments deepened when in September 1385 he was created earl of Suffolk and acquired a grant of most of the East

Anglian lands that went with the old lapsed Ufford family title of Suffolk. Michael de la Pole had achieved nobility, which his wealthy father had failed to do and while Michael was by no means as rich as some of the more ancient titled families with whom he mixed, he had just about enough to sustain a household and entourage fit for an earldom. The new additional grants to his already substantial estates finally gave him enough money to build outward symbols of his success.[1]

On 27 April that year Michael was granted by the king a licence to crenellate his mansion house in Wingfield and two other properties on manors he owned nearby in Suffolk.[2] Within two years, the simmering resentments of more established courtiers about Michael's effective control of the king would lead to his spectacular fall. But for the moment let us share in Michael's pleasure at his sensational success as he and his wife Katherine plan their new fortified manor house.

The Choice of Wingfield. Michael chose Wingfield for obvious reasons. He, Katherine and their children already had a home there, Katherine having inherited property from her father Sir John Wingfield. The sixty-nine acres of land, next to an extensive green, was ideal for creating a hunting deer park. More importantly, twenty years earlier, her father had established a chantry college of secular priests, Wingfield College, which provided an opportunity to display status and power through patronage. Chantry colleges were popular means by which wealthy patrons provided an insurance policy of prayers and masses to shorten time spent in purgatory for relatives, patrons and of course themselves.

The wording of the licence acknowledged Michael's plan to enclose the land that went with the three mansions to create deer parks:-

> Michael de la Pole the elder, that he and his heirs may at pleasure crenellate a place or places in the mansion-houses of their manors of Wyngefeld, Sternefeld and Huntyngfeld, co. Suffolk, with stone and lime or paling of timber, and also enclose all their woods, lands, meadows and pastures several in Wyngefeld, Stradebrook and Sternefeld, co. Suffolk which are without the metes of the forest, and impark the same. [3]

The manors of Sternfield and Huntingfield had been part of the extensive property portfolio brought to the de la Poles' marriage from Katherine's inheritance from her father. But neither estate had the *caché* of Wingfield. In Sternfield there were two medieval manors in the parish, Mandeville's Manor and Virlies or Glanville's manor. Copinger suggested in the nineteenth century that the licence to crenellate was applied to Virlies manor, which seems to be the smaller manor with a trapezoidal moated site detectable by crop marks and the eye of faith.[4] Sternfield Hall has a wing of late sixteenth century date and could be the site of a medieval manor house. This may well be the Virlies Manor House site. Is it possible the trapezoidal moat was laid out by the de la Poles, started but not finished?

In Huntingfield however there is good evidence that the old hall manor house dated from before the date of the licence and was a fortified house. There is an early eighteenth century print that shows the old hall, given by the owners of Huntingfield Old Rectory to Eric Sandon, the architectural historian, in the late 1970s.[5] It was published by Sandon and copied by Emery for his magisterial work on Medieval English Houses but the print is now apparently lost.[6] It shows clearly a house with towers and battlements, so it seems that Michael may have activated his plans for Huntingfield. The medieval house was destroyed in the eighteenth century.

Michael had then several houses in close proximity, common among wealthy medieval families. A large family of sons and daughters required a good legacy of property for the next generation but these houses also provided a lodging

6. Early eighteenth century print of Huntingfield Old Hall.

place to stay while supervising the estate bailiffs managing the manorial demesne and tenanted land. Families moved from property to property in a kind of rotation although they of course had their favourite homes where they spent more time.

Michael and Katherine had four sons and two daughters who survived infancy; the eldest, also Michael, born about 1361, was already 24 years old when his father decided to fortify his manor houses. A second son Thomas was born about 1363, a third named Richard we know of from his burial in Wingfield in 1403 and a fourth, John, was also buried in Wingfield in 1415.[7] Their daughters Anne and Margaret completed the family. A modern fortified manor house would be a fine family base for any of them. But it seems possible that events moved too fast for plans for Sternfield and Huntingfield to be implemented in full.

The meaning of a licence to crenellate. A licence to crenellate is not a straightforward permit for a building to be fortified. In medieval feudal society, the licence was used both by king and recipient as a mutual recognition of someone having acquired lordly stature in the fluid hierarchy below the king. It carried the extra cachet of royal recognition, acknowledgement and commendation. The king's right as overlord to license was a right to grant, not to refuse, permission to crenellate. It was not in reality necessary to obtain a licence to crenellate to erect a fortified building. There was little chance of interference by royal officials. A licence was however prestigious and could be had for the asking only if the petitioner had achieved a certain status.

Fortifications were not restricted by law but the cost of building an apparently impregnable solid stone, brick or flint mansion was high. A fortified building exuded a show of strength and impregnability to the local populace, rather like the gated communities of middle class enclaves do today. Unlike other royal patronage, licences to crenellate conferred no fiscal or other financial advantage but they were as eagerly sought by the socially ambitious as any lucrative privilege. We should though beware giving modern meaning to the medieval use of the term 'licence'. Transcription and translations of the original documents often date to the nineteenth or early twentieth centuries. Licentia is best translated as 'freedom to', rather than 'permission to.'[8]

The building that often, but not always, resulted from these licences had some show of fortification, like battlements, moats and gatehouses. Wingfield Castle, built on a flat plain with no significant geographical advantage against a serious invasion, nevertheless had some serious secure construction. The building could be used defensively if necessary, if not against an army then at least against thieving insurgents, a defence against casual burglary and thuggery.[9] The lower social orders organised themselves remarkably effectively in the Great Rebellion, or 'Peasants Revolt' of 1381; they had no trouble in ransacking castles and palaces. Well-organised, belligerent locals seem unlikely to have been put off by the odd tower or two if in an invasive, destructive mood but most thieves and bandits would be deterred.[10] The castle was and is, the most imposing structure in the vicinity. The deer park, gardens and cultivated fields provided some social distance from the villages nearby that set the occupants and their retainers apart from ordinary folk. It was after all a family home where women and children lived and needed to feel secure.

The historian Charles Coulson pointed out that many later fourteenth century grants were to relatively minor knights for quite small manor houses, many of which could only have had token fortification.[11] Applications to crenellate soared in perilous times, when wealthy men had good reason to want to protect themselves. Marauding bands in the early years of the fourteenth century were followed by deterioration of public order under extreme population pressure in the 1330s and 1340s and in 1381 civil order broke down spectacularly during the terrifying Great Rebellion.[12]

The events of 1381 may well have been significant for Michael de la Pole's decision to make more secure his main family home. Tellingly, Michael's opening speech as the new Chancellor of England in the parliament called to Westminster in October 1383 was about the causes of the insurrection.[13] It was a speech designed to warn the assembled 'gentils' that disobedience to the king's local agents could lead to rebellion against the king himself if the causes of the disobedience were not addressed. There is no evidence that Michael's own manor house was attacked during the week's bloody rising in the summer of 1381 but Mettingham Castle fourteen miles away up the Waveney Valley had been ransacked and looted.

Built and owned by the Norwich family, in 1381 Mettingham Castle was under the trusteeship of Catherine de Brewse, who had left the castle in the custody of agents while settling into a nunnery. A rebel army, five hundred strong, local men from Waveney Valley villages, attacked and ransacked the castle on Tuesday 18 June, stealing £1,100 worth of gold, silver and other valuables but also charters, contracts, official title documents and court rolls, the symbols both of ownership and servitude that the rebels targeted with especial fury.[14]

7. Mettingham Castle, from an 18th century print, c1735.

Mettingham Castle may have been built by a close relative of Michael. His mother, Katherine 'of Norwich', was possibly the daughter of Walter of Norwich, whose son Sir John of Norwich founded Mettingham Castle in 1342. There are significant similarities between the construction of Mettingham and Wingfield that hint that Michael de la Pole's new building at Wingfield was an attempt to improve on what his uncle had built up the road. Katherine Norwich's connections with East Anglia may also have added weight to her son's marriage into the Wingfield family, although his direct connections to Sir John Wingfield were probably more important.

Well, this all sounds plausible but there is in fact no documentary evidence that Katherine of Norwich was the daughter of Walter of Norwich. She could have been from a different Norwich family entirely. Katherine of Norwich appears not to have been an heiress and if she had been Walter's daughter she would surely have brought substantial land to the marriage, of which there is no record. We do not know for sure where she came from. Nevertheless, events of 1381, including the murder of the locally born Simon Sudbury, Archbishop of Canterbury, the slaughter nearby of Sir John Cavendish, Chief Justice of the Kings Bench, the murder of the Prior of the Abbey of Bury St Edmunds and the hacking to death of popular Sir Robert Salle in Norwich must have been a factor in Michael's desire for a secure base for his family. The final structure though may not have provided the defensive certainty that Michael had originally planned.

Castle or Fortified Manor House? From Norman times, castles were always more than defensive structures. They were centres of administration and justice, of land and property. They were expressions of social status where the latest fashions in architecture and the arts reflected the medieval preoccupation with honour, chivalry and courtly romance. They were also family homes, a place where the retinue of servants and administrators worked and often lived, where prestigious visitors could be accommodated and social gatherings held. They were an imposing local symbol of prestige and power at a time when public display and family lineage was important.[15]

As the desire for massive defensive structures waned, new castles emerged that were in truth large manor houses but the old forms, battlements, towers, drawbridges and moats retained meaning and were not to be lightly given up even when their usefulness had declined.[16] Military might was the guiding aspiration of early medieval society and symbols of military prowess had meaning far beyond the obvious, symbolizing status, honour, a continuity with a glorious legendary past. These new castles no longer hosted a military base, indeed earlier residential castles rarely had standing troops, but nevertheless were a potent demonstration of where power lay in the local economy. And as we have seen, rebellious outbursts from the local population were not uncommon in the late fourteenth century. I will return to this theme of when is a castle a 'real castle' in the last chapter. For now I am going to take John Goodall's excellent definition. 'A castle is the residence of a lord made imposing through the architectural trappings of fortification, be they functional or decorative.'[17] If it looks like a castle, well it is a castle! And if this is reminiscent of Humpty Dumpty's scornful remark to Lewis Carroll's Alice 'When I use a word,' 'it means just what I choose it to mean', then so be it.[18]

Why did de la Pole choose this particular site for his castle in Wingfield? The precise location of a castle tells us a good deal about the function of the community of the castle and its park. Wingfield lies towards the northern edge of the clay till plateau in north Suffolk, a flat landscape with little natural drainage. The land is still waterlogged in a wet winter if not artificially drained, unsuitable in the middle ages for arable cultivation. There were small areas with better drainage locally, where the land slopes down to the River Waveney and to streams such as the Dove. There is evidence that these slopes provided some shared common fields in late medieval days. Oddly though, Wingfield Castle is not on one of these good growing areas, it is sited on less good soil.

Like other castles in north Suffolk, such as Bungay, Mettingham, Haughley and Framlingham, Wingfield was sited right next to a large green. Forty acre

Wingfield Green is just south of another large green, Syleham Great Green. Up until the eighteenth century there was a sizeable wooded area called Wingfield Park, the last remaining wooded area in the vicinity that in Norman times would originally have covered the whole plateau. We know that in the Jerninghams' time, in 1597, four hundred oaks and fourteen elms were sold from Wingfield Park, presumably felled for timber and bark.[19]

Castles and fortified manor houses are often constructed over existing seigneurial houses and these were usually built where the greater population was settled, that is around the commons edge, where new village settlements and farms grew up beside the common grazing land.[20] Quite apart from the proximity to the main Wingfield common and population, there are some obvious reasons for Michael choosing the site near the green and that is simply because they already occupied the site. Katherine had inherited a home and land there from her father Sir John Wingfield, which eventually passed to her on the death of her mother in 1375. The sixty-nine acres of land on which the castle sits were held directly from the king as overlord; it had prestige. The land was also ideal for creating a hunting deer park without compromising local agricultural effort.

The boggy plateau may not be ideal for arable farming but it is excellent for creating status-sized moats and fishponds, lined with clay. They readily stay full with seepage from a high water table in an area of relatively little rainfall, although, as we will see later, keeping the eastern fishpond full may have required some engineering. Edward Martin, in his landscape history of Wingfield, has pointed out that the primary settlement in Wingfield around the date of the Conquest was probably where Wingfield College was sited in 1362, perhaps constructed on the foundations of the original manor hall of the de Brewse family, a building in close proximity to St Andrew's church, which later provided the chapel for the college.[21] The old hall and church are sited on rather better land than the castle, being adjacent to the stream that provided the main village water supply. Indeed the stream is still running through the farmland near the College to drain into the River Waveney a couple of miles north.

Wingfield manor, or at least the one belonging to Sir Richard de Brewse, had been transferred in 1357 to the five trustees of the estate of Sir John Wingfield.[22] The transfer was to be effected after the death of Sir Richard's son's wife, Katherine de Brewse, probably by then a childless young widow, who was to retain the property for her lifetime. Soon after, in 1359, the manors of Stradbroke and Wingfield were settled on Sir John of Wingfield and Eleanor

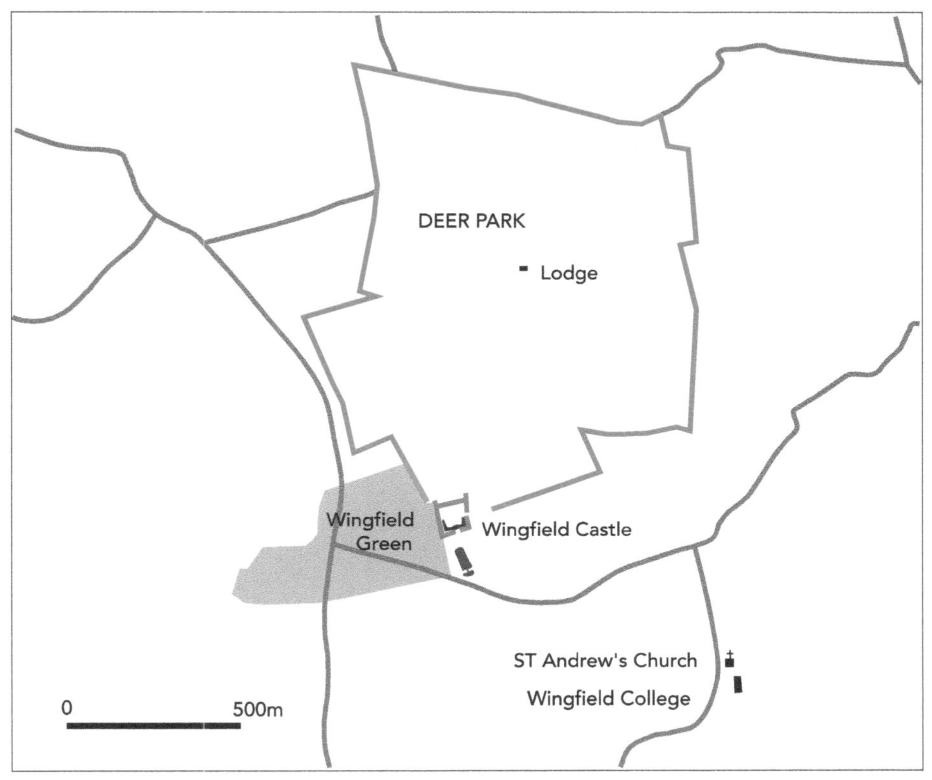

8. Suggested map of Wingfield Castle deer park and possible lodge (after R.Liddiard.)*

his wife by the Brewse Trustees and afterwards were to go to the Wingfield's daughter Katherine, who was by 1359 the wife of Michael de la Pole.[23]

Edward Martin has suggested that Katherine de Brewse, the young widow of Richard de Brewse and Katherine the wife of Michael de la Pole may have been one and the same person.[24] This would explain why the Brewse trustees so readily settled the Wingfield lands on the Wingfield family and how Katherine converted her lifetime interest in the manor to an inheritance for her children in perpetuity. It is an attractive explanation for the continuing intertwining of the names of the de Brewse family and the Wingfields. For example, the de Brewse were named in the list of souls to be prayed for at Wingfield College chantry chapel and de Brewse family silver was itemised in the bequests of Sir Thomas Wingfield (Sir John's brother) in 1378.[25] The argument against this is

* Liddiard, Robert. 2015 Reconstructing Wingfield Castle, pp. 77-95 in Bloore Peter and Martin, Edward (Eds) Wingfield College and its Patrons, Boydell Press, Woodbridge.

that Katherine is always described as 'de Wingfield' and never as a widow but this could be because of the exceptional status of her father.

The donation of property for Wingfield College. Prior to 1357, Sir John de Wingfield and his family were not in possession of the main manor of Wingfield. Their eventual acquisition seems to have been in connection with Sir John's wish to found a Chantry College, acquiring the Brewse's manor house site for the college. John's ancestors may have served the more powerful de Brewse family in the thirteenth century and family connections were maintained.[26] After John died in 1361, his widow Eleanor carried out her husband's wishes to build the chantry chapel in Wingfield church, gave a hundred and seventy acres of land, a messuage (a dwelling house and its associated land and property), five acres of meadow, twenty-four acres of pasture, two acres of wood and twelve shillings of rent in Wingfield, Esham [now Earsham Street], Fressingfield and Weybread together with the advowsons, that is the gift of the church livings, of Wingfield, Stradbroke, Syleham and Esham Chapel.[27]

The Frumbald Fee. Having donated this excellent land and house near the stream to the purposes of Wingfield College, Eleanor Wingfield then needed another home nearby to accommodate herself, her daughter Katherine and her son-in-law Michael. There was other land in Wingfield next to Syleham Green in the possession of the Wingfield family, sixty-nine acres acquired in a rather suspect fashion by John de Wingfield's grandfather, also John, in c1270. This part of Wingfield was called Frumbald's Manor, named in perpetuity after its original owner, Frumbald (or Fromund) le Flemyng. [The manor is variously called Frumbald's Frombald's, even Trumbold's]. It seems that this land was 'held in chief' from the Crown, that is, there was no intervening magnate who could impose service demands or rents. That in itself was a desirable attribute and it also had a certain caché of royal connection. Although the acquisition of the land was agreed between Fromund/Frumbald and Wingfield, neither consulted the Crown nor sought permission. In 1326, the later John of Wingfield sought and was granted a pardon for this oversight.[28]

Perhaps not surprisingly the Frumbald family felt aggrieved by a pardon being granted to Wingfield for his outright land grab. Believing no doubt that their grandfather had been coerced into an arrangement, William Frombald, parson of Grundisburgh, petitioned the Crown to complain that his grandfather purchased rents and services in Wingfield which ought to have descended to him following the death of his father. At his father's death, because the rents and services were held in chief of the king, 'he entered and held them until the king granted them to John de Wingfield of which he is now seised.' Frombald requests remedy so that he can enjoy the right of the services which ought to have descended to him after the death of his father.[29]

The Wingfields had tenure of the land and were not giving it up. In 1362-63, shortly after her husband's death Eleanor Wingfield engaged Richard Damondevill as trustee to look after the sixty-nine acres of 'Fromondeland', securing it against envious local predators.[30]

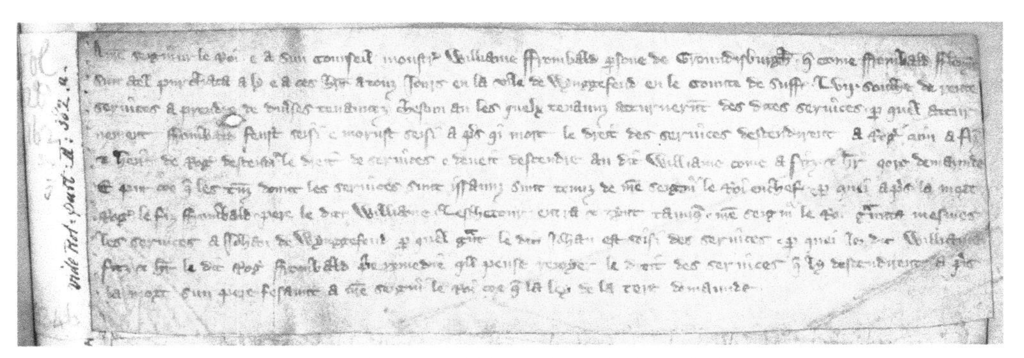

9. Petition by William Frombold, c1326.

On Eleanor Wingfield's death in 1375, these sixty-nine acres passed to her daughter Katherine and her husband Michael de la Pole, who took back possession of the land. Edward Martin has suggested that Sir John Wingfield and his wife may have built their main home on this land, and created a building which was later converted into the castle.[31] Another explanation is that Michael and Katherine decided to create a home there after 1375 and built the house that was to be crenellated officially a decade later.

The three manors of Wingfield. The land on which the castle was built, Frumbald's sixty-nine acres, was part of one of the three medieval manors of Wingfield, and while there is some confusion in the literature, Wingfield Castle manor is one and the same with Wingfield Frumbalds Manor. The de la Pole family eventually procured all the manors around Wingfield, including Syleham Comitis, Fressingfield, Stradbroke, Hoxne, Horham and many further afield in Suffolk, many of them first owned by Sir John Wingfield. The Wingfield family probably first held a manor and hall south of the Church/College complex called Old Wingfield Hall, where the southern part of a small sub-square moat still survives, although the house extant today is much later. Old Wingfield Hall was owned by Sir Richard de Brewse in 1275 and probably later by the Wingfields. The old hall manor had been absorbed into the wider de la Pole estates by 1408. It seems likely that the de la Poles abandoned Old Wingfield Hall when they built their new manor hall at Frumbald's. The third small manor in Wingfield was based at Chickering Hall and remained a separate manor until the twentieth century. Nevertheless it was in the ownership of the de la Pole family from the late fourteenth century, acquired from the de Chickering family.

Wingfield became one of Michael de la Pole's main homes when he married Katherine Wingfield in about 1360. He retained his strong roots and affection for Hull, the town of his birth and old family home but East Anglia became the base of his extensive land ownership and regional influence, and was to remain his descendants' home for one hundred and fifty years.

Who was Michael de la Pole? Where had he come from? His castle is not large, nor particularly ostentatious by the standards of his day, given his personal significance and influence on national events. His home tells us something about his character and priorities and so, before we consider his life story, let us look more closely at the castle itself.

Notes

1 Petitions to the King. Petitioners: Michael de la Pole, Earl of Suffolk. 8 September 1385. TNA SC 8/251/12507.
2 Calendar of the Patent Rolls 1381-5 Richard II Pt II, London 1887, 555. Transcription by Lyte, H.C. Maxwell (ed), 1897.
3 Ibid.
4 Copinger W. A., 1909, *The Manors of Suffolk Vol 5* Taylor, Garnett Evans, Manchester. Sterfield, *Manor of Virlies or Glanville* p. 172. Online at https://archive.org/details/manorsofsuffolkn05copiuoft/page/n5 [accessed 8 June 2019].
5 Sandon, E., 1977, *Suffolk Houses: a Study of Domestic Architecture*, Baron, Woodbridge, p. 189.
6 Emery, A., 2000, *Greater Medieval Houses of England and Wales Vol II East Anglia, Central England and Wales*, Cambridge University Press, p. 117.
7 Napier, H. A., 1858, *Historical Notices of the Parishes of Swyncombe and Ewelme in the County of Oxford*, published Oxford, appendix II, de la Pole pp, 314-315. John de la Pole became a canon of York Cathedral.
8 Turner, T.H. and Parker, J.H., 1859, *Some account of Domestic Architecture in England,* Oxford, Vol. 3 part 2, p. 41.
9 Johnson, M., 2002, *Behind the Castle Gate, from Medieval to Renaissance,* Routledge, Abingdon. Introduction, p. 6.
10 Ibid., pp. 6-8.
11 Coulson, C., 2016, Specimens of Freedom to Crenellate by Licence, Chapter 10 in Liddiard, R. (ed), *Late Medieval Castles*, Boydell, Woodbridge pp. 221-240.
12 Davis, P., 2009, 'Licences to crenellate: additional data, analysis and comment', *The Castle Studies Group Journal, Vol 22* pp. 245-67.
13 Parliamentary Rolls 1383 Vol iii 150. Quoted in Dobson, R. B., 1970, *The Peasants Revolt of 1381*, Macmillan, London p. 362.
14 Ridgard, J., 2009, Mettingham, Suffolk, the building of a religious college with particular reference to the acquisition and production of books for its library, *Proceedings of the Suffolk Institute for Archeology and History*, Vol XVII Part 1, pp. 21-31.
15 Liddiard, R. (ed), 2016, *Late Medieval Castles.* Boydell, Woodbridge. Introduction by R.Liddiard, pp, 1-17.
16 Emery, A., 2000, *East Anglia: Architectural Introduction Vol II*, Chapter 2. pp. 19-34.

17 Goodall, J., 2011, *The English Castle: 1066-1650* Yale University Press for The Paul Mellon Centre for Studies in British Art, p. 7.
18 Carroll, L. (Charles L. Dodgson), 1872, *Through the Looking-Glass*, 1934 edition, Macmillan, chapter 6, p. 205.
19 Bargain and Sale of 400 oaks and 14 elms from Wingfield Park. Staffordshire County Record Office, Ref K007, Records of the Jerningham family, D641/3/A/1/1.
20 Liddiard, R., 2008, Living on the Edge: Commons, Castles and Regional Settlement Patterns in Medieval East Anglia, *Proceedings of the Cambridge Antiquarian Society*, Vol XCVII, pp. 169-178.
21 Martin, E., 2015, A Landscape History of Wingfield, pp. 9-29 in Bloore, P. and Martin, E. (eds), 2015 *Wingfield College and its Patrons*, Boydell, Woodbridge.
22 John de Wynewyk, clerk, David de Wollore, clerk, John de Wengefeld, chevalier, Thomas de Wengefeld and Gilbert de Debenham v Richard Breouse, chevalier, of the manor of Wengefeld with appurtenances, TNA, CP 25/1/221/90, Rye 1900, p220, 1357-8 and 1358-9.
23 John de Wingfeld, knight and Alianora his wife v David de Wollore, clerk and Gilbert de Debenham of the manors of Stradebrook and Wyngefeld (except the advowsons of the churches) TNA, CP25/1/221 91, p223. Rye 1900, p223 1359-60.
24 Ibid. 21, p. 21.
25 Will of Thomas of Wyngfeld of Letheringham, 1378 NRO NCC Will Register 154 Heydon.
26 Ibid. 21, p. 24.
27 Calendar of Patent Rolls 1361-1364 p. 180, 8 November 1361, transcribed Public Record Office 1891.
28 Calendar of Patent Rolls 1324-6 p. 242, 13 February 1326.
29 Petitions to the King and Council. 1326/7 TNA Ref SC 8/1/14/680.
30 Calendarium Inquisitionem Post Mortem sive Eschaetarum (CIPME) Edward III, Vol II note 24, p. 257, transcribed J. Caley, 1808.
31 Ibid. 26.

10. Aerial View of Wingfield Castle, c2000.

The First Building

Michael de la Pole's fortified manor was surprisingly modest for a man of his eminence, at a time when outward show was of consequence. Compared, for example, with other knightly castles of the same period, such as Bodiam in East Sussex, Donnington in Berkshire, Saltwood in Kent and Michael's brother-in-law's magnificent Bolton Castle in Yorkshire, Wingfield is not pretentious or grandiose. Even if today we could see the complete new building with all four of its walls intact, instead of just the south curtain wall and moat, the charm of the place lies not in its size but in the combination of medieval fortifications with the pretty, even delicate, Tudor house along the west interior wall and its setting on the green.

It is quite possible that Michael was not much interested in personal aggrandisement. There have always been ambitious people in public life who court influence, wealth and power but whose personal homes are relatively modest. Money and influence provide sufficient kudos for many a man to feel his life has significance without needing an ostentatious habitation. He may have been sensitive too to the reverses of his father's career and the risks of appearing to have an inflated sense of his family's importance. And indeed he was already subject to resentful murmurings of that kind when he began the construction of his fortified manor. Or perhaps, after all, he did not have anything like the money required for something more showy.

An alternative explanation for the modesty of the house is that, when the earlier house on the site was first constructed, Michael and Katherine's main base and home was still in Hull. It wasn't until about 1379, after the death of Katherine's mother, that Michael started calling himself 'Lord of Wingfield'. It is likely that the family only then focused their attentions on making Wingfield their permanent base. Michael retained his links and his affection for Hull, visiting his home there frequently and requesting to be buried there in the Charterhouse he had established. The Hull property, later called Suffolk Palace, was a vast edifice of brick and timber with a tower, chapel, reception hall, over twenty chambers and a 'somerhalle', thought to be a type of garden house or conservatory.[1] A century later, the lieutenant appointed to upgrade Hull's defences commented, when invited to live there, that 'the rooms were so large he could not furnish even one of them'.[2] It is perhaps not surprising that when Michael was creating his own family home he wanted a manor of a more usable size.

11. A sixteenth century drawing of Suffolk Palace, the de la Pole mansion in Hull, by John Rogers c1542.*

A further likely explanation for the modesty of the new castle is that it was confined by the site of an earlier structure with an existing moat of a shape that pre-defined the new building. The shape is asymmetrical and yet the land on which it is constructed is flat and featureless. The superstructure of the new walls were surely simply redeveloped on old foundations. The licence to crenellate refers to existing 'mansion-houses of their manors of Wyngefeld, Sternefeld and Huntyngfeld'.[3] It seems likely that the new castle was defined by the size of the old hall.

Wingfield in short is a castle that has a quietly defined superiority, constructed without ostentation but of the highest quality workmanship. No one has yet improved on Anthony Emery's detailed description of the building.[4] The narrative here owes everything to his scholarship and that of Robert Liddiard, who with Virtual Past, a company specialising in computer

* this drawing is attributed to John Rogers one of the foremost military engineers of the Tudor period.

generated historical media, bravely and with great gusto, attempted a virtual digital reconstruction of how the building may have looked around 1500. This was a century on after its construction but when we might imagine the de la Poles had finished their work and the castle was at its finest.[5] I have added a tentative suggestion or two.

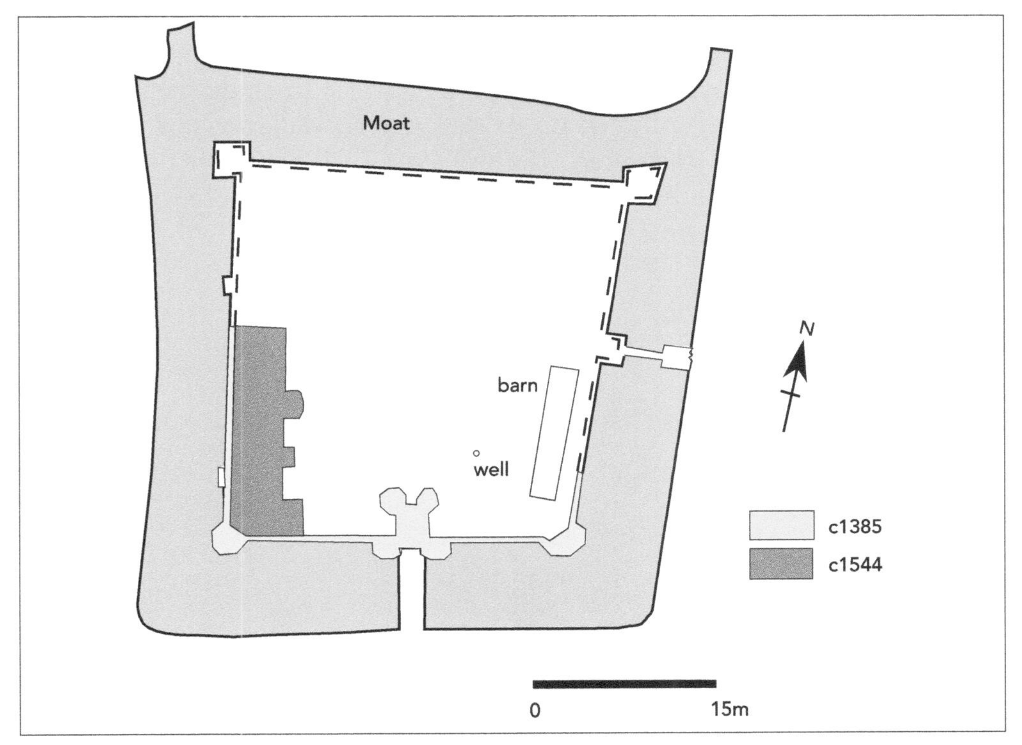

12. Wingfield Castle Site Plan.

Historic England lists the castle as Grade 1.[6] It is four sided but not quite square, as is shown in the site plan above (12). The dimensions are 56.3/65.5 metres by 62.4/65.5 metres surrounded by a broad and deep moat. The entrance front is a three storeyed gatehouse, flanked by two ancillary slightly lower towers linking the gatehouse to the southern curtain wall. At both ends, west and east, there are octagonal towers, again slightly lower than the central gatehouse towers. The west curtain wall has been incorporated into the later sixteenth century house that is the most striking feature of the castle inside the perimeter wall today. A short section of curtain wall extends northwards about 9 metres from the east tower. It is likely that the curtain wall extended around the whole perimeter of the building when first constructed, although the original height of that northern wall is not clear. The east curtain wall shows foundations of another tower and a secondary entrance.

A century ago the castle did not look much like the eighteenth century Buck engraving shown on page 35 (14). Many of its crenellations were gone and the walls were encroached upon by destructive ivy. But, after the restoration by Graham Baron Ash in the 1940s, the castle frontage today looks once more like the Buck depiction. The perspective of the Buck drawing however is seriously awry, the Tudor house inside the westerly wall runs north to south at right angles to that illustrated. The walls are of flint, dressed with stone but with some later nineteenth century patching with brick, especially on the entrance causeway and some battlements.

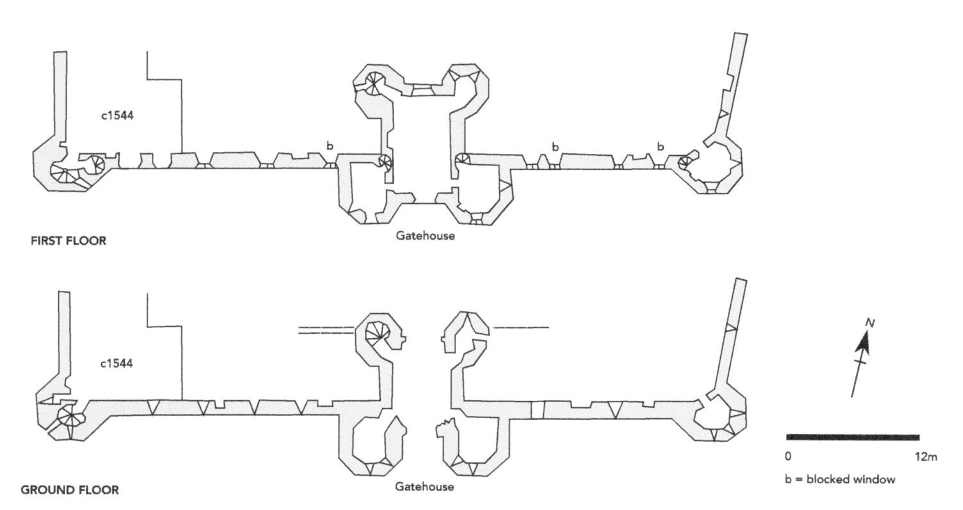

13. Plan of gatehouse and curtain wall.

A brief report written by Philip Aitkens after a visit in 2009 noted that there is uncoursed and unflushed rubble of small stones and brick inclusions at the lower level of the gatehouse range. In contrast, for example, the rear of the south east turret has been constructed differently, largely of red brick at the upper levels although the external faces are in flushed flint.[7] His conclusion was that the original rubble-walled castle was remodelled in the fifteenth century using bricks much more freely, and that areas of the earlier rubble walls were re-faced in flushed flintwork. This would have greatly changed the castle's appearance.[8]

The main entrance on the south now crosses a causeway, not a bridge. There was a brick bridge there until at least 1913, when it was mentioned in an article in Country Life magazine and can be seen in many earlier prints.[9] There are clear implacements visible in the gatehouse for a portcullis to be raised and lowered, so the bridge was probably built in Tudor times when castles were no longer thought of as strongholds.[10]

14. Engraving of South Façade, Wingfield Castle, 1738, by S and N Buck.

There is also a drawbridge crossing the east side of the moat for pedestrian access that nowadays connects the orchard garden on the east side of the demesne to the castle drawbridge tower and courtyard. It is a relatively modern structure, the previous one being destroyed in a gale in the 1990s, but built on the site of and of similar dimensions to an older drawbridge shown in nineteenth century drawings. It is constructed of wide oak planks, held together with large iron bolts and elegantly counterpoised with a substantial counterweight. This was at one time made of stone, according to a letter from G E Buncombe to *Country Life* in 1957.[11] The oak drawbridge carries the initials and date RL 1768, presumably restored by Robert Leman during his tenure and also BA 1958 for Baron Ash. Since there was a fourteenth century entrance to the west of the castle, this may represent a 'twin' on the eastern side to bring foot traffic into the courtyard.

The Gatehouse. The gatehouse stands complete, restored and reroofed by Ash in 1962, the front two towers considerably more dominant than the back two. It is, oddly, not completely central, perhaps another indication that the new castle was a rebuild. Protected by a portcullis, the passage hall has lost its original vaulting. The doors appear to be original, with a small wicket door set in on the west side.

15. The small wicket door in the gatehouse discovered and restored to its rightful place in 1945.

There are doors in the four corners opening into the two tower lodges at the front and a rear newel staircase. The front lodges would presumably provide rooms for the porter and guards. The towers have narrow slits and narrow windows providing light. One of the front, south westerly tower lodges now has a nineteenth century solid pine staircase providing access to the roof and the upper chambers. This replaces what would originally have been the stairs up to the Great Hall. The north side towers are smaller than the southerly towers but the north-east one has an original stone newel staircase winding up to the roof. Ash restored the side fireplace in the surprisingly spacious first floor chamber in the gatehouse with figured corbelled columns from Flanders purchased from Ditchingham Hall, where they had been installed by Sir Rider Haggard. The purpose was to support the canopy above the fireplace. The replacement roof was also installed over new corbels. It is a faithful reproduction of a late fourteenth century roof. Taken all together, the heated rooms in the gatehouse make up a single lodging, possibly occupied by the castle bailiff. We will return to the gatehouse when we consider the detailed decorative alterations made by Baron Ash in the twentieth century

The gatehouse walls are decorated with flushwork panels of trefoil-topped arcading design surmounted by a generous stringcourse. The pattern is formed from a combination of knapped flint and stone in a style first seen about 1320.[12] Small coats of arms of the de la Pole and Wingfield families are discreetly sited on the outer archway. There are remarkable similarities between the Wingfield gatehouse and the gateway c1350 at Alnwick Castle, seat of the great Percy family but whether the architect of Wingfield knew Alnwick is not known.[13]

The ancient oak door in the east side of the gatehouse that gives on to the staircase to the chamber above still has its original door knocker, of iron fashioned into wings similar to the wings on the arms of John Wingfield. There are similar knockers on other doors but they have lost their wings with age.

16. The gatehouse from the courtyard, 1913.

The Perimeter Walls. The curtain wall is about 1.5 metres thick, slightly asymmetrical, being 6 metres shorter on the east than the west, just over 7 metres high from the base to the crenellations. The south front is some 62 metres long. A moulded stringcourse marks the bottom of the crenellations on the towers and the curtain wall. The wall above is of brick, not flint. The crenellations seen in the Buck engraving on page 35 (14) had crumbled away on the westerly tower and west curtain wall by the time Thomas Hearne painted the castle in 1780 (79. p. 277), although a close scrutiny of the Buck picture suggests that the west tower was beginning to look dilapidated in the 1730s. Stone gargoyles for water drainage are still in place on the surviving walls, their lead pipes more recently restored to protect the fabric. A gargoyle dredged from the north-eastern side of the moat in the mid-1980s now stands in the courtyard as ornamental decoration. It reminds the visitor of the unexpectedly large dimension of the gargoyles.

The two south-facing curtain walls either side of the gatehouse have window openings from the fourteenth century although some are now blocked. Other windows are later inserts from the sixteenth and twentieth centuries. The north curtain wall stands no longer but is flanked at either end by two square tower foundation bases, quite different from the southern towers. It may be that they are survivors of an earlier building.

17. Photograph showing stringcourse and trefoil flushwork on the east gatehouse walls.

There is an interesting remnant of an ancillary entrance to the immediate east of the gatehouse on the south east perimeter wall, a blocked up door at ground floor level giving directly on to the moat that can clearly be seen in the Hearne print. This 'water gate' or 'sally port' for emergency egress was a common feature of medieval castles but is unusual in fortified houses. It suggests that Michael de la Pole wanted to ensure he could get himself and his family out in a hurry if necessary.

Another small watercolour of 1791 by Edward Dayes shows no crenellations on the west tower or south curtain wall but there is a surviving tiled roof over the southern curtain wall buildings (84, p. 291). Emery suggests that the crenellations were restored in the nineteenth century and then restored anew by Ash in the twentieth. I am not sure that this is correct. Artists in the nineteenth century took serious licence with the fabric in order to create a romantic picture and the state of the crenellations in a rather grainy photograph in the 1930s suggests that prior to Baron Ash's restoration the castle crenellations were in a sorry state.

Emery pointed out that the gothic tracery of the two light windows across the front of the curtain wall were old fashioned for 1380 but when fashion trends travelled slowly, architectural styles in East Anglia frequently lagged behind the major towns and cities as local designers and craftsmen adhered to older styles. Again this suggests that Michael de la Pole may not have taken a close personal interest in the detail of his new manor, hardly surprising given his responsibilities elsewhere. The windows in both the gatehouse and curtain wall are too large for the building to have been constructed primarily as defensive although the fortifications could be used if necessary against a less formidable foe than an invading army. There is a marvellous view from the top of the towers that would allow any local marauders to be seen clearly for miles.

The two-storey house built inside the curtain wall was clearly designed to be residential with generous windows in the second storey. Emery points out that the internal buildings would have been timber framed, as at mid fourteenth century Maxstoke Castle in Warwickshire, a remarkably similar building in some ways to Wingfield. The upper floor, where the more senior members of the household would have lived, is provided with better windows and a good fireplace and is divided into an inner and outer chamber, the former providing access to a private suite in the corner tower at the west end. The southeast range is similar but with access to the wall walks from the upper chamber. The two-storey range along the southwest wall was covered in, it is said, by a steeply pitched roof until the early to mid nineteenth century. Certainly the roofline of this range is clearly visible today.

The Chapel. The chapel in a castle is usually the apartment next in importance to the Great Hall. Traditionally the chapel at Wingfield castle has been reputed to be between the south-west corner tower and the gatehouse. Baron Ash decided to designate the ground floor uncovered area as a chapel and left the medieval piscina and a small stone head in place for effect. There is therefore no actual chapel extant.

Judging from the number of liturgical and religious song-books that were part of Alice's list of chapel goods to be transferred to Ewelme in 1466, John Goodall has conjectured that there may have been up to four priests and many clerks employed there.[14] Her chapel inventory for transfer also included:

> a crucifix with Mary and John of silver and II silver basyns for the Awmes,[alms] II high chandeles of silver. An high chalys of silver, I pix of gold, I pix of silver, I pix brede of gold, I cruette of silver, square. A holy water scopette [scoop] and holy water spryngell.[15]

The piscina is mentioned in nineteenth century descriptions and was certainly in the castle before Baron Ash's twentieth century renovations. A piscina is traditionally on the south side of an east-facing altar in an east-west chapel and so the piscina in its current location could be in the conventional place, except that the nearest elaborate window is above it facing south. We really do not know if the chapel was at this site but it seems the most likely spot. Nor should we be concerned about which way it faced. Other castles have chapel windows facing in eccentric directions. The only difficulty today is the exposure to the elements that the piscina suffers. It was we assume covered until the early nineteenth century.

The Courtard. It is difficult to be sure how the courtyard space at Wingfield was subdivided, if at all. Emery judges, as does Liddiard, that there was possibly a subdivision into two courtyards, north and south, a residential court and a service court. This would fit with the position of the well and the slightly off-centre position of the gatehouse, with the main residential areas lying on the west side in the front, southerly, court. We can see this design in the ruins at Baconsthorpe Castle, Norfolk, built in the mid-fifteenth century by John Heydon, lawyer and agent of William de la Pole. Heydon would have been very familiar with Wingfield Castle because of his close links with William.

Nowadays there is of course just one courtyard. It is mainly used as an attractive garden. The current owner was told by Roger Groom, the grandson of the pre-second world war tenant, who grew up at the castle and whose family feature in a later chapter, that when the drive inside the courtyard was relaid in the early twentieth century a huge pile of discarded deer bones was found there. A legend had grown up that, during the time of Henry VIII, the castle was ransacked and the deer were providing sustenance for the despoilers. A possibly more likely explanation is that the bones were on the site of a midden. Even in Tudor times domestic waste was not uncommonly deposited near residential buildings. The same unintentional excavation also uncovered some medieval leg-irons, rough crude instruments that still hang inside the gateway.

The attractive sixteenth century timber framed courtyard house of brick and plaster, built in the middle years of the century will be considered in a later chapter as it so clearly belongs to the Jerningham family's time at Wingfield. But this 'new' house incorporates the octagonal southwest tower of the medieval castle with a spiral staircase to the first floor and separate stair to the upper floor, from where there is access to the parapet. It is likely that this house is in the same location as the original residential apartments of the de la Poles. Their apartments would have extended the whole length of the west side of the courtyard to the north-west tower. There is a stone trough marking a garderobe chute, that is a sewage outlet, from near the end of this range. There also remains evidence of a door in the west curtain wall, visible in the kitchen, opposite to the one in the east curtain wall, which may indicate there was once yet another entrance to the courtyards.

Buildings inside the Courtyard. Some architectural historians, who clearly never inspected the site themselves, have suggested that Wingfield did not have a complete curtain wall originally but this is incorrect. The solid foundations of the original east and north walls are very clearly visible along the edge of the moat, indeed about seven metres of the original east wall still stands.

18. Virtual reconstruction of how Wingfield Castle may have looked c1500.

Curiously there is a timber framed building inside the courtyard on the east side that is not included in the Grade I listing of the castle, labelled on plans as 'a barn'. It serves as storage and workshop, with a nineteenth century gallery stair inside. This is considered in a later chapter

The west side of the Castle. The main range is Tudor and will be considered in the chapter on Jerningham House but the western range south of the porch was the probable location of the Great Hall. However, there is a substantial room between the hall and the southwest tower, now housing a library but probably once a main part of the de la Pole family lodgings. The windows are enlarged now into facsimiles of Tudor windows.

The landscape of Wingfield Castle. A castle, and indeed any large house, as Creighton pointed out, is more imposing if it is set squarely in a landscape that draws attention to its grandeur.[16] At Wingfield the approach across a causeway through magnificent fish-ponds and, probably, an outer base court, gave a visual impact that would still be impressive if it were not for the twentieth century mounds obstructing the view. The western edge of the moat abuts on to Wingfield Green where the village settlement would have been and indeed in part still is. There is evidence that there was a substantial deer park to the north of the castle and it has been suggested that there may have been a moated hunting lodge on it. The fun of guessing leads one to all kinds of entertaining ideas but evidence is frankly lacking. We can however deduce from other similar houses of the period what the de la Poles would have aspired to.

One puzzling feature on old maps, which local people can remember being in situ, is a long earthwork running along the north side of the moat.[17] It can be seen on the Ordnance Survey map of 1904 shown below. It is said to have been planted with a line of hornbeam trees running along the top of the 'bund'. The earthwork was flattened in the early 1980s 'because it spoilt the view'. Liddiard points out that it is an unusual feature unlikely to be part of the castle park and that it lies inside the two 'ears' of the moat on the northern side which allow the inflow and egress of water. The fact that the earthwork sits so neatly between them would suggest that it post-dates the moat. The earthwork could represent spoil from a later re-cutting of the moat. Having personally witnessed the huge amount of spoil generated from dredging a sizeable moat, I find this an attractive explanation.[18] The 'bund' could have been created at any time between the sixteenth and nineteenth centuries.

In their re-creation, Liddiard and Virtual Past plumped for a park divided into a coppicing area and an area of grazing wood pasture with oaks. They modelled a hypothetical lodge on the one at Odiham in Hampshire. Perhaps a lodge in Suffolk was more likely to be a relatively simple timber framed building rather like the buildings inside the curtain wall. Whether and how often this deer park was used for hunting is a matter of conjecture. Deer parks were in fact not simply places to hunt, they were venison farms, the meat being highly prized by the nobility. By around 1300 there may have been as many as 3,000 such parks in England. Every nobleman wanted a park; while great magnates and some bishops owned ten or more and the king could boast as many as eighty to a hundred. To prevent deer escaping, parks were surrounded by high wooden fences. Hunting was also a way to hone the military skills required in battle and to learn how to manage horses. Parks were not popular with local people whose access to the pasture or meadow was suddenly denied them. The Wingfield Castle park was not encroaching good arable land and would have been accessible by peasants before the high wooden pales were erected.[19]

The fishponds outside the curtain wall, which are still there although the easterly one has been mostly filled in, were both ornamental and practical. Fresh water fish were expensive and appreciated at a time when sea fish was difficult to acquire fresh and the church dictated so many meat-free days, two hundred or so when Fridays and Lent are included. Carp, perch, pike and tench were kept, also much desired trout and in some places eel.

The approach to the castle is quite short once inside the privacy mound. Lyndon-Stanford has suggested that the visual approach may have been more stirring in times past.[20] An old field boundary that connects the castle to the Wingfield College-Church complex, visible on the 1837 tithe map, may represent the route of an old road from the south that gave the approaching visitor a grander visual impact.

There would also have been barns, a solidly built dovecote and other agricultural buildings outside the wall of the castle, probably south of a gatehouse entrance. Inside the curtain wall there would be a vegetable garden and perhaps an ornamental garden for the family to enjoy. Most of the internal buildings from Michael de la Pole's house have been destroyed over the centuries, replaced by the later sixteenth century house and even later ancillary buildings that were used for agricultural storage. In the late fourteenth century the Wingfield Castle estate demesne and park extended to

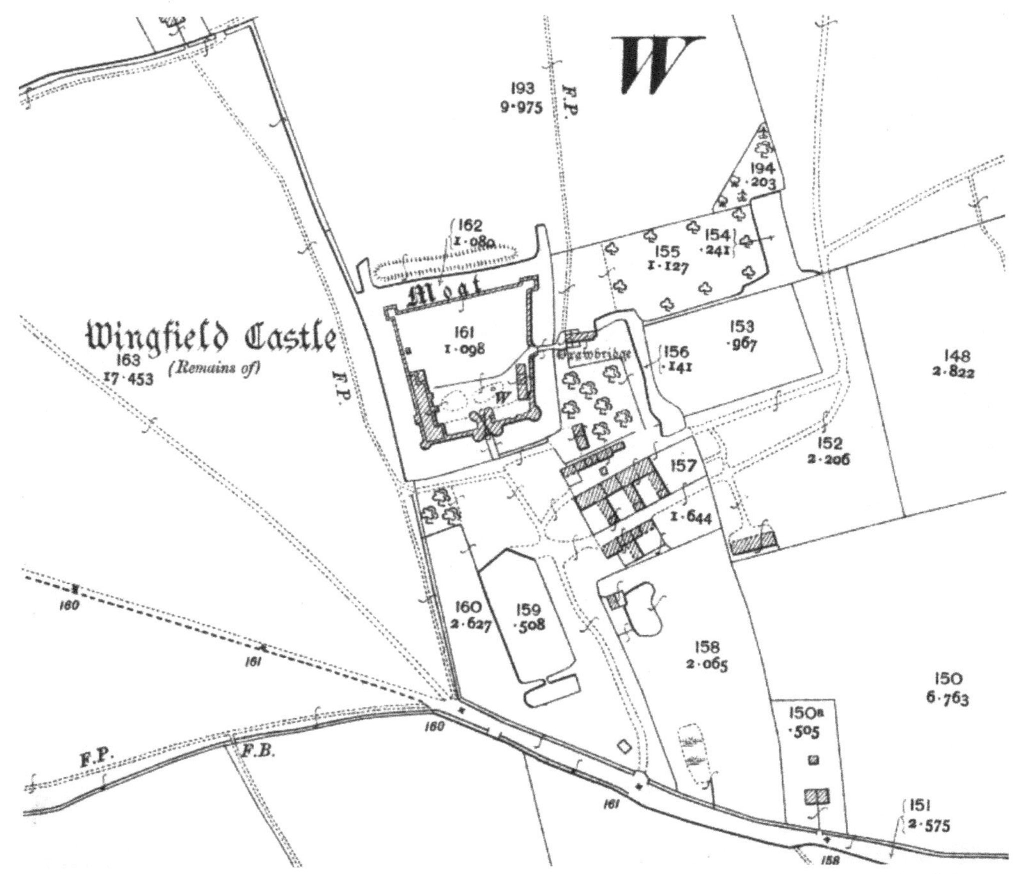

19. Ordnance Survey map Wingfield Castle 1904 showing the earthwork north of the moat.

over four hundred acres and included one hundred and forty acres of pasture, meadow and woodland, along with two hundred acres of heath and marsh and seventy acres of arable land.[21]

Emery speculated that the castle was built as a retirement home for Michael and Katherine but this was surely not the case. Michael had a fair mileage of administrative duties still ahead of him and he certainly did not offer to 'retire' when his administration was under threat in 1385. I prefer to think it was Michael and Katherine's family home built when they were still in their successful middle years, an outward confirmation of what they had achieved. Almost certainly it remained Katherine's and the children's main base when Michael was in Westminster or in the myriad other locations where the king held court or sent his Chancellor on errands.

It would have been Katherine who bore the brunt of the management of the daily life of the castle. The wives of medieval gentry and nobility carried heavy responsibilities for securing supplies, managing stores, supervising household servants, supplying home remedies for sick family members, supervising children, keeping in touch with relatives far and near and coordinating the work of the estate bailiff. They gardened for pleasure, or at least enjoyed the gardens created for them, made fine needlework, played musical instruments and read. We know from the Paston letters that they did a lot of worrying too, about their husbands, their absent children, their property. This was a covetous age beset with envious neighbours ready to encroach if given half a chance. While men were away on military or administrative business their wives and stewards or bailiffs ran the show.[22] Margaret Paston, for example, quite literally 'held the fort' at her home Oxnead in Norfolk, then later at Caister Castle, while her lawyer husband John was away in London, not quite appreciating the physical threats his wife faced. She was one of many women of her class who coped with the many absences of their menfolk during war and peace.[23] If Katherine had learnt well at her father's side Michael would have been confident that his home was safe, at least from local rebellious resentment.

The couple had very little time to enjoy their new home. Barely had construction begun than Katherine died in 1386 and Michael fled the country. Wingfield Castle was then confiscated by the Crown. It was another decade before the de la Poles could claim their country home again.

Notes

1 Clarke, R., 2017, Suffolk Palace Hull. online at http://www.richardclarkelandscapehistorian.co.uk/wp-content/uploads/2017/06/Suffolk-Palace-text-and-formatted.pdf [accessed 24 October 2019].
2 Sheahan, J. J., 1866, (2nd Edn) *History of the Town and Port of Kingston upon Hull*, p. 105. TNA Ref ZLIB 29/23.
3 Calendar of Patent Rolls 1381-5 Richard II Pt II, London 1887, 555. Transcription by Lyte, Maxwell, H.C. (ed), 1897.
4 Emery, A., 2000, *Greater Medieval Houses of England and Wales 1300-1500. Vol II East Anglia, Central England and Wales*, Cambridge University Press, Cambridge. Wingfield Castle, Suffolk pp. 160-164.
5 Liddiard, R., 2015, Reconstructing Wingfield Castle, pp. 77-95 in Bloore P. and Martin, E. (eds). *Wingfield College and its Patrons*, Boydell Press, Woodbridge. Virtual Past is an initiative of the University of East Anglia, at www.virtualpast.co.uk.
6 Wingfield Castle, Historic England Listing number 1032894, 29 July 1955 https://historicengland.org.uk/listing/the-list/list-entry/1032894
7 Aitkens, P. G., 2009, Report on Wingfield Castle visit July 2009 undertaken for Virtual Past and University of East Anglia, unpublished.
8 Ibid.
9 Wingfield Castle, Suffolk, 1913, *Country Life Magazine*, 28 June, pp. 952-958.
10 Jeffery, P. H., 1989, *East Anglian Keeps, Castles and Forts*, The Old Orchard Press, Norfolk, p. 55.
11 Buncombe G. E., 1957, Correspondence. Wingfield Castle, drawbridge survivals, *Country Life Magazine* 28 February, p. 389.
12 Hart, S., 2000, *Flint Architecture of East Anglia*. Giles de la Mare, London, p. 54.
13 Wood, M., 1965, *The English Medieval House*, Bracken Books, London. Chapter 11 The Gatehouse, pp. 155-165.
14 Inventory of Alice de la Pole's goods transferred from Wingfield to Ewelme listed in Bodleian MS DD Ewelme, EMA 47. Goodall J. A. A., 2001, *God's House at Ewelme*, Ashgate Publishing, p. 4.
15 Ibid.
16 Creighton, O., 2009, Castle studies and the European Medieval Landscape: traditions, trends and future research directions, *Landscape History*, 30, pp, 5-20.
17 National Library of Scotland. Ordnance Survey map Suffolk XXVI.10 (Hoxne; Syleham; Wingfield) revised 1903, published 1904.
18 Liddiard, R., 3 March 2020, personal communication.
19 Mileson, S., 2005, The Importance of Parks in Fifteenth-Century Society in Clark, L. (ed), *The Fifteenth Century, V: 'Of Mice and Men': Image, Belief & Regulation in Late Medieval England*, Boydell, Woodbridge pp. 19-37.
20 Lyndon-Stanford, E., 2007, *Wingfield Castle in the 14th and 16th Centuries*. Thesis submitted for a BA degree University of Newcastle on Tyne, p. 10.
21 Calendar of Patent Rolls, 13 Richard II, part ii 29d quoted in Copinger, W. A., 1909, *The Manors of Suffolk: Notes on their History and Devolution, Volume 4*. Manchester, Taylor, Garnett, Evans & Co, p. 110.
22 Archer, R. E. ,1992, Women as landholders and Administrators in the Late Middle Ages, in Goldberg, P.J.P. (ed), *Women is a Worthy Wight: Women in English Society 1200-1500*, Stroud.
23 Gairdner J. (ed), 1904, *The Paston Letters, Vol II* Chatto and Windus, London, pp. 101-102.

20. The Arms of Michael de la Pole

Azure, a fess between three leopards' faces or.

The Origins of the de la Pole Family

Michael de la Pole was the first member of an English government administration to be impeached by the parliamentary Commons. He is surprisingly well known therefore to students of constitutional history in jurisdictions sharing a common parliamentary heritage with England.

In 1386, barely a year after the licence to crenellate was granted, Michael and Katherine faced ruin and a threat to his life. There had been other impeachments but at the instigation of the king or another senior government official, none by representatives of the people. This was a first of its kind. For that reason, his impeachment is more famous than Michael himself. Six hundred years after the event his case and its influence on the framers of the American Constitution were quoted in the legal discussions about Bill Clinton's impeachment on the floor of the US Senate in 1999.[1] Political and constitutional historians have always been fascinated by the unwitting role Michael played in the slow pathway to representative democracy.

Another president Thomas Jefferson remarked, 'In England impeachment has been more of an engine of passion than of justice' and certainly Michael's case demonstrates that all too well. Impeachment has always been a way of attacking unpopular ministers, the sharpest arrow from the quiver of checks and balances. In those days the tensions were between the king and his personal council on one side, and on the other the Commons and Lords. This was an early power struggle between an unpopular absolute monarch and the people's representatives. Impeachment became obsolete in England once a full parliamentary democracy was in place but an impeachable offence has transmuted in the US to anything that appears to be a betrayal of public trust of presidential office.

Michael the man has often become lost in erudite discourse although dozens of academic papers have been dedicated to the question of his guilt or innocence of the seven charges against him. Then there is the thorny matter of the king's and Michael's insistence on the absolute right of the monarch to appoint his own ministers. David Hume, the eighteenth century enlightenment philosopher, thought the charges against Michael were 'frivolous'. Henry Hallam in 1818 agreed and Tout, in the first comprehensive story of Michael's life in the Dictionary of National Biography in 1896, also remarked on 'the paltry quality of the charges'. But expectations of public office have changed. Scholarship has gradually, over the course of the eighteenth to the twentieth centuries, swung from regarding him as an innocent scapegoat to more recent analyses conducted in the puritanical 'blame-game' spirit of our own times, when gifted administrators are more than ever subjected to public obloquy.

Closer examination over the course of the late twentieth and early twenty-first centuries found a case to answer for some of the charges and definite guilt on one or two counts. But, as with Bill Clinton's sexual misdemeanors and attempts to cover up, the underlying charges seemed inconsequential compared with the vindictiveness of the proceedings. In the 1980s J S Roskell dedicated a whole detailed book to an analysis of each charge.[2] De la Pole's most recent biographer, Anthony Tuck, gives a balanced account, avoiding censure but emphasizing the personal and political drivers that ineluctably came together.[3] But the story is moving along too fast. What led Michael to this reckoning with posterity? What sort of a world did Michael de la Pole inhabit? And who was he? This author is indebted to Tuck for his scholarly but accessible life of Michael and to many others who have found insights into the man while researching even grander princes and kings.

England in the Fourteenth Century. Michael lived and died in a century that was both the worst of times and the best of times. England became a successful military nation under the 'good' reign of Edward III and the wool trade brought great wealth to some. On the other hand the two most devastating human disasters to strike England in the millennium from 1000-2000 occurred in the early fourteenth century, the Great Famine and the Black Death. The social economic and political changes that followed undoubtedly shaped Michael but so did the place of his birth, Kingston upon Hull, and his extraordinary father and family.

When Michael was born in Hull, in 1330 or possibly just a little earlier, England was recovering after the Great Famine of 1315-1322, caused by seven years of some of the worst weather northern Europe has ever seen. The rain started in 1315, and continued every summer for seven years. The winters were exceptionally cold. The decrease in food supply was not limited to a drop in grain production but extended to epidemics in herds and flocks and an acute shortfall in the supply of salt needed to cure meats and fish that might have supplemented the reduced supply of grain. Wars diverted resources to military demands that might otherwise have been used to feed the hungry.

England weathered the crisis of 1315 relatively well. It was the continued bad harvests of 1316 and 1317 that brought widespread starvation and disease. It is estimated that fifteen per cent of the population perished. There were stories of starving peasants resorting to cannibalism; certainly people ate dogs and their precious livestock. The displaced swelled local cities looking for work. The manorial courts reveal the anxiety of the times with frenzied litigation over small strips of land, the demands of creditors and arrears in rent.[4] Where landowners paid labourers in bushels of wheat the inflated price pushed landlords into desperation too. The economy did not improve until 1322.

Kingston upon Hull in the Fourteenth Century. The de la Pole family were protected against much of the misery of the famine by their growing wealth but also because they were based in Kingston upon Hull, a town that by the year 1300 was a booming Yorkshire port.

The population of Yorkshire had risen dramatically in the previous two centuries, although not so much as in East Anglia. Surrounding woodland had been cleared for farming and in the famine years Yorkshire countryside was as affected as elsewhere. In the early fourteenth century Yorkshire people also suffered in a long war with the Scots. In 1318 Robert the Bruce burned Northallerton. There were constant raids and destruction of people and livestock. Hull however prospered as a principal supply port for armies and garrisons in the north. Hull ships supported Scottish campaigns throughout the early fourteenth century. In 1334–1336, ships took lead to Berwick, wine to Scotland, and were being requisitioned to supplement the navy. Michael's father William de la Pole played a prominent part in these affairs, collecting and transporting flour, wine, salt and other foodstuffs.[5]

With the onset of the French wars in 1337, ships and supplies from Hull were as often directed southwards as they were towards Scotland. Seven ships were fitted out at Hull in 1337 for service in the south, and in recompense the town was released from three instalments of a tenth (a tax) and from the fine (payment) for the charter of 1334. Again, in 1338, ships were ordered to stop at Hull to carry goods to Aquitaine. Early in 1337 for the fleet was being built at Beverley and at Hull, William de la Pole was responsible for building and manning another ship; 'the king's galley of Hull', which was operating in Scottish waters in 1339.[6] Pole was also, in 1339, assembling victuals at Hull from Nottinghamshire, Lincolnshire and the East Riding. The de la Pole family's rise was spectacular.

21. English warships of the fourteenth century.

Origins of the de la Pole Family. Michael's father, Sir William de la Pole, was one of the most successful men of the fourteenth century. He was a business tycoon, a formidably competent financier, admired but later reviled by King Edward III, who for many years depended on de la Pole's loans to finance the war in France. The king and higher born courtiers, who became seriously financially beholden to William and other wealthy merchants, harboured a festering resentment against a man they considered their social inferior, a prejudice that would bedevil Michael's career too. Fishy jokes at William's expense played on the unfortunate name of his mother's second husband, John Rottenheryng. On the other hand what we know of William's character is not especially endearing. He was often guilty of sharp practice and worse.

William's rise to wealth and influence, later downfall, then partial retrieval of his fortune foreshadowed the careers of his descendants who made Wingfield Castle their home. Many, including Michael, had a touch of the Icarus complex about them. William far outshone most of his ambitious fellow merchants in the social advancement that was possible for wealthy merchants. His son Michael was made earl of Suffolk only 68 years after William and his brothers first appear in the Hull records as traders.

This account of William of Hull relies heavily on three historians who have examined original sources in recent times. A S Harvey, an archivist at Trinity House, Hull, wrote a detailed history of William and his descendants in 1957, now online.[7] Rosemary Horrox' short but brilliant little book brought Harvey's work up to date in 1983 and successfully skewered a goodly amount of hearsay and imaginative twaddle still current on the web.[8] Third, Edmund Fryde meticulously analysed Pole's business accounts and records to give a marvellous overview of what Pole was up to in his trade and banking business career from Hull to London, to the low countries and France and back again through a period at the outset of the 100 Years War.[9] Two older sources provide additional insights.[10]

William is thought to have been born some time between 1290 and 1295 at the highly successful trading port of Ravenserodd, near Spurn Point in East Yorkshire. The name de la Pole (or in English atte Pole or simply Pole) was a common one in the north but also in other areas of England. William was described not long after his death by a monastic chronicler from the nearby Abbey of Meaux, just north of Hull, as 'second to no English Merchant'. Enthusiasm for genealogy did not begin until the sixteenth century, so we simply have no authoritative record from wills or other documents to discover where the family's origins were. A century later, John Paston of the Norfolk Paston family, who was in dispute with a later William de la Pole, claimed to know 'right well' the parentage of the first William de la Pole but 'more I will not tell in this matter but if I be desired or compelled', which seems to suggest he was party to a useful piece of information waiting an opportune time to reveal and one suspects the information was that William was of lowly birth.

William was the middle of three brothers, Richard, William and John. Richard de la Pole established himself and his children as country gentry in Northamptonshire and married his son to the daughter of a peer. The youngest brother John seems to have followed in the more brilliant William's slipstream, acting as his agent in London. At an early age the two elder brothers established themselves as traders in their own right. In about 1310 they moved to Hull, probably because, although then a larger port, Ravenserodd was built on land that was being continually eroded by storms in the early fourteenth century. It was eventually lost to the sea completely in 1362.

By 1317 the brothers were already well set up in Hull; both were Deputies of the Royal Chief Butler, indicating they were well connected and in 1321 to 1324 they were both Chamberlains of Hull. They dealt in foodstuffs in the famine year of 1316, a useful position to be in to protect their own families from want. Most of the extensive monastic lands in Yorkshire were producing wool and soon William began trading in this most valuable of commodities, rapidly becoming very wealthy. He was an astute businessman. He got more for his wool than his competitors and employed better agents at a higher salary to supervise sales. His agent at Antwerp was a well-paid, superior kind of official. He also traded in lead and wine in addition to wool and later bought arms for the king. William's rise to prominence with his elder brother Richard, also a wool merchant who based himself mainly in London, seems to have been due solely to his own abilities and driving personality. He used his lesser associates with some disdain and certainly made as many enemies as friends.

William's financial acumen was astonishing. His main skill was the ability to borrow huge sums of money for the Crown from people who would not lend directly to the government. He was the first English financier to rival in importance, as banker to the Crown, the vastly wealthy Italian merchants, the Bardi and Peruzzi of Florence, who had been financing English kings from 1272. Between June 1338 and October 1339, the total amount raised for Edward III by Pole was at least £111,000, a vast sum that today would be worth more than a billion pounds.

In Suffolk, the de la Poles are noted as a family that scaled the heights of political ambition in the fourteenth and fifteenth centuries. There is a tendency to dismiss Michael's father as 'a wool merchant from Hull' but in Kingston upon Hull, Sir William de la Pole is celebrated as one of the most distinguished fouteenth century local burgers, the first Mayor of Hull and an important figure of national renown, and rightly so.

There is a fanciful Victorian statue of William, on Nelson Street near the Ferry Terminal, gazing over his city, his back to the North Sea. Unveiled in 1879, it was listed in Hull's 'year of culture' in 2017 as an important national landmark, along with the Humber Bridge, Philip Larkin's flat and some rather elegant public conveniences. The statue's sculptor, a local man called William D Keyworth, clearly modelled the facial features on a late fourteenth century tomb in Holy Trinity Church in Hull that for generations has been called the 'de la Pole Tomb'. It is now thought that the tomb is unlikely to be William's although it is definitely that of a wool merchant, most likely Richard de Selby, who died in 1390 and for whom there is convincing documentary evidence of his tomb being placed in this location.[11] If so, then, we have a statue of William de la Pole modelled on someone else entirely. No matter, it is a handsome, if rather crumbling, memorial and probably neither Pole nor Selby looked anything like the features chiselled for posterity.

The facial features and costume of the tomb figures also clearly inspired an 1879 portrait in oils of Sir William de la Pole by Thomas Tindall Wildridge (1858-1928), a Hull antiquarian, although again it is a purely fictive creation, perhaps suggesting a more diffident, sensitive personality than William possessed in reality. It was created to coincide with the statue's unveiling.

The family connections that linked the de la Poles to East Anglia. We know surprisingly little about William's domestic life. Women do not figure in historical chronicles unless they were well-born, powerful or eccentric. It is said that William de la Pole married Katherine, the daughter of Walter of Norwich and that her brother, Sir John of Norwich founded Mettingham Castle. Possibly so but really all we can be sure of is that by 1330, Katherine and William were married and their eldest son Michael born.

The Rise of William de la Pole. William began to loan money to King Edward II to finance his war against the French. Loans of £1000 and £1800 were recorded in 1325. He also financed the rebuilding of Hull's fortifications, the first of many gifts to the town over his lifetime. William loaned money to whoever was in power at the time. After Edward II's enforced removal, William dealt with usurpers of the throne Roger Mortimer and Queen Isabella, but, after they were deposed in the coup that led to the accession of Edward III, William wisely transferred his loyalty and his funds to Edward III for his war against the Scottish, providing loans of £6,000 and £18,000. He was rewarded with the manor of Myton, Hull in 1330, and engineered his own appointment as the first mayor of Hull from 1331 to 1335, one of the favours he extracted from the Crown. This was no trivial appointment; it signified that Hull was granted a degree of autonomy to raise its own taxes and arrange its own affairs under William's control. He represented Hull at various parliaments through the 1330s.

Medieval merchants became rich through private business activity but it was only by service to the Crown and close royal family members that they became powerful. William raised his family through the acquisition of wealth but he may always have been regarded as a social climbing upstart by more established members of the elite.

The Royal Wool Company. William's most ambitious money lending opportunity came in 1337 when Edward III took England into war with France, claiming that he was as of right the king of France, thus intensifying previous intermittent bursts of enmity into a full scale conflict that became the Hundred Years War. With the support of Edward III, Pole and a handful of close associates who were the most important wool merchants in the kingdom, formed themselves into a Wool Company, which controlled exports and also the collection of the tax revenues that went to the king. Pole also instigated the scheme for 'farming the customs', granting a higher rate of tax on exported wool, which became the largest single source of royal revenue but was to the detriment of other traders excluded from the scheme.

In exchange for the money he lent, Pole received more grants of land and property and acquired many manors in his native Yorkshire and across the land. William's demand for grants of land in exchange for loans was usury on a grand scale. Usury, the lending of money for interest, was illegal according to the medieval church. This was why financing was often arranged by Jewish bankers perceived to be outside the Christian ethic. Money lenders could get round the problem by asking the debtor to declare he had borrowed more than the sum required and would pay back that sum, which in reality included interest. Thus William's fortune in land grew and it was said he could reach London from Hull by travelling only on his own land, not quite true, but the notion speaks to his reputation. He had a grand house in Lombard Street, London that he acquired, via yet another royal grant, from the Italian Bardi family but his base remained in Hull, where he built a vast mansion later enjoyed by his son Michael. The home in London was later renamed Suffolk Palace and remained the de la Pole London home until the late fifteenth century.

William also possessed many other properties and manors. He managed to buy the Seigniory of Holderness for £22,650 from the King, which must have caused a little resentment in royal circles. The Seigniory was a holding of monastic manorial estates in Yorkshire including two abbeys, Meaux and Swine, and various lesser nunneries and religious establishments. In 1339 he settled a debt for the King where he had cheekily used the Crown as collateral. Nevertheless in the same year he was made Knight Banneret and a Baron of the Exchequer. A knight 'banneret' was a cut above an ordinary knight in medieval chivalry. The role of Baron of the Exchequer however, a senior judge in financial matters, would have given him money and yet more power.

William seems to have weathered a period of physical or mental ill health in mid 1339 or at least a period of intense worry about his future and fortune. He was working in Antwerp, perhaps disheartened so far away and for so long away from home. He asked for and received five new grants or agreements.[12] First, after his death, his wife was to be allowed to marry whom she pleased. In fact she never remarried. Second, if William died before his heir came of age, and Michael was less than 10 years old at the time, the child's wardship was to be given to his nearest kinsman, who would be his brother Richard, without a claim being made on the estates, which shrewdly prevented Richard from benefitting from Michael's death or disinheritance. Third, his heir was to marry whom he chose, the king could not sell his marriage. At this time William engineered for Michael and his heirs the grant of a reversion of an annuity of £70 from the customs of Hull, already bestowed on his father and uncle. This curious grant, that was worth less than a landholding, would crop up again in Michael's impeachment case.

In the event of William's death, Michael's younger brothers, Thomas and Edmund, were to have the manor of Keyingham, one of the Holderness manors. William demanded he hold on to a ten year grant and his three daughters were to be provided with suitable husbands. Finally William is to be exempted from jury service and:-

> In consideration of being wearied with labours and divers vexations under the burden of the king's service...shall not be sent on the king's service anywhere against his will and shall not be charged with any offices or labours but shall henceforth enjoy his own fireside at his pleasure.

In twenty-first century parlance, this is a man saying he's burnt out, had enough and wants to go home. William recovered from this personal crisis and was soon back in action.

The de la Pole family seemed to have escaped the Black Death, the bubonic plague that arrived in London in 1348 and killed over the next few years between a third and a half of the population. The sudden reduction in the workforce had seriously unpredictable effects on mercantile and banking businesses.[13] It is possible that the recurrent nature of the pandemic, which returned in waves up until 1353, was a subtle contribution to the failure of the English Wool Company. There were other complex reasons that were not Pole's fault but there is no doubt the customs farmers and financiers associated with them behaved in an arbitrary unscrupulous way that made them deeply unpopular. There were repeated complaints to parliament about the abuses and misconduct and in 1353 a Great Council procured from the king an ordinance designed to stop the profiteering by the customs farmers and merchants but also to encourage the English cloth manufacturing trade that was much more profitable than the sale of raw wool. Parliament distrusted the Crown's bankers for good reason and the one they distrusted most was de la Pole.

A Changing Society—Parliament becomes stronger. Men and women's duties became more intertwined after the first wave of bubonic plague, women were needed to fill vital roles. Although men retained their privileges, women achieved stronger property rights for themselves than ever before although they were to lose many of their advances during the later medieval period and in the Elizabethan Protestant reformation.

In both East Anglia and East Yorkshire, arable land was turned to pasture, which required less manpower. Sheep rearing took over whole swathes of the country. It has to be admitted that a reduced population was easier to feed and diets improved as meat became more widely available. The greater availability of land did not halt the continued flight from country to town where work in the clothing industry was an attractive alternative.

Many villages died altogether in the late fourteenth century, leaving only an isolated medieval church standing in today's landscape. Some of these changes were inevitable and not wholly attributable to the plague. The spare manorial land was however available to purchase for ambitious men with money and, where landlords were keen to rid themselves of labour-intensive arable land, there were opportunities for an ambitious tenant or a grand landowner to muscle in to build up their holdings. Thus there were winners and losers following the catastrophe, both the de la Poles and the de Wingfields, whom we will meet soon, were able to profit from the disaster.

Many of the potential economic gains of the aftermath of the plague were however destroyed by the new king Edward III's preoccupation with war and glory in Scotland and France. Frequent taxation weighed heavily on both towns and countryside. Parliament often opposed the King's ambitious taxing plans, and in so doing triggered the increasing desire of parliament to become an effective political assembly. The Commons did not become a regular or permanent feature of the English parliament until Edward II's reign (1307-1327). Representatives had attended assemblies throughout the thirteenth century, but only on an *ad hoc* basis. In Edward I's reign, only eighteen out of fifty parliaments had members of parliament present. But at the very beginning of the fourteenth century an important shift of perspective resulted in much less emphasis on the barons, or 'Lords', as defenders of the 'community of the realm' in political discussion and negotiation with the king. This role increasingly transferred to the Commons. It was the knights of the shires and burgesses of the towns who represented 'the whole community of England' and who alone should grant taxation on behalf of the people.[14]

The downfall of William de la Pole. By 1353 Pole had lost favour with Edward III, who was probably tired of the massive rewards he was giving William in exchange for loans. William was put on trial on a series of charges that would ultimately destroy his fortune. He wasn't the only one; he shared this fate with many other royal moneylenders during the 1340s and 1350s. He survived an initial court proceeding in the early 1340s when both he and his brother Richard were arrested with others. William was imprisoned at Devizes Castle and his lands seized. The charges were dropped in 1344, but before this William had already been scheming to fund the king's wars by the foundation of a new company. All went well until 1350 when the old charges were resurrected and William had to renounce all claims to the Manor of Burstwick and Holderness. He later felt it expedient to cancel all debts owed by the king in return for a pardon but it must have been a bitter loss of his wealth and a reversal of fortune that had a significant impact on the attitudes and careers of his children.

The Death of William de la Pole. William died in 1366, having seen his oldest son Michael well established in a military career and married to a suitably wealthy heiress, the daughter of Sir John de Wingfield, a man even more brilliant than himself. William's wife Katherine died in 1382, 16 years after William. She had probably spent most of her life in Hull, where she is buried. Her life would have been occupied by the care and supervision of her seven children and keeping the household business in Hull under her oversight with William's retainers and agents while he was away on business in London, Antwerp and later in prison.

The Family Arms. William was the first person identified with the arms of de la Pole, 'azure a fess between three leopards' faces or', (20. p.46).[15] The leopards' faces may refer to assay marks and the colour blue to water but we cannot be sure. His brother Richard adopted different arms.

With the next generation, William's descendants moved away from Hull but they never forgot their rise to fame had begun in the town and maintained an emotional attachment to it, especially to the Hull Charterhouse, in spite of their later endowing other religious institutions at Wingfield and at Ewelme in Oxfordshire. William and Katherine were probably buried in the priory church at the Charterhouse, their son Michael and his wife Katherine were too and their grandson Michael wished to be. Finally William and Katherine's great grandson, also William, was interred there.

Notes

1 Cowell, A., 1999, The World; Impeachment: What a Royal Pain, *New York Times,* 7 February 1999.

2 Roskell, J.S., 1984, *The Impeachment of Michael de la Pole, Earl of Suffolk in 1386 in the context of the reign of Richard II.* Manchester University Press, Manchester. See Introduction pp. 1-8 for a review of pre-1984 opinions on Michael's guilt.

3 Tuck, A., 2004, Pole, Michael de la, first earl of Suffolk (c.1330–1389), *Oxford Dictionary of National Biography*, Oxford University Press, online edn, Jan 2008.

4 Rubin, M., 2005, *The Hollow Crown: A History of Britain in the Late Middle Ages*, Penguin Books. Chapter I. Famine and Deposition 1307-1330 pp. 17-56.

5 British History online, *The Town of Hull.* www.british-history.ac.uk/vch/yorks/east/vol1/pp11-85#p35.

6 Harrison, J., 2018, *Past Hull and Around; Medieval Hull, 1300–1400 AD*, online at https://pasthull.com/medieval-hull/

7 Harvey, A. S., 1957, *The de la Pole Family of Kingston upon Hull*, East Yorkshire Local History Society, pp. 2-4. Online at http://www.eylhs.org.uk/dl/115/the-de-la-pole-family-of-hull [accessed 19 July 2018].

8 Horrox, R., 1983, *The de la Poles of Hull*, East Yorkshire Local History Society, East Yorkshire.

9 Fryde, E.B., 2004, William de la Pole, *Oxford Dictionary of National Biography*, doi:10.1093/ref:odnb/22460; Fryde, E.B., 1962, The Last Trials of Sir William de la Pole. *The Economic History Review. 15*, pp. 17–30. doi:10.1111/j.1468-0289.1962.tb02225.x.; Fryde, E.B., 1964, *The Wool Accounts of William de la Pole: a Study of Some Aspects of the English wool trade at the start of the Hundred Years' War*, St. Anthony's Hall Publications, Borthwick Institute of Historical Research no 25; Fryde, E.B., 1988, *William de la Pole: Merchant and King's Banker (d. 1366)*, Hambleton Press, Stockton.

10 Bourne, F., *Henry Richard 1866 II. The de la Poles of Hull (1311–1366), English merchants: memoirs in illustration of the progress of British commerce, I*, Richard Bentley, pp. 50–70; 2nd edition, 1886. Kingsford, C. L., 1896, Pole, William de la (d.1366), *Dictionary of National Biography, 1885–1900, vol 46*, pp. 49–50.

11 Badham, S., 2012, *A Monument in Holy Trinity Church, Hull*, Church Monuments Society, http://www.churchmonumentssociety.org/Monument%20of%20the%20Month%20Archive/2012-09.html [accessed 9 July 2018].

12 Ibid. 8, p. 18.

13 Routt, D., 2008, The Economic Impact of the Black Death *EH.Net Encyclopedia*, edited by Whaples, R., 20 July 2008. http://eh.net/encyclopedia/the-economic-impact-of-the-black-death/ [accessed 4 July 2019].

14 BBC History online, Dodd, G., 2011, *The Birth of Parliament* http://www.bbc.co.uk/history/british/middle_ages/birth_of_parliament_01.shtml [accessed 30 December 2013].

15 Ibid. 8, p. 4.

The Rise of Michael de la Pole

Michael de la Pole's boyhood. Michael was about nine during the year of his father's apparent nervous strain and in his teens when his father was in prison under threat of ruination, only to retrieve a miraculous recovery of his status and further success, to be followed yet again by disgrace and permanent downfall. He learnt early how fickle fortune could be.

To what extent, if at all, Michael was able to salvage any remnants of his father's financial empire is unknown but it seems likely to be minimal. In any case, most of his father's remaining assets were held jointly with his wife, who did not die until January 1382. When William died Michael inherited little beyond an annuity of four hundred marks (£266 13s 4d).[1] He had however married a rich heiress by then so had considerable prospects. Nevertheless, as a youth, Michael was obliged to make his way in the world on his own merit and, given his father's history of a reviled mercantile career, it is unsurprising that Michael moved away from trade and banking to the more respectable military.

Military Service and a Knighthood. England was the foremost military power in Europe when Michael de la Pole served as a soldier, a remarkable achievement for a country with a tiny population, no more than two to three million people after the devastation of the plague. Edward III was a successful military strategist and his eldest son, the Black Prince, was described as the 'flower of chivalry', a military commander admired and revered by nobility and common people alike. For twenty years or more, Michael was often absent from England fighting battles in France, and gradually making himself useful in the administration of campaigns. We know very little detail of his early career but we know he served with Henry of Grosmont, duke of Lancaster and was knighted by 1353. His career probably started when he was in his early teens in the 1340s, after Crecy but well before the siege of Calais.

Acquiring a knighthood was a key recognition for Michael in his early twenties. When life expectancy for those who survived childhood was fifty to sixty, honours often came earlier than today. English society in the fourteenth century was organised in a social hierarchy that was subtly fluid and permeable to upward and downward movement depending on patronage and wealth.

At the top of the social scale stood the king and nobility, about two hundred great lords and magnates forming the ruling elite. Crown, nobility and church owned about seventy-five per cent of English land. Immediately below the nobility were knights like the de la Poles. Knighthood was not hereditary; men were made knights as a reward for outstanding service or because they

22. A medieval siege. Painted miniature from *Ogier le Danois*, ed. Antoine Vérard, Paris 1496–1499.

had become wealthy enough. By the fourteenth century, there were about one thousand knights, owning land worth on average forty pounds per annum.

Michael must have played his part well to be recognised by a knighthood, which was a serious step up the social ladder. The gulf between the nobility, the knights and the rest of the population was accentuated by the fact they spoke different languages. The ruling classes spoke a corrupt form of Norman French, common people used Germanic English. Over the course of Michael's lifetime, and that of his contemporary Geoffrey Chaucer (1343-1400), English became increasingly the language of all, although French continued its cultural dominance. The court had begun to speak Parisian French, an acquired skill, rather than Anglo-Norman French. English replaced French as the language of instruction after the Black Death. English was also becoming the language of government. In 1362 the Chief Justice opened Parliament with a speech in English for the first time since the Conquest. The same year, the Statute of Pleading was enacted providing that the courts and judiciary should conduct all business in English. Fourteenth-century English was spoken and written in a variety of dialects, but by the fifteenth century, London English was firmly established as the dialect spoken by the ruling elite.

Michael's leader, Henry of Grosmont, or Lancaster, was Edward III's lieutenant and captain in southwestern France from 1345 to 1347. He won a notable victory over a superior French force at Auberoche in Périgord in October 1345 and triumphed in a major battle at Poitier in September 1346, afterwards violently sacking the town. In 1349 Henry was appointed captain and vice-regent of Gascony and Poitou. As Edward's commissioner in France, Henry was largely responsible for negotiating in May 1360 the provisional Treaty of Bretigny, ending the first phase of the Hundred Years War. We do not know if Michael was present at Poitier or other battles of the 1340s. He does not appear in the short list of English nobles compiled by the contemporary chronicler Jean Froissart but we know there were many other omissions. If he were present, as seems likely, Michael would certainly have won his spurs in these pitiless and bloody encounters.

Medieval warfare was a pretty barbarous business. Though men set out to war steeped in historical cultural notions of chivalry they soon discovered the vile reality. English armies marched to French battlefields using the chevauchée strategy of cutting a swathe of destruction five to thirty miles wide, burning and pillaging towns and farms en route, murdering any village inhabitants in the way. It was effective in terrifying the French before the battle but naturally led to decades of French hatred of the English. The whole of modern Normandy was a war-torn half-deserted wasteland from where the local population had fled for safety. If one thinks about the twenty-first century wastes of Iraq, Syria, Somalia or Eritrea we can imagine the horrors of medieval northern France. The exponents who used the chevauchée with maximum force were Henry of Lancaster and that 'glamorous' figure, Edward of Woodstock, the Black Prince, Edward III's eldest son and heir. Michael's future was largely determined by the connections he made while serving with the Black Prince's extensive retinue. A successful military career in the fourteenth century brought financial rewards but also more lucrative administrative positions of power.

In 1355, Michael was attached to Lancaster's retinue in an abortive expedition to Normandy. In 1359 he accompanied the Black Prince in a new expedition, was again fighting in France in 1369 and serving in 1370 under the Black Prince in Aquitaine. He took part that year in the famous siege of Limoges, and in December 1370 and January 1371 fought under John of Gaunt at the successful siege of Montpont. John of Gaunt (named after his place of birth, Ghent) was Edward III's third son and became duke of Lancaster after Henry of Lancaster died during the outbreak of plague in 1361, inheriting Henry's fortune and title by marrying Henry's daughter Blanche. John of Gaunt was a critical influence on Michael, who accompanied Gaunt in another abortive expedition in 1372. Gaunt was also the richest man in England with all the revenues of the Duchy of Lancaster at his disposal. By 1373 Edward III's waning powers and the Black Prince's recurrent debilitating chronic illness opened the opportunities for Gaunt to exert influence on policy at home.

Michael's loyalties to John of Gaunt in later years determined his Lancastrian sympathies. It seems to have been through Gaunt's influence that, in 1366, Michael achieved the rank of Knight Banneret, the upper echelon of the knightly class. Shortly afterwards he was summoned to parliament by personal writ, a singular honour.[2] His father had served Hull as member in the Commons; Michael had achieved a place by personal merit.

Capture by the French. During the later impeachment trial, there was mention that Michael had been taken prisoner twice while on the king's service, which had cost him dear. We know that one time was when he was on an errand to negotiate the king's marriage but it is not clear when the other period of imprisonment occurred. We have to assume it was during his French campaigns.[7] Prisoners of war were taken only when the prisoner looked likely to be of sufficient standing to justify the demand for a substantial ransom but there is no record of payment made for this first release or how long he was held prisoner. A period of months was usual, but it could be years before negotiations concluded. Aristocratic prisoners were usually well treated but nevertheless families had to bear the brunt of the huge costs of release.

Captain of Calais and Promotions at home. Michael was also at one time Captain of Calais. Reference was made to this during the impeachment trial. After the capture of Calais by the English in 1347 this crucial gain of French territory demanded a large standing garrison of 1,400 men, virtually a small army, under the overall command of the Captain, who had numerous deputies and specialist under-officers. It was a position of considerable responsibility for a young man. In February 1367, Michael was appointed one of the commissioners of array for the East Riding of Yorkshire, consolidating his power in his native town and its surrounding area. This gave him powers to muster troops locally and sign them up to be paid. Commissioners were usually experienced soldiers, appointed by the Crown to recruit able-bodied men from each shire.

23. Depiction of the Battle of Calais, 2 January 1350—Froissart Chronicles, 1410.

Michael meets Sir John de Wingfield of Suffolk (c1330–1361) and marries Katherine Wingfield. Michael would have met Sir John de Wingfield when they were both serving in the Black Prince's retinue. Exactly when is not known but it was probably in France in 1358 or 1359. Sir John de Wingfield was as extraordinary a man as Michael's own father. He held various unofficial titles but was for over ten years, between 1350 and his death in 1361, the

Black Prince's business manager, fixer and chief administrator. In twenty-first century parlance he was Chief Executive, Chief Operating Officer and also Finance Director. In short, he was crucial for the implementation of the Black Prince's military strategy in France but also in the management of his estates at home.

While the documented facts of Wingfield's life are not extensive, Mark Bailey has constructed a compelling account of what is known and I have drawn on his work and that of other modern historians such as Richard Barber, Michael Jones, and Jonathan Sumption, who have increasingly understood the genius of Wingfield's business brain.[3] He enabled the Black Prince to embark on the Poitier Campaign of the 1350s, one of the most dazzling successes of the Hundred Years War. Wingfield managed to overcome the extraordinary challenges posed by the demographic catastrophe of the Black Death to marshal sufficient men, materials and supplies for the campaign. This was when the prince was at the height of his powers, a military strategist of genius and a national hero. But he needed to generate sufficient cash to embark on the expensive business of war and the older Wingfield, who had campaigned and run errands in France for Edward II as a young man, was an old soldier with vast experience of the organisation, logistics and practicalities of warfare.

Wingfield grew up in the parish of Wingfield, Suffolk, the fourth Sir John in succession. His mother was Elizabeth Honeypot, about whom little is known but is thought to have come from a local Suffolk family. Sometime before 1330, John married Eleanor de Verlay, whose mother was from the wealthy de Glanville family. Eleanor's father Thomas de Verlay was a royal servant.

Wingfield took a very active role in the military campaigns early in the 1330s. He fought at Crecy in the third division alongside Edward III and also at the siege of Calais and gradually grew in esteem and personal fortune, becoming a knight sometime before 1340. He placed his new coat of arms in Brockdish Church, Norfolk in 1335, where his brother Thomas held the advowson, and had a great seal created, which is now in the National Archives.[4] As a reward for this service he was granted the right to hold an annual fair at Saxmundham every June, in those days a real 'money spinner'. He was also exempt from sitting on assizes.

Wingfield continued to fight personally during the Poitier campaign and we know something about his role there from his blow-by-blow letters home that convey the immediacy and reality of war. He personally captured Louis, Sire D'Aubigny, the head of the French king John II's bodyguard. Edward III

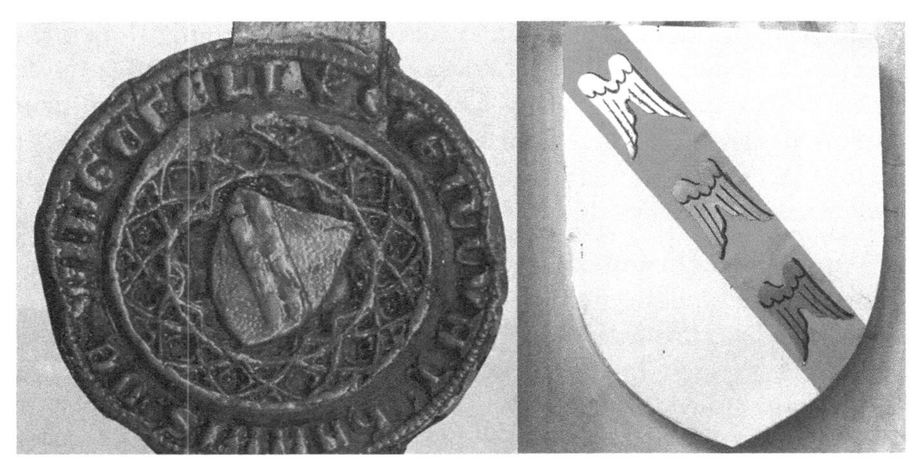

24. left: de Wingfield's Seal 1335. 25. right: the arms of Sir John de Wingfield
right, argent, on a bend gules three wings conjoined in lure of the field, later quartered by de la Pole.

later purchased this valuable captive from Wingfield for two thousand, five hundred marks, about seventeen hundred and fifty pounds, a considerable sum that added to Wingfield's personal fortune.

Though often in England raising cash and supplies, Wingfield travelled extensively in both England and France to wherever he was needed. We know that he was in France in late 1359 and early 1360 when Michael de la Pole was also there. From 1350 Wingfield was also appointed steward of all the lands in the Black Prince's estate. This included the Duchy of Cornwall, the earldom of Cheshire, vast tracts of North Wales, Aquitaine and also the business departments of the Prince's substantial travelling household and in London. Wingfield kept a house in London called Wingfield's Inn where presumably he lived when on business there.

Wingfield's role went far beyond the conventional estate manager. He centralised decision making to an unusual extent and authorisations of expenditure were restricted to himself and a few other royal servants close to the prince. Wingfield held the purse strings, was ruthless in his dealings with lesser officials in peripheral localities and ensured that maximum profit was extracted from the estates to finance the prince's ambitions. Where matters were going wrong he took personal control, reorganised accounting systems, put greater emphasis on cash management and income generation. Perhaps he would not have been able to sustain this over a prolonged period but in the short term he was spectacularly successful, even though he could be guilty of sharp practice and had no tolerance of lesser mortals' failings. Wingfield at times even over-ruled the prince if he thought it was in the best interests of the prince's goals and he appears to have been indulged by the younger man, who seems to have had total trust in him. While on the prince's business he received ten shillings a day, twice as much as his predecessor and a huge amount of pay for the time. He was possibly the first business 'fat-cat'.

The Acquisition of Frumbald's Manor, Wingfield. One might have thought Sir John Wingfield was quite busy enough on the prince's business but he took on other lucrative roles. He had a retinue which was made up largely of neighbouring gentry in East Anglia and he himself took on commissions in Norfolk and elsewhere, serving on the councils of the earls of Salisbury, Surrey and later the earl of Surrey's widow. He was not a trained lawyer but clearly had a deep understanding of the law. Meanwhile Wingfield's fortunes were consolidated in his estate based in north Suffolk. We know from his application for a licence of free warren in 1335 that his main manorial holdings were in Wingfield, Syleham, Esham, Fressingfield, Sternfield, Weybread and Saxmundham.[5] Free warren was a type of franchise or privilege conveyed by a sovereign, promising to hold them harmless for killing game of certain species, usually hare and fox but also other game within a stipulated area. It indicated that the licensee was to be regarded as the virtual owner. Some of these manors Wingfield had acquired through his wife. Over the course of the 1340s and 50s he added further manors in East Anglia and further afield in Hampshire, Cheshire and the north, opportunities that must have emerged from his knowledge of those areas during his work for the prince. It was in 1357 that he finally acquired the Wingfield Frumbald's manor that later became the site of Wingfield Castle.

The historian Mark Bailey estimates that his lands by the late 1350s would have generated about two hundred pounds a year but add to this his other stipends and salaries and he was earning a huge amount.[6] He was also granted the income from the judicial profits of the hundreds courts of Blything and Wangford hundreds, local courts that settled property and land disputes and could impose fines on behalf of the Crown, not too popular with ordinary litigants who felt the fees and fines were imposed in an arbitrary fashion in some of these 'outsourced' courts.[7] By 1359 he was perhaps earning about five to six hundred pounds a year, which puts him in the very wealthiest group of knights, on a par with lesser nobility. Out of this of course he had to fund a very expensive lifestyle but his capital assets made John de Wingfield a very wealthy man.

Katherine Wingfield and marriage to Michael de la Pole. John de Wingfield and Eleanor had one daughter, Katherine, their only child to survive to adulthood and sole heir to her parents' substantial estate. We do not know exactly when she was born, some authorities say 1340s, others think later that decade. She was of marriageable age by 1359, that is, she was over twelve years old. She may have contracted an early first marriage to one of the de Brewse family, who died shortly after. It is understandable that John and Eleanor would be determined to find a new match for Katherine as soon as possible, but by then Katherine perhaps would have had more say in the choice of husband. Even very young widows had more personal property rights than married women, although in Katherine's case, her father held the disposal of his future legacy in his hands and it is likely that Katherine herself would have wished to remarry and have children.

From all we know of Wingfield's personality he would not have contemplated Michael de la Pole as a son-in-law unless he judged that Michael would be a success in life and likely to be a worthy steward of his daughter's inheritance. The Wingfields must have been aware of the disgrace and loss of fortune of Michael's father, who was still alive, ageing at home in Hull but it would be entirely in character for John de Wingfield not to care one jot about Michael's forebears and their trading background if Michael was a sound prospect for maintaining his daughter's future fortune. The marriage took place on 18 October 1361 in Michael's home town of Kingston upon Hull.

Michael was in his early 30s, his bride younger by perhaps 10-15 years. This marriage was a triumph for an ambitious young man. Although Michael had been summoned to Parliament by personal writ, that is, he was appointed to the medieval Commons, he did not become a member of the peerage until a decade later. There are misunderstandings of his position in some accounts. Nevertheless, when Michael contracted a marriage with Katherine he was a seriously successful man already, though he did not have a lot of personal wealth. Did love come into the equation? We shall never know. Marriages among the propertied elite were first and foremost designed to preserve and develop personal estates. They were thus a property contract, although romantic love could and did influence arranged marriages. The Black Prince famously married for love and a good choice his Joan of Kent turned out to be, in spite of early opposition from his relatives and bishops. After his second wife's death, John of Gaunt married his long-term mistress, Katherine Swynford, who had already borne him four children. Couples lucky enough to be paired with someone compatible frequently fell in love after marriage rather than before. We can hope that Michael and Katherine were well-suited and found marital happiness in the twenty five years of their marriage.

Katherine would have spent most of her time overseeing the various households where Michael was living, including Wingfield and of course taking charge when he was away on business, as was frequent. The couple had at least seven children. Anne was born very shortly after their marriage, she went on to marry Gerard de Lisle in 1373 but he died early and she later married Richard Thorley. Michael and Katherine's oldest son, also Michael, was born about 1367, then followed William, who became a canon of Beverley, Richard c1369 who was buried at Wingfield in 1403, John c1370, buried at Wingfield 1415, Margaret c1371, Elizabeth c1372 and finally Thomas c1378. All these dates are estimates, but seem to fit best the likely sequence of events. The dates of their deaths are more secure. All the children except Thomas were born in Kingston upon Hull and it is likely therefore that Michael and Katherine made their main home in Hull in the first 15 years of their marriage. Michael's father died in 1366, leaving a large, well-furnished mansion in Hull. At the time of Michael's disgrace many years later, the inventory of his possessions there included many costly hangings and silver plate, the value of £40 13s 10d suggests a beautifully decorated and sumptuous home.

The death of Sir John de Wingfield. Within a month of his daughter's marriage, on 8 November 1361, Wingfield died. In June, Sir John was still 'busily warranting' letters in London on behalf of the Black Prince but contracted a sudden illness which is thought likely to have been a resurgence of bubonic plague that autumn. There had been other recurrences but this one was particularly virulent among men and young people and was concentrated in the southern half of the country. Henry of Lancaster also died in this outbreak.[8] Wingfield had at least the satisfaction of knowing that his daughter was well settled; he also had time to dictate his will and say how he wished to be buried and remembered. Ever generous to his old friend, the Black Prince paid the magnificent sum of £57 13s 4d for Sir John's funeral and burial at St. Andrew's Church, Wingfield, a church which he was responsible for rebuilding. His tomb, a now very weathered Purbeck marble effigy, shows him to be taller than six feet, lying in full armour below an ogee canopy, his head cradled on his helm, his feet resting on a sadly crumbling lion's head.

John's will expressed his wish that a chantry chapel and college should be established at Wingfield. The purpose was to provide masses in perpetuity for the souls of the benefactor, his immediate relatives and a handful of other named persons. Building a chantry was an act of piety but also in the fourteenth century a fashionable statement of wealth and status. It was a legacy that would be honoured by his de la Pole descendants for generations.

26. Tomb of Sir John de Wingfield, died 1361, St Andrew's Church, Wingfield.

Michael de la Pole's family move to Wingfield, Suffolk. Michael often served abroad, sometimes at sea and was also gathering positions of respect in Yorkshire. In 1362 he acquired the lands of his niece Catherine, who died in that year, the daughter and heiress of his brother Thomas. Katherine's mother, Eleanor de Wingfield, died in 1375, at last bequeathing to her daughter, and therefore Michael, all her husband's estates in Suffolk and elsewhere. Michael had finally come into substantial wealth. He decided to move his base from Hull to Wingfield, probably initially living in the manor house where his in-laws had lived and Katherine grew up. He began to call himself 'Lord of Wingfield'.[9]

There were good practical reasons for the move. The south, and East Anglia in particular, was wealthier than the north of England, it was more populous and it was far less remote from the various palaces where the court resided and nearer to Westminster too. Most travel between East Anglia and Hull was by boat from Yarmouth or Dunwich, far more efficient than going by road all around the Wash, but nevertheless not for the faint hearted in the notoriously poor weather on the North Sea coast. Getting to London from Wingfield on the other hand could be effected in three days on a good mount.

We have some insight into Michael and Katherine's income from their estates from the period when they were first living at Wingfield from two incomplete sets of accounts dated 1369-1370, compiled for the manors of Wingfield and Syleham by Ellis Typeter, servant/sergeant for 'Lord Michael de la Poole', and from 1375 to 1378.[10] The total annual income from Wingfield and Syleham manors, mainly from farm rents, but also from the income from manor courts of 16s and including over £30 in arrears, was £112 14s 9d farthing. Expenses and payments for wages, for ploughing, for equipment, the costs of running the mill came to £80 10s 7d halfpenny, leaving a total reckoning owed to 'the Lord' of £32 3s 1d halfpenny farthing. This would generate an income of about sixteen thousand pounds today although the sums are not easily comparable. Nevertheless with several dozen manors producing this size of income, Michael was making a substantial amount from his land and livestock.

Michael rises in politics; A new king comes to the throne. Michael was increasingly spending time away from Suffolk at the heart of politics in Westminster and at court, wherever the court happened to be, often at Windsor, Eltham or Sheen. In domestic politics he naturally attached himself to John of Gaunt. Edward III was failing and died in June 1377. The Black Prince had died after five years of physical incapacity in 1376. The prince's son, the new king Richard II acceded to the throne, a boy of ten years old. The king's uncle John of Gaunt was clearly the most likely person to exercise power over the new king and indeed there were real fears, probably unjustified, that he would seize the throne or at least exercise illegal regency.[11] But the boy king already had personal counsellors and trusted friends whom he turned to for advice. Sir Simon Burley had long been his most senior tutor and a friend of his father and after Richard's accession was made Vice Chamberlain of the king's household. Burley rapidly became unpopular with the nobles at court, which some years later led to his downfall.

In the so-called 'Good Parliament' of 1376 Michael stood strongly on the side of the Crown and the unpopular duke. Though his relationship with John of Gaunt later cooled, de la Pole never swerved from the policy of supporting the Crown. Loyalty was the fundamental root cause of his downfall, an admirable trait when the king was a revered experienced man, a more difficult principle to maintain in the face of the autocratic, single-minded but weak and petty young tyrant that Richard turned out to be. But Michael was always convinced of the right of his king, whoever he was, to exercise autocratic power as of birthright. As a reward for this early demonstration of loyalty to Edward III, in 1376 Michael was appointed Admiral of the King's Fleet North of the Thames, responsible for the commissioning and deployment of the king's ships in battle. He was gaining ground politically, the future was looking good.

Notes

1 Tuck, A., 2004 online 2008, Pole, Michael de la, first Earl of Suffolk, *Oxford Dictionary of National Biography*, Matthew, H. C. G. and Harrison, B. (eds), Oxford University Press, Oxford.

2 Fildes, K.E., 2009, *The Baronage in the Reign of Richard II, 1377-1399.* Unpublished PhD thesis University of Sheffield, p124.

3 Bailey, M., 2015, Sir John de Wingfield and the Foundation of Wingfield College, Chapter 2 in Bloore, P. and Martin E. (eds), 2015, *Wingfield College and its Patrons.* Boydell Press, Woodbridge, pp. 31-39; Jones, M., 2018, *The Black Prince, England's Greatest Medieval Warrior*, Pegasus books, New York; Sumption, J., 2001, *The Hundred Years War, Volume 2 Trial by Fire*, University of Pennsylvania Press, see especially Chapter IV Scotland and Languedoc 1355-1356; Barber, R., 2002, *The Life and Campaigns of the Black Prince: from contemporary letters, diaries and chronicles, including Chandos Herald's Life of the Black Prince*, Boydell and Brewer, Woodbridge.

4 Blomefield, F., 1806, Hundred of Earsham: Brockdish, in *An Essay Towards A Topographical History of the County of Norfolk: Volume 5,* London, pp. 327-339. British History Online http://www.british-history.ac.uk/topographical-hist-norfolk/vol5/pp327-339 [accessed 16 August 2020].

5 Calendar of the Charter Rolls Vol IV, Edward III, 1327-1341, p 342, published transcription London 1912.

6 Ibid. 3, p. 42.

7 Ibid. p. 41.

8 Mullan, J., 2007, Mortality, gender, and the plague of 1361–2 on the estate of the bishop of Winchester, *Cardiff Historical Papers* online http://orca.cf.ac.uk/3975/1/CHP8_Mullan.pdf; Cohn, S. K., 2008, Epidemiology of the Black Death and Successive Waves of Plague. *Medical History, Vol 52*, pp. 74-100. https://doi.org/10.1017/S0025727300072100 [accessed 7 July 2019].

9 Michael de la Pole addressed as Lord of Wingfield in 1377. The National Archives, Kings Remembrancer Series D ancient deeds E 210/4471, William Godman to Sir Michael de la Pole, lord of Wingfield: Grant of half an acre in Esham [in Syleham]: Suffolk.

10 Account of Ellis Typeter servant/sergeant of Lord Michael de la Poole of the manors of Wynggefelde & Syleham Michaelmas 2—Michaelmas 3 King Richard. Staffordshire Record Office D641/4/D/8/6/1; Suffolk Record Office, Ipswich. Account Roll [8,9,10 Henry IV] Henry IV (April 1367 – 20 March 1413) accounts 1375-1378. HA 411/5/2/1.

11 Saul, N., 1997, *Richard II.* Yale University Press, New Haven, p. 16.

27. Portrait of Richard II, The Westminster Portrait.

The Later Career of Michael de la Pole

Michael's rise to prestige and his second captivity. The accession of Richard II did not at first affect Michael's position. On 14 August 1377 his commission as Admiral of the Fleet was renewed, although in December the same year he and his colleague Robert Hales were superseded in favour of the earls of Warwick and Arundel. Michael then joined Lancaster's abortive maritime operations against the French. Gradually, however, civil responsibilities superseded military ones and he became increasingly prominent at court.

In Spring 1379, Michael was the senior of three officials sent as an embassy to Milan to negotiate a marriage between young Richard II and Caterina, daughter of Bernabo Visconti, Lord of Milan.[14] The other two were Sir John Burley, the older brother of Simon, and Gerard de Lisle, Michael's son-in-law. Nothing came of the Milanese negotiation, for complex reasons involving loyalties to the two rival popes at Rome and Avignon. The envoys, after visiting the papal curia at Rome, no doubt offering Richard's support to the Rome Pope Urban VI, went on to Germany to see Wenceslas, (or Wenzel), king of the Romans and of Bohemia, to suggest Richard's marriage with Wenceslas' sister Anne.[1]

En route home from Germany, having concluded successful initial negotiations, Michael and his party of envoys were waylaid and captured by brigands, who had no respect for the warrant of imperial safe conduct. This was sometime before 14 December 1379, when a royal herald, Richard Hereford, was sent to negotiate the group's liberation.[2] John Otter, Michael's secretary, was dispatched from England to effect his ransom in January 1380.

Michael's younger brother Edmund was intimately involved in raising the high ransom demanded for the hostages' release. John of Gaunt put up seven thousand gold florins, about a thousand pounds, to be sent to Albert, duke of Bavaria, on condition that Sir Edmund and other friends of the prisoners would be promptly reimbursed. The duke of Bavaria seems to have acted as an intermediary, on condition that Michael and the others were released in February or March. Michael did not actually reach England again until May

1380. It was not until he was Chancellor that he was paid for the whole time of his absence abroad, recompensed for his total losses and was able to claim the money to repay Gaunt.

This whole episode must have cost Katherine and their daughter Anne severe anxiety, news travelled very slowly in the medieval period. But the success of the mission in Richard's eyes, producing the highly desired outcome, must have raised Michael in the king's esteem.

Richard II married Anne of Bohemia in 1382. It was a successful marriage, at least in the world's eyes although politically the marriage achieved little in the way of useful alliances. There were mutterings that she probably wasn't worth the considerable investment. Richard was devoted to Anne, never looked at another woman and was later devastated at her death. They had no children.

Richard's sexuality has often been called into question. The young king was a tall and handsome blond but writers noted his 'feminine aspect' and 'stuttering, lisping speech', although we might nowadays suspect this description likely to be invented as slur. Richard and his closest friend Robert de Vere, the earl of Oxford, were certainly emotionally entangled and contemporaries thought that the king and de Vere had a sexual relationship. In 1385 Richard made de Vere marquess of Dublin, and the following year duke of Ireland. These were exceptional, unprecedented honours out of keeping with de Vere's role at court. No wonder de Vere was unpopular and reviled by other courtiers. But Richard and Anne became close friends at least; whether they were married lovers is a question few wished to ask.

Counsellor to the king. In November 1381 Michael was appointed, jointly with Richard Fitzalan, earl of Arundel 'counsellor in constant attendance on the king and governor of his person'. The problem for everyone at court and indeed for the nobility and parliament was Richard's extreme youth. Richard was fourteen, a self-possessed, good-looking, well mannered youth. But even in those days when a youth might marry at fourteen and be expected to fight from his early teens, he could not be expected to be an effective head of government at a time when personal monarchy depended absolutely on the character and behaviour of the monarch. Richard had faced Wat Tyler during the Peasants Revolt and at the tender age of fourteen had appeared to exhibit a kingly, even lofty demeanor, indeed this turned out to be the highlight of his entire career. Nevertheless the depth of his inexperience was clear. It was decided to establish a Council that would govern on Richard's behalf. The rising disagreements between the Council, largely made up of magnates together with the king's own retinue, and on the other side the Commons, led to the maelstrom of political crises that encircled Michael over the next few years.

28. The Coronation of Anne of Bohemia as Queen of England, illustration from Liber Regalis.

Chancellor de la Pole. Michael impressed the young king with his ideas on policy. The withdrawal of John of Gaunt overseas to stake his claim to the throne of Castile removed the only rival counsellor of any influence and Michael soon became Richard's most trusted personal adviser. But Michael's attachment to the court engendered growing unpopularity with both the great barons and the populace at large, who saw him as an over-promoted common man. Tuck judges that there was no obvious ill feeling expressed when Pole was appointed Chancellor of England on the 13 March 1383 in succession to

Robert de Braybroke, Bishop of London, but it would not have been politic to air this.

There were two great departments of state, the Exchequer and the Chancery. By 1345 the Lord Chancellor began to be seen as the leader of the Court of Chancery, as well as a representative of the king, and writs and bills were addressed to him. The Chancellor and his clerks often heard the cases themselves, rather than having them referred to the council itself. Occasionally a committee of lay and church members dealt with them, assisted by the judges of the common law courts. The Lord Chancellor also convened parliament and opened it on behalf of the king. Michael de la Pole was right at the centre of the developing tussle for influence between parliament and the king and his council. He heard petitions addressed to the king, made decisions on behalf of the king and when overwhelmed with the workload, delegated his powers to others, something his enemies resented.

Michael was not the first, nor the last, to feel the burden of the power struggle developing between parliament and the Chancery that intensified during the next century. The Commons regularly complained about the work of the Court of Chancery and after Michael's time in 1390 it petitioned the king to pronounce that the Court could not act contrary to the common law, nor annul a judgement without due process. It would take another three hundred years before relations between king, his parliament and Chancery were reordered and it took a civil war to do so.

De la Pole opened the parliament of 1383 with a speech in which he modestly declared his own unworthiness. This was customary but it became a stormy session. Pole said that besides enemies abroad, the king had to deal with enemies at home among his own servants and officials and proceeded to berate the assembled crowd with lax oversight. While Michael is famous for being impeached, he himself denounced and instituted impeachment proceedings on behalf of the king against the fighting Bishop of Norwich, Henry le Despenser. Despenser as a consequence was deprived of his temporalities, that is, the property assets of the bishopric. It is hard to feel sorry for Despenser, whom Thomas of Walsingham described as 'a man distinguished neither in learning nor discretion' 'unbridled and insolent, incapable of restraint'.[3] That may have been true but he was decisive, effective and successful in putting down the Peasants' Revolt in East Anglia.[4]

Foreign Policy. Fundamental differences in policy between Chancellor Pole and the Commons arose because of their differences on the French war. In the parliament of 1384 Pole wisely urged the need of a solid peace with France but the Commons, who were anxious enough to end the war, were not prepared to purchase peace at a high price and Pole's proposal was ill received. Throughout his career as Chancellor, de la Pole was hostile to pursuing further war with France. The pursuit of peace was clearly the king's wish and Michael, whose attitude may have been influenced by his own experience of war, knew how much war would cost, given France's recent gains in the Low Countries. His attempts to negotiate peace were unwelcome however and he was blamed for England's declining influence. Further, his critics complained that Ghent fell into French hands owing to his slowness in sending relief.

An unfortunate event gave his enemies an opportunity to foment suspicion against him.[5] A fishmonger named John Cavendish appeared before parliament and complained that the Chancellor had taken a bribe from him. Cavendish had an action before the Chancellor, and had been assured by Pole's clerk, John Otter, that if he paid forty pounds to the Chancellor, gave him three yards of scarlet cloth worth forty two shillings and four pounds in cash to Otter himself he would speedily get judgment in his favour.[21]

Cavendish had no money, but he sent to the Chancellor presents of herring, sturgeon and other fish instead. He lost his action anyway. Outraged, Cavendish brought his grievances before the Lords. The Chancellor had no difficulty in making a satisfactory answer, he had been unaware of the bribe until Cavendish' action against him. As soon as he had heard of the presents of fish, he ordered them to be paid for, and compelled his clerk to destroy the contract he had entered into with the fishmonger. Cavendish, instead of gaining his point, was condemned for defamation, and ordered to remain in prison until he had paid one thousand marks as damage to the Chancellor, and such other fine as the king might impose. It was an outrageous miscarriage of justice. Was Otter sacked for his corruption? There is no report, but probably not.

The Scottish Campaign and de la Pole becomes earl of Suffolk. De la Pole failed to carry out his policy of peace; he had misread the enemy and was forced to face a vigorous prosecution of the war against both Scotland and France. In the summer of 1385 he accompanied Richard on the king's only serious military undertaking, the expedition against Scotland, in which Michael commanded a band of sixty men-at-arms and eighty archers. It was his last military engagement although it is said that he did not participate personally in combat. He was after all about 55 years old, considered mature if not elderly at that time. After the failure of this undertaking, he was more than ever bent on peace. Ominously, France had threatened invasion so he renewed negotiations in some desperation.

During the Scottish campaign, the king awarded Michael the title of earl of Suffolk, extinct since the death of William Ufford three years before. While at Hoselaw in Teviotdale in the Borders, presumably where the army was encamped, the king granted him lands worth five hundred pounds a year, which had belonged to Ufford, and which included the castle, town, manor and honour of Eye, Suffolk, with other manors and jurisdictions, mainly in Suffolk, which nicely rounded off Michael's Wingfield inheritance. Since the widowed countess of Suffolk still held part of these estates for her lifetime, and other portions had been granted to the queen, Richard further granted the new earl two hundred pounds a year from the royal revenue and three hundred pounds a year from other estates until the Ufford estates became available. The grant of a small sum from the county revenue completed the formal connection between the new earl and his nomen territorialis. It was at this point Michael acquired the 'licences to crenellate' his mansion houses.

At the parliament that met Richard on his return from Scotland, Pole was formally ennobled, with the sword of the shire, and performed homage for his new office. Walter Skirlaw, Keeper of the Privy Seal and Bishop of Lichfield, delivered an oration to the assembled estates on the new earl's merits. It was a promotion too far for the assembled nobles, 'the murmurs were many and deep'.[6] He was, after all, wrote the St. Albans chronicler, 'a merchant and the son of a merchant; he was a man more fitted for trade than for chivalry, and peacefully had grown old in a banker's counting-house, and not among warriors in the field.' The saying became a commonplace, and is repeated by several other chroniclers. De la Pole's wealth was steadily growing and was exciting widespread envy. He was, they thought, an over-promoted, jumped up parvenu.

Nothing could be more unjust than such a taunt levelled against the old companion in arms of the Black Prince and of John of Gaunt and indeed someone who had just engaged in more fighting alongside the king. But it faithfully reflected the opinion of the greater families. Nor did Michael's former ally, John of Gaunt, support him any more either. Thomas Arundel, then Bishop of Ely, was especially hostile. Arundel tried to get Bishop Despenser's confiscated property restored to him. The Chancellor argued in the parliament of 1385 that to restore the bishop's lands would cost the king a thousand pounds a year. 'If thou hast so much concern for the king's profit,' retorted the bishop, 'why hast thou covetously taken from him a thousand marks per annum since thou wast made an earl?' The Chancellor had no answer, and Despenser recovered his property.

Suffolk, as we should now call Michael, was on the continent between 9 February and 28 March 1386 engaged in yet more fruitless negotiations with France for a truce or for peace. The English unwillingness to include Spain in the truce frustrated the negotiations and England was by now clearly under threat from invasion. The Chancellor did his best to organise defences but in rather a hurry. He acted as commissioner to inspect Calais and the castles of the marches, and as chief commissioner of array in Suffolk. In April and May he visited Hull, where his influence was still significant and he had lately enlarged and beautified his father's old house into a showy 'Suffolk Palace.' He was undoubtedly becoming quite grand in his home town. Local Yorkshire folk still perceived Michael to be their friend. It may be that his accent, manner of speaking and dress were more acceptable in Hull than in London. The north/south divide did not start in the twenty-first century.

By this point, whatever Michael did was judged adversely in Westminster. In June some English warships captured and plundered several Genoese merchant ships off Dover, mistaking their business. When the Chancellor quite rightly gave the aggrieved Genoese traders compensation, he was taunted with robbing the king of his rights and showing more sympathy with traders than with warriors, the old dig at his pedigree.

Impeachment. Opposition to de la Pole was now formally organised. When parliament met, in mid-October 1386, Michael urged as Chancellor that the time had now come to combat the threat of a French invasion by strengthening the south-east coastal defences. Parliament needed to agree the tax necessary to raise the huge amount of money needed. History refers to this parliament as the 'Wonderful Parliament'. Suffolk asked for an unprecedented amount of money to be raised in tax, four-fifteenths, says the chronicler Knighton. The medieval tax system was based on a fraction of a percentage of personal wealth in moveable goods, a complex system designed to achieve some fairness between townsmen and country folk. Parliament was enraged by this tax demand because, after all the peace-making, compromises and appeasements, Suffolk had left king and country exposed to invasion and now demanded an excessive amount of money to combat the threat.

The Commons now united to demand that the king dismiss and impeach the Chancellor but Richard retreated to Eltham Palace and told parliament that he would not dismiss Suffolk and, further, would not at the request of parliament dismiss a scullion from his kitchen. It was his right to choose his own ministers, not parliament's job. Parliament was enraged; this was an example of the arrogant attitude of monarchy that they were fighting against. Bishop Arundel visited the king at Eltham, and hinted that if the king did not agree to Michael's dismissal, he would be deposed.

Richard had little choice; he knew his crown was under real threat. The recollection of the fate of his great grandfather Edward II, deposed and then murdered, must have been lingering at the back of his mind. Richard dismissed Suffolk from the chancellorship on 24 October 1386. The Commons now drew up formal articles of impeachment against him. First, he had received grants of great estates from the king, or had purchased or exchanged royal lands at prices below their value. Second, he had not carried out the ordinances of the nine lords appointed in 1385 for the reform of the royal household. Third, he had misappropriated the supplies granted in the last parliament for the guard of the seas. Fourth, he had fraudulently appropriated to himself a charge on the customs of Hull previously granted to one Tydeman, a Limburg merchant. Fifth, he had taken for his own uses the confiscated revenue of the master of St Anthony's Hospital, London, which ought to have gone to the king. Sixth, he had sealed charters, especially a grant of franchises to Dover Castle, contrary to the king's interest; and seventh, he was remiss in conducting the war which had led to the loss of Ghent together with a large sum of treasure stored up within its walls.

The charges fell into two broad categories, those that accused him of failing in his duty as Chancellor and those that accused him of misusing his office for personal benefit. Michael spoke briefly but with dignity in his own defence, but left the burden of a detailed answer to his brother-in-law, Richard, lord Scrope, a former Chancellor himself, who applauded Michael's thirty years of service in the field and in the council chamber, denied the allegations of his mean origin and estate, and gave what seem to be impressively satisfactory answers to the seven heads of accusation. Many of the failings as Chancellor were decisions made by the whole governing king's council and were joint decisions for which Suffolk had only been partly responsible. There was however no doubt that while some of the personal benefits that he had accrued were common-enough perks of medieval high office and may have been modest in size compared with others' takings, nevertheless these perks neither looked well nor were honest.

The Commons, while silently dropping the charge of misappropriation of supplies, pressed for a conviction on the other six, and brought forward some fresh evidence against Suffolk. He was committed to the custody of the constable of the Tower but released on bail. The Commons having battered him, the Lords then gave their judgment: Suffolk was convicted on three of the charges but on the other four the Lords declared that he ought not to be impeached alone, since his guilt was shared by other members of the council. The legal arguments tossed back and forth by the Lords touched on the rights of monarchs and the position of parliament. While the Commons appeared unreasonable, the Lords and Judges appeared careful and fair.

Loss of office and the death of Katherine. Sentence was pronounced in the name of the king. Suffolk was to forfeit all the lands and grants which he had received contrary to his oath, and was committed to prison, to remain there until he had paid an adequate fine. The chronicler Thomas Walsingham, who had a very poor opinion of Michael, said the fine was 20,000 marks, (£13,333 6s 8d). Walsingham was a Benedictine monk who may have had an allegiance to clerical figures against whom he felt Michael was unreasonably prejudiced. But it was expressly declared that the judgment was not to involve the loss of the name and title of earl, nor the twenty pounds a year that the king had granted him from the issues of Suffolk for the title. Nonetheless, the fine was enormous, the loss of office a huge blow to Michael's self esteem.

Another terrible blow hit Michael that year. His wife Katherine died, we do not know the cause. The date given in one genealogical site is 10 October, just immediately before the crisis that led to Michael's impeachment. All his accomplishments that had been crowned with the plans for Wingfield Castle, must have seemed hollow and meaningless at that point. Many would have despaired. Michael though still had the support of the king.

The King's support. Parliament ordered Suffolk to be imprisoned at Corfe Castle, but Richard remitted the fine and invited Suffolk to join him for Christmas at Windsor. It was an act of kindness to a bereaved friend, an outrageous affront to the members of his parliament and nobles who clearly wanted Michael out of the way. As soon as the 'Wonderful Parliament' came to an end, Richard released Michael from custody and again listened to his advice. If not the boldest spirit, Suffolk was certainly the wisest head of the royalist party now formed against the new ministers and council set up by parliament. He dwelt in the king's household and seems to have accompanied Richard on his hasty progress through the land to win support for the impending civil war between king and council against parliament and nobles. It seems unlikely that Michael saw much of Wingfield and his Suffolk lands during this time.

The tensions dragged on, relations between king and his supporters on one side and nobles and parliament on the other were deteriorating. In August 1387 five judges declared at Nottingham that the existence of a new perpetual council established by parliament contravened the king's prerogative, and that the sentence on Suffolk ought to be reversed. Suffolk's name appears among the witnesses to this declaration of war against parliamentary government. But his enemies were resolute in their attack. He was accused of attempting to prevent reconciliation between Richard and his uncle the duke of Gloucester when Bishop William Courtenay of London went to promote peace between them. 'Hold your peace, Michael,' said the bishop to Suffolk, who was denouncing Gloucester to the king; 'it becomes you right evil to say such words, you that are damned for your falsehood both by the lords and by parliament.' Richard dismissed the bishop in anger but was not prepared to push things to extremes. By then he must have been seriously fearful of being deposed.

Suffolk goes into Exile. Richard was forced to promise the hated council, made up of Gloucester, Arundel and the earl of Warwick, that Suffolk and Robert de Vere, earl of Oxford, and three other close advisers should be compelled to answer for their conduct before the next parliament. The charge was an 'appeal' of treason. Hence the accusing nobles have always been called the 'Lords Appellant'. The original three appellants were joined by the earl of Derby and the earl of Nottingham. There is some indication from the record that Michael's eldest son, also Michael, had some sympathy with the Lords Appellant, although he must have realised that his future title and wealth depended on the judgment.

There was only one outcome for a guilty verdict of treason and Michael de la Pole saw instantly that to save his own life he needed to flee; the days of political negotiation were over. The support of this damaged and weak king was now useless. Suffolk hastily fled the realm although quite when he left is not clear. It may have been after an abortive attempt by incompetent de Vere to settle the matter by force with an ill-led army at Radcot Bridge, an ignominious defeat that made matters worse. De Vere escaped to Belgium where he had the sense to stay.

Suffolk and his four chief associates were accused of general malfeasances such as having withdrawn the king from the society of the barons, having conspired to rule him for their own purposes, inciting civil war and attempting to pack parliament. The declaration of the judges that the form of the appeal was illegal was brushed aside on the ground that parliament itself was the supreme judge in matters of this sort.

29. Robert de Vere fleeing Radcot Bridge after the 1387 battle.

The court imprisoned, exiled, or executed most of Richard's court in 1388. One victim was Sir Simon Burley, although there were many voices raised that his execution was unjust. Even the queen begged for his life but he was beheaded anyway. Despite Richard's efforts to save him, Sir Nicholas Bembre, a former Mayor of London, was also executed for treason. Chief Justice Robert Tresillian went into hiding but unfortunately hid in his father's house in London, where he was readily discovered and also quickly executed. On 13 February 1388 sentence was passed on all four absent accused by members of the well-named 'Merciless Parliament'. Suffolk was condemned to be hanged. His estates and title were of course to be forfeited.

Escape. A knight named William atte Hoo is said to have helped Suffolk to escape across the Channel. Michael disguised himself by shaving off his beard and hair and putting on shabby clothes. In this state he presented himself at Calais Castle, dressed like a Flemish poulterer carrying a basket of capons. The image of Michael accompanied by squawking chickens turning up to seek refuge is a compelling one. Michael's brother Edmund was at that time captain of Calais Castle, and not surprisingly, after a moment's scrutiny, he recognised him. Only in Shakespearean comedies do brothers fail to recognise each other, beard or no beard.

The de la Poles had always been a close-knit family, and Edmund never failed to show a well-developed sense of responsibility for his parents and brothers and sisters.[7] Michael and Edmund had worked very closely together as envoys sent to treat for peace with France in 1385; and a year later he and Michael were given special authority to make a survey of the town and fortresses at Calais and its marches, studying the administration, security and state of repair of the English possessions.

Following their father's death in 1366, it was Edmund who assisted his mother, with whom he jointly held property at Cringleford in Norfolk, to conduct her affairs satisfactorily, and eventually he took on the executorship of the will she made in 1381. Edmund was that solid, reliable member that every family needs, a predictable rock. Evidently he was on the best of terms with his brother. Michael would not have gone to seek refuge in Calais if he had thought Edmund would not protect him.

Edmund was faced with a terrible dilemma. He naturally felt a certain ambivalence about what to do with Michael and told the governor of Calais, William Beauchamp, of his arrival. Michael was after all a convicted traitor. Edmund is reported to have said *'frater meus es, sed noveris, quod pro ulla consanguinitate nolo deprehendi falsus regno Angliae'*. 'You are my brother, but I know that I do not want any ties to the kingdom of England that are found to be false'. Edmund's reluctance to aid Michael, albeit his own brother, proved to be in the best interests of the de la Pole family in the long run. Certainly, the triumphant appellants took no action against Edmund personally, and, indeed, even kept him on at Calais, at least until May 1388, when they empowered him to negotiate a truce with the Flemings.

Beauchamp, the governor, immediately arrested Michael and after some dithering and no doubt tortured discussion with Edmund, sent Michael back to England, to the king. Richard was not only surprised but angry at Beauchamp's officiousness. The king decided to allow Michael to escape a second time. This time Michael headed north to Kingston upon Hull, knowing he would find friends there. In late December 1388 the king's sergeant-at-arms was despatched to arrest him but Michael got wind of it and set sail, if Jean Froissart's account can be trusted, over the North Sea and along the coasts of Friesland, ultimately landing at Dordrecht. From there he found his way to Paris.

The death of Michael de la Pole. Michael was exhausted and ageing, Katherine was dead. Paris was far from his adult children, whose inheritance he had lost. His son and heir Michael had not really supported him as he might. His castle in Wingfield, his palace in Hull and lands were all gone. The future must have seemed bleak. He had survived but at what cost? King Richard managed to reassert some power in spring 1389 but he made no attempt to help his former Chancellor, who died at Paris on 5 September 1389.

The contemporary chroniclers rejoiced over Michael's death. Walsingham remarked nastily that 'his spirit deservedly departed from its earthly pilgrimage'.[8] Froissart had criticised him throughout, referring to de la Pole in the Chronicles as a devious and ineffectual counsellor, who dissuaded Richard from pursuing certain victory against French and Scottish forces and fomented unreasonable suspicion against John of Gaunt.[9] Froissart is frequently wrong and his opinions are highly personal; he invented dialogue he could not possibly have heard. As historian Jonathan Sumption has remarked, 'Chroniclers are episodic, prejudiced, inaccurate and late. Froissart is particularly unreliable.'[10] But sometimes we have no other source to consult.

At his death Michael left a legacy of Wingfield Castle and also a group of religious institutions that he had supported and enriched. His ultimate legacy, however, was a place in the history of English parliamentary democracy. He was on the 'wrong' side through loyalty to a weak, autocratic and ineffectual king who eventually was deposed and replaced. It would be five hundred years before the philosopher David Hume rescued Michael's reputation from ignominy.

The Maison Dieu and Charterhouse Hull. Michael's father William de la Pole had sufficient remaining wealth in 1350 to found a hospital (almshouse) in Hull called the Maison Dieu; he also obtained a licence to build a religious house. William died before the priory was completed but Michael completed the Carthusian priory, which like others of that order in England was known as a 'Charterhouse'. He also provided a hospital, we would call it an almshouse or retirement home, to accommodate thirteen poor men and thirteen poor women. Situated to the north of the city, beyond the walls, in de la Pole's manor of Myton, William endowed it with the rents from lands in Myton and in Hessle and some other nearby properties. Michael added substantial funds from the manor of Sculcoates.[11] The priory was demolished at the Dissolution in Tudor times but the hospital survived. The building has been redeveloped many times and the endowment still provides an income for the almshouse charity that exists today. It provided thirty-five sheltered flats for older people

30. The Charterhouse, Hull, woodcut by Thomas Gent, 1735.

in 2020.

Michael originally intended that the foundation would serve as a family mausoleum and his mother asked in her will to be buried there although we are not sure if she was. Michael's wife Katherine was buried there in 1386 and at some point in the 1390s, Michael's body was brought back from Paris and interred there. Their tombs were lost when the priory was destroyed.

Michael de la Pole's contribution to Wingfield College. The Chantry College of priests at Wingfield, whose Great Hall still survives, has recently been subject to detailed research. An authoritative book covers its foundation by Sir John de Wingfield, its construction and history until the Dissolution and after, when it became the private house that it now remains.[12] Peter Bloore's fascinating attempt to reconstruct a digital image of how the College looked at the end of the fourteenth century shows a building quite different from the apparently Georgian house we can now see from the road. The Georgian façade successfully masks the earlier house. It stands just south of the church of St Andrews, which provided the chapel for the college.[13] The timber framed north end shows a little of the original construction.

The chantry college was founded by Sir John de Wingfield but it was his widow Eleanor who oversaw the beginning of the construction of what was a substantial building. How much did Michael de la Pole add to the original construction? Did he have the time, energy and resources to invest

31. Wingfield College from the churchyard showing the Georgian façade and the end of the 1380 great hall.

in an educational religious foundation? The answer is yes, he did. There is documentary evidence that for the first twenty five years of its existence, the College was a stable and successful enterprise. His mother-in-law Eleanor died in 1375, the dendro-dating of the great hall gives a date of the early 1380s when Michael was at the height of his powers and increasingly wealthy.[14] The hall's north arcade plate timber was felled in 1379, the upper tie beam in 1383. Peter Bloore thinks it probable that work on the College and work on Wingfield Castle were going on at the same time, indeed at the same period that Michael was funding the construction of the Charterhouse in Hull.[15]

Notes

1 This was not the Good King Wenceslas of the Boxing Day carol, who lived in the 10th century.

2 Roskell, J. N., 1984, *The Impeachment of Michael de la Pole Earl of Suffolk in 1386 in the context of the Reign of Richard II*, Manchester University Press, pp. 130-131.

3 Clark, J. G. (notes) and Preest, D. (transcription), 2009, *The Chronica Maiora of Thomas Walsingham (1376-1422)*, Boydell and Brewer, Woodbridge online at https://www.jstor.org/stable/10.7722/j.ctt163tc0v.

4 Prescott, A. ,2004,The Hand of God': the Suppression of the Peasants' Revolt of 1381', in Prophecy, Apocalypse and the Day of Doom, Morgan, N. (ed), *Harlaxton Medieval Studies 12,* Shaun Tyas, Donington, pp. 317-41.

5 The Cavendish case appears in Parliamentary Rolls, 3, 1384, 168. The role of this case in the development of English Appeals Law is discussed in Stephens, J. F. 1883 *A History of the Criminal Law of England* Chapter V, p. 151, Cambridge University Press, online 2014 at Google Books.

6 Tout T. F., 1896, Michael de la Pole, Earl of Suffolk, *Dictionary of National Biography Vol XLVI* Lee, S. (ed), Macmillan and Co, London, pp 29-33.

7 The account of his brother Edmund's involvement in Michael's life and his capture in exile is taken from Woodger, L. S., 1993, Sir Edmund de la Pole (c.1337-1419), of Boarstall Castle, Bucks and Dernford in

Sawston, Cambs, in *The History of Parliament: the House of Commons 1386-1421*, Roskell, J.S., Clark, L., Rawcliffe C. (eds), Boydell and Brewer, Woodbridge.

8 Walsingham, T., c1380, *Historia Anglicana Vol 2* 1862–64, Riley, H.T. (ed), p. 187.

9 Froissart, J., c1380, Chronicles II, f 173. Quoted in *Tales from Froissart*, Translated by Muhlburger, S., Dept History, Nipissing University, online at http://faculty.nipissingu.ca/muhlberger/FROISSART/TALES.HTM

10 Sumption J. P. C.,1989, *The Hundred Years War, Volume I: Trial by Battle*, Faber and Faber, London. Comment on Froissart in Preface.

11 Calendar of Patent Rolls membrane 16, f 52, November 8, 1378 at Gloucester.

12 Bloore, P. and Martin E. (eds), 2015, *Wingfield College and its Patrons*. Boydell Press, Woodbridge.

13 Bloore, P., 2015, Historical Digital reconstruction: The Role of Creativity and Known Unknowns—A Case Study of Wingfield College, Chapter 6, pp 97-133, in Bloore, P. and Martin E. (eds), 2015.

14 Ibid. 12, pp. 106-7.

15 Ibid. pp. 107-8.

The de la Poles Recover Their Home, 1387–1415

The 2nd and 3rd Earls of Suffolk

We do not know for certain whether the construction of the castle commenced before or after the granting of the licence to crenellate in 1385. We can be confident that the building was not finished by 1387 when Michael was impeached and his property confiscated. It was to be another ten years before Michael's heir, also Michael, was able to claim back most of the old family property and was reinstated as the 2nd earl of Suffolk. There would have been therefore a hiatus of about ten years before the completion of the castle allowed the second Michael and his family to use it as their home. The half-finished fortified manor probably just sat there waiting and in ten years could well have become somewhat dilapidated. A bailiff would possibly be employed to supervise the confiscated lands but no one would have spent much money on new construction.

32. Michael de la Pole, 2nd earl of Suffolk and Katherine Stafford, his wife, tomb monument in St. Andrew's Church Wingfield c1415.

Michael de la Pole, 2nd earl of Suffolk. The second Michael is a puzzling figure. The only hint of his character is from a comment made after his death that he was 'a knight of excellent and most gracious name', conventional obituary praise.[1] Rather unusually he gave very practical instructions to his executors about what to do with his body after death, which provided options depending on where he died, suggesting perhaps that he was considerate of other people's convenience or perhaps simply a man who paid attention to detail. During his father's impeachment, he had been left in a quandary about his personal loyalties and then later placed in a position of mistrust by Richard II for being too acquiescent with the parliamentary Lords Appellant who had persecuted his father. Michael was not alone in this predicament of loyalties, all aristocratic families had to choose sides in the later stages of Richard's reign and in this respect he was no different to many other noblemen.

Michael does not seem to have supported his father through the crisis that led to his downfall. Possibly he agreed with the Appellants' desire for parliament to have greater influence on the Crown, a laudably high-flown ambition. He would not be the first son and heir to be at political loggerheads with his father's ideas. These lofty justifications seem a less likely rationale than that he was trying to save his own neck and hang on to what he could of his family fortune by being perceived as unsympathetic to his father's cause. And most importantly he had developed other family loyalties through marriage to Katherine Stafford, a niece of Thomas Beauchamp, earl of Warwick, a leading Appellant.

Michael tries to retrieve his inheritance. From the moment his father was impeached in 1388, young Michael, ably supported by his solidly reliable uncle Edmund, launched a campaign to get his properties and title restored. Michael was just twenty-two years old when his father died in Paris; his mother had died three years earlier. Michael had recently married Katherine, a younger daughter of Hugh, the late earl of Stafford. Her father had only a year earlier died while at Rhodes on a pilgrimage to the Holy Land.

Michael and Katherine were not quite penniless when his father died. After the impeachment, Parliament had granted them three manors in the East Midlands, Blyborough and Harpswell in Lincolnshire and Grassthorpe (Gresthorp) in Nottinghamshire. These manors were supposed to generate an income of £100 a year to support them. It was on that basis that the marriage was contracted between Michael and Katherine, with the support of the late earl of Stafford's family. It turned out the manors were not worth that much so the couple petitioned the king to provide other manors, lands and tenements to the value promised them.[2] A commission to enquire into the matter dragged on for some years.[3]

The National Archives hold a dozen or more petition documents presented by Michael and his uncle Edmund between 1389 and 1392 for Michael to repossess piecemeal all such properties, manor by manor, acre by acre. Drip by drip, manors were restored to him, but it was not until January 1398, five years after the de Vere family heir had been restored to his Oxford earldom, that Michael finally became the 2nd earl of Suffolk.[4] More petitions followed in 1398 and 1399 to claw back other properties that went with the title, particularly those that he should have inherited after the death of Isabel Ufford, the old dowager Countess of Suffolk.[5] These included the manor of Costessey, one of the most prosperous manors in Norfolk, which he was refused, Orford Castle rents and the manors of Stradbroke, Benhall and Faxfleet, which he did regain. A year later he was granted the manors of Winchester, Hampshire; Rockingham, Northamptonshire; Haughley, Suffolk and Thorndon, Suffolk.[6] The substantial Hull family home and Yorkshire property were also restored. Thus most of his property was eventually returned to Michael although he was still pursuing some at his death.

The Lithuanian Crusade 1390-1392. Meanwhile, in between all this litigation and supplication, Michael made his living as his father had before him, as a soldier. The fact that he served under Thomas of Woodstock, duke of Gloucester (1355-1397), another of the Lords Appellant, was enough to delay the restoration of Michael's title by the king. Gloucester was the last of Edward III's fourteen children and Richard II's nephew. He was eventually murdered at Richard's behest.

33. The Murder of Thomas of Woodstock, duke of Gloucester.

Michael joined Gloucester on the extraordinary crusade to Lithuania sometime between 1390 and 1392.[7] Most people have never heard of this 'crusade' although the fictitious Knight in

Chaucer's Canterbury Tales had also been there, so perhaps the crusade was better known in the late fouteenth century than now.

> In Lettow hadde he reysed and in Ruce, (*He had campaigned in Lithuania and in Russia,*)
> No Cristen man so ofte of his degree. (*No Christian man of his rank so often.*)
> General Prologue, The Canterbury Tales, Geoffrey Chaucer c1400

The Baltic Crusades, fought in Russia, medieval Livonia (Estonia and Latvia), then in Lithuania, one of the largest states in Europe at that time, were a long-term phenomenon lasting for about three hundred years (1147–1525). The crusades were controversial from the start, as they aimed at conquering new land, expanding and consolidating the borders of Christendom, as well as converting the local pagan population.

A key figure in the Lithuanian crusade was Henry of Bolingbroke, John of Gaunt's youngest son and the future king of England. He had a fractious relationship with his cousin Richard II and had good reasons for keeping out of the way of the king, as did Michael de la Pole.[8] Despite the efforts of Henry and his English crusaders, two years of attacks on Vilnius proved fruitless. The 'crusade' was a brutal war of raid and retaliation over an uninhabited, swampy and densely forested no-man's-land. Bolingbroke described the city as built of wood with no defensive wall but a very solid stone castle. The attacking crusaders burned the city but failed to seize the castle. Michael returned home unharmed from this diversionary venture, to continue his assault on the king with more petitions.

Michael and Katherine's family. It is thought that Michael and Katherine had up to twelve children, of whom 5 sons and 5 daughters survived infancy. Their oldest son, yet another Michael, was born about 1395. Their second son, William, eventually became 1st duke of Suffolk and will figure prominently in this narrative with his other unfortunate brothers, John, Alexander and Thomas. The family served the usurper Lancastrian king Henry IV and his successors with unflinching loyalty and suffered terribly as a result. Their oldest daughter Isobel married Lord Morley; their second Katherine became Abbess of one of the most important abbeys in England, Barking Abbey in Essex. Their third daughter Elizabeth married Edward Burnell. There were other daughters too, including Philippa and Joan, but here the family story is a little hazy.

Wingfield becomes home to Michael and Katherine. Richard II is replaced by the usurper Bolingbroke who becomes Henry IV. A decade of persistence paid off. By 1398 Michael had retrieved almost all the property his father had lost and, crucially, his earldom; all that is except for the valuable Costessey manor and a handful of other manors, a matter that continued to irk him for the rest of his life. He had enough wealth now to finish the house his father began. Meanwhile Michael seems to have stayed away from politics and the court altogether until the national crisis of 1399, when just like the rest of the aristocracy, he was faced with unpalatable choices.

Richard II's deposition had been brewing for years and in 1399 he was finally overthrown. From 1397 Richard's policies became increasingly arbitrary, rejecting any counsel from his advisors. Instead of guaranteeing order, he seemed to threaten it.[9] The final crisis was provoked by his treatment of the house of Lancaster. In 1398 Richard banished his cousin Henry Bolingbroke, whom he correctly perceived as a threat. In the following year, on the death of Bolingbroke's father John of Gaunt, the king seized Bolingbroke's estates and extended his cousin's exile for life. This peremptory action shocked the nobility and landed elite. These actions threatened the entire social order, for if Henry Bolingbroke was not safe, then who was?

Bolingbroke seizes the throne. In the summer of 1399, Richard went on an expedition to Ireland, leaving yet another uncle, Edmund, duke of York, as Custodian of the Realm. Richard II had always made it clear that he favoured Edmund as his heir in spite of Bolingbroke and the earl of March having stronger claims. In late June of that year, the exiled Bolingbroke landed at Bridlington on the Yorkshire coast. Edmund of York raised an army to resist him, then decided instead to join him, for which he was well rewarded.[10] He thereafter remained loyal to the new Lancastrian regime when Bolingbroke overthrew Richard II to become king Henry IV.

Michael, who had only become 2nd earl of Suffolk a year earlier, was in a major quandary like so many others but decided to obey Edmund's summons to defend the kingdom, raising a force of twenty nine men-at-arms and one hundred and nine archers. Michael also consented to the deposition and imprisonment of Richard II and the disbanding of the York army. He recognised that Henry Bolingbroke's successful coup enabled him to seize the throne and we might conjecture that Michael knew sufficient about Bolingbroke's strength of character to see that he would be a better king than Richard. Henry IV's first parliament technically re-imposed the decisions of the Merciless Parliament, making Michael penniless again but his titles and property were swiftly restored 'in consideration of his services after the king's advent'.[11] And then Michael commenced his new onslaught on the task of acquiring the final bits and pieces of his father's original estate. He was nothing if not tenacious.

A Modest Role in National Life but a significant power in East Anglia. Michael concentrated his efforts on re-establishing a base in Suffolk, thus reviving and consolidating the family power and influence in the area. His biographer Simon Walker judges that he chose peace and respectability, consciously and successfully removing the taints of treason and usury that had bedevilled his ancestors.[12] He was a justice of the peace in Norfolk and Suffolk from 1399 and a frequent commissioner of array for raising troops. He played only a very minor role in national parliaments, definitely a back seat observer, although he was an assiduous attender at parliaments and served as a trier of Gascon petitions in 1404, 1411, 1413 and 1414.[13] (Gascony was ruled by the English from 1152 to 1453 in their capacity as dukes of Aquitaine). He was appointed member of the Privy Council in 1402. One gets the impression of a solidly reliable administrator who could be asked to take on some modestly important but tedious work, a safe pair of hands.

In the main, leaving national politics to others, and probably never offered any preferment as even a minor officer of state, Michael gathered gentry and titled families around him as friends in Suffolk, including the career soldier Sir John Fastolf and the Bardwells of Bardwell. He married two of his daughters into local money, Isabel to Thomas, Lord Morley, Elizabeth to Edward, heir to Lord Burnell. His oldest daughter Katherine did not marry but later became abbess of the royal Abbey of Barking, an impressive woman who was to have some influence on Henry VI.[14]

By 1403 Michael's eldest son, the third generation Michael, though still only about nine years old, was married to Elizabeth Mowbray, the daughter of Thomas Mowbray 1st duke of Norfolk, whose colourful career had ended in exile and death of the plague in Venice just before Henry IV's accession. Michael and Elizabeth, while still in their teens, produced three baby girls as grandchildren for the 2nd earl and countess of Suffolk.

The estates in Norfolk and Suffolk were supervised meanwhile with pernickety attention to accounting detail; miraculously some of the de la Pole family accounts have survived and are held in the British Library and in the Suffolk Record Office.[15] Between 1407 and 1409, and probably for a lot longer, Roger Grys was the 'receiver' responsible for collecting and maintaining the family accounts.[16] Grys was probably one and the same as Roger le Grice who was living in Brockdish just north of the Waveney in 1392, from a long established Norfolk family who became substantial owners in Brockdish.[17] Roger Grys collected money from half a dozen other manorial stewards and added a charge for his own expenses of £10. £20 was received from Lady Isabel Ufford, the dowager countess of Suffolk for annual rents from Orford Castle and also other rents from the manor of Costessey that had originally been part of the Ufford estates. The total for the manors was £40. Other monies received added up to a staggering £1,064 16s 8d farthing. Out of this was paid to Lord Morley a part payment of £100 owed to him for the marriage of Isabel 'sister of the lord' as part of her dowry of £433 6s 8d. Further payments were made to Lord Morley, sent via the chaplain William Beford.

A payment of £200 was made to Sir Thomas Erpingham, to whom Michael owed money, sent via John Phelip, of Dennington, a relative by marriage of Erpingham. Thomas Erpingham (1357-1428), who later built the Erpingham gate at Norwich cathedral, became famous at Agincourt as commander of the English longbow archers and a cheerily loyal old soldier in Shakespeare's Henry V.

A total of £381 19s 6d halfpenny was paid to various tradesmen in London:

> 'To Thomas Symond executor of the will of John Somer of London *draper* in part payment £7 17s 8d …
> to John Whitwell of London jeweller, William Twyer & his associates provosts of the church of St Michael in Cornhill London...
> William Erneton of London, mercer…
> John Grafton of London malemaker (chain mail armour maker)
> Roger Wangford citizen & pannarius (draper) of London...
> Thomas Rolff citizen & pelliparius (skinner) of London...
> Thomas Hunden of London cissor (tailor)
> John Wade of Ipswich
> John Orkesley of Ipswich'

Michael had incurred other financial and legal administration expenses in London, a total of £32 5s 4d halfpenny. Roger had incurred expenses himself for journeying from London to Wingfield 'to speak with the lord & his counsel: 5 days with 2 horses, 6s 4d, then journeying from London to Hasilberi [?] to enter the manor there in the name of the lord, with expenses there, for 10 days, 13s 1d and further journeying to and from Wingfield, total: £28 3s 3d halfpenny'.

Provisions for the Lord's household in London in the month of August

(1407), were 71s 10d, the lodging of the Lords household at London £7 13s 4d.

Then there were the travelling expenses for the family, for example 'Michael de la Pole son of the Lord going from Wingfield to Fifet in Berkshire to the wedding of lord Thomas de la Pole the lord's brother with 14 horses in the month of April 9th year (1408) 68s 6d.' This was presumably a re-marriage. 'Expenses of this same third Michael from Wyngefeld to London, his three day sojourn there and onward travel thereafter to Canterbury together with expenses of William his brother accompanying the same Michael to London & then to Exeter etc etc, total: £10 15s 5d.'

Then the wages of household servants and messengers, musicians and lawyers:

> 'Henry, Messenger riding from London to Gestingthorp in November
> Total: £6 15s 9d halfpenny
> John Appilyerd servant/serjeant of Master Michael the lord's son for his fee
> William del Chambre
> Robert del Chambre valet of the wardrobe
> Richard el Chambre
> John Motte the lord's valet
> Mary Bokkyng
> Elizabeth Boston
> William Wilbey garc' of Michael de la Pole the lord's son
> total: £12 13s 4d
> Fees of the minstrels: 33s 4d
> William Prentyng trumpet at Wyngefeld
> Richard Gren? Bumbard (Bombard = woodwind instrument)
> Henry Brigeford shalmoser (possibly schalmei or shawm, double reeded instrument forerunner of oboe)
> Thomas Lyon shalmoser
> Fees of men at law: £16 3s 4d
> John Staverton baron of the Exchequer
> Richard Norton sergeant at law
> William Ludyngton apprentice at law [barrister]
> Walter Askham apprentice at law
> Thomas Derham apprentice at law
> James Andrew
> Robert Palgrave lord's attorney in King's Bench
> John Clere attorney in Chancery
> Religious offerings/payments: 35s 6d

To church of St Mary Aldermanbery London (and others)
'Gifts with rewards':
1 pipe of wine bought & given to Simon the steward ... of the Archbishop of Canterbury etc etc
total: [illeg]
Annuities with fees for accounting: £31 13s 4d
to lord Robert Belton clerk etc etc
Other payments. Money handed over:
To Katherine Countess of Suffolk..... £6 13s 4d
to Robert Bolton junior, the lord's chamberlain £127 11s 10d
to Edmund Drury steward of the lord's household £36 16s 4d
to John Wilteshire steward of the foreign household... £46 13s 4d
to the Earl for his expenses going overseas.... £103 6s 8d'

Whenever there was soldiering work to be done, however, Michael the 2nd earl was willing to join the action. In 1400, now in his late 30s, he campaigned with Henry IV in Scotland, supplying the earl of Westmoreland with a large force of two hundred men-at-arms and a thousand archers. The same year Michael funded a ship with twenty men-at-arms and forty archers for the defence of the Channel. It is not clear whether he participated in naval warfare himself; it is thought he may have done round about 1405. But the expenditure in 1408 for 'going oversees' was probably for an unusual trip to Pisa.

The Council of Pisa. Michael was sent to Pisa between December 1408 and August 1409 to act as the king's senior English representative at the Council of Pisa.[18] This controversial ecumenical council of the Catholic church was convened unofficially by some influential cardinals to attempt to bring to an end the western schism between the two popes, one in Rome and one in Avignon. England was firmly on the side of the Pope of Rome. The College of Cardinals, composed of members of both the Avignon and the Rome adherents, who were recognised by each other and by the Council, then elected a third papal claimant, Alexander V, who lived only a few months. He was succeeded by John XXIII.

The gathering in Pisa was enormous. Four patriarchs, twenty-two cardinals and eighty bishops assembled in the Cathedral of Pisa under the presidency of the Cardinal Bishop of Palestrina, the senior cardinal bishop in both 'obediences'. Then there were the hangers-on, representatives of a hundred absent bishops, eighty-seven abbots with the proxies of those who could not come, forty-one priors and generals of religious orders, and three hundred doctors of theology or canon law. The ambassadors of all the Christian kingdoms, like Michael, completed the assembly. Probably no one had any great hopes of a breakthrough. Michael's was an observer's job, a role which a ruler might give to someone easily spared from more important work.

The assembly made some modest progress and although it did not end the schism, indeed it produced three itinerant popes instead of two, it was a modest step forward by the united cardinals towards ending the split, finally resolved in 1414. Quite what role the observing ambassadors took is not obvious, it must have been an unusual experience at least, trying to keep up with the ebb and flow of clerical discourse, which the transcript suggests was largely legalistic and obscure in nature, about the justifications of the two existing popes. We don't know what report Michael made afterwards when he got home but Henry IV decided to support the election of the third pope, presumably on the advice of the English cardinals and Michael.

The duomo at Pisa, where all the meetings were held, was already more than three hundred years old and one of the most spectacular buildings in Europe. The campanile tower, even then famously and dangerously leaning, had been completed only thirty years earlier and the stupendous baptistery was not long finished. They are still among the most strikingly beautiful buildings in the world. How extraordinarily impressive they must have looked to Michael then.

Endowments at Hull and Wingfield. Both the Charterhouse at Hull and the Maisondieu at Myton in Humberside, started by his father, were completed by an endowment from Michael. He also gave generously to Wingfield College chantry and considerably enlarged the church of St Andrew Wingfield. This could have included the chancel clerestory and the lady chapel.[19] In 1401-2 he donated the land and rents of manors in Wingfield, Stradbroke, Syleham, Essham (Earsham Street, Syleham) to The Master and Chaplains of the Church of Wingfield, worth ten shillings a year.[20] When his brother Richard died in 1403, he commemorated him by a further gift to the College of the manor of Benhall, south of Saxmundham, and rent from the manors of Sweffling, Cransford, Great Glemham and Farnham, to fund a priest to pray for Richard's soul.[21] Richard's splendid brass memorial is still in Wingfield Church though it has lost its figure. Michael and Katherine donated the church font in about 1405.

In his will, Michael left to the college 'one vestment of white cloth of gold, with everything belonging, viz 3 copes, 1 amictus (outer layer of priest's clothing), 1 chasuble, 3 amices (caps), 3 albas (surplices), 3 stoles, 3 fanons (napkins), 2 altar cloths with one frontal, 2 pillars (a dorsal cloth extending the chasuble), 1 canopy, 2 curtains of Tartaryn and 2 towels'.[22]

Master John de la Pole, Michael's uncle, had become a cleric and rose to become Canon of the cathedral Church of York and the collegiate church of Beverley. When he died in 1414 he was also buried at Wingfield, where his gravestone can still be seen although the ornamental brass image is long gone. He had requested in his will, proved in February 1415, that he be buried in Wingfield and no doubt there would have been a family funeral to honour him.

Fair stood the wind for France. Michael and his sons join Henry V's campaign to win the crown of France. Not long after John's death in early 1415, at the age of 48, Michael de la Pole joined the extensive planning operation for Henry V's invasion of France. Money, supplies, and crucially, men-at-arms and archers had to be recruited for Henry's great venture to win the French crown. Michael raised a company of one hundred men-at-arms and one hundred and twenty mounted archers. His eldest son, Michael, just twenty years old, joined him and raised a further twenty men-at-arms and sixty archers. Michael's second son William, then about 19 years old, also joined the campaign. The three younger boys did not join the expedition because they were too young

The three warriors said their goodbyes to their families in Wingfield and Benhall just south of Saxmundham, where the younger Michael had set up home with his wife and children. Michael and Elizabeth would not have had their own establishment or be expected to consummate the marriage until their early teens but their third baby, a daughter, was born in June 1415; their other two daughters were still toddlers.

On Sunday 11 August 1415 the invasion fleet of fifteen hundred ships, mostly provision ships recruited for the passage, set sail from the shelter of Southampton water to cross the Channel. Most had no idea where they were going, only that it was somewhere in France. Henry was in fact heading for Harfleur, a port town of strategic importance to the French. Heavily fortified, with vast outward sloping stone walls encircling the hill town and its harbour with twenty four armed watchtowers. Only a fragment of the ruined walls survives today and Harfleur is no more than a hilly suburb of Le Havre built centuries later. It is now surrounded by the industrial wasteland of a container port's overspill. It is hard to imagine the daunting scene that greeted the English soldiers. Were they really going to vanquish this heavily fortified bastion?

There were good reasons for choosing Harfleur for the invasion. It was a base from which raids struck at English coastal towns and was said to be a nest of pirates threatening English shipping. It also controlled military and commercial shipping up the Seine, one of the main arteries of French commerce to Paris. Calais was one English bridgehead into France, the capture of Harfleur would be another.

The six-week siege of Harfleur is especially well documented by a detailed eyewitness account provided by an anonymous author, now thought to be an English chaplain, in the Gesta Henrici Quinti (The Deeds of Henry V), which enables us to reconstruct the main sequence of events. [23] For anyone wanting a meticulous, exciting moment-by-moment account, Juliet Barker's book about Agincourt and the military campaign that preceded it is the best account yet of the siege of Harfleur.[24] She spares us nothing of the horrors, but also conveys vivid portraits of the men and their characters. Anne Curry has also published several indispensable works about Agincourt.[25]

The Seige and the Bloody Flux. The Seige of Harfleur and the extraordinary triumph of the Battle of Agincourt are probably the best known battles of the medieval period, but largely as a result of Shakespeare's rousing play Henry V. The triumph of Agincourt of the English 'few' over the vast numbers of French has become part of an idealised story about the ordinary yeomen of England, led by a magnificent military royal commander. The legend was circulating soon after the battle and has been used down the centuries as a symbol of righteous determination, immense inspirational leadership, English courage and character. This has understandably irritated the French, who even today complain about the sacrifice of their history on the altar of English myth. The propaganda licence used by Shakespeare on behalf of the Tudors in his great play was reused by Churchill in 1940 for Lawrence Olivier's film, Henry V. The film was created to stiffen the sinews of a blitzed Britain preparing for the D Day landings. There can be few of us who have not said, usually in jest at some challenging point, "Once more unto the breach, dear friends, once more",[26] not realising that the 'breach' Shakespeare referred to was a breach in the walls of the heavily fortified hill town of Harfleur.

Death and Repatriation. The siege was long, bloody and much more gravely depleting of army stores, arms and men than was intended. It was meant to last eight days; it went on for eighteen. The siege in fact lasted until 22 September when the townsmen and garrison surrended. Harfleur was where Michael de la Pole, 2nd earl of Suffolk died, not of wounds but of dysentery. Dysentery was the scourge of every army on campaign. It was known as the 'bloody flux' because its main symptoms were of profuse watery and bleeding diarrhoea. A bacteria, Shigella, usually causes the episodic sort, although there are several other types caused by amoebae and other bacteria that are less immediately debilitating. Dysentery kills by causing pain, cramps, profound dehydration, septicaemia and kidney failure. It is passed from one person to another where there is inadequate sanitation, poor hygiene and lack of safe fresh water. It is still a scourge in undeveloped tropical countries. Of course Henry V did not know the cause of the outbreak but every commander dreaded it.[27] They knew that they should try to avoid humid marshy low ground, maintain a flow of fresh air to convey away evil humours and maintain hygiene but, at Harfleur, that was impossible. What they did not realise was that they should keep the sick away from the healthy.

The epidemic seems to have started in early September. One of the early deaths was of Humphrey, lord Fitzwalter, a youth serving with the duke of Clarence but his malady does not seem to have been recognised as dysentery. The first prominent death was of 35 years old Richard Courtney, bishop of Norwich. He was a soldier, not a churchman and never visited his diocese. He was a brilliant man, a doctor of civil and canon Law, twice elected Chancellor of the University of Oxford, diplomat, financier and close companion of Henry V. The king attended his deathbed, bathed his feet and sat with him while he died.

Sir John Phelip, a wealthy knight in his late 30s, also died on 2 October of the bloody flux. A significant death for the history of Wingfield Castle because he had been married, for just one year, to young Alice Chaucer, a girl of just 10 years old when her husband died. Both Alice and her third husband William de la Pole play an important part in the next chapter of the castle's history.

Michael de la Pole died on 18 September, almost certainly his son, young Michael, would have been with him at his death and his second son William too. He had made his will before setting out for France. He said if he died in the north of England he would like to be buried in the Charterhouse at Hull with just a flat stone between him, the tomb of his parents and the altar. But if he died elsewhere he would like to be buried in the collegiate church of St Andrews in Wingfield on the north side of the chapel of the Virgin. To his son Michael he left a small Latin primer owned by his uncle John. To his wife he left a small book and the coronet once owned by her father, the earl of Stafford. Katherine was left in charge of his estate to be administered by her with his elderly uncle, Edmund, until his son Michael could take over.[28]

After his death, Michael's body was quartered, then boiled until the flesh fell off the bones. This grisly task may perhaps have been done by a surgeon, or possibly a cook but we know it was the way bodies of noble birth were dealt with unless there was time to eviscerate and then pickle the remaining body. Contemporary chronicles reported that both Michael and the duke of York's bodies were dealt with by boiling.[29] The bones were then sent home to Wingfield for interring, with an escort from his own retinue of two men-at arms and other retainers. It was reported in the late fifteenth century that his bones had yet to be interred.[30] Why there was a delay we do not know and the specific location his bones were kept has not been identified.

Nevertheless, a splendid tomb monument was erected to Michael and Katherine in St Andrew's church, Wingfield, in an arch between the chancel and the Lady Chapel, rebuilt in the 1460s under the direction of Alice, duchess of Suffolk, his daughter-in-law. The monument has been altered over the years but remains a splendid tribute; Michael in his battle armour, droopy moustache falling over his bascinet, Katherine wearing a fashionable reticulated headdress and expensive silk or woollen outer garment called a houppelande or sometimes simply goun (gown), with a long, full body and flaring sleeves. This could be worn by both men and women. The effigies themselves are carved from wood but painted over many times. They look and feel like stone until you tap them. Originally they would have been in bright colours and an effort would have been made to make them lifelike.

We few, we happy few, we band of brothers. The siege of Harfleur ended on 22 September. Between a quarter and a third of Henry's great invasion army died of dysentery, far more than on the battle field. The great army Henry had assembled at Southampton was reduced to about nine hundred men-at-arms and five thousand archers. Henry had decided to leave at Harfleur the minimum troops necessary to man the garrison and to send home any sick who were not likely to be able to fight efficiently. Ship after ship originally carrying supplies in to Harfleur left for England with the sick, many of them mortally ill. One of those who were invalided home from Harfleur was nineteen years old William de la Pole, but it is likely that he was wounded rather than sick since his armour needed to be repaired when he got home.[31] He made a full recovery. Twenty year old Michael de la Pole, now the 3rd earl of Suffolk, marched on with his comrades.

The majority of Henry's council, seasoned experienced soldiers, including his brother Clarence, thought the invasion should be abandoned at that point; they had achieved a new bridgehead into France, they could retreat to England with honour and fight another day. Henry, with extraordinary if not deluded optimism, buoyed up with an unshakable belief in the holy righteousness of his cause, decided to march his weary battle-worn troops north to Calais, tracing his grandfather's steps through Normandy, crossing the Somme at the same place Edward III had before Crecy. They knew they were likely to meet stiff French opposition that had been assembling specifically to fight them. Henry seems to have calculated that his well trained professional army, if in the right frame of mind and well led, though small, could triumph over a much larger force. Henry's determination to continue prevailed over his council. Whether his troops and assorted civilians, minstrels, heralds and chaplains felt confident as they set out from Harfleur round about 6 October 1415 is doubtful. They were accompanied by up to twelve thousand horses, which were never used.

The column heading for Calais was repeatedly attacked by French armed bands but beat them off, making good progress against their planned eight days to Calais, successfully attacking the garrisons in Normandy to head for the crossing of the Somme, requiring them to take a lengthy detour. By the time they reached Azincourt, the French name for the village we know as Agincourt, Henry's Welsh and English army was sick, starving and exhausted. They already knew they were facing a battle with a French army that vastly outnumbered them, perhaps up to twenty thousand men.

The fighting took place on 25 October 1415 on a strip of muddy rain-soaked ground sandwiched between two woods. It was difficult terrain and the French were fresh and ready for the battle. Henry heard mass three times on the eve of battle but also went round his camp encouraging his troops, engaging them with the cause he was fighting for. Shakespeare caught perfectly the genius of Henry as inspirational leader. He and his chief commanders made a clear plan of action. Every man knew the strategy and was trained to follow instructions. They deployed the archers. A well-trained archer could fire many more than the ten arrows a minute that was the qualifying standard. Under a murderous hail, the poorly led French cavalry was cut to pieces. Horribly injured horses fell before opposing French and English forces. When the more heavily armed French knights began to advance on foot, staggering through the mud, they were slaughtered at point-blank range, falling on the bodies of their comrades. When the archers ran out of arrows, they turned axes, swords and even mallets against the helpless mass of French chivalry wallowing in the mud.

The truth is the French were poorly organised, ill-led and no match for Henry's highly trained fighting band. Everyone agrees it was a massacre. Many French knights, trapped inside their expensive armour, suffocated or drowned in the mud. The English breakthrough seems to have been comparatively swift. There were hundreds of French prisoners taken and quite against the chivalric code of battle, Henry ordered that they should all be slaughtered. The barbarity was justified, some historians have said, since Henry realised he could not supervise the huge number of prisoners and they remained a threat to his smaller number of troops. Others have pointed out it was considered a war crime even then; Shakespeare did not shirk from the question but left the matter unresolved. The French are still understandably aggrieved. Christophe Gilliot, head of the Agincourt museum, railed against a 2019 remake of the story of Henry V, pointing out that the king's cold-blooded execution of his French prisoners included 'their throats slit and heads crushed with sledgehammers' or 'faces slashed with daggers'.[32] Overall, the French death toll was appalling. French sources suggest that they lost between four thousand and ten thousand men, although there is no official number recorded. The whole of the French nobility was wiped out that day; the entire governing elite, including dukes and bishops, was annihilated. It would take decades for a new generation to recover from the devastation.

The Death of Michael de la Pole, 3rd earl of Suffolk. Estimates of the English dead, range from an improbably small one hundred to a plausible fifteen hundred. There were only two deaths among the nobility. One was the king's uncle, Edward, the 2nd duke of York, leading the charge on the vanguard wing at the head of his troops. The other was Michael de la Pole, 3rd earl of Suffolk, an earl for only thirty-seven days after his father died on 18 September. We know very little about the facts of Michael's death, although we know he was described by the English chaplain observer "as strong, as active and as daring as any member of the court" and lamented some weeks later as "a brave young knight".[33] We can borrow some lines from Shakespeare here. Exeter reports the death of Suffolk to Henry…

> Suffolk first died: and York, all haggled over,
> Comes to him, where in gore he lay insteep'd,
> And takes him by the beard; kisses the gashes
> That bloodily did spawn upon his face;
> And cries aloud 'Tarry, dear cousin Suffolk!
> My soul shall thine keep company to heaven;
> Tarry, sweet soul, for mine, then fly abreast,
> As in this glorious and well-foughten field
> We kept together in our chivalry!'

Henry V, Act IV, Scene 6

When the news eventually reached Wingfield Castle via a herald that both young Michael and his father were dead perhaps some kindly soul may have invented some similarly consoling words for Michael's wife Katherine, her young daughter-in-law Elizabeth and the three infants, Katherine, Elizabeth and Isabel. Katherine received home alive her second son William but he may well have needed good nursing care for many weeks, a disabling injury did not heal fast.

I'd like to think it was reliable uncle, Edmund de la Pole, who was there to help this bereaved family through their grief. In 1400 Sir Edmund, then aged 63, and 'so languid that he cannot labour', had obtained exemption from holding royal office.[34] Yet the government still expected him to serve on the Cambridgeshire bench for many years more and also sent him summonses to attend great councils in 1401 and 1403. In the early years of the fifteenth century, Sir Edmund joined with his nephew Michael in making further benefactions to the Carthusian priory of Mount Grace near Hull and to the hospital annexed to it. Continuing to show a concern for the interests of his nephew, in July 1415, although nearly 80 years old, he was prepared to take on the executorship of the will that Michael had made on the eve of his departure for France. Edmund died at a very advanced age in late July or early August 1419, the same year that Katherine Stafford also died.

Katherine Stafford oversaw personally the proceedings to execute the will of her husband, welcoming Matthew Assheton, the archbishop of Canterbury's commissioner to Wingfield Castle in November 1415. He had the power to approve the administration of the will.[35] Assheton remarked that he could not collect the earls' seal, because it had been left overseas. Katherine said she could get it for him, but does not say how. Katherine seems to have developed into a confident matriarch during the years of her marriage and widowhood.

Some years after her young husband's death, Elizabeth 3rd countess of Suffolk entered Bruisyard nunnery. This was an acceptable move for a widow but her residence there had to be funded by someone. Her two older daughters died young before marriage. Alice de la Pole, the new 4th earl's wife paid a pension of £150 for some years to Elizabeth and her daughter Katherine, who followed her to Bruisyard.[36] Finances were probably tighter than the family status would suggest. The treasury was never prompt in settling soldiers' accounts. Another year passed before the 3rd earl's payments for the Agincourt campaign were authorised.[37]

It seems strange that the three young de la Pole girls, who should have inherited some property from their father, notably the manor of Costessey and property in Hull, were apparently left to the charity of their uncle William, the new earl. One sceptical historian has suggested that their inheritance may have been negotiated away from them over the several years it took to confirm his inheritance.[38] From the story that follows of William's life, it is clear he was capable of taking ruthlessly decisive action in his own best interests when he wanted. In his nieces' case, he provided some compensation in the form of an annuity.

There is no clear evidence on where the last Michael was buried. Ewelme Church claims him and if he was buried there, it would have been after his brother William married Alice Chaucer in 1431. William and Alice built a new church at Ewelme in 1436, said to be in East Anglian style. Bringing Michael's remains there would be a fitting tribute for the new church. But really Michael had no connections to Ewelme at all and it seems an unlikely choice. An alternative suggestion is that he may have been buried at Butley Priory, near his home at Benhall in Suffolk. More likely than either of these suggestions is that he was buried at Wingfield alongside the other earls of Suffolk. Against this though is the lack of a tomb or cenotaph to this third Michael.

Jane with the Blemyssh. There is one curious tale that has long puzzled historians of the de la Poles. It may be completely without foundation but it can scarcely be ignored. There is a manuscript in the National Archives dated about 1490 that was first publicised by a Victorian local historian, Henry Napier, writing about the history of Ewelme.[39]

This extraordinary story tells of Michael and Elizabeth's first daughter Jane, disfigured in a fire when a baby, rejected by her parents and then hidden in a monastery but later allowed to marry some worthy local yeoman. The tale is not impossible and intrigued the historian Rowena Archer to explore it in greater detail.[40] If she existed then Jane would have been born before 1410, when her father was only thirteen or fourteen. This is not impossible because he was married at the age of eight, although the marriage would not have been consummated until he was twelve at the earliest. It is probable that the author of the document was more interested in hypothetical Jane's grandson John by her second son William and that it was written to make claim to some inheritance. The document was written right at the end of the fifteenth century, or beginning of the sixteenth, and for some reason found its way into safe keeping in the public record. This was a time when the de la Pole family was perceived to be a threat to the Tudor throne of Henry VII. Was someone official collecting information on the genealogy and properties of the de la Poles for some reason we cannot yet fathom?

This was the age of false pretenders and spurious claimants. This may be another piece of hearsay from an old wives' tale or a piece of romantic nonsense as is sometimes created around a long dead heir. History is littered with such cases, be they false pretenders to a throne, such as the several Anastasia Romanovs, Perkin Warbeck, the servant boy who was mistaken for the missing boy Richard duke of York or Lambert Simnel who attracted an extraordinary following, as we shall see.[41] For now this author is keeping an open mind; if poor Jane existed then she took a brave stance in insisting on making a life for herself outside the convent. And her tough grandmother in this story is highly consistent with what we know of Lady Katherine's personality. But Katherine died in 1419; a child of 10 or younger is unlikely to have had the determination to pursue a life outside the convent until much later. There are undeniably inconsistencies and improbabilities. The story remains an unsolved and probably unsolvable mystery.

Notes

1 Anonymous contemporary author, *Gesta Henrici Quinti* (The Deeds of Henry V), translation Taylor, F. and Roskell, J. S. (eds), 1975, Oxford University Press, Oxford.

2 1388 Petitioners: Michael de la Pole; Catherine de la Pole, wife of Michael de la Pole. TNA SC 8/21/1026. Calendar of Patent Rolls, Ric II, vol. IV, 1388-1392, (Public Record Office, 1902), p.58, (commission to re-assess the value of the three manors mentioned, in the light of this petition). Full original petition at Parliamentary Rolls, petitions and proceedings, vol. III, Ric II and Hen IV, (Record Commission, 1783), p.274a (no. 1)

3 Calendar of Patent Rolls 1388-92, p. 58. Another later petition on this matter is now at TNA SC 8/173/8637.

4 TNA SC 8/250/12455 Michael de la Pole, Earl of Suffolk, son and heir of Michael de la Pole, late Earl of Suffolk. The petitioner requests that the King grant him and the heir male of his body the title of Earl of Suffolk with £20 yearly from the issues and farms of Suffolk with the arrears since Easter last, of both of which he was possessed until by judgment against him in the parliament held at Westminster in the eleventh year of the King's reign [1388] the money was seized into the King's hand and the name of earl taken from him, because by a statute published in the last parliament all judgments and statutes made at the said parliament of the eleventh year were revoked and annulled. 1398, with reference to CCR 1396-9, p. 336, an order to pay Earl of Suffolk £20 yearly in response to the petition. This is also the date of the Chancery warrant with which it was formerly enclosed (C 81/574 no.12148A). For another petition enclosed with the same Chancery warrant SC8/251/12516, related petition SC8/251/12511, SC8/250/12498, Chancery warrant with which this was formerly enclosed C81/574, no 12148A.

5 TNA SC 8/250/12498 1398 De la Pole requests that whereas the King granted his father the reversion of the manor of Costessey with other lands and rents after the death of Isabel, Countess of Suffolk to have to him and his heirs forever in exchange for yearly rents of 400 marks and £50, which rents his father gave to him and his heirs to be taken yearly from the ancient custom in the port of Hull, which lands and rents in his father's possession by the said exchange the King seized into his hand by judgment returned against his father at the parliament held at Westminster in the tenth [sic, for eleventh] year of the King's reign which was annulled in your last parliament, that he can have execution by writs to the tenants of £20 yearly rent from Orford castle, 40 marks for the fee farm of the manor of Stradbroke and of the manors of Benhall and Faxfleet.

6 TNA SC 8/134/6662 1399 Grant of manors to Michael de la Pole of Winchester, Hampshire; Rockingham,

Northamptonshire; Haughley, Suffolk and Thorndon, Suffolk.

7 Walker, S., 2004, Pole, Michael de la, second earl of Suffolk, *Oxford Dictionary of National Biography* online at https://org/10.1093/ref:odnb/22453.

8 Ehlers, A., 2001, The Crusade of the Teutonic knights against Lithuania reconsidered. Chapter 2 in Murray, A. V. (ed), *Crusade and Conversion on the Baltic Frontier 1150–1500*, Ashgate, pp. 21-44.

9 Saul, N., 2017, *Richard II and the Crisis of Authority* online at https://www.bbc.co.uk/history/british/middle_ages/richardii_crisis_01.shtml.

10 Tuck, A., 2008, Edmund, 1st duke of York 1341-1402. *Oxford Dictionary of National Biography*, Oxford University Press. doi:10.1093/ref:odnb/16023. [accessed 23 July 2019].

11 Parliamentary Rolls 3, 668 Collected and arranged by R. Blyke, P. Morant, T. Astle, & J. Topham. (ed.) J. Strachey. 6 vols. London: 1767-1777. Transcription at *The Parliament Rolls of Medieval England, 1275-1504.* (ed.) Given-Wilson, C., Curry, A., Horrox, R., Martin, G., Philips, S. & Ormrod, M. Boydell Press, Woodbridge; National Archives, 2005 and *Calendar of Close Rolls, Henry IV: Volume 1, 1399-1402*, ed. Stamp, A. E. London, 1927, pp 58-59. British History Online http://www.british-history.ac.uk/cal-close-rolls/hen4/vol1/pp58-59 [accessed 22 July 2019].

12 Ibid. 7.

13 Michael de la Pole's role in hearing Gascony petitions is online at The Gascon Rolls Project. http://www.gasconrolls.org/en/solrsearch/?&query=Suffolk#q=Suffolk.

14 Bush, R., 2012, Pole, Katherine de la, *Oxford Dictionary of National Biography* online 04 October 2012 [accessed 21 July 2019].

15 Accounts for the de la Pole earls of Suffolk 1406-1505 Suffolk Record Office, Ipswich, HA411/5/2/1. British Library Egerton Rolls. 1404 Michael De la Pole, 2nd Earl of Suffolk: List of his debts; BL Egerton Roll 8777, 1404; Accounts for Michael De la Pole, 2nd Earl of Suffolk: Roll of expenses, incurred on behalf of: Fragment, BL Egerton Roll 8778, c 1405.

16 Account Roll [8, 9, 10 Henry IV] Henry IV (April 1367 – 20 March 1413) accounts 1407, 1408, 1409. HA 411/5/2/1 Suffolk Record Office, Ipswich.

17 Blomefield, F., 1806, Hundred of Earsham: Brockdish, in *An Essay Towards A Topographical History of the County of Norfolk: Volume 5,* London, pp. 327-339. British History Online http://www.british-history.ac.uk/topographical-hist-norfolk/vol5/pp327-339 [accessed 15 August 2020].

18 A complete list of those attending the Council of Pisa is given in Lenfant, Jacques, 1724, *Histoire du concile de Pise,* in French and Latin, Pierre Humbert Vol II, pp. 167-188.

19 Aitkens, P., Easton, T. and Martin E., 1999, Wingfield, *Proceedings of the Suffolk Intsitute of Archeology and History, Vol XXXIX*, pp. 392-397.

20 Aldwell, S.H.W., 1925, *Wingfield, its Church, Castle and College*, Harrison, Ipswich, p. 81.

21 Ibid., pp. 38, 81.

22 Tataryn was a kind of costly silk cloth. A glossary of terms for vestments and clerical costume is given in Chapter 2, pp 11-23 of Baumgarten, *Vestments for all Seasons.* Dee, B. 2002, Morehouse Publishing, New York.

23 Gesta Henrici Quinti 1975.

24 Barker, J., 2005, (new edition 2015) *Agincourt: the King, the Campaign and the Battle Little*, Brown, London.

25 Curry, A., 2005, *Agincourt: a New History*, Tempus, Stroud, is one of Curry's more recent publications. Curry, A., *2009, The Battle of Agincourt, Sources and interpretations*, Boydell Press, Woodbridge, includes translations of key documents relating to the Agincourt campaign. Curry's most useful co-authored book for a serious student of the battle is Curry A., Hoskins P., Richardson, T. and Spencer D., *The Agincourt Companion: A Guide to the Legendary Battle and Warfare in the Medieval World,* 2015, Andre Deutsch, London.

26 Shakespeare, W., 1599, *Henry V*, Act III, scene 1.

27 Henry V himself is said to have died of dysentery in 1422, at the Château de Vincennes, supposedly having contracted the disease during the siege of Meaux.

28 Inquisitions Post Mortem Suffolk, Michael de la Pole, son and heir of the late Michael de la Pole, earl of, TNA C 138/16/48B.

29 Curry, A. and Foard, G., 2016, Where are the dead of medieval battles? A preliminary survey. *Journal of Conflict Archeology, Vol. 11*, pp. 61-77.

30 College of Arms: MS L8, fol 75.

31 Expenses for repair of William's armour—Curran, 2011, p. 52, quoting Suffolk Estate accounts Suffolk Record Office Ipswich, HA 411/5/2/1.

32 *The Daily Telegraph,* 4 November 2019, online at https://www.telegraph.co.uk/news/2019/11/04/director-agincourt-museum-says-netflixs-king-anti-french-will/

33 Ibid. 1, pp. 51, 75.

34 Woodger, L. S., 1993, Pole Sir Edmund de la (c.1337-1419), of Boarstall Castle, Bucks and Dernford in Sawston, Cambs. *The History of Parliament: the House of Commons 1386-1421*, Roskell, J. S., Clark, L., Rawcliffe, C. (eds), Boydell and Brewer, Woodbridge.

35 Archer, R. E. and Fenne, B. E., 1989, Testamentary procedure with special reference to the executrix, in Medieval Women in Southern England, *Reading Medieval Studies, Vol 15* p. 9.

36 Chrimes, B. S., Ross, C., Griffiths, R. A. (eds), 1972, *Fifteenth-century England, 1399 -1509; Studies in Politics and Society*. Manchester University Press, Manchester, p. 102, original document, Alice Duchess of Suffolk support for Katherine de la Pole abbess of Barking, Alice late the wife of William de la Pole, Duke of Suffolk to Thomas Tyrell, knight, and others: Grant indented, of an annuity of 10l. for the life of Katharine de la Poole, the duke's sister, Abbess of Barking, charged on the manor of Langham, Essex, Records of the Exchequer: King's Remembrancer: Ancient Deeds, TNA Series E 29 Henry VI E 210/5183.

37 Account and official: Michael de la Pole, earl of Suffolk, the son, deceased TNA, E 358/6 Rot 2, 3 Henry V

38 Archer, R. E., 2003, Jane with the Blemyssh: a skeleton in the de la Pole closet. *The Ricardian Vol 13*, pp. 12-26 online at http://www.thericardian.online/downloads/Ricardian/13/03.pdf

39 Napier, H., 1858, *Historical Notices of the Parishes of Swyncombe and Ewelme in the County of Oxford*, printed for the author by James Wright printer to the University of Oxford.

40 Archer, R. E., 2003, original document 'Notes on the descent of the dukes of Norfolk' TNA E163/9/28.

41 See Gell A. blog on *Impostors*. https://aarongell.com/impostors

34. Foliate initial 'S' with the heraldic arms of William de la Pole at the beginning of John Lydgate's Siege of Thebes, 1425-50.

The Most Despised Man in England

William de la Pole, 4th earl, then 1st duke of Suffolk (1396-1450) and his wife, Alice Chaucer, duchess of Suffolk (1404-1475). William de la Pole, or simply 'Suffolk' has been vilified by historians and storytellers more than most. Shakespeare has Queen Margaret carrying William's severed head around the stage in *Henry VI part 2* in what is surely one of the most tasteless if not plain silly Shakespearean scenes, usually cut from modern productions.[1] Shakespeare's Suffolk, developed over the course of the first two parts of *Henry VI*, is an ambitious, arrogant, spirited nobleman with an erotic obsession for Margaret that largely drives the plot. But while the real Suffolk may have been genuinely fond of Margaret of Anjou, thirty-four years his junior, there is no historical evidence of impropriety between them. Like many men in the public eye, stories grew up around William that are now very difficult either to verify or refute. A created myth may well be oft repeated by unsympathetic chroniclers and sometimes by his defenders, a bit of spice for the gossipmongers; 'fake news' was rife then as now. William was interesting enough without adding scandalous relations with the Queen, unidentified bastard children and secret marriages.

He has been described as 'the most despised man in England' and certainly he was generally hated in Norfolk and Suffolk because of his failure to control his henchmen on his East Anglian estates.[2] Eventually he was also reviled by the men surrounding the unpopular king, not simply because of William's singular personal influence with the monarch but also because of the foreign policies he espoused.

Popular opinion at the time judged him a traitor and later legend added his supposed obsession with Margaret. Even his modern biographer John Watts is cool, somewhat detached about his good points, although he admits that Suffolk was an exceptionally competent administrator for Henry VI for many years.[3] The evidence points to Suffolk being an unfortunate scapegoat for an unpopular administration and policies for which others were as much responsible as he. His careless management of the estates in East Anglia however leaves one infuriated with his inaction and tolerance of his bullying henchmen. William has belatedly found a worthy champion for his positive qualities in a modern biography by Susan Curran, who does not gloss over his failures nor inadequacies but understands him as a war weary peacemaker sympathetic to his peaceable king's own yearning for an end to the destructive wars in France.[4]

While William's career closely mirrored that of his grandfather Michael, he rose even higher and then finally crashed further in tragedy. Here is a man who was a competent if not brilliant military commander, a romantic poet, a loyal and dedicated servant of his king and whose gift for friendship and sustained desire for peace make him both understandable and likeable. Like his grandfather, he had the bad luck to serve a youthful and weak un-kingly king who could not control the resentful circle of ambitious men around him.

How much did William contribute to Wingfield Castle? Though he grew up in Suffolk and Wingfield was his family's main home, he left to fight in France in his late teens, then spent twenty years there. He acquired property in France and rarely visited England until after his marriage in 1430 to Alice Chaucer, the twice widowed countess of Salisbury. There had been no resident owner at Wingfield Castle since the 2nd countess of Suffolk had died thirteen years earlier. And there were very good reasons for the newly married couple to spend more time at her father's old estates around Ewelme, Oxfordshire rather than at Wingfield. The newly built, modern home in the Thames Valley was much better situated for the political machinations at Windsor, London and Westminster, and "For love of her and the commoditie of her landes, (the earl) fell much to dwelle yn Oxfordshir and Barkshir wher his wifes landes lay".[5]

Ewelme Manor, later often referred to as a 'palace', was the home that William and Alice created for themselves. They visited Suffolk and Hull, indeed Alice was responsible for much church building work in Suffolk as well as in Oxfordshire, but Wingfield Castle was probably a secondary home. During their ownership it may have seen little development. Nevertheless there is ample evidence that they did use Wingfield as one of their homes and their son John liked it well enough to make it his main home. Their estates in Norfolk and Suffolk were far too valuable to stay away for long. They also maintained a large house in London, the Mansion of the Rose in Candlewick Street, commemorated now in Suffolk Lane. They also maintained a house in Norwich, the regional capital and prosperous centre of the worsted wool manufacturing industry. In addition they owned secondary manor houses in a dozen or more locations in Norfolk and Suffolk.

35. Ewelme Manor or Palace, extended after 1430 by William and Alice de la Pole.

William's early years. Noble ladies often had a favourite manor where they retreated to give birth accompanied only by women attendants. William's mother Katherine Stafford chose the de la Pole manor at Cotton, just sixteen miles away from Wingfield, for many of her 'lyings in'. His father Michael was about thirty four, his mother in her mid twenties when their second son William was born on 10 October 1396. Katherine returned to Cotton for the birth of several other children. It must have felt a reassuring place. Legend says he was born in an October gale, likely enough in this easterly village. He was baptized in the magnificent church in Cotton, a beautiful building even before the double hammerbeam roof was installed.

William grew up in Suffolk, perhaps at Wingfield but if not there, he would have been a regular visitor to his parents at the castle. The children of noblemen were sometimes cared for by relatives in other noble houses, a means of strengthening family connections. His parents must often have been absent travelling round their estates. The children would not have travelled with them. William was the second oldest son but there was at least one sister, Isabel, later Lady Morley, who was older than him. His other sisters, Katherine and Elizabeth were born more than a decade later. After William, Michael and Katherine had three more sons, John, Alexander and Thomas, who would all play an important part in William's life. He would have grown up knowing that his older brother Michael was the most important son, the heir to the earldom, the future owner of all the major estates in East Anglia and Yorkshire, the house in London, the mansion in Norwich. He would also have learnt that his father had only regained the title and some of the estates when William was just two years old. The family's total commitment to king Henry IV, his son Henry V and the Lancastrian cause would have been drummed into him early.

William became a soldier, like Michael, as did John and later Alexander. Thomas was destined for the church and studied at Oxford to that end, soon after becoming a prebend at St Paul's Cathedral, supported by an income from the manor of Brownswood (now part of Finsbury Park), then owned by St Paul's and the Bishop of London. Thomas remained there all of his short life until called to aid William. William may also have gone briefly to university at Cambridge in his teens, as Alexander did.

The impact on William of the events of 1415. Barely nineteen, wounded at Harfleur, William was brought home to Wingfield to recover. His mother and siblings were there grieving his father and his older brother. His sister Elizabeth had also lost her husband Edward Burnell at Harfleur. William did not have the consolation of being one of the 'happy few' at Agincourt. And now he was the 4th earl of Suffolk, with the responsibility of managing the vast estates but also of supporting the dowagers, younger siblings and nieces as best he could, although he did not formally reach his majority and the control of his money for two years.[6] His father had left sufficient wealth to his widow to support her and she could live at Wingfield Castle and Court Hall in Hull until her death. But the family was not hugely wealthy. William had little choice but to return to soldiering as soon as he could, at least it gave him an income and opportunities for advancement. His mother was a competent negotiator; she moved swiftly to secure title of the property for William.[7]

In the next couple of years, there being no new military initiative in France, William would have got to know his estates better and the families and retainers who had traditionally supported them and acted as agents in their absence, collecting the rents and managing the estates. Two families, the Tuddenhams and the Heydons, affluent and well set up in East Anglia, were to become loyal Suffolk retainers, naturally William turned to them for support. He could not know then that his near contemporary, young Thomas Tuddenham, who came into his Oxburgh manor estate in Norfolk only in 1423, was to prove, together with John Heydon, an ambitious lawyer from Baconsthorpe, a major cause of William's later unpopularity in East Anglia.

Remarkably we know something of the business of the Wingfield Castle household through surviving fragments of 'the wardrobe accounts' of Lady Katherine, William's mother.[8] In 1416-1417 Thomas was studying at Burnell's Inn at Balliol College, Oxford, where Katherine was in part supporting him. She sent his tutor Thomas Rowebury eight shillings for her son's 'play and his small expenses', together with 'one purse to put his money in' and money to buy two yards of violet cloth. Younger brother Alexander was studying in Ipswich under Master William Bury. John Heydon was paid for riding out to fetch Alexander back from Ipswich to Wingfield in the summer of 1417.

The accounts include gifts for Elizabeth, Lady Burnell and young Philippa, who was at the time staying with a maid in Bungay Priory and money for another sister Joan to go to London to get William's armour repaired. That cost a hundred shillings, no small amount at the time. Older brother Michael's widow Elizabeth was given some help with her three children, who were farmed out to local people to look after. This was the way at the time, it indicated a desire to see the children expand their contacts and gain an education about how young women should behave. In 1416 young Elizabeth stayed with Christian Fastolfe at Bungay (surely a kinsman of Sir John Fastolf who would soon build Caister Castle) for a cost of 8d per week. Isabel stayed with Joan Baker of Fressingfield from August 1416 to May 1417 for 6d a week. Young Elizabeth got some education from a friar called 'Le President'. The young girls visited Wingfield when Lady Katherine sent for them. John Heydon organised one such trip, an undertaking that required seven horses and men to collect Elizabeth, possibly because of the lawlessness of the countryside or maybe simply an appropriate entourage for noble children.

Katherine was still adding to her substantial wardrobe, investing in silver vases, livestock and other goods, donating offerings and alms to the poor and providing goods for her three granddaughters. It may have been her decision that her young widowed daughter-in-law entered Bruisyard Nunnery. But Katherine died in 1419 and while one might have thought her three nieces Elizabeth, Katherine and Isabel would have received a substantial inheritance, in fact they did not.

The wheels of bureaucracy turned mightily slowly in the fifteenth century. It was not until 1421 that the 'Inquisition Post Mortem' was confirmed on the assets of deceased Michael de la Pole, 2nd earl of Suffolk was agreed. By then Michael's wife Katherine, the 3rd earl and his three young daughters were all dead. William, the male heir to his brother's property, was in France but probably had legal representation at the hearing, held at Weybread on 14 July. Edmund Wynter was the King's 'escheator' in Suffolk, the local official responsible for 'escheats', that is upholding the king's rights as feudal lord, and who held the majority of IPM hearings. It was agreed at the hearing that the king had not taken possession of Michael's lands and tenements in general but that the Manor of Frumbalds Fee, that is Wingfield Castle and the sixty-nine acres that were held directly from the king, were now at the king's disposal, valued at twelve shillings per annum.[9]

William de la Pole fights in France 1417–1431 and acquires French property and a nickname. Suffolk went back to France to serve with Henry V in 1417 and did not return for fourteen years. The only way he would have known what was going on back home in Wingfield was through news carried back and forth by heralds and messengers employed for that purpose. But he may well have employed lawyers to help sort out the inheritance of his property after Katherine Stafford died. William was present at the sacking of Caen, a bloody and prolonged battle that ended in most of the townsmen being massacred but also the butchering of perhaps two thousand women and children.

After Caen, Henry split up the English army, Suffolk accompanying the commander Humphrey, duke of Gloucester, 'Good Duke Humphrey', as he was called by the general populace. Younger brother to Henry V, Gloucester in his youth was a warm and charming figure, good looking too, although an unpredictable hot head, sometimes frankly rash. He was a patron of the arts and learning, eager to know the influential poets and musicians of his day. He was not a brilliant soldier but he was strongly committed to the conquest of France by any means. He seems to have worked well with Suffolk at his side in the early days and for many years they appeared to be good friends. They turned west after Caen to take the city of Bayeux, then suppressed and conquered the Cotentin promontory.

From 1418 until the truce with the Burgundy in 1421, their main enemy was the duke of Burgundy, the ruler of the Valois faction who had superseded the Armagnacs, whose power had been destroyed at Agincourt. Suffolk was rewarded for his military success with the lordship and captaincy of two Normandy strongholds, Hambye and Briquebec. A French chronicle reports that the king gave them to William 'in exchange for a shield of the arms of St George annually'. The chateau at Briquebec was a substantial Norman castle, grander than Wingfield by a long way, which was considered in 1857 a grandly picturesque place for a visit by Queen Victoria. It is now a hotel. These estates were valuable spoils of war.

Rejoining the king, the whole army took part in the appallingly cruel siege of Rouen. William was learning the realities of war. The townsfolk of Rouen, starving and unable to support the women and children of the town, forced them out through the gates. They believed Henry's reputation for chivalry and that he would allow them to pass through his army unmolested. However, Henry refused and the expelled women and children died of starvation in the ditches surrounding the town over many desperate weeks.

36. The Seige of Rouen, 1419.

Jackanapes. Soldiers in medieval times, as now, frequently gave each other nicknames; William's was Jackanapes or sometimes Jack Napes. The name probably derived from 'Jack of Naples', a slang name for a monkey at the time. His heraldic badge was an 'ape's clog', a wooden block chained to a pet monkey to prevent it escaping. Heraldic badges were used as personal emblems worn on the livery on the battlefield to identify heavily armed men to their comrades when the full arms would perhaps be too complex for instant recognition.[10]

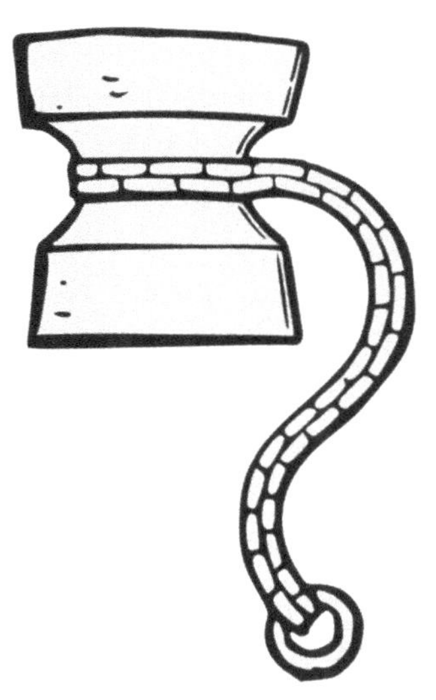

37. William de la Pole's personal heraldic emblem, an ape's clog.

William's nickname became so well-known that the word 'jackanapes' was absorbed into the English language as a derogatory term to mean an impertinent or conceited person, reflecting the popular if unjustified perception of Suffolk as a newly ennobled upstart.

Garter Knight. After Rouen, in May 1419 Suffolk was created Admiral of Normandy, a significant command. The French by then were paralysed by disputes between Burgundians and the remnants of the retrenching Armagnacs. Henry skilfully played them off one against the other without relaxing his warlike approach. When Henry returned to England in 1421 with his Valois bride, Catherine, he left Suffolk behind as conservator of the truce with Brittany. The alliance with the Burgundians was cemented by the marriage of Henry's brother John, duke of Bedford, to Anne, the daughter of duke John the Fearless of Burgundy in 1423. William was next made a knight of the Garter, a highly treasured honour and became the warden of the lower marches of Normandy. His garter stall plate with his coat of Arms was placed in St George's Chapel at Windsor Castle in his absence and is still there.

After Henry V's death in 1422, the succession of his baby son Henry VI demanded a competent regent. On his deathbed, Henry had named his oldest brother, John, duke of Bedford as regent. He was a man of far greater common sense than Gloucester. Bedford frequently entrusted Suffolk with area commands and diplomatic missions. William was sent to Hainault to mollify the hurt feelings of the court there about the improper 'marriage' of Humphrey of Gloucester with Jacqueline, countess of Hainault, a pretty, popular member of the English court who was in exile in England. It would have been a great match, Jacqueline being a woman of wealth, if only she was not already married to her cousin John of Brabant, from whom she had run off to England. She had requested an annulment from the pope in Rome, who had declined, so she had then sent to the alternative Avignon pope hoping for a different result. When she married Gloucester, half of Europe did not recognise the marriage, believing her to be still married to her cousin. Bedford and the English court knew Gloucester had made one of his rasher decisions. Gloucester and Jacqueline invaded Hainault to rescue her lands and did manage to get most of them back but when Gloucester returned to England without her, the marriage was over. He was by then tired of her and accepted the marriage had been incautious. Poor Jacqueline was shoved from pillar to post, betrayed by Gloucester with one of her ladies in waiting, Eleanor Cobham, whom he subsequently married, although that ended badly too.

The English alliance with Burgundy was threatened by the hostility between Gloucester and Philip, duke of Burgundy. Bedford was obliged to return to England in 1426 to arrange a reconciliation between his increasingly quarrelsome younger brother Gloucester and the Chancellor Henry Beaufort. William was a fervent Bedford man; his relationship with Gloucester slowly worsened over the years.

The English Court at Paris. By the early 1420s William's brothers John and Alexander de la Pole were both fighting alongside him. Only one of the de la Pole brothers, Thomas, remained in England, working at St Paul's Cathedral. Now that their mother Lady Katherine was dead, Wingfield Castle and the estates in East Anglia and Yorkshire were left entirely to the mercies of agents.

William and his fighting brothers' focus was France. Paris was their capital, not London. Although Paris had been deserted by up to half of the original French population and it was an impoverished sort of capital, it was the headquarters of the English territory from the early 1420s to 1436. The English held almost all the lands north of the Loire. William put in 'a respectable performance' as the historian John Watts put it and he further received grants of land in France at Dreux, becoming count of Dreux and acquiring yet another impressive fortified chateau.[11]

William and his brothers often fought under the direction of the earl of Salisbury, an experienced senior general who also had a base in Paris and brought over his countess, Alice to be with him. Bedford set up court for himself in Paris and also in Rouen, also then in English hands. It is likely that William had an establishment in Paris. William brought into his personal service one of the finest musicians of his day, Gilles de Binchois.[12] Born in Mons in the Low Countries, Binchois' father was employed at the Court in Hainault and it may have been through the connection to Jacqueline of Hainault and Gloucester that the musician came to be known to the Burgundian and English courts in France. He was one of the most influential composers of the fifteenth century of chansons of chivalric love, sung masses and other religious music.

Meeting Alice, countess of Salisbury. Wingfield must have felt a world away from William at this point. The tone of court life in France for the English nobility was established by Bedford's Burgundian duchess and by Alice, the beautiful young wife of the earl of Salisbury. As Salisbury's second in command, William would have become well acquainted with the strikingly elegant tall slim Alice. He would also have known about, indeed may have witnessed Alice's beauty having caught the amorous eye of Philip, duke of Burgundy at a wedding reception in Paris in November 1424. She turned Philip down but did not have the good sense to keep quiet about the duke's amorous overtures and told her husband. Alice was the advance guard of the 'Me-Too' generation.

She was an embarrassment for the English and the Burgundians. Alice's father, Thomas Chaucer, was in Paris at the time, a wealthy and influential Speaker of the House of Commons with several lucrative public appointments. But he was also from a lowly commoner background. The Chaucer family lineage may have made both father and daughter touchy about any perceived slight. Furious about the episode, the story goes, Salisbury became an implacable enemy of the amorous Burgundy. The incident does not seem to have lessened Salisbury's good opinion of Alice. We do not know what William thought.

William and Jacqueline of Hainault; Malyne de Cay. There is very little certainty about William's love life in these French years. There was a story that William became the lover of the discarded Jacqueline of Hainault, who gave birth to his daughter Beatrice and that the child was sent home to Wingfield to be brought up there. It was common enough for noblemen like William to sire children out of wedlock and to make respectable arrangements for their upbringing. He may have been Jacqueline's lover for a while but the story seems to have become conflated with that of another woman, Malyne de Cay. She was a French nun and more convincingly his mistress before the English defeat at Orléans. She gave birth to a daughter, some say Jane, others Joan, who was apparently brought up in England and later married Sir Thomas Stonor of Oxfordshire.[13]

The final years of William's military career. Suffolk's brother John de la Pole was taken prisoner after a failed insurgency against the Valois, an unauthorized chevauchée in the territory of Anjou. His men were killed. William's priority at this point would be to produce sufficient money for the ransom; John would not have been expected to raise it all himself. The brother of an earl would be quite a prize but raising the heavy ransom would take some months. William may have sold land back home but more probably he would have sold some of his estate in France. John would have been obliged to sell most of his own estates in France but probably held onto Moyon where his French wife, Marie de Sicile and their daughter lived. After John's release, William kept his young brother close to him in his own company of soldiers.

Salisbury managed, after a persuasive visit to Bedford in England, to raise reinforcements to replace the 2700 or so dead in recent campaigns and get agreement for an onslaught on the great city of Orléans. Bedford later acknowledged his doubts about whether it was possible to take Orléans, indicating he would have preferred a campaign into Anjou. Taking Orléans was indeed an ambition too far and would prove to be the turning point in the Hundred Years War between France and England. William shared Bedford's scepticism but Salisbury was determined. The early part of the campaign went well, some lesser towns were taken, Beaugency, Meung and Jargeau. They also took the fort of Tourelles at the gates of Orléans in an opening gambit.

On 27 October 1428, Salisbury and a few others, probably including Suffolk, went to the top of the Tourelles to survey the town and its landscape from a window. A cannonball struck the iron lintel of the window as Salisbury leaned out; the iron bar flew at Salisbury's head and tore away much of his lower face.[14] For a week he lingered, before dying at Meung sur Loire on 3 November. Salisbury and Alice had no children, although he had a daughter by his first wife as well as an illegitimate son. Alice served as the supervisor of her husband's will. He left her half of his net goods, a thousand marks in gold and three thousand marks in jewellery and plate, as well as the revenues of his Norman lands, as long as they could be collected. William de la Pole, earl of Suffolk, took up Salisbury's command in France.

Suffolk's personal assessment was that they could not take the city of Orléans without many more men. Bedford refused to supply them, but perhaps hinting that he thought William was not up to the task alone, sent Lord Scales and Lord Talbot as co-commanders. It is true that Suffolk appeared to be sitting on his hands reluctant to proceed; we might judge him appropriately cautious.

Orléans was important because it lay in a border region between the zone recognising Henry VI of England as king of France and the zone recognising the dauphin, Charles VII. The campaign restarted with Talbot and Scales. Impressive siege works, including forts, were undertaken. Weeks went by; a French attempt to cut the besiegers' line of supply was defeated in February 1429 and the defenders were considering capitulation when a fanatic girl, 16 year old Joan of Arc, persuaded Charles VII to send an army to relieve the city. Diversionary action against one of the English forts enabled Joan to enter Orléans with supplies on 30 April. In the following week the principal English forts were stormed and Suffolk abandoned the siege.

38. Thomas Montagu, 4th earl of Salisbury is fatally injured at the siege of Orléans in 1428.

Joan or Jeanne d'Arc, 'La Pucelle', was an extraordinary figure. How did this obsessive visionary, a slight girl in boy's clothing, come to be the figurehead of the Valois and their weak king? Just as Henry V's near delusional belief in the righteousness of his cause at Agincourt spread like wildfire round his troops, so Joan's godly vision about the removal of the English from French soil gave a new impetus to the Valois army. There is no space here to explore Joan's history but there is a recent biography by Helen Castor that explores her fascinating life, death and relevance to the making of France.[15] William de la Pole and his companions must have been astonished by her as an opponent.

The Battle of Jargeau and Captivity; the Deaths of John and Alexander de la Pole. Suffolk and his men retreated to Jargeau, the small but heavily fortified town on the Loire, about ten miles east of Orléans. The French force, commanded by Joan and duke John II of Alençon, attacked the suburbs; Suffolk for a while held them there. They eventually fell back, but Joan again rallied her troops, which included many volunteers inspired by this apparently fearless slip of a girl. She fought on even after having been wounded by a heavy stone. The English at Jargeau were heavily beaten.

Suffolk had brought perhaps fifteen hundred men with him from Orléans. By the end of the battle about one hundred and fifty survived. William's brothers John and Alexander were killed. Suffolk surrendered, not to Joan but it is said to some minor captain, an unconventional choice because noblemen were meant to surrender to noblemen. Perhaps it was to avoid surrendering to a mere woman. One chronicler records that to preserve chivalric proprieties, William 'knighted' his captor before handing over his sword, which seems an unlikely tale but a pleasingly stylish gesture. He probably thought it scarce mattered to whom he surrendered at that moment. He knew he would be in captivity for months; a ransom would be ruinous and hard to arrange.

William was allocated as prisoner to Jean Dunois, the bastard of Orléans and fervent supporter of Joan. In this respect William was lucky. The Bastard was the illegitimate son of Louis I, duke of Orléans, himself a son of King Charles V of France and his mistress Mariette d'Enghien. His nickname, the 'Bastard of Orléans', was a term of respect, since it acknowledged him as a first cousin to the king and acting head of a branch of the royal family during his half-brother's captivity. He later became count of Dunois. In 1407, Jean's father, the duke of Orléans was assassinated. Eight years later, his half-brother, Charles duke of Orléans was captured at Agincourt. When William was taken prisoner, Charles of Orléans had been a prisoner in England for fourteen long years. This left Jean the only adult male to represent the house of Orléans.

Given that Jean's half brother Charles was still held in England there was no guarantee that William would be released even if it were easy to raise the ransom, which it would not have been. He was held somewhere in a stronghold on the Loire, we do not know where. Jean was a youngish man, about twenty seven years old, younger than William but he seems to have been a competent, fair commander. When he eventually came to meet William, in fact he probably met him many times over the negotiations for his release, he found his prisoner writing poetry.[16] Many others have commented that even though the few remaining poems attributed to William, written in both English and French, while they do not have the yearning, brilliant imagery of Jean's prisoner brother Charles, duke of Orléans, they are competent courtly poems about love. Charles' poetry was known and admired throughout France and Europe, and William's style suggests that he admired Charles too. Would that perhaps have endeared him to Charles' half brother?

In April 1430 William was freed but for a stinging ransom of twenty thousand pounds, which would have necessitated selling all his lands in France and a substantial number of manors in England. He lost Hambye, Briquebec and probably Dreux. There were other conditions too. First, he had to do everything in his power to secure the release of Charles, duke of Orléans and secondly, in order to hold him to that promise, William's brother Thomas must come and be a prisoner in exchange for William's freedom. Thomas agreed to this, it was a duty owed to his older brother. This may have engendered some considerable guilt in William, who was forced to leave his brother in France when he returned home to his inheritance and his life in England, hoping to free Thomas as soon as he could. Thomas never came home but died in captivity in France in 1433. William was going home to Wingfield Castle and a new future.

Notes

1 An analysis of Shakespeare's dramatic intentions for Suffolk and Margaret is given in Williams, G., 1974, Suffolk and Margaret: A Study of Some Sections of Shakespeare's Henry VI, *Shakespeare Quarterly, Vol. 25*, pp. 310-322.

2 Wise, M., 23 January 2014, William de la Pole, the most despised man in England. In *The de la Pole Family, the Wars of the Roses*, online at https://mattlewisauthor.wordpress.com/2014/01/23/william-de-la-pole-the-most-despised-man-in-england/

3 Watts, J., 2004, Pole, William de la, first duke of Suffolk (1396–1450) *Oxford Dictionary of National Biography*, online at https://doi.org/10.1093/ref:odnb/22461.

4 Curran, S., 2011, *The English Friend: A Life of William de la Pole, first duke of Suffolk*, Lasse Press, Norwich.

5 Quoted without source in Greening Lamborn, E. A., 1940, *Oxoniensis 5*, 78-93, in Papers of Greening Lamborn E .A., Bodleian Library, University of Oxford, GB 161 MSS Eng.Misc. Top. Berks. g 1; Top. Oxon. d. 457.

6 William's age and inheritance formerly recognised in Court of Chancery, Inquisitions Post Mortem Series 1,

Henry V, TNA C138/29/63.

7 Lady Katherine petitions king for estates to pass to William de la Pole. Granted 8 December 1415. Curran 2011, p. 50.

8 Suffolk Estate Papers HA411, 1408-1506. Suffolk Record Office Ipswich HA411. Curran 2011, 51-54; County of Suffolk: Compotus rolls for lands of the Earls of Suffolk in: 1403, 1454.County of Norfolk: Compotus-rolls 1403-1522. Michael De la Pole, 2nd Earl of Suffolk: Compotus rolls for his lands in counties of Norfolk and Suffolk: 1403-1416. BL Egerton Roll 8776.

9 Michael de la Pole IPM TNA C 139/2/26 [Latin document] 1421.

10 The ape's clog emblem is shown in Fox-Davies, A. C., 1909, *A Complete Guide to Heraldry,* Illustrator: Johnston G., Project Gutenberg ecopy December 13, 2012 [EBook #41617].

11 Chateau de Dreux is still a family home occupied by the current Comte and Comtesse de Dreux, whose guidebook acknowledges that for 17 years the castle was 'under the yolk of the English'.

12 De Binchois' patron was mentioned in a line in the funeral motet composed in Binchois' memory in 1460 by the composer Johnannes Ockeghem.

13 Kingsford, C. L. (ed), 1924, recent edition Carpenter, C. (ed), 1996, *Kingsford's Stonor Letters and Papers 1290-1483* first published by Royal Historical Society, reissued Cambridge University Press, Cambridge. A discussion in the footnote examines the various claims and likelihood of Suffolk's relationships and illegitimate progeny p. 5, online at https://books.google.co.uk/books.

14 The death of Salisbury is recounted in two chronicles and by various modern authorities. One is *The Chronicles of Enguerrand de Monstrelet. Vol VI* pp. 234- 237, translated by Johnes, T., 1853, London, online at https://archive.org/details/chroniclesofengu01mons/page/n9. See also Hunt, W., 1894, Montacute or Montague, 4th earl of Salisbury 1388-1428 in Lee, S. (ed), *Dictionary of National Biography Vol 38*, Smith Elder and Co., London.

15 Castor, H., 2014, *Joan of Arc, a History*. Faber and Faber, London.

16 An appraisal of William de la Pole's poetry is in Neilly, M. 2011 The 'Fairfax Sequence' Reconsidered: Charles d'Orléans and the Anonymous Poems of Bodleian MS Fairfax, *16 Fifteenth century studies, Vol 36*, pp. 127-136.

William de la Pole's Rise and Fall 1430–1450

Marriage to Alice, countess of Salisbury. William now needed a wife, a rich one. Alice, the good-looking widowed countess of Salisbury was the ideal candidate. We have only one image of Alice, a rather unsatisfactory one, a seven foot alabaster effigy which she commissioned for herself for her elaborate tomb in Ewelme church, showing a tall, thin smooth faced impassive figure, a formal grandiose monument to an extraordinary life. The inscription reads 'a serene princess'. Underneath the coffin is carved her semi-naked cadaver, a pious if showy reminder of the fleeting nature of earthly things. There was nothing fleeting about Alice's ambitious strategy for her family's future.

39. Alice, duchess of Suffolk, alabaster tomb effigy St Mary's Church, Ewelme, Oxfordshire.

Alice and William must have already known each other well, so neither embarked on the marriage unaware of the qualities of the other and there seems no doubt that they chose each other. Within a few months of William's return to England on 11 November 1430 they contracted to marry. The complex legal agreements between Alice, her father and William took two or three years to finalise but before these were completed they were married, probably in early 1431. Alice was an extraordinary woman, clever, self-important, vain, a force always to be reckoned with and a dominant force on his side for the rest of his life. From now on William would be trying to manage Alice as well as his career. Theirs seems to have been a strong partnership, a successful marriage.

Alice was born about 1404 and died in 1475, the only child and heir of Thomas Chaucer and his wife Maud Berghersh and granddaughter of the poet Geoffrey Chaucer, who died before she was born.[1] Maud was co-heir to the wealthy Berghersh estates including the manor of Ewelme, Oxfordshire, where Alice was probably born. Thomas Chaucer was 'a self-made man of great wealth, acquisitive yet circumspect, politic and affairé, well versed in all branches of administration and diplomacy, a practised chairman and envoy, influential and respected.'[2] Elected Speaker of the Commons on five occasions, Chaucer held the position of Chief Butler but exactly where all his money came from, apart from his wife's estate, is unclear.

Thomas' daughter had many of his qualities without the diplomatic reserve. She could be wilful, interfering, charmless and greedy. Sometimes her behaviour was shocking, demure she certainly was not. Her childhood marriage to Sir John Phelip ended when he died of dysentery at Harfleur and she returned home, being still a child. Her second marriage to Thomas Montague earl of Salisbury was a great coup for her father and brought both status and wealth. Salisbury's death at Orléans increased her personal wealth by a modest additional eight manors but when her father and mother died in the 1430s she acquired the whole Chaucer estate. Alice had continued to buy land for her own enlarging portfolio after Salisbury's death, and would again after William's. She always kept a watchful eye on her domains.

Home to Wingfield Castle and the Norfolk and Suffolk manors; growing ambition. Coming home to Wingfield after 14 years in war-torn France must have been a strange experience. The house had been occupied by a bailiff but no family members had lived there. In early 1432 Alice may well not have been very impressed with this rather remote home of her new spouse. It was not especially grand compared with his lost estates in France and Alice's previous English home she shared with Salisbury. Bisham manor, the Salisburys' main home had been expanded and modernised only recently. While personal family servants may have been welcoming, the couple would quickly have been beseiged by numerous local petitioners seeking redress for all manner of wrongs that had been dealt with inadequately in Suffolk's absence. William and Alice must then have become acquainted with the agents whom he had relied on for so long to manage his business in his absence, John Heydon and Sir Thomas Tuddenham.[3,4] How did he react when he learnt that these men were mistrusted and reviled by the population over whom they wielded so much power?

Heydon was a major landowner in north Norfolk around his castle at Baconsthorpe; the same man or possibly the son of the John Heydon who had acted as servant to the family for an earlier generation.[5] Thomas Tuddenham (1401-1462) was an ambitious lawyer with an unfortunate marital history. He had married, about 1418, Alice Wodehouse, the daughter of his guardian, John Wodehouse. The couple lived together until about 1425, during which time Alice gave birth to a son who died young. Both Tuddenham and his wife later denied that the marriage had been consummated, and Alice admitted that her father's chamberlain was the father of her infant son. By 1429, Tuddenham and his wife were formally separated, and Alice became a nun at Crabhouse Priory in Norfolk. The marriage was annulled in 1436. The separation case was a very public humiliation for Tuddenham, who never remarried.

As an ally of Suffolk and a member of Henry VI's household, Tuddenham was the recipient of numerous appointments and grants of land in East Anglia. He was Sheriff of Norfolk and Suffolk in 1432, and Member of Parliament for Suffolk in 1431. He was member for Norfolk in 1432, 1435 and 1442. In 1443 he and William, now generally called Suffolk, were jointly appointed to the chief stewardship of the north parts of the Duchy of Lancaster. In 1446 Tuddenham was appointed Keeper of the Great Wardrobe in the royal household. These appointments were clearly engineered by William, who throughout his life regarded Tuddenham as a close friend. He and Alice were either blind to their retainers' faults or did not much care as long as their own interests were served.

The great rivals of the de la Poles for land and influence in East Anglia were the Mowbrays, earls and dukes of Norfolk. In the 1420s East Anglia had been ruled by the Lancastrian kings linking together a local gentry network focused on the Duchy of Lancaster's huge estates in Norfolk, managed by Sir Thomas Erpingham and Thomas Beaufort, duke of Exeter. Other magnates had been more or less excluded. But with Exeter's death in 1426 and Erpingham's in 1428, there was a vacancy into which William could step with alacrity when he returned home. It was made possible by his advancement at court. But the newly inherited 3rd duke of Norfolk, John Mowbray arrived on the East Anglian scene in 1432. Mowbray's marriage to Eleanor Bourchier in the early 1430s drew him into the highly partisan and complex politics of East Anglia, and he became a bitter rival of William.

Mowbray had been an unruly and notoriously uncontrollable youth and in later life prosecuted his feuds with vigour, often taking the law into his own hands. His violent tactics drew the disapproving attention of the king, and he was bound over for huge sums of money and imprisoned twice in the Tower.[6] It should be said that de la Pole also resorted to violent tactics, though not personally. Rather he allowed his retainers to use force. Local gentry looked to Mowbray for leadership, but often in vain. Mowbray is a curiously anonymous figure, who seems to have been difficult to get on with. Some retainers deserted him and some like Sir Robert Wingfield, his own steward at Framlingham Castle, were on grumbling bad terms with him. De la Pole was a powerful local force and favourite of the King, while Mowbray was neither.

One incident, the murder of James Andrew in 1435, reflects badly on the rival nobles.[7] Andrew was a wealthy elderly man, a knight of the shire, MP for Suffolk and closely associated with William. During a dispute between the two lords of Norfolk and Suffolk, Andrew was ambushed and attacked near Bury St Edmunds by a gang led by Sir Robert Wingfield of Framlingham of the Norfolk faction. Other 'Gentlemen of Suffolk's faction' gave fight and another general affray resulted. Wingfield fired a hail of arrows at the Alderman of Bury who came to arrest them all. Andrew died of his wounds and his widow Margery appealed for justice. The duke of Norfolk and earl of Suffolk appeared together before the king's council in February 1435. Each had been asked to give security to keep the peace. They were compelled to promise not to prevent an enquiry into Andrew's death. The case dragged on for five years and it is probable that Wingfield eventually paid some financial compensation to the widow. The case however speaks to the continuing tensions and violent exchanges that both factions indulged in, to the detriment of the general peace in Norfolk and Suffolk, where the population sought fairness and justice in their private dealings.

Heydon and Tuddenham were the twin engines of control of Suffolk estates and kept other lords and landowners under their repressive thumb, extracting money where they could. Mowbray never did get the better of William, which is why, as William's influence grew at court, Mowbray shifted his allegiance towards supporting Richard, duke of York, the king's cousin who arguably had a stronger claim to the throne than Henry VI.

The Feud with the Paston family. The Pastons of north Norfolk were one family that suffered from the bullying and greed of Heydon and Tuddenham. The family's celebrated personal letters have thrown much light on the lives of the gentry in East Anglia in the fifteenth century. Although John Paston inherited a substantial estate, in the latter 1440s the family suffered 'a series of reverses', including the loss of the manor of East Beckham in 1445. The circumstances of these reverses are recounted in the letters, and it is hard not to read the events through the eyes of these mostly likeable people, who hated Suffolk with a passion. Suffolk's dominance and the consequent continuing troubles of the Paston family demonstrated the extent to which gentry society in East Anglia was terrorised by Heydon and Tuddenham. Some authorities suggest that the Paston family's difficulties during this period were a direct result of the power struggle between Norfolk and Suffolk, and perhaps also as a result of personal animosity between John Heydon and the Pastons.

In February 1448, almost certainly on Heydon's initiative, the Paston's manor of Gresham was invaded and taken over by Robert, Lord Hungerford. Paston attempted to recover the manor through both negotiation and legal action. When these proved fruitless, he sent his wife, Margaret, to reside in a house in Gresham in October 1448. In the following January, Hungerford's servants assaulted and damaged the house, forcing Margaret Paston to leave. Hungerford remained in possession of Gresham for the next three years. Among Paston's associates during this difficult period were the courtier Thomas Daniel, Margaret Paston's kinsman Sir John Fastolf, and the duke of Norfolk. However none of these connections afforded Paston any practical support, and in May 1449 Paston's wife Margaret wrote to him advising that local opinion was of the view that he should try to reach a rapprochement with Suffolk. She wrote that she thought John Heydon was 'a false shrew'.[8] But so long as Suffolk was alive, his two henchmen dominated East Anglia. Their come-uppance came only after his death.

One very odd incident, if true, sheds light on the characters of Alice Chaucer and Sir Thomas Tuddenham, We do not know exactly when it occurred but it was before June 1448, when William was made duke of Suffolk. Officials of the city of Norwich complained:

> It was so, that Alice, Duchess, that time Countess of Suffolk, lately in person came to this city, disguised like a country housewife. Sir Thomas Tuddenham, and two other persons, went with her, also disguised; and they, to take their disports, went out of the city one evening, near night, so disguised, towards a hovel called Lakenham Wood, to take the air, and disport themselves, beholding the said city. One Thomas
>
> Ailmer, of Norwich, esteeming in his conceit that the said duchess and Sir Thomas had been other persons, met them, and opposed their going out in that wise, and fell at variance with the said Sir Thomas, so that they fought; whereby the said duchess was sore afraid; by cause whereof the said duchess and Sir Thomas took a displeasure against the city, notwithstanding that the mayor of the city at that time being, arrested Thomas Ailmer, and held him in prison more than thirty weeks without bail; to the intent thereby both to chastise Ailmer, and to appease the displeasure of the said duchess and Sir Thomas; and also the said mayor

> arrested and imprisoned all other persons which the said duchess and Sir Thomas could understand had in any way given favour or comfort to the said Ailmer, in making the affray. Notwithstanding which punishment, the displeasure of the duchess and Sir Thomas was not appeased.

This extraordinary incident, if true, reflects badly on Alice, cavorting round the countryside with a retainer, the whole party in fancy dress, in disguise. The appalling treatment of Thomas Ailmer is repeated as an illustration of Alice and Tuddenham's disregard for niceties. We have only the city's version of events, not Alice's. Nor do we know what Suffolk thought of his wife 'disporting' herself with Tuddenham. The story was written down some years later and many have challenged its authenticity.

Returning home to Suffolk also allowed William to become re-acquainted with his sisters, Isobel Lady Morley, based at the Morley estates at Hingham in Norfolk and Elizabeth, who had remarried after her first husband's death to Sir Thomas Kerdeston. Thomas and Elizabeth must have been keen on hawking and hunting as they commissioned an East Anglian scribe to write a book on hawking.[9]

Little is known about the lives of William's other sisters apart from Katherine, who became the Abbess of Barking.[10] They would have made connections with the other great families in the region, rivals or no; many of them were connected by marriage. Alice's stepdaughter by her first marriage was married to a Neville, brother of Mowbray, duke of Norfolk. So in spite of rivalries and power struggles there were Mowbray and Beaufort connections to be remade and polished with social gatherings, perhaps in Norwich, the great regional centre where noble families kept homes.

Advancement at Court. William became a member of the king's council in November 1431, his first step on a ladder that would take him to the very top. It is likely that his father-in-law Thomas Chaucer had some hand in this preferment and that William's advancement was also much assisted by Alice's connections to Cardinal Henry Beaufort, a wealthy cousin of Thomas Chaucer. As her husband became a prominent figure at court, so did Alice. In 1432, she was made a Lady of the Garter. There are still female members of the Order of the Garter in the twenty-first century, three in 2021, and it remains a mark of the highest royal favour.

Charles duke of Orléans (1394-1465), a prisoner friend. For four years, from 1432 to 1436, William was given the custody of the most important French prisoner, the poet Charles duke of Orléans, half brother of William's own captor the Bastard of Orléans. William's release had been contingent on making efforts to have Charles released. Charles was someone whose poetry William admired greatly and on which perhaps he modelled his own work. The negotiations necessary to acquire Charles must have been complex and the motive surely could not simply to have been to exchange poems. Charles had now been in captivity for eighteen years, he had acquired a substantial library; he was allowed a modicum of freedom, could even travel with an escort and had personal servants. A stream of goods and servants moved to and fro between the French duke and his home, at least in the early years. William and Charles became close friends and clearly discussed politics, the future of the war in France and of course, Charles' release.[11]

Charles had been captured at the battle of Agincourt, found unharmed but trapped beneath a pile of bodies on a battlefield where many of his fellow French were slaughtered. He was newly knighted and just short of twenty-one years old. Brought to England he was handed round from one aristocratic jailer to another, being held in the Tower of London, then in the castles at Pontefract, Fotheringhay, Bolingbroke, Ampthill and Donnington, Berkshire, among others, before coming to Wingfield in 1432. He often accompanied his captors to London and indeed travelled with William and his family on their trips to Ewelme. It is thought that he was with the de la Poles for at least four years, mainly at Wingfield.

40. Portrait of Charles duke of Orléans 1472 from Statutes, Ordonnances and armorial of the Order of the Golden Fleece.

William undoubtedly played a special role in Charles's captivity. He was near Charles' age and William was a francophile, sympathetic to the French cause, or, more accurately, interested in making peace between the English and the French. They were both bilingual in French and English. Indeed by the time Charles went home he spoke better English than French. Both William and Charles must have been sick of war by then, having both lost so much at Agincourt and after. They had both witnessed the destruction of northern France by the English. Suffolk was thus acquainted both with Charles' condition as prisoner and with his family and home and probably shared many of his aspirations. The friendship between William and the duke lasted beyond 1440 when Charles was belatedly returned to France. We know that Suffolk visited Charles at Blois in 1444.

Charles was highly thought of in his own time, both as a man and as a poet but scholars who write literary history, after ignoring him for centuries, have often been less than kind to the duke. In the early twentieth century he was seen as refined but ineffectual, weak-willed and self-centred. His reputation among English readers and even some French scholars was besmirched by Robert Louis Stevenson's condescending essay on his life and works.[12]

But we know that Charles was an able administrator and a good politician who worked tirelessly from prison to free his brother, govern his lands and protect his property. He was a loyal friend, worked for peace between France and England and suffered much sorrow in his life, not least because of his long imprisonment. Charles's books reveal a devout, serious, reflective turn of mind, one more interested in philosophy, science and theology than in chronicle and romance. But he wrote romantic poetry, poetry about loss and imprisonment. Many are charming and playful. We do not know which poems, if any, were written at Wingfield but the following example seems appropriate.

> Strengthen, my Love, this castle of my heart,
> And with some store of pleasure give me aid,
> For Jealousy, with all them of his part,
> Strong siege about the weary tower has laid.
> Nay, if to break his bands thou art afraid,
> Too weak to make his cruel force depart,
> Strengthen at least this castle of my heart,
> And with some store of pleasure give me aid.
> Nay, let not Jealousy, for all his art
> Be master, and the tower in ruin laid,
> That still, ah Love! thy gracious rule obeyed.
> Advance, and give me succour of thy part;
> Strengthen, my Love, this castle of my heart.

Charles, duke of Orléans (1394-1465)

Building Churches and Religious Foundations; supporting Wingfield College. William's finances had been left in a sorry state by the vast ransom paid to release him. He had sold many manors, including his birthplace at Cotton. By the mid 1430s however he had repaired his fortunes as a result of Alice's wealth and had attracted other preferments and grants from the Crown. The couple began to invest in supporting religious foundations and building churches. They endowed Wingfield College with one hundred shillings a year for two chaplains to say masses for his mother Lady Katherine and for his uncle Richard. They substantially rebuilt Wingfield Church, extending the chapel and chancel eastwards, which later Alice would extend again. They gave the church its striking creamy arch between the chancel and the Lady Chapel.[13]

Alice also added a pretty porch on to Syleham Church and after William's death, in his memory, she contributed a substantial amount to build the new tower at the Church in Eye, later adding the magnificent porch. They established a charitable hospital and school at Ewelme in Oxfordshire and William gave further money to the Charterhouse in Hull, his grandfather's foundation. William was a benefactor of a thousand marks (£666) to Eton College Chapel, having supervised the building of Eton College on behalf of the king. He also supported Oxford University, becoming Protector in 1447. He furthered the king's building ambitions at Cambridge and laid the first stone of Kings College Chapel for the king.

Suffolk rises to the heights at Court. Following the end of Henry VI's minority in 1437, Suffolk became a favoured royal councillor. The acceptance of this role came at a time when those who knew the king were aware that while he was nominally, from the age of fourteen, a responsible adult and in charge of policy decisions, this was a fiction. In reality decisions had to be made by agreement of the great magnates around the king. While everyone of influence was in agreement this was fine, but when factions developed maintaining any united policy or holding to the pretence that Henry personally was making the decisions was challenging.

William trod a careful path at first, allying himself to those close to the king and consulting them. Irritatingly, Henry VI held onto the purse strings and distributed largesse to favourite causes without consultation or sense, seemingly influenced by the last person who had spoken to him. William, gradually building his influence throughout the early to mid 1430s, had been awarded in 1434, jointly with Alice, the role of Constable of Wallingford Castle, a highly prestigious appointment at one of the greatest medieval castles in England, just a stone's throw from Ewelme and a far more prestigious site than Wingfield. Alice's father had held the role of Constable, so Alice would have known Wallingford well. The couple added Wallingford to the growing list of manors and castles they used as homes. Wallingford Castle is now a modest ruin but the earthworks provide witness to its former grandeur.

William attended the king's council assiduously. He was eventually appointed as Steward of the Household, becoming the dominant figure in the government. He was at the forefront of the main policies conducted during the period. He and the king eventually pursued a policy of peace with France, which neither of them unfortunately seem to have had the skill to implement successfully. It was unpopular with other magnates, especially Humphrey of Gloucester, who continued to hark back to his brother Henry V's death-bed exhortations to conquer France. William may have had other Lancastrian aims in pursuing peace with France. I think we can safely assume he was no pacifist but he did pursue a policy of peace consistently in the face of considerable opposition.

It seems likely that William's long experience of war in France had convinced him of the wisdom of drawing the fighting to a close and his conviction was no doubt strengthened by his association with the captive Charles of Orléans. He was working actively for peace when Hue de Lannoy came to England as ambassador from Philip of Burgundy. Lannoy and his colleagues met Orléans at Suffolk's house in London and Suffolk seems to have worked with Orléans in forwarding the negotiations. In 1435 the peace negotiations had progressed enough that a general congress was arranged and Suffolk was appointed one of the chief English representatives together with Cardinal Beaufort. The English however failed to compromise and were not prepared to yield to French demands. After the English withdrew from the congress, the French strengthened their own cause almost immediately by Burgundy forming an alliance with the French king. Then, shortly after this, the steady and wise John of Bedford died.

These two events, the new French alliance and the death of Bedford changed the whole face of English politics. Gloucester, seeing an opportunity to resist peace, gradually assumed more power. Suffolk inevitably became chief opponent of Gloucester and the remainder of William's life centred on his rivalry with the king's uncle. Meanwhile William was nominated to several responsible posts at home. In April 1437 he was appointed steward of the Duchy of Lancaster north of the Trent. In 1440 he was chief justice of North Wales and Chester and then of South Wales. In 1441 he was directed to make inquiry into the royal lordships in the county of Monmouth and in July that year into the government of Norwich. In this same year he was one of the commissioners to inquire into the charges of necromancy and sorcery against Eleanor Cobham, Gloucester's wife, a painful story concerning a barren, desperate and foolish woman, treasonable ideas and her inevitable disgrace. Gloucester had good reason to hate William.

A baby son and a childhood bethrothal. William must have thought it unlikely that he would have children by Alice. They had been married for eleven years without her becoming pregnant and she had borne no children by her second husband. But at a relatively late age, perhaps thirty-eight years old, Alice was delivered of a healthy son in September 1442. Baby John was not called by the traditional names for an older de la Pole son, such as William or Michael but probably after William's rash but much loved younger brother. Baby John was baptised as his father had been at Cotton Church. Before long, the infant was betrothed to a little girl Lady Margaret Beaufort, the orphaned child of the duke of Somerset, whose wardship William and Alice were granted by the king, a seemingly supportive royal way of approving the infant betrothal between a girl of royal blood, a descendant of John of Gaunt and the heir of his main minister. It was an ambitious step for the Suffolks, too ambitious it turned out.

William of Suffolk meets Margaret of Anjou and negotiates her marriage to the king. It was clear that Henry VI needed a wife and it had to be an advantageous one with dynastic potential. In 1442 a marriage was projected for the young king with a daughter of the count of Armagnac but Suffolk was instrumental in defeating the plan, which had been favoured by Gloucester. Suffolk had decided that the king should marry Margaret of Anjou, the daughter of the count of Anjou. This match with Margaret was suggested by Charles of Orléans, who had finally been released and returned to France in 1440. Charles also suggested that Suffolk should be the chief negotiating ambassador. William had already incurred some unpopularity and was sufficiently aware of his standing to urge objections to his appointment. These were finally overruled, but at his own request a formal indemnity was granted exonerating him from all blame for what he might do in the matter of the peace or marriage. He was quite unsure of this project.

Suffolk's mission, which included his wife Alice, landed at Harfleur on 13 March 1444. On 8 April conferences were opened at Vendôme, and a week later Suffolk and his colleagues joined Orléans at Blois. Thence they sailed down the Loire to Tours, and on 17 April were presented to Charles VII at his castle of Montils-les-Tours. It soon became clear that terms for a permanent peace could not be agreed upon, but a truce was nevertheless arranged to last until April 1446. On 24 May Margaret of Anjou, then just 14 years old, was formally betrothed to Henry with Suffolk standing as proxy. The truce was signed on 28 May and on the next day Suffolk started home. As a reward for negotiating this deal, Henry VI made William a marquess, a rare appointment in those days, making Alice a marchioness of course.

Alice went with her husband to France, as the principal lady of Margaret's escort, to accompany Margaret back to England. As well as Alice, Margaret's entourage had five other lords and their ladies, seventeen knights, sixty-five esquires and two hundred and fifteen yeomen. When Margaret, travelling through English-occupied France, fell ill in March 1445, Alice, dressed in the queen's robes, took her place in the ceremonial entry into Rouen. But there was a setback. The French extracted from Suffolk further concessions about the projected truce before allowing Margaret to depart, including the surrender of all that the English held or claimed in Maine and Anjou. Later Suffolk laid the blame for this transaction on Adam Molyneux, (or Molyns), Bishop of Chichester, who was accompanying them. William did not realise at the outset what a disaster this casual concession would be perceived by his countrymen. Margaret finally landed at Portsmouth in April, still poorly and looking ghastly with a blotchy rash. There was a high swell on the sea as they landed and William had to carry Margaret ashore himself. The wedding between Margaret and her king took place at Tichfield Abbey for convenience. It was an inauspicious start to the marriage.

Suffolk defended his conduct in the next parliament. It met in June and he received the active support of William Burley, the Speaker, for the 'ryght grete and notable werkys whiche he hathe don to the pleasir of God'.[14] Even Gloucester found it expedient to express his approval at that time. It was something of a relief to everyone that a bride had been secured and an heir might be expected at some point soon.

The king was apparently delighted with Margaret and, even though the alliance proved to be of little use politically in the longer term, Margaret turned out to be an indomitable woman who matched Alice in her imperious wiliness. She was described as beautiful, presumably the rash abated, and furthermore 'already a woman: passionate and proud and strong-willed'. But her character was not yet fully in evidence until after William's death in the following civil wars that saw Margaret leading the Lancastrian faction. Margaret had all the strength of character that her husband, eight years her senior, lacked. She undoubtedly played a role in supporting Suffolk's policies with the king.

41. Margaret of Anjou, Queen of England from the Talbot Shrewsbury Book.

The Death of Gloucester. Under Suffolk's influence, negotiations for peace were continued throughout 1446, with no clear result. The government, however, passed more and more into Suffolk's hands. The king became alienated from his uncle, who made Suffolk the object of open and repeated attack. To Suffolk and the queen, the complete overthrow of Gloucester's power appeared a necessity. On 14 December a parliament was summoned to meet at Bury St. Edmunds, a place where Suffolk was strong, and where Gloucester would be far away from his London friends. Parliament met in February 1447, intending some formal action against Gloucester. He reached Bury on 18 February and was at once arrested, to his total surprise. Either that day or the following Gloucester suffered what was reported to be a devastating stroke. He lingered in a coma until 23 February when he died. His body was placed on public display before being buried at St Albans Abbey because rumours had already sprung up that he had been murdered, perhaps poisoned. There is in fact no evidence to support this but the belief that Gloucester had been wronged lingered for years and his death was undoubtedly convenient for the government. Popular belief laid his death at Suffolk's door, though no definite charge was ever formulated. Perhaps he was partly guilty for creating such fear that the poor man became apoplectic. The nearest approach to blame is in the petition of the Commons for Suffolk's attainder in November 1451.[15] The death of Cardinal Beaufort, which took place six weeks after Gloucester's, left Suffolk without a rival.

William's unpopularity grows. Suffolk's tenure of supreme power, second only to the king, was questioned at once. Mutterings and criticism about the loss of Maine and Anjou were raised again. Suffolk formally defended his action in the council, and on 18 June a royal proclamation was issued, declaring the king's satisfaction with what he had done. But Gloucester's death had brought the troublesome Richard, 3rd duke of York, a step nearer the throne, and made him the leader of the party opposed to the court. Suffolk engineered that the command in France was now taken away from Richard, who was sent into exile in effect as lieutenant of Ireland, and the lands in France were given to Edmund Beaufort, duke of Somerset. Both appointments were ascribed to Suffolk's influence and were in hindsight a dreadful mistake on William's part. They certainly served to diminish his popularity, and made Richard his mortal enemy.

At this point, Suffolk was so confident of the king's favour that he ignored his rising unpopularity. On Gloucester's death he had obtained the earldom of Pembroke, the reversion (inheritance after death) to which had been granted to him four years previously. In 1447 he was made chamberlain, constable of Dover, and lord warden of the Cinque Ports, then later admiral of England, and in 1448 governor of Calais. The much longed for accolade of a dukedom was granted that year, making Alice a duchess and putting the family at the very pinnacle of aristocracy and the summit of his power.

Maine was formally surrendered in February 1448 and a truce concluded for two years. The fact of the surrender increased Suffolk's unpopularity. The truce was ill observed, and Suffolk found it impossible to carry out his policy of peace in full. War with France was resumed. He may well have colluded in the treacherous capture of Fougères in Brittany. Unsurprisingly the attack on Fougères was followed by open war. One after another the English strongholds in Normandy were lost and Rouen itself was taken on 29 October. This string of disasters stirred a warlike mood in England, and finally discredited Suffolk and his policy. A storm of recriminations broke over Suffolk's head, destroying his long held hopes for a lasting peace. Suffolk had been careless about the enmities that he excited.

Parliament was fomenting against him. He was charged with pride and avarice, and with having disposed of bishoprics and other preferments from corrupt motives. The parliament of 1449 insisted that two of Suffolk's principal supporters, Adam Molyneux, bishop of Chichester and Marmaduke Lumley should resign their posts. Their removal marked the beginning of the end of his influence. In the first weeks of the parliament no public action was taken against Suffolk but on 28 November, just as Ralph, lord Cromwell, who appears to have been the duke's chief adversary in the council, was entering the Star-chamber, he was hustled in Westminster Hall by William Tailboys, a thoroughly disreputable Lincolnshire squire and local supporter of Suffolk in East Anglia. Tailboys was one of the people who had done Suffolk's dirty work in the localities where Suffolk held sway; he was a violent, reckless and poor friend.

In 1450, Lord Cromwell accused Tailboys and Suffolk of intending his death. Tailboys, supported by Suffolk, denied the charge, but was committed to the Tower. There were other charges of violence against Tailboys, and in these also it was alleged that he had profited by Suffolk's patronage. Afterwards Suffolk's connection with Tailboys formed part of the charges brought against him. William's importuning and attempted engineering of Tailboys' pardon were profoundly unwise.

East Anglian problems continue. There was indeed mounting evidence of disorder and injustice in Norfolk and Suffolk, which William was ineffectual in intervening to put right. It might be pointed out that a man's energies cannot be everywhere at once. While he was maintaining his power base at court he was ignoring all kinds of vile deeds done in his name back on his estates. He was often at Ewelme, Alice's favourite place, and was probably not as often at Wingfield as he might have been. The Commons called him 'of Ewelme in the countee of Oxenford' in 1450.[16] There is some evidence he tried to intervene in East Anglia but too late. The historian Colin Richmond has described William as head of a powerful 'mafia' in the region, but this is to ignore that historians have taken their attitudes to William and the de la Poles from the Paston letters and the Pastons were antipathetic to Suffolk, believing John Mowbray, duke of Norfolk was rightful leader in the east.[17] Helen Castor reads William's position in East Anglia somewhat differently. It was his central position at the heart of the court that made William so unassailable at home.[18]

William de la Pole was no gangster, in spite of the Pastons' beliefs, but he failed to rein in his deputies, that much must be admitted. And there is ample evidence of high-handed demands, seizures of property, denials of justice and the perverting of due legal process. Tuddenham and Heydon were at the root of these problems. From the time he was appointed Recorder of Norwich in 1431 Tuddenham had become deeply unpopular with the townsmen, and was dismissed from the position before May 1437. It was alleged that during his tenure as Recorder he had informed Norwich Cathedral Priory of information concerning the City of Norwich's dispute with the priory. By the mid-1430s he was acting as legal counsel for the priory, and by 1445 was the priory's chief steward. When William was appointed to arbitrate between the City fathers and the Priory, in a dispute that had been going on for decades, the evidence seemed to point conclusively to the guilt of the priory and the right of the City. William found for the priory in what was an extraordinarily shameless piece of favouritism to Tuddenham. The resentment of the city folk towards William was justified and accounts in large part for his continuing unpopularity in East Anglia.[19]

On 9 January 1450 Adam Molyneux was murdered at Portsmouth. Before Molyneux's death he made an accusation that it was Suffolk's fault that Maine and Anjou were lost during negotiations over Margaret of Anjou. A few days later William made his will; he must have been well aware of the danger he was in. He did not itemise his possessions, he left Alice, his 'best beloved wife' as his sole executor 'for above all the earth my singular trust is most in her'. He wished to be buried at the Charterhouse in Hull established by his family in their home town, not at Wingfield and not at Ewelme. He hoped eventually Alice would wish to be buried with him.

When parliament reassembled after a Christmas break, Suffolk, in anticipation of attack, at once made an eloquent and impressive speech in his own defence. Odious and horrible language was running through the land to his 'highest charge and moost hevyest disclaundre.' He appealed to his long and faithful service, and begged that any accusations against him might be preferred openly.[20] The Commons accused Suffolk of having sold the realm to the French and treasonably fortified Wallingford Castle. There was no mention of Gloucester's death so it seems parliament accepted that he had died of natural causes.

Enemies close in. Suffolk was committed to the Tower.[21] On 7 February 1450 a long indictment was presented by the Commons. The chief charges were that Suffolk had conspired to secure the throne for his son, John de la Pole, by marrying him to his ward Margaret Beaufort; that he had advised the release of Charles of Orléans, which was true, promised to surrender Anjou and Maine, betrayed the king's counsel to the French, failed to reinforce the English armies, and estranged Brittany and Aragon. In short that he had a treasonable relationship with the French. As his grandfather had pleaded before, the decisions made ultimately by the king had been made with many other people's involvement. It was unreasonable to blame him at this point. That made little difference. A desperate Alice hastened to marry the two betrothed young children, her son John and Lady Margaret Beaufort. She thought this would afford protection for John from zealous Yorkists. It was an insurance policy that did not work.

On 12 February the articles were brought before the king's council, and Henry ordered the matter to be put aside. It was clear that both he and the queen were horrified by the turn of events and the king clearly intended a pardon for Suffolk. The Commons refused. On 9 March the Commons presented eighteen additional articles, charging Suffolk with maladministration, the promotion of unworthy persons and with the protection of William Tailboys. On the same day Suffolk was brought before the king, and received copies of the accusation. On 13 March he again appeared before the parliament. He denied the charges utterly, and said: 'Savyng the kynges high presence, they were fals and untrue'. Four days later he once more appeared and repeated his denial. At length, on the first bill, the king held Suffolk 'neither declared nor charged;' on the second bill 'not by way of judgment,' but by force of his submission, the king ordered his banishment for five years from the first of May. The decision was a compromise intended to save the duke's life and satisfy the Commons. Surely William now must have felt the weight of his grandfather's fate lying on his shoulders.

William's final visit to Suffolk. On 19 March Suffolk was set free, with a safe conduct from the king. He at once left the capital, pursued by a mob of two thousand angry Londoners who tried to intercept him as he left London through St Giles' Fields. Some of his servants were manhandled but he escaped. He did not return to Wingfield but retreated to his manor at Westhorpe, where he was less detectable and far more private than he might have been at Wingfield. The record says he went to 'Est Thorp' but there was no such place nor manor and it seems likely that he went to Westhorpe where we know the couple frequently lived. He passed six weeks on this estate, probably with only close members of his family and trusted servants. On 30 April he went to Ipswich, and in the presence of the chief men of the county took an oath on the sacrament that he was innocent of the charges brought against him. He then received a safe conduct to take him to Burgundy.

That same evening he addressed a touching letter of farewell to nine year old John. Its content became well publicised, by Alice perhaps, and rightly so. The Pastons recorded it in full.

> My dear and only well-beloved son,
>
> I beseech our Lord in Heaven, the Maker of all the World, to bless you, and to send you ever grace to love him, and to dread him, to the which, as far as a father may charge his child, I both charge you, and pray you to set all your spirits and wits to do, and to know his holy laws and commandments, by the which you shall, with his great mercy, pass all the great tempests and troubles of this wretched world.

And that also, knowingly, you do nothing for love nor dread of any earthly creature that should displease him. And there as any frailty maketh you to fall, beseech his mercy soon to call you to him again with repentance, satisfaction, and contrition of your heart, never more in will to offend him.

Secondly, next him above all earthly things, to be true liegeman in heart, in will, in thought, in deed, unto the king our aldermost high and dread sovereign lord, to whom both you and I be so much bound to; charging you as father can and may, rather to die than to be the contrary, or to know anything that were against the welfare or prosperity of his most royal person, but that as far as your body and life may stretch you live and die to defend it, and to let his highness have knowledge thereof in all the haste you can.

Thirdly, in the same way, I charge you, my dear son, always as you be bounden by the commandment of God to do, to love, to worship, your lady and mother; and also that you obey always her commandments, and to believe her counsels and advices in all your works, the which dread not but shall be best and truest to you. And if any other body would steer you to the contrary, to flee the counsel in any wise, for you shall find it naught and evil.

Furthermore, as far as father may and can, I charge you in any wise to flee the company and counsel of proud men, of covetous men, and of flattering men, the more especially and mightily to withstand them, and not to draw nor to meddle with them, with all your might and power; and to draw to you and to your company good and virtuous men, and such as be of good conversation, and of truth, and by them shall you never be deceived nor repent you of.

Moreover, never follow your own wit in nowise, but in all your works, of such folks as I write of above, ask your advice and counsel, and doing thus, with the mercy of God, you shall do right well, and live in right much worship, and great heart's rest and ease.

And I will be to you as good lord and father as my heart can think.

And last of all, as heartily and as lovingly as ever father blessed his child in earth, I give you the blessing of Our Lord and of me, which of his infinite mercy increase you in all virtue and good living; and that your blood may by his grace from kindred to kindred multiply in this earth to his service, in such wise as after the departing from this wretched world here, you and they may glorify him eternally amongst his angels in heaven.

Written of mine hand,
The day of my departing from this land.
Your true and loving father [22]

The letter was heartfelt and earnest. William must have feared his exile might end as badly as his grandfather's.

The next morning 30 April, William set sail from Ipswich with two ships and a pinnace, that is a small boat carried aboard merchant and war vessels to serve as a tender, usually rowed but could be rigged with a sail for use in favourable winds. When he was off Dover, he sent the pinnace towards Calais to learn how he would be received but the small boat was intercepted by a ship called Nicholas of the Tower, which was lying in wait. One report says that the large vessel was captained by Robert Wennington, a ship-owner from Dartmouth but this seems unlikely given that Wennington had a royal commission to patrol and protect the seas. He was known to be an ally of John Fastolf and had connections with the Pastons in East Anglia but the connections do not add up to a likelihood of his ignoring the king's safe conduct. The Captain of the ship sent some of his men in a small boat to meet Suffolk. The men said to Suffolk that he must come with them to speak with their master. Suffolk agreed, got into the small boat with two or three of his men and went to the Nicholas. The rest of the story was described in a letter from William Lomner to John Paston.

The master bade the duke come on board.

The master badde hym, 'Welcom, Traitor,' as men sey". "and thanne his herte faylyd hym, for he thowghte he was desseyvyd, and yn the syght of all his men he was drawyn ought of the grete shippe yn to the bote; and there was an exe, and a stoke, and oon of the lewdeste of the shippe badde hym ley down his hedde, and he should be fair ferd wyth, and dye on a swerd; and toke a rusty swerd, and smotte off his hedde withyn halfe a doseyn strokes".[23]

Some accounts reported that Suffolk was given a sort of mock trial, and that he spent his last hours writing to the king. Most agree that he was captured on the Thursday and died two days later on 2nd May 1450. Another report commented that the man who executed him was a Sussex man called Richard

Lenard, who subsequently in 1453 was accused of the execution although possibly never convicted.

William's body was taken to shore and thrown on the beach near Dover. Some say his head was stuck on a pole and his body abandoned. News of the murder reached London very quickly by way of a handful of William's men who were deposited on the beach alive and quickly informed the Sheriff of Kent. By Henry's orders, the body was removed to Wingfield for burial, presumably Alice's wish. It was also said that Queen Margaret grieved openly, weeping and unable to eat for three days, or was that part of the rumour mill suggesting an extramarital attachment? Margaret had indeed lost a major friend of her hopelessly weak spouse; she had cause for upset and was probably deeply attached to this man who had been her champion ever since she arrived in England. After William's death, her intransigent determination in her husband's cause led eventually to civil war.

The identity of the culprits who ordered Suffolk's murder remains a mystery. The historian Roger Virgoe judged that his murder was part of a wider plot to aid Richard, duke of York, in his bid for supremacy.[24] Probably the crime was instigated by some of Richard's supporters. It is sometimes said that Suffolk was attainted after his death, that is, he had his titles and property confiscated, but the petition of the Commons to this effect, in November 1451, was refused by the king and Alice and her son held on to their titles.[25]

The dramatic story of William's murder has caught the imagination of several artists, notably James William Edmund Doyle, a Victorian historian, antiquary and illustrator who sketched the scene for his 1864 Chronicle of England B.C. 55–A.D. 1485. An earlier eighteenth century copper plate engraving catches the scene of his beheading over the gunwale.

42. Murder of the duke of Suffolk, by James William Edmund Doyle, 1864.

Perhaps we should let William have the last word here. Shakespeare knew how to give dramatic effect to an underserved death at the hands of worthless people. As he is led to his death, Suffolk says:

Great men oft die by vile bezonians.[26]
A Roman sworder and banditto slave
Murdered sweet Tully; Brutus' bastard hand
Stabbed Julius Caesar; savage islanders
Pompey the Great; and Suffolk dies by pirates.

Henry VI, Part II. William Shakespeare

Suffolk's murder was regarded by contemporaries as the worthy end of a traitor. Public indignation expressed itself in a host of unkind and inaccurate satirical verses. Suffolk himself foresaw and endeavoured to forestall the dangers before he embarked on his embassy in February 1444. His conduct at that time was open and straightforward throughout although sometimes inept. He was not blind to the advantages and dangers of becoming close to the king and exercising power on behalf of the monarch. Like his grandfather he believed strongly that service to the Crown was morally the right thing to do. His main difficulty was that service to Henry VI meant stepping in to make decisions that the king himself was unable to make for himself through his deficient intellect and personality. For a while William held the reins of power for the general good but he paid a dreadful price for it.

It is hard to excuse William's behaviour in his heartland of East Anglia. But anyone who has served in public office will know that one person has only so much energy to go round and cannot be everywhere at once. The important personage to whom an official is accountable will always take precedence of time and effort over geographically more remote concerns. It is necessary to delegate wisely and to be sure that the underlings who exercise that power have wisdom and good character and are capable of exercising sound judgment. On that score William failed. William de la Pole neglected to control the thuggish men who ruled East Anglia in his name with little heed to justice or fairness. And Alice must take her share of the blame. She was a strong-minded woman who could have influenced William for the better; it seems she did not.

Alice is thought to have honoured William's desire to be buried in Charterhouse at Hull.[27] It must have been a profoundly sad procession from Wingfield to Hull to his final resting place. Alice lived on for twenty-five more years, enduring turmoil, accusations of treachery and threats all around her while trying to secure her son John's future.

Notes

1 Alice's story is taken from many sources but especially the work of Rowena Archer, in her piece no 54434 in the *Oxford Dictionary of National Biography* 2004, revised 2011, Oxford University Press, printed 2018, and also Archer, R. E., 2015, Alice Chaucer, Duchess of Suffolk and her East Anglian Estates. Chapter 9 in Bloore, P. and Martin E. (eds), *Wingfield College and its Patrons*. Boydell Press, Woodbridge, pp. 187-206.

2 McFarlane, K. B., 1945, *Henry V, Bishop Beaufort and the Red Hat 1417-1421*, p. 337.

3 Richmond, C., 2005, East Anglian Politics and Society in the Fifteenth Century: Reflections, 1956–2003, pp. 183–208 in Harper-Bill, C. (ed), *Medieval East Anglia*, Boydell, Woodbridge.

4 Castor, H., 2004, Tuddenham, Sir Thomas (1401–1462). *Oxford Dictionary of National Biography* (online ed.). Oxford University Press. doi:10.1093/ref:odnb/50241.

5 Smith, A., 2004, Heydon, John (d.1479). *Oxford Dictionary of National Biography* (online ed.). Oxford University Press. doi:10.1093/ref:odnb/52787.

6 Virgoe, R., 1997, Three Suffolk Parliamentary elections of the mid 15th century, Chapter 3 in *East Anglian Society and the Political Community of Late Medieval England*, pp. 53-60. *Selected Papers of Roger Virgoe,* Barron, Caroline, Rawcliffe, Carole and Rosenthal, J. (eds), 1997, Centre for East Anglian Studies. Copy in Norfolk Record Office.

7 The story of James Andrew's murder is described in Virgoe, R., The Murder of James Andrew: Suffolk Faction in the 1440s, Chapter 7 in *East Anglian Society and the political Community of Late Medieval England. Selected Papers of Roger Virgoe.* Barron, Caroline, Rawcliffe, Carole and Rosenthal, J. (eds), 1997, Centre for East Anglian Studies, pp. 109-115 Copy in Norfolk Record Office.

8 Ibid. 3.

9 The Kerdeston Hawking Book. British Library Add MS 82949 c 1430–1445.

10 William, and later Alice, supported Katherine de la Pole abbess of Barking. Alice late the wife of William de la Pole, Duke of Suffolk to Thomas Tyrell, knight, and others: Grant indented, of an annuity of 10l. for the life of Katharine de la Poole, the duke's sister, Abbess of Barking, charged on the manor of Langham. Essex. Records of the Exchequer: King's Remembrancer: Ancient Deeds, Series E 29 Henry VI TNA E 210/5183.

11 The life story of Charles duke of Orléans is well described in Arn, M-J., 2019, *Oxford Dictionary of National Biography* online at https://doi.org/10.1093/ref:odnb/92434. Also see Arn, M-J. and Taylor J. at Oxford Bibliographies Charles d'Orléans https://www.oxfordbibliographies.com/view/document/obo-9780195396584/obo-9780195396584-0194.xml 31 March 2016; also Mcleod, E., 1969, *Charles of Orléans: Prince and Poet*, Chatto & Windus, London, updated Viking Press 1971; Arn, M-J., 2008, *The Poet's Notebook: The Personal Manuscript of Charles d' Orléans Paris*, Bibliothèque nationale de France (BnF) MS fr. 25458, Turnhout, Brepols.

12 Stevenson, R. L., 1882, *Familiar Studies of Men and Books*, Chatto and Windus, online 1896 edition at Project Gutenberg free books, http://www.gutenberg.org/files/425/425-h/425-h.htm p 236.

13 Scarfe, N., 1986, Wingfield, Fressingfield, the Hundred Years War and the funding of Medieval Church Building, Chapter 12 in *Suffolk in the Middle Ages*, Boydell, Woodbridge, pp. 156-162.

14 Parliamentary Rolls 1450 v. 73–4.

15 Parliamentary Rolls 1450 v. 226.

16 Parliamentary Rolls 1450 v.177.

17 Richmond, 2005.

18 Castor, H., 2000, *The King, the Crown and the Duchy of Lancaster: Public Authority and Private Power 1399 -1461*, Oxford University Press, p. 91.

19 Litigation between the City of Norwich and Priors 1441. Drafts of letters, petition and bonds relating to the disputes with Bishop William and Prior John of Norwich are in a series of documents held in Norfolk Record Office. City of Norwich Records NRO, NCR 9c/13. There are other easier to read accounts in Smith, A. 2004. Heydon, John (d.1479). *Oxford Dictionary of National Biography* (online ed.). Oxford University Press. doi:10.1093/ref:odnb/52787 and in Castor, Helen 2004. Paston, John (I) (1421–1466). *Oxford Dictionary of National Biography* (online ed.). Oxford University Press. doi:10.1093/ref:odnb/21511.

20 The subsequent story of William's downfall is documented in the parliamentary roles blow by blow, beginning at Parliamentary Rolls v. 176.
21 Parliamentary Rolls 1450 v. 176–177
22 The Paston Letters 1422-1509 Gairdner J. (ed), 1904, Volume I, 121–2
23 The Paston Letter 1422-1509 Gairdner J. (ed), 1904, Volume II letter from William Lomner to John Paston Letter 120, 5 May 1450, online at http://www.gutenberg.org/files/40989/40989-h/40989-h.htm#note146_1.
24 Virgoe, R., 1965, The Death of William de la Pole, Duke of Suffolk, *Bulletin of the John Rylands Library, Vol 47*, 489-502. Online at https://www.escholar.manchester.ac.uk/uk-ac-man-scw:1m2071 [accessed 21 October 2019].
25 Parliamentary Rolls 1450 v. 226.
26 Bezonian means a beggar, a worthless person, from Italian bisognoso, a pauper or needy person; Tully was Marcus Tullius Cicero, great writer, orator and statesman of late-republican Rome, murdered by a Roman soldier on the orders of Mark Anthony. Note by John Derbyshire, 2008 https://www.johndebyshire.com/Opinions/Diaries/2008-06.html.
27 The Charterhouse in Hull claimed to have William de la Pole buried there. Tickell, J., 1796, *The History of the Town and County of Kingston Upon Hull*, Thomas Lee and Co, Hull.

43. Sketch of Wingfield Castle from south west.

Surviving William

Alice, duchess of Suffolk and her son John de la Pole, 2nd duke of Suffolk.

The golden age of the de la Poles ended with William's death. The marriage that his widow Alice negotiated for her son John to Elizabeth Plantagenet brought John and Elizabeth's sons perilously close to threatening the Crown itself. Within a generation the de la Poles had been eliminated as a force to be reckoned with. While Alice's nifty transfer of allegiance from the house of Lancaster to the house of York served her and John well early in his lifetime, when the house of York fell at the battle of Bosworth, John's heirs had neither the brains nor the political skill to ensure the family's survival. John's sons set out willingly if unwittingly on the road to self-destruction. They spent their lives as potential 'white rose' Yorkist heirs to the throne of England and died as traitors. Diarmaid MacCulloch summed up the later fortunes of the de la Poles. 'Up to the first duke's time his family might be said to have not enough genealogy. Henceforth, their problem was to have too much...'.[1]

Alice lived on for twenty-five years until 1475 and proved to be even more formidable as widow than wife.[2] After William's death, Alice needed all her wits about her to get through the following months. Less than a week after his murder, she moved to secure the safekeeping of all the de la Pole lands, to ensure nine year old John's inheritance during his minority. Alice had already engaged in dozens of suits all over the country to chase claims, unpaid rents, missing goods, property and other rights.[3] Historian Rowena Archer has made a detailed study of Alice's properties.[4] Alice held one hundred and thirty manors across twenty-two shires, one hundred and forty-four parcels of land, some of them several thousand acres, two London residences and five castles (Wingfield, Eye, Claxton in Norfolk, Ewelme and Donnington, Berkshire). Her properties in Norfolk, Suffolk and Essex brought in an annual income of at least thirteen hundred pounds in 1453-1454.[5] All these properties would have been richly furnished in a manner that suited her status. In addition she had jewellery previously estimated to be worth 3000 marks (two thousand pounds). Surviving accounts suggest that her income was at least fifteen hundred pounds per annum and probably more like double that.

When the duke of Norfolk moved in on her estates at Stockton she swiftly got him out using a posse of her retainers. Throughout the summer and autumn of 1450, and over the next two years, poachers repeatedly raided Wingfield deer park; the castle was in a state of near siege against an angry local population who resented her deeply. She was dependent on the support of Tuddenham, Heydon, Edward Grimston, John Ulverston and Philip Wentworth, all named in petitions in the Commons against Alice, the very people who had got her into this uncomfortable mess. At the same time Alice was determined to see the completion of the magnificent new church tower and porch at Eye as a tribute to her husband, a memorial that remains one of the glories of the perpendicular age.

Medieval noblewomen were trained from an early age to manage their families' property and households. Their task was to arrange the marriages and careers of their children, create, sustain, and exploit the local and national relationships that were an essential element in politics at the time. They were also often responsible for the transmission and distribution of property from one generation to another, since most wives outlived their husbands.[6] Alice swiftly used all her skill to show she was in charge. Cleverly, she seems to have sustained the all-important support of the king throughout these early years of widowhood.

Besides the duke of Norfolk there were other nobles jostling for the vacancy as East Anglia's premier locus of power, Thomas, lord Scales, and Miles Stapleton. It seems that Scales was a close friend initially whom Alice trusted with the administration of her lands. Three or four years later she realised that he was as avaricious as she was and retrieved her property from his control.

There is little evidence of Alice building at Wingfield Castle and she seems to have favoured Ewelme as her main home, although clearly she continued to build at the College and other religious buildings in Suffolk. She certainly continued to spend part of the year at Wingfield Castle until 1466, when she transferred to Ewelme a long inventory of tapestries and furniture, it is thought because she intended to base herself at Ewelme for the future.[7] The fact that she moved her precious gold and silver chapel items suggests a wish to move permanently. There is evidence that she also lived in Eye and at the manor in Westhorpe when she was in East Anglia.

The Great Slump. Between 1440 and 1480 the county of Suffolk, like the rest of England, was enduring the Great Slump, an economic recession that began in the 1430s in the north of the country.[8] The downturn took place against a wider trading crisis in northern Europe driven by shortages of silver, essential for the money supply, and a breakdown in trade. Multiple harvest failures in the 1430s and disease amongst livestock also drove up the price of food and damaged the wider economy.

44. Scything hay 15th century.

Cloth exports fell by thirty five per cent nationwide in just four years at the end of the 1440s, up to ninety per cent in some parts of the south-west. Prices of other trade goods fell dramatically as well. Declining revenues from directly managed manors led landowning families like the de la Poles to reduce their risk by leasing out their manorial assets. This stabilised their rental income but left the lessees exposed to the vicissitudes of agrarian income. This only worked for so long and gradually income from rent declined severely and it became difficult to find tenants.[9] The general consensus seems to be that landowners and the wealthier sections of society were seriously affected by the downturn even though the value of land held up quite well. Suffolk was far more urbanised than most counties, providing some protection from an agricultural slump.

Manorial tenants and peasants became more 'uppity' and demanding in the late fifteenth century. They wanted and enjoyed more leisure. They increasingly resisted the formerly obligatory labour service and liability for holding office on the manor as a constable or reeve. Landlords were forced into a better understanding of the hardship of their workers. The power of the manorial courts, which had regulated daily life on the manor, simply withered away as the courts became less respected; their coercive powers of land seizure had less force. Farmers became increasingly independent of their manorial lords and gradually renegotiated their subservience.[10] It was not an easy time to be a grand landowner and family members were often quite short of ready cash, having few other sources of income but their land. Alice of course was far richer than most but her son John was not so fortunately set up and he and his children often borrowed and importuned others to fund their political ambitions. The economy finally recovered at the tail end of the century.

Jack Cade's rebellion. Shortly after William's murder, unrest exploded in Kent. 'Jack Cade's rebellion' began quite suddenly. It was the largest popular uprising to take place in England during the fifteenth century.[11] The local population apparently thought they might be blamed for William's murder off the Kentish coast and feared reprisals by the king. Economic recession was at the heart of the matter but the general populace also believed that William's unjust administration was at the root of their problems. William's murder provided the rebels with the spur to reckless violence. Cade, originally from Ireland, organised a rebellion among local small property holders angered by high taxes and prices. He also identified himself with the king's rival, the duke of York.

Cade and his followers defeated an army sent to Kent to suppress them and headed for London. Once inside the city gates, Cade and his men initiated a series of tribunals dedicated to seeking out and convicting those accused of corruption. At the Guildhall, the Lord Treasurer, James Fiennes, Lord Saye and Sele was brought before a sham trial. Found guilty of treason he was summarily beheaded in Cheapside alongside his son-in-law William Crowmer. The heads of the two men were put on pikes and unceremoniously paraded through the streets of London while their bearers pushed them together so that they appeared to kiss. Their heads were then affixed to London Bridge. The citizens of London turned on the rebels and forced them out of the city in a bloody battle on London Bridge. Cade's followers dispersed on being offered a pardon. Cade himself was mortally wounded shortly after. The rebellion contributed to the breakdown of royal authority that led to the thirty year civil unrest we call the Wars of the Roses.

Alice was one of the rebels' targets. When the rebels entered London in July 1450, they forced members of a commission of 'oyer and terminer' (a loose translation of the French 'to hear and determine', in effect a court of assize) to indict a number of supposed traitors, Alice among them. It is unknown what charges were pressed against Alice, but it seems possible that they were connected with the marriage of her son, John, to Margaret Beaufort, daughter of the deceased John Beaufort, duke of Somerset. One of the charges against Suffolk had been that he was planning to proclaim Margaret as the childless king's heir and make his own son king through this marriage.

During Cade's rebellion, Alice was probably safe at one of her own manors, or possibly with the queen, to whom she was always close. But the news that the rebels had murdered at least five men must have shaken her. Even after the crisis of the rebellion passed, she found herself the target of popular hatred. At the parliament that convened in November 1450, the Commons brought a petition that certain persons be banned from coming into the king's presence. Edmund Beaufort, duke of Somerset, headed the list; Alice was second. An attempt was also made to attaint William retrospectively as a traitor, which would have prevented his son from inheriting his title and estates. Fortunately the king resisted both petitions. It may have helped that, in October 1450, Alice lent the Crown three thousand, five hundred marks toward the war effort in France. Yet Alice's problems were still not over, for sometime before March 1451, Alice was tried for treason before the assembled Lords, perhaps on the indictment that had been brought in July. Little is known of Alice's trial or other state trials that were held at this time, probably, because the defendants, including Alice, were acquitted. She was lucky.

Alice's life eventually returned to a semblance of normality, a round of visiting her various estates, although how often she visited Wingfield is difficult to say. Her son John eventually settled at Wingfield Castle as his main home and one might guess that it was a place he had been happy as a child, away from the London/Berkshire/Thames Valley axis of royal politics. Alice may also have decided that he needed to be visible on the extensive East Anglian estates to which she and William had paid insufficient attention. Alice was probably doing some quiet thinking about her allegiances and where to put her loyalties. More serious political thinking went on in Alice's head than in many other de la Pole skulls.

The King's Insanity. In 1453, Alice was among the great ladies summoned to attend the churching of Margaret of Anjou, who had at last borne Henry VI a son. Henry was absent because he was incapable of participating. He had fallen into a catatonic psychotic state in August 1453, which was to last eighteen months, missing the birth of his heir because of it. Stuporose, mute, barely eating and needing total care and supervision, it is likely that he inherited a genetic predisposition to psychosis from his French grandfather Charles VI, who was frankly raving mad for a good part of his life. Henry probably had some symptoms of chronic mental disorder for many years before the descent into overt mental illness. His socially inept personality, religiosity, eccentric dress, odd enthusiasms and obsessional rituals all suggest that he was profoundly troubled from his mid teens. He recovered after a fashion from the 1453 crisis but was never really able to muster for long the necessary leadership skills that would have saved him from the inevitable loss of the Crown.

The War of the Roses begins; Alice and John change sides. Readers unfamiliar with the factional struggles of the Plantagenet family that blighted England for thirty years may be relieved to know that this author is not going to go into any further detail here. There are a myriad readable modern accounts. A good place to start to appreciate the Wars of the Roses is through the letters of the beleaguered Paston family in 'Blood and Roses' by Helen Castor. A more general narrative account is Dan Jones' 'The Hollow Crown: The Wars of the Roses and the Rise of the Tudors'.[12] The account here is confined to what is essential for understanding Wingfield Castle and its owners.

There is certainly no doubt that violence and lawlessness flourished during the Wars of the Roses and the nobility could be as morally reprehensible as those lower down the social scale. Soldiers brutalised in France behaved with a ferocity that their commanding officers were powerless to control. Some magnates were little better than sadistic ruffians. The men employed by Alice did not fall far short of that description. Thousands of men died horribly in the handful of battles, or were mercilessly butchered while trying to escape. Yet the wars were by no means continuous, nor did England experience the economic devastation like that suffered later in the seventeenth century civil war. Agriculture, trade, manufacturing and commerce flourished in the final years of the fifteenth century at the end of the recession, inspirational building in 'perpendicular' style continued at a pace.

There were, at most, thirteen weeks of active fighting in the thirty-two years of the Wars of the Roses. The problems of keeping an army fed and watered meant that individual campaigns lasted for a matter of hours or days, not months. Some of the battles were very short affairs, and none lasted longer than a day. Most took place in open countryside and hardly affected life in the towns and villages. Nor did the castles, halls and manors of the aristocracy suffer greatly. Only the great defensive castles of the north became targets for military action.[13] Nevertheless, John Edward, the Wingfield Castle bailiff and his successors would have been busy keeping the towers and battlements in good repair in case of attack from marauding bands of discharged soldiers.

The majority of people regarded the battles as a dispute between noble factions and aimed to avoid committing themselves wholeheartedly to either party unless obligated to fight by kinship or loyalty to a lord taking sides in the dispute. The large towns of Norwich and Ipswich showed a marked disinclination to take sides, more concerned with maintaining their wool trade and paying taxes when required, whichever side was governing at the time.[14] But if Wingfield men did join the fighting the likelihood is that they were fighting on the Lancastrian side at first, then later the Yorkists. For the bailiffs and the families who worked the land on de la Pole manors, the social changes in the fifteenth century, engendered by changes in the economy, were probably more important than the wars.

Plague remained endemic, a recurrent unavoidable hazard. Villein labour service had largely disappeared, to be replaced by copyhold tenure, that is tenure by copy of the record of the manorial court. There was a well-developed land market among peasants, some of whom managed to rise above their neighbours and began to constitute a class called yeomen. Wingfield Castle and the other estates were subtly changing as expectations of fair dealing were demanded by tenants who felt they had more of a stake than previous generations.

Alice's last supporting role for the house of Lancaster. In 1455, as constable of the prestigious Wallingford Castle, an office Alice held jointly with her son, she was entrusted with a state prisoner, the troublesome Henry Holland, duke of Exeter, son-in-law of Richard, duke of York, who had been taken into custody following the Yorkist victory at St. Albans in 1455. In this relatively modest battle, Richard duke of York, and his allies the Nevilles, defeated the royal army led by Edmund Beaufort, duke of Somerset and then captured the king. This was the first battle of the ensuing thirty years conflict. This may have been the last time that Alice overtly supported a Lancastrian issue on behalf of the incompetent king. It is perhaps worth pointing out here that the Lancastrian regime did not use their red rose as a national symbol in the way the Yorkists used their white rose. The Yorkists' white rose was a successful attempt at 'branding' a cause. The red rose was probably not used at all until the 1480s. Only with the later creation of the joint Tudor rose, another potent brand, were the Lancastrians with hindsight allied in the public mind to the red rose.[15]

After St Albans, parliament decided to appoint Richard duke of York as lord Protector and an uneasy truce ensued for a while. After Richard was killed in 1460, his son Edward of York deposed Henry and became king Edward IV in 1461, with the help of the earl of Warwick. Henry was briefly restored for six months from 1470 to 1471 but was finally ousted and murdered in the Tower of London in May 1471. His redoubtable queen, Margaret of Anjou, never gave up the fight for her own son Edward to be recognised as king and carried on the fight, drumming up support where she could.

John de la Pole's second marriage. In early 1453, the childhood marriage of John de la Pole and Margaret Beaufort was dissolved without any valid rationale, apparently at the whim of king Henry, who gave Margaret's wardship to his own half-brothers, Jasper and Edmund Tudor. Alice must have felt piqued by this, a great deal of effort having gone into acquiring the correct papal dispensation to allow the children's cousin marriage in the first place. Ironically it was Margaret Beaufort's next marriage, to Edmund Tudor, which would have momentous consequences, for in 1485 her son by Edmund, born when she was about thirteen and a half, eventually became Henry VII.

Young John therefore needed another wife and this time Alice's perspicacity on the likely drift of politics decided her to move her allegiances from the house of Lancaster to the house of York. All around her the nobility were dividing in support of one of these houses, coalescing around the two branches of the Plantagenet family descended from children of Edward III. Both these branches had claims to the throne. Alice was fortunate in holding her son's wardship and gift of marriage, this in an age when the wardships of wealthy young heirs were sought-after commodities. In 1458, she and the duke of York entered into an agreement for John de la Pole, age 16, to marry Elizabeth Plantagenet, 14, the second of York's four daughters. Whatever Alice's motives, this decision would prove to be well-judged. Three years later, York's son, Edward IV, was sitting on the throne of England. John de la Pole thus became brother-in-law to the king. Alice had done all she could to promote young John's interests and this was the crowning success. John and Elizabeth's children would be in line for the throne itself.

45. The arms of John de la Pole, 2nd duke of Suffolk (1442–1491/2), KG in a 15th century stained glass window at the Church of St Mary the Virgin, Iffley, Oxfordshire. John donated the gothic windows to the church after becoming owner of nearby Donington manor.

Alice's Property Grab. Alice did not relax into midlife retirement. Throughout the 1450s and 1460s she proved adept at looking after her own and her son's interests, even where there was minimal right on her side. She was notoriously predatory and grabbed manors she hankered after. Singly or with her son, she seized the manors of Cotton, Dedham, Hellesdon and Drayton from the Paston family, despite having a highly dubious claim. Historian Colin Richmond has suggested that she was partly motivated by devotion to the memory of her husband, who had coveted the manors himself. Cotton, William's birthplace, had been sold to pay his ransom to the French. Unsurprisingly the Pastons did not see the Suffolks' actions as anything but unjustifiable 'carpet-bagging'. Margaret Paston had good reason to advise her son not to approach the duchess without his counselors, on the ground that the duchess was 'subtle and has subtle counsel with her.'

Alice then engaged in unscrupulous methods to avoid the Pastons re-acquiring Cotton, Drayton and Hellesdon. She left Cotton manor decaying rather than let it go and eventually stripped the tiles off the roof to reuse at her manor of Westhorpe. Her illegal claims to the Norfolk manors, so conveniently near the manor of Costessey, were not pursued through the courts but through the violent interventions of her bailiffs and retainers and parties of men employed for the purpose. One wit has recently referred to wealthy smash and grab theft by Alice and her like as 'fur-collar crime'.[16] It could not have been a very comfortable life for the tenants and labourers on manorial land subject to these knightly predations. John Cossey, the bailiff at Monks Hall Manor at Syleham, owned by the monks of Thetford Priory, must have kept a watchful eye for any incursions.[17] Monks Hall had a watchtower for good reasons. Its land was surrounded by de la Pole manors and its own outlying pieces of manor land in Denham, Chickering and Hoxne were especially vulnerable.

We know who some of Alice's bully boys were as they are named in various accounts, Paston letters and petitions, referred to by Margaret Paston as Alice's 'doggeboltes'. James Blondell was a Norman farmer at Cotton who acted for Alice. John Andrew and his servants were also employed by Alice at Cotton. William Harleston, her surveyor at Westhorpe, invaded and ransacked Hellesdon in the company of John Andrew and her bailiff from Costessey. John Dogett, the bailiff of Drayton, was involved in enforcing her demands. Her bailiff at Eye castle manor, John Bottisford, stole Paston goods from Drayton and took away Paston's men by force to be prisoners at Eye castle. The Pastons appealed to the new king, Edward IV, but he was far too concerned elsewhere to do anything to upset his brother-in-law, the young 2nd duke of Suffolk, or his mother.[18]

The birth of a new generation. Alice's son John and his new wife Elizabeth needed their own establishment when their first son, also John, was born at Ewelme some time between 1462 and 1464. Alice was determined to supervise Elizabeth's lying-in where she felt it was safest. A unique set of inventories of the palace at Ewelme, preserved in the Bodleian Library, list a sumptuous collection of materials and a cradle clearly designed for the new duke. [19] The items were delivered by a servant, Alison Croxford, to Ewelme and also included a pane and 'headshete' of blue velvet cloth of gold for a bed, along with a matching set for the child's cradle in the nursery. Both were trimmed with miniver (white fur) and powdered ermine fur (powdering was the process of cutting a slit in the skin, inserted a tail through it, and sewing it in place). Mistress Croxford also delivered several pillows, a swaddling sheet of Rheims cloth and sheets of lawn cloth for both a bed and couch. But after the birth, the young couple and their new baby returned to Wingfield and made their home there. We have no idea if Wingfield was their choice or Alice's but Alice's withdrawal to Ewelme left Wingfield and the East Anglian estates to be enjoyed by John and Elizabeth and in due course their eleven children.

Alice also lived occasionally in Eye and at the manor in Westhorpe when she was in East Anglia. The Norman motte and bailey castle at Eye was largely destroyed in the fourteenth century although parts of the castle continued to be maintained as a prison, where Alice imprisoned the unfortunate Paston retainers. Despite the ruined nature of the castle, the local estates previously subject to the castle-guard system continued for many years to return their dues, now converted into monetary rents, to the owners of Eye castle. A windmill was built on top of the motte between 1561-2, which can be seen in early nineteenth century prints, before the Victorians reassembled the keep walls we see today. The 'honour of Eye' comprised dozens of manors and there would probably have been another manor house for Alice at Eye, although it is so near Wingfield one has to wonder why it was necessary. Meanwhile her estates ticked over but were not very profitable. In 1453, the bailiff of Wingfield, John Edward paid £11 3s to the treasurer of Alice's household, while the manors of Old Wingfield and Fressingfield were in the hands of a farmer who owed £36 19s 4d, more than half in arrears. The treasurer also paid out the annuity of twenty marks from Alice's coffers to the Abbess of Bruisyard for maintaining Katherine de la Pole.[20]

Like her husband and grandfather, Alice was a collector of books and a poetry lover.[21] She may have commissioned the poet John Lydgate's The Virtues of the Mass. Lydgate was a nationally revered poet who lived in Bury St Edmunds. Alice's 1466 inventory lists a number of books: fourteen were religious texts of the sort that would be used in her chapel, but seven others, in

English, French and Latin, were clearly for Alice's own use. The Latin book, for 'the moral instruction of a prince,' was likely acquired for John's education. The others included Christine de Pizan's Livre de la Cité Des Dames, and the Ditz de Philisophius. On one occasion Alice wrote from London, worried that her books might be damaged on the ground in the closet where she had left them and asked her servant William Bylton to move them to a safer location. Presumably, the floors in Wingfield could be damp.

Alice's later life. The upheavals of the second round of battles in the 'wars' from 1469 to 1471 seem not to have affected Alice directly but in 1472 she acted as 'host' jailor at the castle of Wallingford to the now deposed Queen Margaret of Anjou, taken prisoner by the victorious Yorkist forces after the battle of Tewkesbury. It is quite possible that just as Charles of Orléans accompanied William and the family as they progressed round their manors so Margaret also came to Wingfield with Alice.[22] Margaret's only son, seventeen year old Edward, had been killed at Tewkesbury. Alice had been Margaret's friend since before her marriage to Henry VI. They were both extraordinary women surviving in a man's world on their wits and their indomitable spirits. Alice would probably have been sympathetic to Margaret's plight. Margaret was eventually rescued by being ransomed by her cousin, King Louis XI of France. She went to live in France as a poor relation of the French king, and died there at the age of 52.

The death of Alice de la Pole, 1475. Alice probably died at Ewelme, aged about 71. We know she was thought to be ailing in August 1469 when Margaret Paston wrote to her husband that 'The duchess of Suffolk is at Ewelme, in Oxfordshire, and it is thought by your friends here that it is do that she might be far and out of the way, and the rather fine excuse because of age or sickness'.[23] Alice's will does not survive, but she made a grant to John and Elizabeth in 1471, four years before her death, of her precious fine things, the way older people do when they want to ensure their treasured objects go to the right home.

> To my dere and welbeloved sone John duke of Suffolk and to my Lady Elizabeth his wife suster to our soveraigne lord Kyng Edward the fourthe alle my stuffe of plate of sylver of gilte and of golde. And all my beddys of clothe of gold and of silke and of arras and of tapiserye werke. And all my tapices of arras and of tapiserye. Excepte the plate and the olde beddes and olde tapices of silke and of tapiserye that dayly serven me. Which also after my decesse I yeve to my seide sone and my seide lady his wife. To have and to holde to my seide dere and wellbeloved

> sone and to my seide lady his wife and to their chyldyr of their bodyes comyng alle the seide plate beddys and tapices with goddess blessing and myn for ever.[24]

Alice's unusual tomb at the church of St. Mary the Virgin at Ewelme was certainly made to her own specifications before death. The tomb is besieged by small angels, intricately carved, in a feminine style. It contains an upper effigy of Alice, who wears the coronet of a duchess with the Order of the Garter wrapped around her left arm. The effigy was originally painted and would have looked life-like. Below the upper effigy is an enclosed cadaver effigy in a cage-like enclosure, showing the naked, shrivelled corpse of Alice lying in an opened shroud. You have to crouch down to get a good view of this macabre likeness. The architectural historian John Goodall notes that it is the only life-sized female cadaver sculpture in England to have survived intact.[25] While many medieval monuments have been lost to us, Alice's tomb still has the power to enthrall by its sheer artistry. But it can also shock and surprise. It is perhaps typical of Alice that she chose not to be buried with any of her husbands but to fashion a memorial to her individuality and independence. Encountering her tomb is like absorbing the essence of Alice. She was a tough

46. Tomb of Alice de la Pole, duchess of Suffolk, St Mary's Church, Ewelme.

and resilient woman who survived personal tragedy and disappointment, but had neither compassion nor kindness for her neighbours. She was not conventionally likeable but admirably fashioned for survival in the aristocratic world of the late fifteenth century.

The most enduring act of piety associated with Alice and her husband William is God's House at Ewelme, founded by the couple in 1437. God's House was an almshouse for thirteen paupers; later the couple added a school. The foundation survives today as the Ewelme Trust. The almshouse and school are still used for their original purposes. The village primary school is the longest established continuously run publically funded primary school in the country. It still occupies the building constructed in 1455 by the Suffolks.

What happened to Tuddenham and Heydon? The City of Norwich did not take long after William's death to avenge themselves on Tuddenham and Heydon. The city fathers raked up the story of Alice cavorting in Lakenham Wood and the two profoundly hated men immediately found themselves under attack by their principal opponents in East Anglia. Sir John Fastolf, a kinsman of John Paston's wife, Margaret, immediately requested a servant to provide him with a list of the wrongs that Heydon had done to him over the previous thirteen years. A special commission swiftly followed in October 1450, empowered to inquire into complaints in East Anglia. Indictments were drawn up which itemized details of Heydon's and Tuddenham's actions during the previous fifteen years. These allegations were perhaps biased. Fastolf, John Paston, and the City of Norwich were among the principal informants and it is likely that much of the shire was hostile to the pair of them. During the years 1450 to 1451 the duke of Norfolk, with John de Vere, earl of Oxford, and Fastolf had exerted efforts to remove Suffolk's former agents from positions of local power. These efforts were ultimately unsuccessful though they curbed their power for a while. By the spring of 1451 Alice had personally regained Suffolk's former dominance in East Anglia nominally for her son and she continued to support her two closest allies.

After the setbacks, Heydon was never again quite as influential in East Anglia, although he retained his offices and stewardships and was a member of various commissions from 1452 onwards. When the Lancastrian regime was overthrown in 1460 to 1461, the Pastons hoped that Heydon would be destroyed. Tuddenham was executed in 1462, for participating in a treasonous plot against Edward IV, Heydon however kept mostly out of trouble and survived. He had continued to enjoy Alice's patronage and was able to obtain a pardon from the Yorkist regime on payment of five hundred marks. For the remaining eighteen years of his life he was not prominent in public affairs, although he continued to practice law and to administer his clients' estates as well as his own.

John de la Pole, 2nd duke of Suffolk (1442-1492) and Elizabeth Plantagenet of York. John de la Pole emerges from this history as a rather weak, ineffectual man, but with an explosive temper. Certainly he inherited none of the driving passion and ambition of his parents. But during his early years as duke he must have been unusually beholden to his mother for her largesse to support his own household. I think we can assume that while his mother was alive John was held firmly under her thumb. John was among the poorest of English dukes on his accession to the title. The endowment of the earldom of Suffolk was worth only about a thousand marks (£666 13s 4d) per annum.[26] While Alice had inherited a considerable estate from her father and held substantial dowers from all three husbands, the dowers from her first two husbands went back to her husbands' families after her death. And during Alice's lifetime she retained a third of the dower from her marriage to William. John did not inherit two thirds of his father's dower or other estates until after his mother's death.

While he was allowed to keep the title of duke, John's boyhood had been blighted not only by his father's murder but repeated threats by the Commons to attaint his father as a traitor, which would have removed all his titles and inheritance. Fortunately the king resisted but the royal grants that William had accrued personally were 'resumed'. That is they became subject to a project devised by the Commons to claw back to Henry VI's own coffers hundreds of grants under the Acts of Resumption. The parliamentary resumptions of 1450 to 1456 were a direct consequence of the king's political inanity, having previously distributed largesse almost entirely among his immediate entourage, including William of course, but left his own household unable to support itself. By 1449 the Commons saw resumption as a panacea for all the nation's grievances. The idea was that the king would be able to cover the costs of his household by being supported by the resumed revenues and sensible management of his lands. John de la Pole was not the only person afflicted by these resumptions. The lists in the National Archive are lengthy and complex.[27]

John also lost the various offices that he had held, some jointly with his mother, such as the constableship of Wallingford Castle. His income has been estimated at less than two hundred and eighty pounds per annum, which was less than the minimum required for an earl, let alone a duke. This state of relative poverty was a circumstance John felt acutely. On more than one occasion, he refused to come to London to serve at some grand event because he could not afford the costs of maintaining a retinue to 'look the part'. One of the Pastons remarked in 1478, no doubt with some satisfaction, that John 'must make shift for money and that in all haste'.[28]

John de la Pole's early career. John was included in various official commissions from around 1457 but he was only 15 and his biographer Michael Hicks suggests that this may have been simply a symbolic public 'launching' to get him started.[29] John and Elizabeth's marriage had taken place at a politically turbulent time. In reality John wasn't much of a financial catch for a daughter of Richard of York, even a younger one, but the king was attempting to make a peace between York and his allies and the families of those lords who had died at St Albans. Elizabeth was by far the wealthier party to the union. On marriage, Elizabeth brought John about £1533. This was not going to make John as rich as most dukes but it was enough to keep him going. Nor was it much compared to other dowries of the period. Worse, Elizabeth's father, Richard of York, whose wages from his various offices were almost permanently in arrears, often could not keep up the instalments.[30] York had pledged payment in bonds to Alice over four years, on the proviso that his daughter did not die in the mean time.

Elizabeth's brother becomes king Edward IV. After the overthrow of Henry VI, Yorkist Edward IV, Elizabeth's brother, became king with the help of the earl of Warwick, the 'kingmaker'. One of de la Pole's first commissions under the new regime was to accompany Edward on his campaign against the Scots in winter 1462. He had returned to Norwich by early the next year.[31] He was also a trier of petitions at parliament later that year. In 1465, the king granted Suffolk an annuity of 100 marks (nearly £67 a year), although this was only during Elizabeth's lifetime.

John's infant son becomes earl of Lincoln in 1464. Two years later, in a clear mark of royal favour and one of the few royal recognitions of his status that John ever received, his eldest son John was created earl of Lincoln and henceforth was always referred to as Lincoln or the earl of Lincoln. Baby John would have been about four years old at the time. Suffolk himself regained his father's Wallingford and Chiltern Hundreds offices, with a forty pounds per annum salary for it. In 1467 he acted as administrator for his sister-in-law Anne duchess of Exeter, Elizabeth's oldest sister, also of course the king's sister, who was separated from her quarrelsome and treacherous husband.

The Yorkist Allegiance and Strife with the Pastons. Although he was politically aligned to the House of York by virtue of his marriage, John de la Pole avoided participating in the battles of the 1450s, not taking up arms until Edward IV had claimed the throne. John seems to have regarded himself from the age of eighteen as a potential force in English politics, although it must be admitted no-one else did. In the late 1450s he seems to have deliberately avoided intimating support for either faction. He finally came off the fence in early 1461 when he came out firmly for the Yorkists.

In fact de la Pole appears to have spent much of this period feuding with his neighbours the Pastons over conflicting interests in the inheritance of Sir John Fastolf, even interfering in parliamentary elections in an attempt to gain the upper hand. John inherited this feud from his mother and never wavered from her course. Most historians have judged the de la Poles to be culpable in pursuing claims that were totally bogus. The duke also made other disputed and in some cases outright illegal claims on other properties in the region over the following decade, and, in 1465, a group of his retainers destroyed the manor house of Hellesdon, also ransacking its church.

John was still pursuing his claim in 1478 at the manor court at Hellesdon. An eye witness at the public hearing, there for the sport it seems, watched John venting his spleen on the Pastons: 'His bearing there that day there never was no man that played Herod in Corpus Christi play better and more agreeable to his pageant than he did'.[32] Where his father William had conducted his property claims in absentia, John dived in personally. Suffolk escaped retribution even when the courts found against him, probably because of his royal connections. On the other hand, he was never able to use his kinship to his advantage or persuade the king to intercede in any disputes on his behalf. He was like one of those irritating relatives who has to be rescued from folly every now and again but is not considered worth rewarding with any major benefits. Suffolk did not receive major grants of any kind from Edward IV, in spite of John continuing to support him in arms when necessary. One gets the impression that Edward was not overly concerned about the wellbeing of his sister Elizabeth or her husband, perhaps because he had ten siblings to worry about and others were in even narrower straits.

John de la Pole's regional and national roles. Suffolk later played a prominent role in Commissions of the Peace in Norfolk and Suffolk, and these became a permanent position from 1464. He was also a justice of the peace in Berkshire and Oxfordshire in the late 1460s. But these were local and rather lowly positions for a duke.

Although Suffolk was receiving minimal financial benefit from Edward's regime, he still took conspicuous part in all the major state ceremonies. These included the 1465 royal wedding and various tournaments. Suffolk always remained loyal to his brother-in-law and appears to have taken no part in the Neville/Woodville feud that occupied much of the second half of the decade. Suffolk participated at the Battle of Empingham in 1470. He also helped the king crush the Neville inspired Lincolnshire rebellion the same year.

Francis, Lord Lovel becomes a ward of John and Elizabeth. Edward lost his throne and was forced into exile in 1470, leading to the short-lived restoration of Henry VI. Suffolk of course was not trusted by the new Lancastrian regime, hardly surprising given his connection to the exiled king and the fact that his mother had a history of shifting sides. However John's wife Elizabeth kept in touch with her royal brothers exiled in Flanders, then part of Burgundy, where her sister Margaret was married to Charles duke of Burgundy.

When Edward IV returned to England in March 1471, Suffolk joined him on the campaign that led to Edward's restoration. But, even though he fought for Edward at the battles of Tewkesbury and Barnet, John was not invited to join Edward's inner circle during his second reign. He did however receive some rewards, such as the wardship and income of the estates of Francis, Lord Lovel. Wardships were lucrative because the guardian had access during the minority to the income from the estates of the ward. Francis, then fifteen years old, had been passed from the earl of Warwick's guardianship to the Suffolks'. Francis was just four years older than the Suffolks' oldest son John and it is likely that young John was much influenced by the impressive Lovel, who was to become Richard III's best friend and eventually one of the wealthiest members of the nobility. It is likely that Francis Lovel spent some time at Wingfield Castle during his adolescence. The boyhood friendship between Lincoln and Lovel provides the background context for Lincoln's later behaviour.

Suffolk received a number of other offices and minor promotions. In 1472 he was appointed High Steward of Oxford University and the following year was made a Knight of the Garter. He was also the King's Lieutenant of Ireland (in later centuries the post came to be known as the Lord Lieutenant of Ireland) between March and July 1478 although he probably never took the position in person and it was a short-lived appointment.[33] None of these positions improved his financial situation much, so in the first parliament after Edward's return from exile in 1471, Suffolk refused his summons to attend parliament because he claimed he felt himself unable to sustain the status and maintain the retinue of a royal duke in London for however long the parliament lasted. Or so he said. Was he just reluctant to gather even more irksome jobs with no real additions to his income? With the exception of the Lovel estates, Suffolk's lack of favour was in stark comparison to king Edward's brothers, George duke of Clarence and Richard duke of Gloucester, and even for the king's Woodville in-laws. Suffolk's continuing poverty was reflected in the fact that, although he again took loyal part in King Edward's 1475 French campaign, possibly the only occasion he ever went abroad, he could muster only forty men at arms and three hundred archers. Alice died shortly after John's return from France and, by 15 August 1476, John st last came into possession of her dower lands, and finally, his whole estate.

The accession of Richard III and John de la Pole's son rises. Edward IV died suddenly in April 1483, leaving his young son, Edward, his heir and his brother Richard, duke of Gloucester, as Lord Protector of the new king and the country. Suffolk may have been in attendance at court at the time but he kept his head down and seems to have waited to see which way the wind was blowing. Pretty soon the young king had been declared conveniently illegitimate and Richard of Gloucester seized the throne. Suffolk was at Westminster Hall on 26 June 1483 when Gloucester claimed the throne and he carried the royal sceptre at Richard III's coronation. He was acquiescent in the usurpation. The new king was his brother-in-law of course, just as Edward IV had been.

John and Elizabeth de la Pole may have been supportive of the turn of events at first. Like many others they probably felt that another young and possibly inadequate king was far less desirable than a strong, intelligent and generally well-regarded adult. But young prince Edward and his brother, the child duke of York, were not seen in public after August that year. It has long been assumed that they were murdered although not necessarily at Richard's behest. At the time their disappearance was deeply suspicious. Two boys' skeletons of the right age were found in the Tower centuries later in 1674, but their identity has never been confirmed. Someone murdered the boys, and that someone was probably working on Richard's behalf.

Richard III was immortalised by Shakespeare as a tragic but evil hunchback, but the play was fashioned for a Tudor audience's prejudices and he gave them what they expected. There can be few readers now who do not know that Richard III's remains were found under a car park in Leicester in 2012. He did indeed have a mild scoliosis.

Richard's reputation has steadily improved in the past century. His magnificent reburial service at Leicester Cathedral was a bizarre but surprisingly emotive event. He was probably no worse than many medieval kings and introduced during his short reign several changes to improve the court system for ordinary people. His importance for this story and especially that of John de la Pole and his heirs is simply that Richard's destruction led to theirs.

Notes

1 MacCulloch, D., The Wars of the Roses, the Downfall of the de la Poles and the Dissolution of Wingfield College. Chapter 10 in Bloore, P. and Martin, E. (eds), 2015, *Wingfield College and its Patrons*, Boydell, Woodbridge, pp. 207-219.

2 Archer, R. E., 2011, Chaucer, Alice, duchess of Suffolk (c.1404–1475), *Oxford Dictionary of National Biography*, Oxford University Press, 2004; online edn, May 2011.

3 Archer, R. E., 2015, Alice Chaucer, Duchess of Suffolk (d 1475) and her East Anglian Estates, Chapter 9, pp. 187-205 in Bloore, P. and Martin, E. (eds), 2015, *Wingfield College and its Patrons*, Boydell, Woodbridge.

4 Ibid., p. 192.

5 County of Suffolk: Compotus rolls for lands of the Earls of Suffolk in: 1403, 1454. County of Norfolk: Compotus rolls rel. to: 1403-1522. County of Essex: Compotus roll of lands of the Duchess of Suffolk in: 1453-1454. Alice de la Pole, widow of William. British Library Egerton Roll 8779: 1403-1522.

6 Harris, B. J., 2002, *English Aristocratic Women, 1450-1550: Marriage and Family, Property and Careers*, Introduction, Oxford University Press.

7 Inventory of Alice's goods transferred from Wingfield to Ewelme listed in Bodleian MS DD Ewelme, EMA 47.

8 Hatcher, J., 1996, The great slump of the mid-fifteenth century, Chapter 12 in Britnell, R. and Hatcher, J. (eds), *Progress and Problems in Medieval England, Essays in Honour of Edward Miller*, Cambridge University Press pp. 237-272 online 2012 DOI: https://doi.org/10.1017/CBO9781139170956.013.

9 Bailey, M., 2015, *Medieval Suffolk*, Boydell, Woodbridge. Chapter 10 The World Turned Upside Down: Rural Society 1350-1500, pp. 242-263.

10 Dyer C., 2007, A Suffolk farmer in the fifteenth century, *Agricultural History Review Vol 55*, I, pp. 1–22, https://bahs.org.uk/AGHR/ARTICLES/55_101Dyer.pdf.

11 Useful reference sources for Jack Cade's rebellion are Kaufman, A. L., 2009, *The Historical Literature of the Jack Cade Rebellion*; Burlington, Ashgate; Harvey, I. M. W., 1991, *Jack Cade's Rebellion of 1450*, Oxford, Clarendon Press and Harvey, I. M. W., 2004, Cade, John (Jack) d 1450, rebel leader. *Oxford Dictionary of National Biography* (online). doi:10.1093/ref:odnb/4292.

12 Castor, H., 2004, *Blood and Roses*, Faber and Faber; Jones, D., 2014, *The Hollow Crown: The Wars of the Roses and the rise of the Tudors*, Faber and Faber.

13 Williamson, M., 2013, *Destruction in the Wars of the Roses*, online at http://weaponsandwarfare.com (accessed 17.11.13).

14 Haward, W. I., 1926, Economic Aspects of the Wars of the Roses in East Anglia, *English Historical Review Vol XLI/CL: XII*, pp. 170–89.

15 Sadler, J., 2014, *The Red Rose and the White: The Wars of the Roses, 1453–1487*, Routledge p. 17.

16 Hanawalt, B. A., 1975, Fur-Collar Crime: the Pattern of Crime among the Fourteenth-Century English Nobility, *Journal of Social History Vol VIII*, pp. 1-17.

17 Murphy, E., 2018, *Monks Hall, The History of a Waveney Valley Manor*, Poppyland Publishing, pp. 53-61.

18 The Paston Family Letters can now be read online at http://www.medievalhistories.com/the-paston-letters-online/ [accessed 21.7.2017] or at The Project Gutenberg www.gutenberg.org, Gairdner J. (ed) *The Paston Letters*, in 6 volumes.

19 Delman, R. M., 2019, Gendered viewing, childbirth and female authority in the residence of Alice Chaucer,

duchess of Suffolk, at Ewelme, Oxfordshire, *Journal of Medieval History Vol 45*, pp. 181-203. Bodleian Library, MS D. D. Ewelme, a. 7, A. 47 (1)–(6) These inventories were transcribed by Goodall J. A. A. , 2001. *God's House at Ewelme, Oxfordshire: Life, Devotion and Architecture in a Fifteenth-Century Almshouse*, Aldershot, Ashgate Publishing, pp. 281–291, and in Ramsay, N. and Willoughby. J. M. W. (eds), 2009, *Hospitals, Towns, and the Professions*, British Library in association with the British Academy pp. 42–9.

20 Accounts in British Library, BL Egerton Roll 8779. Payments to Bruisyard Abbey in Archer, R. E., 2003, Jane with the Blemyssh: A Skeleton in the de la Pole Closet, *The Ricardian Vol XIII*, pp. 12-26, Bury St Edmunds.

21 Jambeck, K. K., 1998, The Library of Alice Chaucer, Duchess of Suffolk: A Fifteenth-Century Owner of a 'Boke of le Citee de Dames,' in *The Profane Arts of the Middle Ages*, Misericordia International, pp. 106-135.

22 Bloore, P. and Martin, E. (eds), 2015, *Wingfield College and its Patrons*, Appendix p. 225, Boydell, Woodbridge.

23 Quotation from Paston Letters, Vol 5, no 704.

24 'Deed A. 11118', in A Descriptive Catalogue of Ancient Deeds in the Public Record Office, Vol. 5, edn. H.C. Maxwell Lyte 1906 His Majesty's Stationery Office, London, 93–108, quoted in Delman, 2019, note 19 above.

25 Goodall, J. A., 2001, *God's House at Ewelme: Life, Devotion and Architecture in a Fifteenth-Century Almshouse*, Aldershot, Ashgate Publishing.

26 Hicks, M., 2004, John de la Pole, second duke of Suffolk (1442-1492). *Oxford Dictionary of National Biography*, Oxford University Press; 2015 edn online at https://doi.org/10.1093/ref:odnb/22450 .

27 Resumed Lands. Account of sheriffs, escheators, and mayors for lands resumed under the various acts of Resumption passed by the parliaments of Henry VI between 1450 and 1456. TNA. Kings Remembrancer Series E 101.

28 Paston Letters Vol 2, no. 228.

29 Ibid 26.

30 Thomson, J. A. F., 1979, John De La Pole, Duke of Suffolk, *Speculum 54*, pp. 529-532.

31 Ibid., p. 532.

32 Quotation from Paston Letters, no 817.

33 Ibid. 31.

The Last of the de la Poles at Wingfield Castle

47. The Arms of John de la Pole, earl of Lincoln.

John, earl of Lincoln assumes the role of heir to the throne. The new king Richard III's son, Edward of Middleham, died in 1484. He was always a sickly child and at the age of 10 died after a short unexpected illness, to the profound grief of Richard and his wife Anne. It is often claimed that Suffolk's son, John earl of Lincoln, then became Richard's heir but this is not clearly stated anywhere in the written record and he was never proclaimed as such.[1] Lincoln carried the orb at Richard III's coronation in 1483, when he was twenty-three years old. He supported Richard against rebels in October 1483 and was rewarded with land worth £157 and the future reversion of Beaufort lands worth £178. To compensate for his having to wait for the reversion of Beaufort lands, he was granted an annuity of £177 13s 4d from the duchy of Cornwall. A few months after Richard's son died, Lincoln was appointed to the Lieutenantship of Ireland.

It has been suggested that the appointment in Ireland signalled Richard's recognition of Lincoln as his heir. A further appointment as President of the council in the north, acting on Richard's behalf, seemed to strengthen his position and he was with the king at Nottingham in August 1485. Perhaps most importantly Lincoln himself seems to have decided he was Richard's heir and while there were other claimants in the wings, notably the young earl of Warwick, Lincoln perceived himself henceforth as the bearer of the torch for the Yorkist cause. Lincoln had already gained far more positions and favours from Richard III than his father Suffolk ever had from Edward IV. He seems to have had the personal charm and self-confidence that always eluded his father.

The new Tudor Dynasty. In August 1485, Elizabeth de la Pole's Lancastrian nephew, Henry Tudor, the exiled earl of Richmond (and son of John de la Pole's first planned bride Margaret Beaufort) invaded England to claim the throne. Whilst he had tried previously, it was this effort that appeared to the king to be seriously threatening. Suffolk, like so many of the nobility, failed to participate at the ensuing Battle of Bosworth. However his son Lincoln fought for Richard.

We could read this division between Suffolk and his son as simply a difference in degree of commitment, the younger man being far more keen to fight on the side of the Yorkists than his less enthusiastic father, but it could also imply that Suffolk was not convinced that Richard was the right man to fill the throne. Many former Yorkists failed to rally to Richard's side at Bosworth. Historian Colin Richmond has estimated that only six peers turned out for Richard and 'several' for Henry, while the rest of the nobility stayed at home.[2] Richmond points out that many of those present at the battle did not actually fight, but like the Stanley family men stayed on the sidelines nearby until the battle was almost over. Many of Richard's northerners may have been inactive too. While he may not have shouted Shakespeare's 'A horse, a horse! My kingdom for a horse!' he might well have shouted for more men when he saw so many standing about watching the developing spectacle.

It is not clear why Richard did not get the support he expected. Possibly one reason was the shocking rumours about the princes' disappearance and a further totally false allegation that Richard had a hand in the death. in March '85, of his own wife Anne, who in fact probably died of TB. Plenty of 'fake news' tainted the medieval air. Theoretically Richard, an experienced and successful military commander who had the greater number of men, should have triumphed. Instead, Richard was killed with a heavy blow to the head, the last English king to die in battle.

There was an early incorrect report of Lincoln's death in combat but he emerged unscathed from Bosworth and surrendered to triumphant Henry Tudor, who was declared King Henry VII on the battlefield. The York royal dynasty was officially dead, the Tudor dynasty had begun. It is hard to conceive what a bitter blow this turn of events was for Lincoln and his parents and indeed for the Yorkist faction in Wingfield and throughout East Anglia.

Both Suffolk and Lincoln sensibly very rapidly offered their support to the new king. How genuine their feelings were must be queried, at least on

Lincoln's part. Generously but no doubt warily, Henry VII does not seem to have held their previous allegiances against them. At this stage he knew he had to win over former Yorkists. Neither of the de la Poles was sanctioned for any part they had played in the previous regimes. Suffolk almost immediately regained Wallingford Castle and played an active role in Henry VII's first parliament. But, in the main, Suffolk seems to have retreated to Wingfield with Elizabeth and wisely kept his head down, leaving his oldest son to take centre stage for the de la Poles.

Lincoln joins a rebellion. In 1485, Suffolk and Elizabeth had nine of their known eleven children still alive. The youngest, Richard, was only five years old, William was just seven. They would be growing up at Wingfield Castle or living in one or more of the de la Pole manors nearby. Some of these children died young, predeceasing their parents. The dates are not always reliable. The list below is the consensus of dates given by recognised authorities.

John, later earl of Lincoln (1462-1487)
Geoffrey, (born circa 1464) may have died young, we know nothing further about him.[3]
Edward (1466–1485) joined the church and became Archdeacon of Richmond, Yorkshire.[4]
Elizabeth (c. 1468–1489) married Henry Lovel, 8th Baron Morley but had no issue.[5]
Edmund (1471-1530) 3rd duke of Suffolk, see below.
Dorothy (born 1472, died young)
Humphrey (1474-1513) took holy orders at Cambridge in 1490 and eventually became a country rector in Hingham, Norfolk.[6]
Anne, (1476-1495) became a nun but died young.
Katherine (1477-1513) married William, Baron Stourton, no issue.
William (1478-1539) imprisoned in the Tower of London from 1502 until his death.
Richard, (1480-1525) see below.

John, earl of Lincoln marries. The family travelled regularly to Ewelme and Lincoln seems to have made his base there rather than at Wingfield. At some point in the late 1470s or early 80s he married Margaret Fitzalan, whose mother was a sister of Edward IV's queen Elizabeth Woodville, strengthening his Yorkist attachments. Ewelme provided the young couple with a comfortable home of their own just as Wingfield had for his parents.

Lincoln's apparent attachment to the Tudor regime continued through 1486 and he was with Henry VII's court at Greenwich on New Year's Day in 1487 and at the royal palace at Sheen, Richmond, in February. Privately he was fomenting rebellion. Surely the Suffolks must have been deeply anxious for their own and their children's welfare as their eldest son's life unfolded over the next two years.

Yorkist supporters were not simply driven by attachment to a family cause but were looking to their property and hegemony in their traditional lands. As historian David Baldwin has pointed out, the regional supremacy of Yorkist families shifted as a result of Bosworth.[7] In East Anglia, John Howard, 1st duke of Norfolk, had been slain and his son the earl of Surrey taken prisoner. Removing the Howards and their allies the Mowbrays from control of Norfolk and Suffolk left the de la Poles in a position to dominate the region again, if the Yorkist cause regained supremacy. Lincoln would be 'king' in East Anglia if nowhere else.

48. The Tudor Rose emblem adopted by Henry VII and used throughout the Tudor period.

Henry VII, well aware of the split loyalties of his kingdom, had sensibly tried to gain the acceptance of the Yorkist faction by his marriage to their heiress, Elizabeth of York. Moreover the creation of the new Tudor symbol, the Tudor rose with Lancastrian and York roses combined, was a deliberate attempt to demonstrate the union of the formerly hostile factions within the state, a stroke of genius on Henry's part. Henry's hold on power was not entirely secure however. Throughout his reign his suspicions hovered on the edge of paranoia. He saw plotting Yorkists all about him. So it is all the more strange that he never seems to have felt John de la Pole was a credible threat. The chief thorn in Henry's side was the principal claimant to the throne Edward earl of Warwick, who was kept safely confined in the Tower of London.

Then an extraordinary plot was hatched, and it seems Lincoln was at the heart of it. He seized the opportunity offered by a man called Symonds or Simon who knew a youth called Lambert Simnel, a cobbler's son, who was able to pose as the earl of Warwick. Later there was a second impostor, Perkin Warbeck. Both acted as stalking horses for Yorkist rebellions. The whole story of these pantomime like figures seems to rely on three post-hoc chroniclers, all of whom were writing many years later and whose credibility has been called into question.[8] Modern historians have struggled to make sense of the story, even suggesting that the impostors were actually really the people they pretended to be.[9] It seems incredible that rebellions could have been raised on such flimsy, obviously ludicrous bases. But we live in an age where laughably inaccurate 'celebrity stories' are lapped up by a gullible public glued to their social media information silos; we can scarcely be dismissive of a credulous populace looking for a cause in the late fifteenth century.

Lincoln personally could have had no doubt whatsoever about the imposter's false identity because he would have known Warwick well, but he saw an opportunity for rekindling the Yorkist cause and perhaps even gaining the throne. Something changed quite suddenly in Lincoln's psyche. He must have seen how possible it was to persuade enthused supporters to rally around the would-be pretender and how deeply rattled Henry VII was by the threat. It is also possible that Lincoln had fallen out of favour with Henry and saw his chances of preferment slipping away. He and his friend Francis Lovel decided to gamble everything.

The Battle of Stoke, the death of Lincoln. Lincoln fled the English court on the 19 March 1487. He made his way to Flanders, where he and his co-conspirator Lovel were given two thousand Swiss and German mercenaries, provided by Margaret of York, dowager duchess of Burgundy, sister of both Edward IV and Richard III but also of course sister to Lincoln's mother Elizabeth. While Elizabeth is quite hard to pin down in the archives, not so her impressive younger sister Margaret, who kept the Yorkist flame burning in her lands for many more years and had the money through her marriage to do so.

Having got what they came to Flanders for, Lincoln, Lovel and their army sailed for Ireland, where Simnel (or quite possibly another boy) was crowned Edward VI at Dublin. On 4 June the rebels, mercenaries and some additional ill-trained Irish forces led by Thomas Fitzgerald landed at Furness in Cumbria. They then headed into the heart of Richard III's territory in Yorkshire and finally turned south to Tadcaster. There they beat off a force loyal to Henry but found that the steadfast Yorkists they had expected to join them did not materialise.

Confronting Henry's army at the Battle of Stoke, near Newark, Nottinghamshire, Lincoln was killed in the fighting, as probably was Lovell. It was said that Henry had wanted Lincoln taken prisoner but it seems the first hour or more of the battle was ferocious and he was killed quite quickly, one of perhaps four thousand slain by royal forces that day, far more than at Bosworth. The Irish forces were slaughtered, but some continental mercenaries may have got back home after the battle. Henry was near the scene but did not fight personally.

49. Margaret of York, duchess of Burgundy, wife of Charles the Bold.

Lambert Simnel was captured. He ended up as a kitchen boy in Henry's kitchens, regarded by the king as a foolish dupe. Lincoln was buried on the battlefield in an unmarked grave. Stories circulated for years about Lovel disappearing after the battle and escaping but he almost certainly had not survived the fighting. There were mass burial graves on site and after looting of armour and clothing, bodies were hard to identify even twenty-four hours after death. The battle of Stoke marked the end of the Wars of the Roses for good. Henry Tudor then had the confidence to crown his wife Elizabeth of York Queen.

John and Elizabeth de la Pole's last years. The loss of Wingfield and their children's inheritance. In spite of the rebellion and Lincoln's death in battle against the king, his father continued to serve Henry and did not apparently suffer any recriminations aimed at his son while he was still alive. Suffolk continued to attend parliament, and mustered men for Henry's expeditions. Around the same time though he lost the constableship of Wallingford again. The lucrative constableship of the great royal fortress at Wallingford was an appointment that demonstrated royal favour. Winning and losing the job was a kind of weather-vane of royal support. So Suffolk was not particularly favoured at this point and understandably so. Nevertheless Suffolk did not actually lose too much under Henry Tudor. His heirs however did.

Lincoln was attainted for treason at the 1487 parliament that his father

Suffolk attended. Suffolk had to sit through a catalogue of treachery and attainders doled out to his dead son. There is no report of him dissenting, presumably through fear and anxiety for his family. Suffolk kept his own lands and also those he had granted Lincoln; but this was only for his lifetime. On his death, these estates were all to revert to the Crown. The de la Poles were thus going to lose Wingfield, Ewelme and all their other remaining manors on Suffolk's death. It was accordingly a very seriously diminished inheritance that would pass to their heir, Edmund. Elizabeth still had her dower and she seems to have continued to live at Wingfield until her death in 1503. But the de la Poles were well and truly defeated.

The Death of John de la Pole. Although Suffolk seems still to have been alive on 14 May 1492, when he sat as county JP in Suffolk, he was certainly dead six days later. He was just 50. His splendid tomb far outshines the man himself. His biographer says he spent his final years in 'discreet obscurity' but I do not think that is quite the case. The Suffolks were still active in East Anglia. John had found court life irksome and unpredictable and after his mother died he simply could not summon the personality or brains to engage in the political shifts that bedevilled his life. He and Elizabeth were probably much grieved by the death of their hotheaded and rebellious son and may have preferred to mourn him quietly at their Wingfield home.

Perkin Warbeck and Ralph Wulford. Henry VII could never relax his guard against Yorkist plots. During the spring of 1491 yet another false son of Edward IV appeared, this time Perkin Warbeck, 'Pierrequin Werbecque' from Tournai, the son of a boatman. He fomented several insurgencies from 1491 to 1497. With help from the compliant Margaret of Burgundy, he became a greater threat than Lambert Simnel, managing to raise money and recognition as 'Richard IV' from Margaret and king Maximilian of Vienna and mounted several unsuccessful invasions. In the end he abandoned the struggle and his ambitions, throwing himself on Henry's mercy. Henry kept him in prison for two years, until another impostor Ralph Wulford appeared, claiming to be the earl of Warwick. Wulford was frankly insane and not much of a threat but the king realised that he would have no peace while the Yorkist claimants remained alive. Their mere existence encouraged rebellion. There was clearly continuing support for the Yorkists in the general populace. They would always be ready to latch onto any excuse for further rebellion. In November 1499, therefore, Warwick and Warbeck, the real earl and the false duke, were tried for treason, condemned and executed.

Edmund de la Pole, 3rd duke of Suffolk (1471-1513) John's dukedom descended to his fourth son, twenty-one year old Edmund, in 1492, possibly one of the most feckless and reckless characters to emerge from this story. No one was touchier about his status than the new 3rd duke of Suffolk. Edmund was his own worst enemy. He was haughty, most likely not terribly intelligent and 'of an hasty and choleric disposition' which exploded in uncontrollable tempers. Contemporary historian Polydore Vergil called him 'bold, impetuous, readily roused to anger'. 'Stout and bold of courage, and of wit rash and heady' wrote a later Tudor chronicler Edward Hall.[10] Despite having been sent to Oxford in his teens, Edmund's surviving letters are often barely comprehendible. So eccentrically crafted and misspelt, even for the day, his clerk Thomas Killingworth had to rewrite them. They were mainly dashed off in haste and consisted mostly of begging letters or orders to his agents. He is noted however among linguists for the modern use of 'you' rather than the conventional 'ye'.

Edmund seemed to enjoy nursing his grievance. When his father John had died the de la Pole lands became forfeit to the Crown under his brother Lincoln's attainder as a traitor. The king allowed Edmund to inherit them but only on payment in instalments of £5,000. This forced him to mortgage a large proportion of his heritage. While his mother was alive he was able to maintain Wingfield Castle and Ewelme; there wasn't much else left.

Edmund reduced from duke to earl. Edmund took part in the siege of Boulogne in October 1492, supporting Henry VII, for which he was made a knight of the garter. But six months later Edmund agreed reluctantly, by an Indenture dated 26th February 1493, to surrender the Dukedom (and, apparently, the Marquessate) of Suffolk, and to be known henceforth as the earl of Suffolk only. This was ratified by Act of Parliament in 1495. The pretext was that his estates were so diminished and impoverished that he could not afford to maintain the status and livery of a duke. Edmund had been plunged into debt. No doubt correctly, he felt deeply insulted by his 'degradation'. His mother retained her title of dowager duchess.

Edmund showed no outward signs of disaffection in the early and mid 1490s. He played his role on ceremonial occasions and was admired for his prowess at jousting, the great spectator sport of the age. A herald's account gives us a colourful glimpse of him at the tournament held at Westminster in 1494 to celebrate Prince Henry's investiture as duke of York. Edmund led the competitors as they rode out of Westminster Hall, his red silken banner bearing his motto, 'For to accumplisshe', while the crest on his tilting helm was a golden lion. During the tournament, he broke his sword on Sir Edward a Borough 'furiously and notably', and performed no less effectively in breaking his lance when charging an opponent. After supper, the five-year-old Princess Margaret, King Henry's eldest daughter, awarded the prize to 'the right noble lord, the earl of Suffolk', a ring of gold with a diamond.

When the tournament was resumed a few days later, he 'gave such a stroke to Sir Edward a Borough that his sword was almost out of his hand and bruised his gauntlet'. His opponent lost control of his horse, many people thought that his arm had been damaged, but he recovered and managed to give Suffolk a light tap on the helmet with his own sword. This time it was Sir Edward who was given the tourney prize, another diamond ring. The earl was still only twenty-three, while the other competitors were all seasoned veterans.

In September 1495 the king paid Edmund the supreme royal compliment of visiting him at Ewelme Palace. Edmund was surviving. He married, some time before 10 October 1496, Margaret, daughter of Sir Richard Scrope. They had a daughter, Elizabeth, who became a nun and died of the plague in the Convent of the Minoresses without Aldgate, London in 1515. A second daughter Margaret may have been born and died in 1498. Sadly Edmund and Margaret scarcely had a marriage at all, because, within two years, Edmund's downward slide into catastrophe gained momentum.

Flight to Guisnes. There is a story recounted by Hall in about 1540 that, in 1498, Edmund was indicted for murder 'for slaying of a mean person in his rage and fury', and was rapidly prosecuted in the Kings Bench, a common court for ordinary folk.[11] The story goes that Edmund was affronted by being prosecuted like a common criminal, and though afterwards pardoned, fled overseas in a panic. There is however no evidence of this murder in the public record. Edmund was embroiled in a lawsuit with a wealthy yeoman of Rishangles in Suffolk called Rivet, whom Edmund claimed was his villein. Edmund was humiliatingly defeated in the court of the Kings Bench and heavy damages were awarded against him. Without royal permission, he left the country, going to Guisnes, where Sir James Tyrell, a prominent supporter of Richard III, was fomenting a Yorkist cell.[12]

What was Edmund thinking? He had spent years regaining the king's tolerance, if not active support, and overnight had thrown it away. Naturally alarmed that he was planning to ally himself with the downright dangerous Margaret duchess of Burgundy, the king sent Sir Richard Guildford to persuade Edmund to come back, on a promise the king would overlook the defection.

So Edmund returned to England some time after September 1499. The king was alert to Edmund's deviousness but clearly felt he was better inside the court circle where he could keep an eye on his activities. Lord Oxford, the Essex based chief supporter of the king, wrote to one of the Pastons, telling him to try to find out who had accompanied the earl abroad and what his intentions were. He also instructed Paston to keep a watch for 'any suspect person nigh unto the sea-coasts which shall seem unto you to be of the same affinity . . .'

Thomas Killingworth of Wingfield. Throughout this period, until Edmund's death, he employed Thomas Killingworth, gentleman of Wingfield and London, as his house steward and clerk, for which Killingworth later received a Royal Pardon. Many of the letters Edmund exchanged with Killingworth about shortage of money and his plans have survived in the National Archive. The story of Edmund de la Pole can be followed through a transcription, published in 1861 by James Gairdner, of contemporary documents held in the National Archive, now online.[13] Killingworth lived at Wingfield Castle as a close servant of the family but clearly often travelled with Edmund and was burdened with trying to implement his master's demands. He travelled back and forth carrying messages to and from England as Edmund required. He must have wondered if he would ever see Wingfield again when he left with Edmund to go into exile.

Edmund steps over into Treason. 'England has never been so tranquil and obedient as it is at present,' reported the Spanish ambassador in January 1500.[14] With pretender Perkin Warbeck executed alongside the benighted earl of Warwick, all looked fair for the king's throne. Edmund was present in May 1500 at Canterbury to witness the treaty for the marriage of Prince Arthur, the king's eldest son, with Catherine of Aragon. Edmund then left for France, arriving there on 13 May, and attended the King at his meeting with the Archduke Philip, at Calais, on 9 June. But in August 1501 he and his younger brother Richard again left England, without Royal leave, apparently assisted again by James Tyrell, who was subsequently executed for the support he gave. MacCulloch reckons that harassment triggered Edmund's flight in 1501.[15] He joined the Emperor Maximilian I in the Tyrol, assumed his former title of duke of Suffolk, and also the alias the 'White Rose'. Hall records, 'Solicited, allured and provoked by that old, venomous serpent the duchess of Burgoyne, ever being the sower of sedition and beginner of rebellion against the King of England, or else stimulate [d] and pricked with envy ... with his brother Richard [he] fled again.' There is no direct evidence that aunt Margaret was plotting again but she may have been.[16]

Disaster for the de la Pole brothers; desperation at Wingfield Castle. In 1501 Elizabeth de la Pole was living still at Wingfield Castle; her 23 year old son William was at home with her and probably also William's wife Katherine. We must assume that all of them were profoundly concerned about Edmund and his youngest brother Richard. All the surviving sisters had been married or were in nunneries, the other brothers in holy orders. As a result of his actions abroad, Edmund was proclaimed an outlaw at Ipswich, on 26 December 1502.

William de la Pole (1478–1539) was his mother's companion and referred to always as 'of Wingfield Castle'. In 1501 he was arrested on suspicion of treasonous activity, although there was no evidence of William ever plotting against the throne. He was sent to the Tower of London, where he remained for 37 years until his death in 1539. Henry VII and then his successor Henry VIII basically left him to rot, well away from anyone who might latch on to this last White Rose. William has the dubious distinction of being the Tower's longest held prisoner. Prisoners in the Tower were not held in dungeons but lived in quite comfortable apartments. They could have servants and buy food and luxuries such as books to ease the tedium. Hall's chronicle says he was well treated by Henry VII. Prisoners could read, receive visitors and sometimes mixed with others in the same predicament. But a prison is a prison and William's life was effectively destroyed by the Tower.

William had married only three years earlier, to the daughter of Lord Stourton but they had no issue.[17] Twice widowed and aged about 42, Katherine was more than twenty years older than William, so the motive for the marriage may have been financial. The de la Poles needed every bit of cash they could lay their hands on to survive, given their diminished property. It is likely that William and Katherine were living at Wingfield with his mother before his arrest and it would have been Katherine who kept Elizabeth company in her final years.

The Death of Elizabeth de la Pole, countess of Suffolk. Elizabeth, dowager duchess of Suffolk, lived eleven years as a widow and died in 1503, having seen six of her children predecease her. Her three youngest sons were either in exile or in the Tower of London. It is almost impossible to say how much Elizabeth colluded with or supported her children's involvement in the hopeless Yorkist cause. Her more powerful sister Margaret, who never abandoned the cause, died the same year as Elizabeth.

Elizabeth never saw Edmund or Richard again after their exile and may not have visited William. She was fifty-nine when she died, not a bad age for the fifteenth century but her life had been peculiarly unfulfilling. As sister, wife, mother, she had been 'a candle in the wind', blown hither and yon by the political winds of the warring Plantagenets blowing round her. If she had character, we cannot fathom it from the record. She certainly did not match in forcefulness her sister Margaret of Burgundy. She had drawn the short straw in her marriage to John de la Pole, and the children who might have given her life meaning, frankly, turned out badly.

The Tomb of John and Elizabeth de la Pole, 2nd duke and duchess of Suffolk.

50. The alabaster tomb effigies of John 2nd duke of Suffolk (d. 1492) and Elizabeth, duchess of Suffolk (d. 1503), St Andrew's church Wingfield.*

John and Elizabeth's tomb is one of the finest in St Andrew's Church, Wingfield, an outstanding example of a tomb chest with the alabaster figures of a late fifteenth century robed knight of the garter with his lady.[18] John lies complete with funeral armour and a line of cresting. John and Elizabeth's faces were clearly both done as portraits. His wavy hair is bound with a jewelled band and he has an earring in his right ear. His head rests on a helm surmounted by the Saracen head crest of the de la Pole family. His feet are on a lion with a curly mane. The duchess has a pillow supported by (now headless) angels. These are just like the angels holding the pillow on John's mother's tomb in Ewelme. They are set under an arch with a decorated top. Above are heraldic beasts and a tilting helmet. Elizabeth is wearing a neck scarf, or barbe, as worn by widows.

Who commissioned and paid for the magnificent tomb? Probably Elizabeth

* Badham, 2015 p 171 Photo by Tim Sutton.

herself commissioned it before her own death. Surely it would be her wish to give her husband the grandeur he was denied in life. Historians have noted the difference between Suffolk's effigy and surviving effigies of some of his contemporaries and it has been suggested that the nobility in general, or perhaps Suffolks' in particular, were increasingly anxious 'to set themselves apart from their social inferiors.' The de la Poles were always touchy about their social status; the tomb is defiantly noble.

The game is up for Edmund and Richard de la Pole. Maximilian signed a treaty at Augsburg whereby, in return for ten thousand pounds, he undertook not to assist the English rebels. Nevertheless Edmund was allowed to remain at Aix, from 1502-1504, though on leaving he had to leave behind his reluctant brother Richard as hostage for his debts.[19] After leaving Aix about April 1504 Edmund was imprisoned first by the duke of Gueldres at Hattem and then secondly, in 1505, by Philip, Maximilian's son, at Namur. Then extraordinarily, while sailing in the Channel, Philip was blown off course and was forced to land for safety on the English side of the Channel. He therefore unexpectedly became an enforced 'guest' of Henry VII, who craftily persuaded Philip to hand over the earl of Suffolk in exchange for letting him continue on his journey. Philip did so. Edmund had been persuaded that he would be treated well if he returned home, so return he did.

On his arrival in London, in late March 1506, Edmund was committed to the Tower. Meanwhile he had fallen out with his younger brother Richard, who was penniless in exile and sending Edmund desperate requests for money. Killingworth was often tasked with paying Edmund's debts too for board and lodging. When Edmund told him to find some more money from supporters, Killingworth said it was impossible, he should try asking for the money himself!

The de la Poles and Henry VIII. Though a 'White Rose' faction would continue to scheme and plot until long after Henry VII's death, he had learnt how to control the English magnates by suspended threats of attainder or ruinous fines and by restricting their recruitment of retainers. Henry died in 1409 having secured his throne. But the new king Henry VIII, even as a young man, having witnessed his father being mentally tortured by the Yorkist opposition, took a characteristically robust approach to the de la Pole 'White Rose' risk.

Edmund, still in the Tower, was, with his two brothers, excepted from the King's general pardon on his accession in April 1509. Perhaps, as Montaigne said in his Essays, Henry VII in his will instructed his son to put Suffolk to death immediately after his own decease. Montaigne criticised Henry VII for requiring that his son do what he himself would not do. After being a prisoner in the Tower for seven years, in the company of his brother William, Henry VIII ordered Edmund's execution. In 1513, without further ado he was beheaded on Tower Hill. He was about 42. It is said Edmund was buried in Wingfield Church, alongside his second daughter Margaret (or Anne?) who died in 1498 and eventually also his widow Margaret.[20] But there is little certainty about his or his family's final resting place. Edmund's motto was 'For to accumplisshe', but he was one of life's failures.

Richard de la Pole's last years.[21] The youngest de la Pole brother Richard, in exile with Edmund, was attainted in Parliament in January 1504. All his honours were forfeited, backdated to 1 July 1499. Chronicler Hall may not have admired Edmund but of Richard he says 'But Richard his brother, being an expert and politic man, so craftily conveyed and so wisely ordered himself in this stormy tempest that he was not attrapped, either with net or snare.'

51. Richard de la Pole 1480-1525, wearing French clothing. A portrait once thought to be a French nobleman, but the hat badge is of a white hart, the emblem of Richard II.

Richard made quite a life for himself as exile and led an adventurous life, sidestepping his brother's creditors at Aachen in 1504, escaping and taking on military service with King Vladislas II of Hungary. He established something of a reputation as a mercenary leader or condottiere. After Edmund's death in 1513 he took over the claim to the crown, taking on the Yorkist cause by calling himself the 5th earl of Suffolk. Although treated with some equivocation by Louis XII of France, Louis's successor, Francis I used him as a weapon in his complex diplomacy and he served the French king well as a commander.

The mischief-making French King recognised Richard as the legitimate

English monarch and referred to him as 'Richard IV'. In spite of plotting and raising support and funds, Richard never returned home. As far as Henry VIII was concerned, Richard de la Pole remained a threat as long as he was alive. He tried hard to have him assassinated but failed. Ultimately Richard died at the Battle of Pavia on 24 February 1525 fighting for the French cause. It is said he died by being buried alive under a pile of dead bodies.[22] Burke's Heraldry describes him as 'the last heir of this gallant race', and records that the duke of Bourbon 'honoured his remains with splendid obsequies'.[23]

Farewell to the de la Poles. This is as far as we travel with the de la Pole family. For near on one hundred and twenty years Wingfield Castle had been their family home, where they could escape the intrigues of court and the perils of war. The first Michael de la Pole and his grandson William achieved the highest political rank England had to offer but their descendants' stubborn loyalty to a defeated Yorkist cause destroyed them completely. The fault line running through their characters down the generations was misplaced constancy to the monarchs who failed them.

Notes

1 Moorhen, W., 2003, The Career of John de la Pole, Earl of Lincoln, *The Ricardian 13*, pp. 341–358.

2 Hammond, P., 2013, *Richard III and the Bosworth Campaign*, Pen and Sword, Barnsley, p. 173.

3 Chrimes, S. B., 1999, *Henry VII*, Yale University Press, New Haven, p. 92.

4 Kingsford, C. L., 1919, *Kingsford's Stonor Letters and Papers 1290-1483*, Cambridge University Press, Cambridge, p. 393.

5 Ibid. 3, p. 92

6 Humphrey de la Pole, Cambridge Alumni Database ACAD online at http://venn.lib.cam.ac.uk.

7 Baldwin, D., 2006, *Stoke Field, the Last Battle of the Wars of the Roses*, Pen & Sword, Barnsley, Kindle version, pp. 423-657.

8 Bennett, M., 1987, *Lambert Simnel and the battle of Stoke*, Sutton Publishing, Stroud.

9 Smith, G., 1996, Lambert Simnel and the King from Dublin, *The Ricardian Vol. 10*, pp. 1-24.

10 Hall, E., 1548, *Hall's Chronicle. The Union of the two Noble and Illustre Famelies of Lancaste and Yorke*, London.

11 Hall, E., c1540 transcribed and printed 1809, *Hall's chronicle : containing the history of England, during the reign of Henry the Fourth, and the succeeding monarchs, to the end of the reign of Henry the Eighth, in which are particularly described the manners and customs of those periods. Carefully collated with the editions of 1548 and 1550.* Printed for J. Johnson and others, London. Murder recorded p. 495, online at https://archive.org/details/hallschronicleco00halluoft/page/494.

12 Hanham, A., 1988, Edmund de la Pole, defector. *Renaissance Studies, Vol 2*, pp. 240-250.

13 Gairdner, J., 1861, *Letters and papers illustrative of the reigns of Richard III and Henry VII*, Longman, Green, Longman, Roberts, London, index at https://archive.org/details/letterspapersill02gair/page/400.

14 Spain: January 1500 in Calendar of State Papers, Spain, Volume 1, 1485-1509, ed. Bergenroth G. A. (London, 1862), pp. 213-216. British History Online http://www.british-history.ac.uk/cal-state-papers/spain/vol1/pp. 213-216 [accessed 4 December 2019].

15 MacCulloch D., 1986, *Suffolk and the Tudors, Politics and Religion in an English County, 1500-1600*, Oxford University Press, Oxford, p. 54.

16 Ibid., 10.

17 Mowbray, C. B. J., 1899, *History of the noble house of Stourton, of Stourton, in the county of Wilts, Vol I*, p. 100.

18 Badham, S., 2015, Medieval Monuments to the de la Pole and Wingfield families. Chapter 7, 135-176, in Bloore, P. and Martin, E. (eds), 2015, *Wingfield College and its Patrons*, Boydell Press, Woodbridge.

19 Cunningham, S., 2004, Pole, Richard de la (died 1525) *Oxford Dictionary of National Biography,* Oxford University Press.

20 MacCulloch, D., 1976, *The Chorography of Suffolk*, Suffolk Records Society, p. 73

21 Ibid., 19.

22 Walsh, R. and Smith, J. J. (eds), 1831, Francis the First. *The Museum of Foreign Literature, Science, and Art, Volume 18*, p. 483.

23 Burke, J. and Burke, J. B., 1844, *3rd Ed'n Encyclopedia of Heraldry or General Armory of England, Scotland and Ireland*, Bohn, London.

Glamorous New Tenants for Wingfield Castle, 1514–1544

There can be few more glamorous couples than Charles Brandon, duke of Suffolk, and his wife Mary Tudor, former Queen of France. Like other celebrity couples whose determined passion transcends duty and common sense, their mutual happiness may not have endured for many years, but while it lasted they brought a touch of Camelot to Wingfield and Suffolk.

Brandon was Henry VIII's best friend, and retained Henry's regard even after Brandon had risked his ire by marrying his sister in secret. He was popular, exceptionally good looking, personable and athletic with a gift for getting along with other men well and women far too well. But he 'kept his head' in Henry VIII's fraught court 'when all around were losing theirs' and undoubtedly had an instinctive sense of how to keep Henry mollified. Perhaps cleverest of all, Brandon harboured no great ambitions to run the realm or challenge Henry's absolute royal power. He did what Henry wanted him to do and did it well. Mary was beautiful, gifted and determined. There are many

52. Charles Brandon, duke of Suffolk.

53. Mary Tudor sketch in the Ashmolean Museum, Oxford, after a French portrait.

portraits of both of them but two sketches from life are thought to be the most accurate.

Brandon and Mary were an asset to Wingfield because they not only lived at the Castle for a few years while building more spectacular residences, they maintained it and also supported Wingfield College and church. Their story has been the stuff of romantic historical novels since the 19th century.[1] A comically anachronistic version was portrayed in a 1953 Walt Disney movie still online, 'The Sword and the Rose'. It is excruciatingly inaccurate but played with some dash by Richard Todd and Glynis Johns, with James Robertson Justice as a suitably irascible Henry VIII.[2]

Wingfield Castle in the doldrums 1503–1509. Before we meet the Brandons though, there were others for whom Wingfield was a coveted acquisition. Long before the deaths of Edmund de la Pole in 1513 and Richard de la Pole in 1525, Wingfield Castle and the extensive north east Suffolk estates of the de la Poles had been seized by the Crown as a result of the attainders of the de la Pole men. Henry VIII began to distribute the various former de la Pole estates to whomever took his fancy, a problem that Charles Brandon had to tackle in building his East Anglian empire.

An 'attainder' was an Act (or Bill) in which Parliament passes judicial sentence on an accused person as if it were a court of law against a person convicted of or suspected of treason. It allowed the monarch to seize the titles and all the material assets of the individual and disinherit his heirs. In the late 15th and early 16th century attainders were used both as a way of circumventing the courts and allowing the Crown to accumulate assets but also as a means of control of threatening subjects. As we have seen, acts of attainder could be and frequently were reversed. Thomas Killingworth for example, Edmund de la Pole's steward, whose main fault had been to serve his master well, was attainted but later forgiven and seems to have had his property restored.[3] Edmund himself negotiated a restoration of some of his father's lands after Lincoln's attainder and his father's death but was attainted a second time after his flight abroad.

Attainders were implemented separately in every county where the victim held property, so in the cases of the earl of Lincoln, Edmund and Richard de la Pole, there are numerous official documents noting when the king's local bailiff was in possession of the forfeiture of property and had delivered the ownership to the Crown via the king's Receiver-General. Although the process started in official documents in 1504, it continued in some far-flung parts of the country until 1522. The de la Pole properties in Suffolk, including Wingfield Castle and manor were mainly seized between 1504 and 1509. The long list of de la Pole attainders for property taken over by the Crown held in the National Archive are listed below in note 4.[4]

William Stafford, (died 1521) keeper of the Castle. In 1509, Henry VIII, having gathered to the crown all the Suffolk de la Pole lands including Wingfield Castle, appointed one of his receivers, William Stafford, as 'keeper of the Castle'.[5] William Stafford was warden of the Tower (of London) from 1485 until his death in 1521 and paid 2s 6d a day. He must have known prisoners William and Edmund de la Pole quite well. As warden of the Tower he was also warden of the Mint, which then operated in the Tower.[6]

Sir John Sharpe (died January 1519), keeper of the Castle. Stafford may have found he had too much to do, or someone else decided for him, because a few months later Stafford was replaced by one of the king's trusted courtiers Sir John Sharpe. At the time Sharpe held Brockdish Hall as a tenant of the king, for an annual rental of one red rose, so it was a convenient appointment, Brockdish being only 3 miles from Wingfield.[7] His main home was at Coggeshall, Essex.[8] He almost certainly never moved into Wingfield Castle but supervised the bailiff and ensured that the land and property was secure and productive. Sharpe was exactly the calibre of experienced administrator the castle needed while the Crown found a new owner. Sharpe had been a gentleman usher at the court of Henry VII and present at his death at Richmond Palace, shown in a contemporary sketch by Thomas Wriothesley, Garter King of Arms.[9]

The sketch is hardly a portrait but confirms his role as a trusted courtier. Sharpe had been appointed as the receiver for the duchy of Lancaster in Norfolk, Suffolk and Cambridgeshire in 1460 and was evidently a highly trusted medium level official.[10] Other offices he held were 'Engraver of the King's dies for gold and silver coinage' and 'Keeper of the change and exchange'. As a gentleman usher, he received a legacy of £100 from King Henry VII and was knighted by the young King Henry VIII in 1513.

Much repeated on the web is a claim that the northern and eastern curtain walls of Wingfield Castle were pulled down in 1510 but there is no written record of this and it seems highly unlikely. The castle was far too valuable a property to be casually demolished, even in part. The Crown would have ensured that it was kept in good repair, and that was Stafford and then Sharpe's responsibility.

54. Scene at the death of King Henry VII at Richmond Palace, 1509. Sir John Sharpe is shown bottom row, far right.

Wingfield Castle grant to Sir Thomas Howard, later 3rd duke of Norfolk and his wife Anne Howard, 1510-1512. It may have been Sharpe who suggested when the time was ripe for the disposal of the castle to a new owner. There was one ambitious family lurking in the East Anglian wings, former rivals of the de la Poles, the power loving Howards, earls of Surrey and dukes of Norfolk. The Howards were probably themselves pressing for the property to be theirs. When the dispossessed de la Pole brothers heard of the transaction they must have felt furious that their ancestral home had ended up in the hands of their parents' and grandparents' detested rivals. The king had his reasons; he wanted something from Anne Howard. Anne had inherited substantial lands from her father king Edward IV and it was probably the king himself who decided on the grant to Anne Howard, in exchange for her covenanting her inheritance from Edward IV to the king.

The grant included the castle and manor of Wingfield, the manors of Syleham, Veales, Stradbroke, Frostenden and Creeting St. Olave in Suffolk, and the manors of Costessey and Stockton in Norfolk. These were some of the richest lands in East Anglia and substantially enlarged the Howard control of the region.[11] The grant also included estates in remote counties, Cudlington, Lewkenor and Nuneham Courtenay in Oxfordshire, Langley and West Bradley in Berkshire, Grassthorpe, Northleyston and Normanton in Nottinghamshire, Bliburgh and Westwoode in Lincolnshire, Faxfleete in Yorkshire, Norton Sub Hampden in Somerset, Wilmyndon, Kent and Evington, Leicestershire.[12]

A further indenture in the Letters and Papers of Henry VIII makes it clear that these manors were given by Henry VIII on condition that Anne's husband Thomas Howard, earl of Surrey, the heir to the Norfolk dukedom, promised not to ask for Anne's inheritance to be returned, as 'tenant by curtesy' 'after the decesse of the said Dame Anne.'[13] The covenant by the king declared that 'if the said manors be under the yearly value of 1,000 marks, he will make up the said value to Anne by the grant of other manors, etc.; further the king grants that he will by other letters patent, before the said date give to the said lord Howarde the manors of Claxton, co. Norfolk, and the manor of Fyndon, co. Sussex, to hold to the said lord his heires and assignes for ever.' In fact Anne died quite soon after in 1512 but Thomas Howard held on to her lands, as was the custom.

Wingfield Castle estate 1510. In 1510 the castle and manor of Wingfield, the manor of Syleham with Veales and Stradbroke, included a mill, 600 acres of (arable) land, 60 acres of meadow, 253 acres of pasture, 60 acres of wood, 100 acres of heath and 100 acres of marsh and brought in £52 in rent from tenants in Wingfield, Syleham and Stradbroke.[14]

Thomas Howard already had an inheritance in Norfolk and Suffolk. It was not large because he and his father were still retrieving lands from their own attainders as a result of being on the wrong side at Bosworth.[15] Some lands though were inherited from the Mowbrays, others acquired by his father the 2nd duke. Wingfield and the northeast Suffolk estates were an important addition to their portfolio if they were to regain their domination in the region.

In the early days of their marriage Thomas and Anne Howard lived mainly on their manor at Stoke by Nayland and in Lambeth, London, where the wily Howard was beginning his slow crafty rise to eminence. Howard is one of the more unattractive personalities of the Tudor age, a competent, conservative but not brilliant administrator whose talents did not match his ambition and who never adapted to the coming Reformation. Anyone who has been in public life or served in a public institution such as a university or a department of the civil service will have come across numerous men like smooth, affable but devious Thomas Howard, plotting and jockeying for position. His bland but shifty courtier aspect was captured perfectly in the well-known Holbein portrait shown above. It is unlikely that he ever lived at Wingfield but enjoyed the fruits of the manor. Readers who want a more sympathetic description will enjoy his biography by David Head.[16]

55. Thomas Howard, 3rd duke of Norfolk by Hans Holbein the Younger.

The East Anglian Economy. North East Suffolk remained arable and dairy country long after the south of Suffolk had turned to sheep and the wool industry. By 1460, Suffolk was the largest textile producing area in the country, producing fourteen per cent of the country's output. The main reason was the sophisticated entrepreneurial spirit of Suffolk producers, who rapidly comprehended the market for cheap, mass-produced clothing.[17] The workforce did not need to be particularly skilled to make these coarse cloths and low cost production could be set up in small villages. Lavenham and Hadleigh had grown with this trade, as did Long Melford and Waldringfield. The lower quality Suffolk wool was used, rather than best Lincolnshire wool. By 1500 Suffolk was the leading cloth making county in England, making 5,000 broadcloths a year. The London market was crucial to this success. In the years 1480 to 1500 Suffolk had one hundred clothiers, whereas Essex and Kent had about fifty each.[18]

But in the north of the county, the rise of dairying and the production of cheese were far more important by 1500 than wool. Bailey points out that by about 1500 Suffolk was the most industrialised and urbanised county in England.[19] It was the most likely county to become the first industrialised region of Britain, having taken over from Norfolk and the Lincolnshire fenlands, which in 1300 had been the thrusting commercial centres of England. By 1500 Suffolk shared this distinction with Devon. It took two hundred years for Suffolk to decline into rural agricultural backwater again. The owners and tenants of Wingfield Castle were beneficiaries of this regional plenty during the Tudor years.

Anne Howard died quite soon after the Howards acquired Wingfield castle. Anne was a sickly tuberculous young woman and while ostensibly a good match for Howard, being the ninth child of Edward IV, she had almost no dowry and no income. Anne and Thomas were married in Westminster Abbey on 4 February 1495. She had four sons who did not survive early childhood and when Anne died of consumption in 1512, all of her sons were already dead. Wingfield Castle's brief association with Thomas Howard however was not over yet. Howard, as 3rd duke of Norfolk, was chiefly responsible for the overthrow of both Cardinal Wolsey and Thomas Cromwell. If Brandon emerges from this chapter as unscrupulous and ruthless towards women, he did not plumb the depths of calculating cruelty and mercilessness of Howard, who inflicted untold misery on his young second wife before she left him.[20] Earl Marshall of England and Lord Treasurer, Howard was lucky to survive the scandals involving his nieces Ann Boleyn and Katherine Howard, unfortunate marital choices for the king, fatal for the women, their affairs were almost as disastrous for Norfolk.

Much later Thomas, as 3rd duke of Norfolk, built a spectacular Tudor palace at Kenninghall, Norfolk, where he lived mainly with his long-term mistress Bess Holland. He also owned a substantial town house in Norwich. Thomas Howard still keeps good company; his 1539 portrait by Holbein hangs in the Queen's private apartments at Windsor Castle.

Charles Brandon, 1st duke of Suffolk (second creation of the title) becomes a tenant at Wingfield castle, 1516. Thomas Howard retained a life interest in Wingfield and other local manors until 1544. He found a tenant or rather it seems likely that the king found a tenant for him and Howard may not have been too pleased. The new duke of Suffolk, Charles Brandon, elevated to the dukedom in February 1514, had been gradually acquiring the titles vacated by the de la Poles. As Henry VIII's close friend, he had been made his jousting partner, his Master of the Horse and marshal of his army in France in 1513. A year later, 'for the support of his title', Brandon was granted virtually all the lands formerly held by the disgraced de la Poles, including the reversion of the manor of Wingfield Castle and the patronage of Wingfield College.[21] Reversion is the right, especially of the original owner or their heirs, to possess or succeed to property on the death of the present possessor or at the end of a lease. In other words, on Howard's death, Brandon would secure the castle, the demesne and associated manor lands. But Howard was not dead yet.

Brandon accepted this possibly long-haul 'expectation' at first but events intervened. He acquired a wife, not his first but a very expensive one and then wanted the whole estate for his own use. In 1516 he secured a "ruinous lease" from Howard for the privilege of using Wingfield Castle as a home.[22] Thomas Howard, usually by then referred to by his title of the earl of Surrey, held about seventeen per cent of the former de la Pole lands but he wanted to milk Brandon for all he could squeeze out of him. Before renting to Brandon, Surrey cut down a hundred oaks from Wingfield Park, a typically mean act of despoliation to make a quick buck when the estate was moving out of his hands.[23] He charged Brandon £413 6s 8d a year for Wingfield and four other manors although the income was only £431 per annum.[24] By then Brandon and his wife were in deep debt to the king. How had matters come to this sorry pass? Here is the full romantic tale. But let us learn a little about the protagonists first.

Charles Brandon's early life. Brandon's story has been told countless times because his life was played out on the small stage of Tudor court politics, where Henry VIII totally dominates the narrative, alongside the brilliant men who made him – Cardinal Wolsey, Thomas Cromwell, Thomas More and the royal wives whose families pushed and shoved for preferment. Brandon seems to have had no great interest in the religious subsidence caused by the Reformation, indeed if he had religious instincts he kept them to himself. While he had the necessary ambition to accumulate property befitting his station, he was not consumed by a desire for power or excessive wealth. He was not especially gifted intellectually and was no book reader. His gift was to be a reliable friend to the most powerful man in the realm. His biography has been admirably researched by Steven Gunn, whose detailed analysis of Brandon's properties I have drawn on extensively, but Tracy Borman and David Head have written psychologically insightful accounts of his career and abysmal treatment of women.[25]

Charles was the second and only surviving son of Sir William Brandon, who had famously been killed by Richard III at the Battle of Bosworth while bearing the royal standard, achieving instant fame and glory for him and his family. In reality William was a reckless and violent man. In 1478 Sir John Paston wrote that Brandon had been arrested for an attempted rape: "yonge William Brandon is in warde and arestyd ffor thatt he scholde have fforce ravysshyd and swyvyd an olde jentylwoman ..."[26] According to Paston there were rumours he would be hanged for his offence but the elder Brandon apparently escaped prosecution and was pardoned in March 1484. He wisely defected abroad and then joined Henry Tudor's band assembling for invasion to topple Richard III. Charles' grandfather in contrast, also Sir William, was a respected and trusted figure in Suffolk, based in Wangford, who did not die until 1491. He was related by marriage to the Wingfield family of Letheringham and elsewhere in Suffolk.

Charles was no more than a baby when his father died and he went to live with his uncle Thomas Brandon, another hero of Bosworth who survived the battle. Sir Thomas was a leading courtier to Henry VII so it was natural that Charles grew up serving the king. By 1503 Charles was waiting on Henry VII at table and by 1507 an esquire of the body and one of a company of young gallants active in jousts and tournaments. The family was influential in Southwark, where they kept a large house on the main thoroughfare south of London Bridge, later called Suffolk Place, but also held the role of Marshal of the Kings Bench prison, a lucrative and responsible position.[27]

Seven years older than Henry VII's second son Prince Henry, Charles and Henry formed a strong early bond because of their love of horses, hunting, jousting and tournaments. When the heir to the throne Prince Arthur died and then young Henry inherited the throne in 1509, Charles' prowess at jousting brought him into the limelight alongside a number of other young male contemporaries, Edward Howard, Thomas Knyvet, Henry and Edward Guildford. They were a rowdy bunch of playboys with a love of sport and combat. Howard and Knyvet's untimely deaths in naval battle left Brandon in a central position and he began to dress like the king and indeed looked almost uncannily like the king. The king approved of this 'twinning'. Both were large, athletic men and dressed magnificently. Young Charles Brandon was about the only member of Henry VIII's entourage capable of standing up to Henry VIII in a tournament. He proved his personal courage in the 1513 campaign against France, for which he received a viscountcy. Many years later, he was trusted with a military command in 1523 and his army came within 30 miles of Paris. He successfully laid siege to Boulogne in 1542–44. He was not a born soldier nor especially brilliant but he was a loyal and reliable one. His marital expeditions were far less conventional than his military ones.

Charles' amorous adventures. Charles' first embarrassing marital situation reveals his careless callousness to women. In 1505, he had become engaged to Anne Browne, a young woman from a knightly family, who was a suitable match for him. They were betrothed *per verba de praesenti*, a binding contract

56. Suffolk Place on the west side of Borough High Street, Southwark.

under canon law. In such cases, there was no ceremony or witnesses; inevitably this could lead to men and occasionally women repudiating their betrothed if they changed their mind. Charles and Anne slept together, Anne became pregnant and gave birth to their daughter in 1506, but, to her family's horror, he did not marry her. Instead, completely unexpectedly, he married her aunt, a wealthy widow named Margaret Neville Mortimer, the widow of Sir John Mortimer, Knt., and daughter of the earl of Northumberland. Margaret herself was no gullible young woman; she was forty years old and she too had borne a child out of wedlock. She knew very well that her money would largely become Brandon's when she married him.

Their match must have suited Charles quite well financially but the marriage was annulled later in 1508, mainly under pressure from Anne's family, who were threatening a lawsuit and because of the disapproval of his own friends. The grounds of annulment were his previous contract and carnal knowledge of Anne and the near kinship between Margaret and Anne. Margaret did not seem to hold Charles' odious behaviour against him in the long term. He supported her in a lawsuit many years later when she had remarried. As soon as Margaret had been dispatched in 1508 he married Anne, first in a private ceremony in Stepney and then in a well attended public ceremony at St Michael Cornhill. Anne bore another daughter in 1510 but the long suffering woman died only two years later. Anne's two daughters were brought up by Charles and his later wife and both made good marriages.

57. Henry VIII, c1520, Joos Van Cleve c1530-35.

No sooner had Anne died than Charles went looking for another wife. He found one very conveniently in his own household, an eight year old girl who had been made his ward. Elizabeth Grey, 5th baroness Lisle, 3rd viscountess Lisle (25 March 1505–1519) was the daughter of John Grey, 2nd viscount Lisle and Lady Muriel Howard.[28] After the death of her stepfather, Sir Thomas Knyvet in August 1512, Elizabeth was left an orphan and became Brandon's ward, a 'gift' of the king. In 1513, Elizabeth and Brandon were betrothed; she of course had absolutely no say in the matter. The king, who approved of the match, gave Charles the Lisle title for his viscountcy, formerly used by Elizabeth's father. Of course he could not marry the eight year old immediately but he could enjoy the title while the bethrothal lasted. Almost certainly Charles was already in love by then with the woman who became his next wife. He cared little for poor Elizabeth. When he married Mary Tudor he was obliged to surrender the title, the betrothal and Elizabeth's wardship but by then he was a duke, he had no need of the lesser viscountcy. Elizabeth was passed like a parcel to the countess of Devon who married Elizabeth to her son, Henry Courtenay. Poor Elizabeth died aged fourteen before the marriage could be consummated.

A friendship consolidated, a dukedom and a flirtation too far. In 1513, by then officially the king's Master of the Horse, Charles accompanied the young king on a campaign to seize more of France inland from Calais. They took Therouanne and then marched into Tournai, which they successfully captured. Brandon had led the successful assault on the city gates, which led to the city's eventual surrender. Brandon and Henry were now brothers in arms as well as close sporting friends. Charles' position was unassailable.

Brandon moved a further few score places up the precedence list when created duke of Suffolk on 1 February 1514, at the very same time the earl of Surrey was at last restored to his father's title of duke of Norfolk. A dukedom was a very high honour. The traditional link between royal blood and ducal status made a duke special. In a ducal household away from court, for example, the duke's steward and treasurer ranked equal with barons. Such were the heights to which he was being elevated that he and Norfolk had to be created separately, since there were not enough peers of comparable status to accompany them both at once. The duke of Buckingham, the only duke in the country since 1504, absented himself from the ceremony, probably piqued at the creations. Others were shocked. The historian Polydore Vergil noted that 'many people considered it very surprising that Charles should be so honoured as to be made a duke' and Erasmus, the great Renaissance thinker, made a comment so insulting that it was edited out of the 1519 Basle edition of his letters. He compared the Master of the Horse to a drunken stable-hand whose new trappings could not hide his true nature.

The glorious success of a dukedom and his military exploits may have given Charles 'ideas above his station'. Soon after his triumph at Tournai, Henry decided to visit Archduchess Margaret of Austria, duchess of Savoy and regent governor of the Hapsburg Netherlands, holding the regency for her young nephew the future Charles V. Henry took Charles with him. Margaret was living at her newly built palace in Mechelen, Flanders. Margaret was known to have been grief struck and attempted suicide after her husband died and kept his embalmed heart with her always. When Henry turned up with Charles Brandon, Margaret had already heard that he was referred to as 'a second king'. His brash self-confidence seems to have been more ostentatious than usual and he flirted openly with this powerful princess of impeccable pedigree. She knew his reputation as a womaniser and tolerated his amusing style until she heard rumours that he intended to marry her. Margaret was horrified and demanded Henry put a stop to the notion at once. This was one woman who was not overly dazzled by the amorous duke, who retreated unabashed. No matter, there was another princess back home waiting in the wings.

Meanwhile, offstage, Charles fathered three other children by various ancillary mistresses and casual liaisons. He acknowledged all his children and they all went on to do fairly well for themselves. His illegitimate son Sir Charles Brandon became a member of parliament for Westmoreland. Charles' reputation, as his biographer noted, was 'scarcely unspotted'.[29]

If Brandon was Henry's companion in his personal and military exploits, another man, Cardinal Thomas Wolsey, dominated the political, strategic and ecclesiastical realms at court. Wolsey and Brandon became unusual allies and friends, both recognising the value of the influence of the other. Wolsey was to prove a useful friend to both Charles and Mary Tudor in their great scandal.

58. Archduchess Margaret of Austria as widow, by Conrad Meit.

Brandon would have known Princess Mary from a young age and, in the claustrophobic atmosphere of Henry's court, their mutual admiration would have been known to everyone, including her brother. But no one expected that the commoner duke and the royal princess would go further than mutual regard and chivalrous flirtation. Mary was far too valuable an asset to the king to throw away on a marital alliance without political strategic advantage.

Mary Tudor, (1496–1533).[30] Mary was the fourth child of Henry VII and Elizabeth of York, born at Sheen Palace in early 1496. At age six, she was given her own household, complete with 'a staff of gentlewomen assigned to wait upon her', a schoolmaster and a physician. She learnt French, Latin, music, dancing and embroidery. She played the lute and clavichord with expertise. She was a quick, clever child who learnt fast. Erasmus was impressed with her accomplishments when he visited her in the nursery when she was four. As children, Mary and her brother Henry shared a close friendship and he remained deeply attached to her all her life, even when she defied him. He named his first surviving child, the future Mary I, in her honour.

Mary's health was fragile and she suffered bouts of illness, which included recurrent episodes of severe pain in her side, increasingly troublesome as she grew to adulthood. She was often treated by a court physician Master Peter. Her ill health did not mar her looks. She was regarded as one of the most beautiful princesses in Europe. Erasmus commented 'Nature never formed anything more beautiful.' Mary was slight with the pale golden-red hair colouring characteristic of the Tudors, shared with her brother Henry and his daughter Elizabeth I. Upon her arrival in France, Mary was described as being 'handsome and well favoured, were not her eyes and eyebrows too light;

she is slight, rather than defective from corpulence, and conducts herself with so much grace, and has such good manners, that for her age of 18 years—and she does not look more—she is a paradise.' Mary was described as 'very lively', one nobleman noting '[she] is never still.' She was also said to be cheerful and affable; upon meeting her future husband king Louis for the first time, she blew him a kiss.

Henry's sister grew up knowing that her brother would use her for a marital alliance between England and some foreign monarchy. It was her destiny to marry whom Henry chose. Mary was betrothed in 1507 to Philip of Castile's young son Charles, who would become Holy Roman Emperor. Throughout her teenage years Mary expected to marry Charles, although they never met. But in July 1514 eighteen year old Mary, under instructions from her brother, and on Wolsey's advice, formally renounced her marriage with Charles of Castile. The political tides were changing and England no longer sought a Spanish alliance. Holy Roman Emperor Maximilian I had been making excuses as to why his grandson could not marry Mary and Henry grew tired of waiting. Within a matter of months a new treaty had been signed between England and France and the marriage of Mary and the French king Louis XII was a key part of the deal.

It is one thing for an eighteen year old woman to contemplate marriage with another teenager, as Charles of Castile was, quite another to find herself allied to Louis, a sickly ageing fifty-two year old suffering from gout and numerous other ailments. And she was already in love with Charles Brandon. Louis was delighted at his prize, having heard nothing but good things about the English princess and when they finally met was even more enchanted with his 'Nymph from Heaven'. As was the custom Mary and Louis married by proxy first in an elaborate, rather comical ceremony presided over by William Warham, Archbishop of Canterbury. Louis XII had his own proxy wedding one month later, on 14th September.

Mary did not leave England until the end of September 1514, not before Charles had staged a showy jousting tournament in honour of the marriage. Her journey from Dover to France was delayed due to terrible storms. While she was detained at Dover, with her brother for company, Mary extracted a casual promise from Henry that if Louis died before her and she was childless, Henry would allow her to marry the man of her choice, 'to marry where my mynd is'. She said if the king broke his promise, then she would enter a convent. If she took the veil, Henry VIII would lose control over her dower and any financial benefits from her remarrying and he wouldn't want that to happen.

Henry knew very well she was thinking of Charles but promised anyway, no doubt thinking if he indulged her it would all blow over. Charles' previous romantic enthusiasms had not lasted long.

Mary married Louis XII of France at Abbeville in October 1514. She was accompanied to France by four English women, one of whom was Ann Boleyn. Shortly after the marriage, Louis despatched these Englishwomen back to England and substituted French women. Mary was left isolated without women friends although Charles was not far away, indeed he was very much present. Nevertheless she tried hard to please Louis and she did. Despite two previous marriages, Louis had no living sons, and sought to produce one. He boasted that on their wedding night he had 'thrice crossed the river and would he have done more had he desired'.[31] The public required confirmation of consummation. Curiously, Charles Brandon having accompanied Mary to France, stayed on at the French court until December making himself generally popular with Louis, then returning to the English court for a week or two. A letter carried by Charles from Louis to Henry in December suggests the French king at least had no suspicion of Brandon and Mary's affair.

> (You) have heard by the said bearer of the joy you had in hearing from my Cousin, the Duke of Suffolk, of my news, and the content which I have in the Queen, my wife, your good sister, who has so conducted herself towards me, and continues so to do daily, that I know not how I can sufficiently praise and express my delight in her. More and more I love, honour and hold her dear; therefore you may be certain that she is, and ever will continue to be, treated in such a manner as shall content her, and you likewise. And as touching the reception and good cheer which my Cousin of Suffolk has told you I have made him, there is no need, my good Brother, Cousin, and Comrade, to give me thanks; for I beseech you to believe that besides what I know of the place he holds about you and the love you bear him, his virtues, honesty, and good qualities merit that he should be honoured and received as much for what he is, as for your own honour; so I have made him the best cheer that was in my power.[32]

Three days after he wrote this letter, Louis died, less than three months after marrying Mary. Salacious gossip sniggered he was worn out by his exertions in the bedchamber, but more likely he died from complications of gout. Following Louis's death, the new king Francis I thought he should arrange a second marriage for the beautiful widow, he did not want to send back Mary's considerable dowry. Henry was adamant that she must come home and immediately sent Charles back to France to fetch her. Henry actually warned Charles not to propose marriage to his sister before he set off. So Henry knew very well what Charles had in mind, and indeed was putting Charles in a position to do the very thing he forbade.

I think we have to be very careful in interpreting why Henry did this. He may simply not have believed that Charles and Mary would defy him but this author does not think this is psychologically reasonable. Henry knew that his own council, not wishing to see Charles Brandon gain further power at court, also opposed the match. But Henry may well have been playing a long game with his friend, realising he could claw back the investment he had put into Mary and in reality not being personally deeply offended that his best friend would become his brother-in-law. Brandon's comparatively lowly birth would not have troubled Henry. His key councillors Wolsey, and later Thomas Cromwell and Thomas More, were all men of much more humble origins. Henry would have been more troubled by the loss of his sister as a strategic pawn and the possible loss of her jewellery, plate and dowry.

Charles and Mary both realised they had to act quickly if they wanted to marry and gambled correctly that Henry's affection for them would eventually smooth over his hurt feelings. They wed in secret at the Hotel de Clugny sometime before 3 March 1515 in the presence of just ten people. Technically, this was treason as Charles Brandon had married a royal princess without the king's consent. Henry was apparently outraged, but perhaps only apparently. The Privy Council urged that Charles be imprisoned or executed. Charles wrote pleading letters saying the marriage was at Mary's begging, he 'never saw a woman so weep' until he acquiesced to her wishes. Brandon wrote to Thomas Wolsey for advice, who replied that he should beg forgiveness, be patient and accept the fine likely to be imposed. Mary also wrote to sympathetic Wolsey to ask him to intervene on her behalf, which he agreed. Henry's immediate rage abated quite quickly. The pair married openly in a second ceremony in Paris. Henry met the pair of them at Birling in Kent as they travelled home.

Surely the king wanted the world to think he was furious with the pair but in reality he was not personally very upset. His apparent rage may have been contrived to convince a restive council. But he imposed an extraordinarily heavy fine of £24,000 on the couple, a debt that would constrain the Brandon coffers for the rest of Charles' life.[33] This made the whole business look convincing to the court. The sum was to be paid to the king in yearly installments of £1,000, as well as the whole of Mary's dowry from Louis XII of £200,000, together with the gold plate and jewels Louis had given or promised her. The £24,000, approximately equivalent to £7,200,000 today, was later reduced by the king but Charles was still conveniently in Henry's debt for many years.

Henry accepted the marriage as a '*fait accompli*' and staged an official third grand wedding ceremony on 13 May 1515 at Greenwich Palace. Eventually in 1528, Charles secured a papal bull legitimizing the marriage. The famous 'marriage portrait' of Charles and Mary (59. p. 202) may not have been done for their wedding at all, but painted in the early 1520s. Probably by Jan Gossaerts, also known as Jan Mabuse, there are two versions of the picture, one at Woburn Abbey and one in the collection of the earl of Yarborough. It is loaded with symbolism but no one has quite established what the symbols represent. The figures bear only a passing resemblance to the real people, Mary was a gingerish blonde rather than the fashionable brunette shown in the portrait and both seem a little wooden. It seems to be an elaborate visual pun showing the 'downgrade' of her status. Instead of holding an orb/globe she is holding a globe artichoke, perhaps indicating her realm is considerably less than it was. She is now the ruler of a mere physical estate representing Charles' land holdings in England, rather than the realm she previously ruled. And instead of holding a sceptre, she is holding her husband's hand. But artichokes were also thought to be aphrodisiac. Really we have no idea what was in the artist's mind.

Charles and Mary come to Wingfield Castle. When they first returned to England as a married couple, it is thought the Brandons stayed at Suffolk House in Southwark, which became their London home when not at court. It was lavishly furnished. Charles and Mary needed a suitably luxurious base to call home in the lands of his *nomen territorialis,* Suffolk. Having acquired the title, Charles needed the de la Pole estates to provide him with an income and suitable trappings of a dukedom for his new duchess and to establish a foothold on power in East Anglia. Even while still in France he began buying up the old de la Pole manors. Brandon's own Chancellor Oliver Pole and his attorney Humphrey Wingfield were both distantly related to the de la Poles and would have been chosen as acceptable to Suffolk people. In early 1515 Henry granted Charles the manors that he had still under his control but he had to buy out many of those who had been granted reversionary rights.

Brandon eventually came into possession of the lands still held by Edmund de la Pole's rather competent widow Margaret and the majority of the de la Pole former manors. But the people of East Anglia did not know either Charles or Mary and the couple realised that if they were to replace the de la

59. Charles Brandon and Mary Tudor, with artichoke, c1520s.

Pole dynasty as regional magnates they needed local people's support. For two years they conducted an extended 'progress' round Norfolk and Suffolk visiting grand estates and lesser gentry as they went. Mary was the glamorous draw; he followed in her wake as consort. Cambridge sent gifts of pike and tench in 1515. They received even more generous gifts in Norwich and Eye, and were entertained for three days in Yarmouth. They re-established good relations with the king quite quickly and both were frequently at court. Charles and Henry jousted together again as leading opponents. Mary had always been close to the queen, Catherine of Aragon, and spent time in her company.

Gradually, Charles won more commissions and grants in East Anglia, although it was difficult to win local hearts while Richard de la Pole was still alive. While Mary was a natural charmer, Charles worked hard at it. He took into his own retinue some lesser gentry who had served the de la Pole family. The Tyrell and Grimston families took on roles in which they had traditionally served the former magnates. The king had an interest in Brandon's ability to gather and maintain loyalty locally because of the continuing threat of Richard being the living focus of Yorkist aspirations.

The years at Wingfield. Even after her second marriage, Mary was normally referred to at the English court as 'the French Queen', whereas the French referred to her as 'The White Queen' or *la Reine Blanche*, because she had worn the traditional white during her short widowhood before marrying Charles. She was not known as the duchess of Suffolk in her lifetime. In the early years of their marriage, they certainly used Wingfield Castle as a base but like other noble families, travelled extensively round their estates, staying only a few weeks at each location. Mary was a prolific letter writer and dated each with the date and place of composition. It is impossible to be exact about how much they used Wingfield, not all her letters have been preserved but there are at least two surviving letters written by Mary while staying at Wingfield Castle.[34]

Mary had her first baby, a son called Henry, in March 1516 in Bath Place, London, a house owned by Wolsey although the child was baptised at Suffolk Place. In summer 1516 the Brandons were staying at Butley Priory, one of their favourite places in Suffolk, which they used most years as a place to enjoy the country. A visit to the woods and countryside round the surviving gateway will allow the reader to comprehend exactly why they loved it. Mary was a favourite with the Prior, who referred to her as *"excellentissima domina Maria Francorum regina venustissima" (excellent Lady Mary of France, most attractive queen).*

Perhaps one of the couple's happiest times were the picnics they enjoyed in the grounds at Butley in summer 1527. Mary spent a month there and, the following summer, she returned for two months and took her furnishings with her. Brandon joined her at Butley and the monk-chronicler there noted that they were enjoying foxhunts and picnics in this long beautiful summer. One hot August evening, Mary ordered her supper to be laid out in a shady part the garden on the east side of the gatehouse. This she so enjoyed that picnic suppers in the priory gardens became a regular feature of her stays. Brother Nicholas noted in his diary that the royal party were overtaken by a tremendous storm one evening and had to rush to the church for shelter.[35]

The Brandons and their entourage often travelled to their manor at Donnington in Berkshire and also regularly sojourned at the manor of Letheringham Hall, Suffolk, the family home of Sir Anthony Wingfield, Henry's Vice-Chamberlain and later Comptroller of the Household to Edward VI. The Wingfields were faithful friends to the Brandons. The Brandons second child, Frances, was born unexpectedly at Hatfield while Mary was making her way on a pre-confinement pilgrimage to the shrine at Walsingham in Norfolk.

A splendid new home at Westhorpe. But while Wingfield was a useful base in the early years of their marriage, it was neither grand enough nor modern enough for the style the Brandons aspired to, although they continued to stay at Wingfield from time to time until at least 1530 on their regular progresses round their estates. The couple began to plan a very grand home at Westhorpe Hall to replace the old manor, which they had acquired as part of the de la Pole estates in 1515. It took several years to build the house at Westhorpe and it was probably finished about 1523.[36] Its magnificence and importance is indicated by the scale of the expenditure alone. Brandon claimed it cost him £12,000, a huge sum for the time. The approach led through a three-

60. Butley Priory, Suffolk, the remaining Gatehouse.

storey gatehouse with a brick bridge crossing a dry moat. The bridge itself was elaborately decorated with stone pillars mounted with stone beasts. The palace was encrusted with fashionable terracotta plaques and battlements, ornate chimneys and a statue of Hercules.[37] The gardens were laid out in the French style. The couple enjoyed hunting and Charles stocked the park at Westhorpe with red and fallow deer. Westhorpe Hall was demolished in the late 1760s.

Only a few buildings remain and now form part of a care home. The bridge over the huge moat is however still visible.

The Brandons built a second mansion at Henham near the Suffolk coast in the parish of Blythburgh. Originally the lands at Henham were hunting grounds for the de la Poles where they built a timber-framed structure. Charles and Mary Brandon built a new mansion house 200 yards (180 m) in front of the old medieval timber-framed structure, said to be one of the finest Tudor buildings of its age. The house was flanked on two sides by extensive walled gardens and incorporated a large courtyard. It was replaced centuries later by a fine Georgian mansion but that was later demolished.[38] The park is now well known for an annual music festival.

The former queen attracted more attention in Suffolk than a mere duke. Every year Mary held a kind of public court at the annual fair in Bury St Edmunds. She sat in a tent with her retinue and musicians and received a stream of admirers. By being out and about in the vicinity, Mary gathered a devoted local following. Charles Brandon's role locally took second place to his role as a courtier and over the years it is clear he spent increasing amounts of time away from Mary and their children. Charles was busy at court, meeting foreign dignitaries, sitting in Star Chamber and attending the king's council meetings. In the mid 1520s, Charles was charged with putting down the civil unrest that broke out in various parts of the country, such as the rising in Essex and Suffolk known as the Amicable Grace. Mary spent much of her time at Westhorpe or visiting around the county and retired from court.

Mary's health was declining. The episodes of pain in her side worsened and an ague like shivering fever debilitated her. But there was another upsetting matter to keep Mary away from court. She did not approve of her brother's relationship with Anne Boleyn. Mary was close to Henry VIII's first wife, Catherine of Aragon, who Mary had known since Catherine had first arrived in England in 1502. They were sisters-in-law, first through Catherine's short-lived marriage to Prince Arthur, and then through her marriage to Henry VIII. There is ample evidence they enjoyed each other's company.

Mary knew Anne Boleyn well enough as a lady from her own retinue; she was furious to see Catherine cast aside for ambitious Anne. In the late 1520s, relations between Henry VIII and his sister became seriously strained when she opposed his attempt to obtain an annulment. In March 1532, Venetian Ambassador Carlo Capello wrote of an incident where 'one of the chief gentlemen in the service of the said duke of Norfolk, with twenty followers, assaulted and killed in the sanctuary of Westminster Sir William Pennington chief gentleman and kinsman of the duke of Suffolk. In consequence of this, the whole Court was in an uproar. Though it was said to be caused by a private quarrel, Capello was 'assured it was owing to opprobrious language uttered against Madam Anne by His Majesty's sister, the duchess of Suffolk, Queen Dowager of France.'

Mary, the French queen dies. Mary's health deteriorated further in 1532 and she retreated to Westhorpe. Charles last visited her in May 1533. Further visits were prevented ostensibly because he was preparing the coronation of Anne Boleyn. Charles had no more fondness for Anne than his wife but duty to Henry came first. Mary died at Westhorpe on 25 June 1533. Her embalmed body lay in the chapel for almost a month whilst her chaplains sang daily mass. After a final mass on 21 July, her coffin left Westhorpe and processed to Bury St Edmunds Abbey. One report said her entrails were buried in the chancel of the church at Westhorpe but if so there remains no local record.

A delegation from France joined the gathering for the lavish funeral ceremony. Neither Charles nor the king attended the funeral, her daughter Frances was the chief mourner, accompanied by her husband and siblings and Charles' two daughters by Anne Browne. It was not unusual for a spouse to be absent from a funeral. Both Charles and Henry attended a requiem mass held afterwards at Westminster Abbey. Five years later, when the abbey at Bury was closed in Henry's great Dissolution, Mary's body was removed to nearby St Mary's Church, where she lies still. In 1784, her remains were disinterred, her coffin opened, and locks of her hair were taken by Horace Walpole, the duchess of Portland and several others. One of these locks of hair found its way to the Moyse's Hall museum in Bury St Edmunds, where a locket containing Mary 's hair is still on display. It was reported that when Mary's coffin was opened her hair was some two feet long and a 'reddish-gold' colour. It is now faded but a strangely moving relic of this lovely woman.

Mary and Charles had four children, two daughters and two sons, brought up mainly at Westhorpe Hall. Their older son Henry Brandon (1516–1522) was only six when he died. A second Henry was born a year later in 1523 but he died a year after his mother in 1534. Their two daughters lived to be adults. Frances (1517–1559) married Henry Grey, marquess of Dorset and would become the mother of the 'nine days queen' Lady Jane Grey. Frances' husband was executed shortly after his daughter. Frances later found happiness, marrying for love like her mother, by wedding a young yeoman, Adrian Stokes, who was her master of horse and later a member of parliament.

Charles and Mary's second daughter Eleanor (1519-1547) married Henry Clifford, earl of Cumberland.

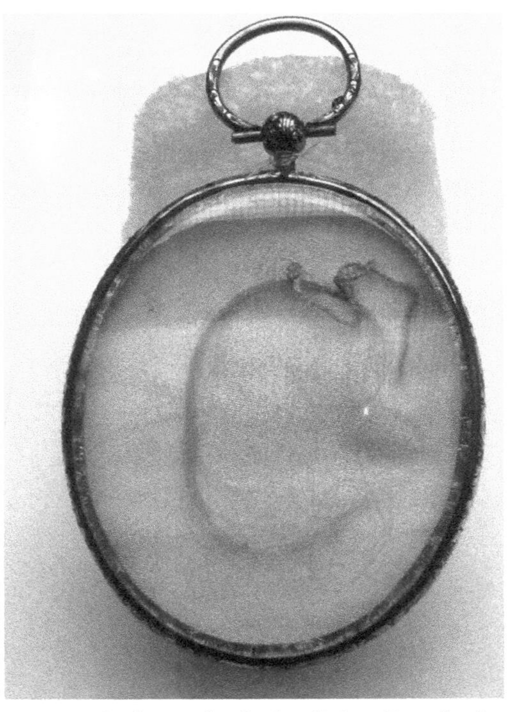

61. A locket with a lock of Mary Brandon's hair.

Brandon was still in debt to the king. Though his major debts had been cancelled, he had lost a good deal of Mary's income on her death. The duke lost all his Oxfordshire and Berkshire estates and Suffolk Place in Southwark. Three months after Mary's death in September 1533, forty-nine year old Charles married his fourteen year old ward Catherine Willoughby, daughter of late Lord Willoughby of Eresby. Charles had paid £2266 13s 4d (c £860 thousand today) for her wardship, purchased originally from the Crown in 1528 with the idea of marrying her to his son Henry. Catherine had thirty large estates in Lincolnshire and some in Norfolk and Suffolk too. She was the asset Charles needed to top up his coffers. There was talk about the unseemly haste of the marriage but it seems to have been a successful one. Catherine turned into an effective and personable duchess and gave Charles two sons, yet another Henry and a second Charles. They are now most famous for their exquisitely pretty childhood portraits by Hans Holbein the Younger.

Charles Brandon gives up his Suffolk estates to become a Lincolnshire magnate. Wingfield Castle is exchanged with dozens of other manors and Wingfield reverts to the Crown.

Brandon was brought back to the forefront of national affairs by the outbreak of the Lincolnshire revolt in October 1536 and the ensuing Pilgrimage of Grace, the rebellion across the north against Henry's break with Rome and the dissolution of religious houses. Appointed the king's lieutenant to suppress the Lincolnshire rebels in 1536, he advanced fast from Suffolk to Stamford, gathering troops as he went. Although by the time he was ready to fight the rebels had disbanded, he stayed on in Lincolnshire to put down any further rebellion. By all accounts Charles negotiated quite skilfully with some rebels to leave the affray but most rebels were viciously punished by Henry and by the duke of Norfolk.

The king commanded Charles to move his home to Lincolnshire and in April 1537 gave him Tattershall Castle as an imposing base.[39] By late summer Brandon was preparing for a wholesale exchange of his East Anglian estates, including Wingfield Castle and its associated manors. 'Wyngfeld *alias* Wynkfeld' and other de la Pole estates came back under the control of the Crown in 1537-8.[40]

62. Portraits of Catherine Willoughby, duchess of Suffolk, flanked by her two young sons, left Henry and right Charles, all by Hans Holbein the Younger c 1540-41.

This is just one of dozens of entries in the official record of exchanges of manors. He also gave up the lands of Leiston Abbey and Eye Priory granted to him in April 1537 in reward for his service against the rebels, for monastic property and other Crown land in Lincolnshire and elsewhere.[41] Negotiations took until September 1538 but the result was to make Suffolk indisputably the greatest landowner in Lincolnshire, with a dense belt of estates spread across the centre of the county. The lands he had been granted in other counties he sold off, ready to invest in more Lincolnshire land as it became available in the years ahead. Effective lordship also required the duke's presence, and after spending May and June 1537 in East Anglia he spent much time in Lincolnshire.

What was happening to Wingfield Castle buildings? By 1537 the castle had become a minor secondary home for the Brandons and when Charles moved to Lincolnshire it was snaffled by the Crown and sat in the king's control until Henry decided whether to sell it or give it to someone else. Whenever the Crown took over property they invested time in documenting its extent and expenditure. Wingfield was no exception and accounts survive for the Wingfield Frumbald's manor and seven other manors associated with the property for the period between 1538 and 1547.[42]

63. Charles Brandon, duke of Suffolk c 1541, Hans Holbein the Younger.

There are reports on the web that an angry Henry VIII, after Richard de la Pole's death in 1525, had the east and north walls of the castle demolished. Liddiard on the other hand has suggested the demolition and asset stripping may have taken place before Brandon took over the castle. Given that the castle was always used by Charles Brandon as one of his bases in Suffolk and one of Mary's letters from Wingfield was dated as late as 1530, it does not make sense to have wasted money, time and effort in pulling some of the building down. Surely it was because the old medieval castle was so old fashioned and uncomfortable that they decided to build Westhorpe and Henham in the extravagant modern Tudor taste but it seems unlikely that Wingfield would have been partly destroyed.

That still leaves the important question of when the medieval buildings were removed and the north and east walls dismantled. Liddiard has suggested that the barn inside the curtain wall could only have been constructed after the demolition of the south and east walls.[43] But this only holds if the barn, which though medieval in appearance and construction stands on nineteenth century footings, was imported from outside the main curtilage of the castle. If the barn was built from medieval oak timbers re-used from the westerly medieval range taken down when the new Tudor house was constructed, it could have been built before the dilapidations of the curtain wall. This will be considered further when we come to the new Tudor house built by the Jerninghams.

But Wingfield Castle had been only intermittently occupied for more than a decade when the Brandons left and now needed a new interested owner to take it on and lavish some care on it. The castle found that person in Sir Henry

Jerningham, a very different character from Charles Brandon but one who played a fleeting but important role on the national stage.

Notes

1 The story was first made into a novel by Caskoden, E. (a pseudonym for Charles Major), 1898, *When Knighthood Was in Flower*, Bowen-Merrill, New York.

2 The Sword and The Rose. Walt Disney, 1953. Available online at many sites, including https://www.justwatch.com/us/movie/the-sword-and-the-rose.

3 Lander, J. R., 1961, Attainder and Forfeiture, 1453 to 1509. *The Historical Journal Vol. 4*, pp. 119-151.

4 1468 (Lincoln's attainder later retrieved) 23 Suffolk Estates seized. Act concerning Edmund de la Pole, with writ Parliamentary Rolls VI, 474-477 TNA E175/5; 1504-1505 Norfolk property, de la Pole, Edmund, earl of Suffolk, attainted. Norfolk TNA E 150/612/2; 1504-1505 Norfolk property, Edmund de la Pole, earl of Suffolk attainted Landed Estates TNA C142/23/229 and TNA C142/23/240; Sep 1504-29 Sep 1505 Norfolk and Suffolk properties taken by the Crown listed in the Compotus of Sir Robert Lovell, kt, the King's Receiver-General for the demesnes, manors, lands and tenements lately of Edmund de la Pole, late earl of Suffolk. Included property in Burgh-next-Aylsham (Norfolk); Stockton (Norfolk); Lowestoft; Lothingland East Leet, North Leet and South Leet; Gorleston (Norfolk); Mutfold; Eye; Huntingfield; Haughley; Westhorpe; Benhall; Hempnall in Cotton; Braiseworth; Nedging; Cawston (Norfolk); Saxlingham (Norfolk); Kettlestone (Norfolk); Sedgeford, Ringstead and Moundevilles (Norfolk); East Ruston (Norfolk); Hundreds of Hartismere and Stow; Combs and Swannes; Thorndon, Saxmundham and Wattisfield; Virlies [in Sternfield]; Winston; Walsham (Norfolk); and Orford Compotus of Sir Robert Lovell, kt, the King's Receiver-General. September 1504-29, September 1505 Suffolk Record Office Ipswich (SROI) HA411/5/2/1/429; 1506-1507 Suffolk property, Edmund de la Pole, earl of Suffolk, attainted, Suffolk TNA C 142/23/272, C 142/23/274 and C142/23/275; 1507-1508 Suffolk property, Edmund de la Pole, earl of Suffolk, attainted, Suffolk TNA C142/23/267, C142/23/268, C142/23/289; Suffolk TNA C142/23/303 and C142/23/317, TNA SC 6/HENVIII/345; Norfolk TNA E 150/612/2; 1519-1520 Oxford, Berks and Somerset property: Kidlington and other places, possessions of the Edmund de la pole, late earl of Suffolk TNA SC 6/HENVIII/6911.

5 Brewer, J. S. (ed), 1862, *Letters and Papers, Foreign and Domestic, of the Reign of Henry VIII, Volume I part 2*, p. 669, British History Online www.british-history.ac.uk/letters-papers-hen8/vol1.

6 Challis, C. E., 1975, Mint Officials and Moneyers of the Tudor Period, *Journal of the British Numismatic Society Vol 44*, pp. 51-76.

7 Blomefield, F., 1805, 'Hundred of Diss: Burston', in *An Essay Towards A Topographical History of the County of Norfolk: Volume I*, London, pp. 125-130. British History Online http://www.british-history.ac.uk/topographical-hist-norfolk/vol1/pp125-130 [accessed 10 December 2019] and grant of Brockdish Hall manor, *Letters and Papers, Foreign and Domestic, Henry VIII, Volume I*, 1509-1514, 1920, Brewer, J. S. (ed), London, British History Online http://www.british-history.ac.uk/letters-papers-hen8/vol1 [accessed 27 December 2019].

8 Beaumont, G F., 1890, *History of Coggeshall in Essex*, printed Potter, London. Brockdish connection mentioned in Blomefield, F., 1805, 'Hundred of Diss: Burston', in *An Essay Towards A Topographical History of the County of Norfolk: Volume I*, London, pp. 125-130. British History Online http://www.british-history.ac.uk/topographical-hist-norfolk/vol1/pp125-130 [accessed 3 November 2020] and Will of Sir John Sharpe 12 February 1519 TNA PROB 11/19/204.

9 Wriothesley, Thomas 1509 The Death of King Henry VII, British Library, Add. MS 45131, f 54 The dying King is in his Privy Chamber, surrounded by his most intimate courtiers and household. John Sharpe's arms are depicted below (three rooks' heads). Drawn contemporaneously from witness accounts by the courtier Sir Thomas Wriothesley.

10 Brewer, J. S., 2015, *Letters and Papers Foreign and Domestic, of the Reign of Henry VIII Vol 3*, Cambridge University Press, Cambridge, p. 864.

11 Copy of a grant by Henry VIII to Anne Howard of the castle and manor of Wingfield, the manors of Syleham, Veales, Stradbroke, Frostenden, and Creeting St. Olave in Suffolk, and the manors of Costessey and Stockton

in Norfolk, 1510. Jerningham Collection, Norfolk Record Office JER 242, 55X1 Historical Manuscripts Commission reference 24.

12 Copy grant by Henry VIII to Thomas Howard Kt. and Anne his wife, daughter of Edward IV of manors of Wingfield, Silam als. Sileham and Veales, Stradbrooke [co. Suffolk]; Frostenden and Cretynge St. Olave, Costessey and Stockton [co. Norfolk]; Cudlington, Lewkenor and Nuneham Courtney [co. Oxford]; Langley and West Bradley [co. Berks.]; Gresthorp, Northleyston and Normanton [co. Notts.]; Bliburgh and Westwoode [co. Lincoln]; Faxfleete als. Flaxflete [co. Yorks.]; Norton Subtus Hampden [co. Somerset]; Wilmyndon [co. Kent]; and Evington [co. Leics.] 1510, Staffordshire County Record Office D641/3/A/1/1.

13 Counterpart indenture, 1 July 1510, 2 Henry VIII, being the memorandum of an agreement. Signed Thomas Howard, Anne Howard. Memorandum endorsed of enrolment in the Bench, in the first roll of Charters, etc. Easter Term, 3 Henry VIII, Suffolk etc, Letters and Papers, Henry VIII, vol. I, no. 1129.TNA E 40/13566

14 Ibid.

15 Vokes, S. E., 1988, *The Early Career of Thomas Lord Howard, earl of Surrey and 3rd duke of Norfolk*. PhD thesis, University of Hull.

16 Head, D. M., 1995, T*he Ebbs and Flow of Fortune, the Life of Thomas Howard, 3rd duke of Norfolk*. University of Georgia Press, Athens.

17 Bailey, M., 2009, Technology and the growth of Textile Manufacture in Medieval Suffolk, J*ournal of the Suffolk Institute of Archeology and History Vol XLII, Part 1*, pp. 13-20.

18 Amor, N., 2016, *From Wool to Cloth, the Triumph of the Suffolk Clothier*, Bungay.

19 Bailey, M., 2007, *Medieval Suffolk, an Economic and Social History,* Boydell Press, Woodbridge, Chapter 12, Conclusion, pp. 290-302.

20 Robinson, J. M., 1982, The Dukes of Norfolk, a Quincentennial history, Chapter 3, *The 3rd Duke of Norfolk*, pp. 23-40.

21 Letters patent of inspeximus 21 June 1515. Henry VIII inspects his own assent to a petition of the Commons asking for confirmation of a grant made to Charles Brandon duke of Suffolk of all the lands formerly of Edmund de la Pole duke of Suffolk including the manors of Claxton and Hillington co. Norfolk and the reversion of Huntingfield, Suffolk. Lincolnshire Archives 2ANC3/B/1.

22 Ibid. 15, p. 156

23 Ibid. p. 157

24 Ibid.

25 Gunn, S. J. , 1988, *Charles Brandon, Duke of Suffolk: c.1484-1545*, Blackwell; Borman, T., 2018, *Henry VIII and the Men who Made Him*, Hodder and Stoughton, London.

26 Gairdner, J., 1904, *The Paston Letters, 1422-1509. Vol 6,* Chatto and Windus.

27 Smith, T. P., Watson, B., Martin, C. and Williams, D., 2014. Suffolk Place, Southwark London: a Tudor palace and its terracotta architectural decoration, *Post-Medieval Archaeology 48*, pp. 90–132.

28 *Cracroft's Peerage*, online at http://www.cracroftspeerage.co.uk/online/content/suffolk1514.htm.

29 Gunn, S. J., 2015, Brandon, Charles, first duke of Suffolk, *Oxford Dictionary of National Biography*, online at https://doi.org/10.1093/ref:odnb/3260.

30 The story of Mary Tudor is well covered in in several authoritative texts. Loades, D., 2008, Mary I (1496–1533) *Oxford Dictionary of National Biography*, online at https://doi.org/10.1093/ref:odnb/18251, 03 January 2008; Richardson, W. C., 1970, *Mary Tudor: the white queen*; Sadlack, E., 2001, *The French Queen's letters*, Palgrave Macmillan, London and Bryson, S., 2018, *La Reine Blanche: Mary Tudor, a life in letters*, Amberley, Stroud.

31 Visentini, F. (ed), 1902 *Sanuto, Marino Diarii, Vol XIX*. CPSV 508.

32 Letter Louis XII to Henry VIII, *Ellis' Original Letters, Second Series, Vol. I.,* Paris, December 28, p. 1514.

33 Debts to be paid to king by Brandon and Mary 1517. Indenture of agreement King Henry VIII, agrees with Mary the French queen, his sister and Charles Brandon duke of Suffolk, her husband. Lincolnshire Archives Ref 2ANC3/B/2/.

34 Bryson, S., 2018, *La Reine Blanche: Mary Tudor, a life in letters*. Amberley, Stroud. Kindle ed'n 3 August 1525 Mary to Wolsey asking for help with restoration of French pension denied her and Brandon since French

war, loc. 3745. Sadlack, E., 2001, *The French Queen's letters*, Palgrave Macmillan. August 1528 Travels London to Wingfield (Sadlack location 4321) then to Butley Abbey between September and November. Writes to Montmorency from Wingfield Castle in August 1528. SP1/59/126 and BNF MSS Francais 2932 folio 3 and 3002, fol 48r.

35 Butley Priory www.butleypriory/history and Sadlack, 2001, fn 219.

36 Gunn, S. J. and Lindley, P. G., 1988, Charles Brandon's Westhorpe: an Early Tudor Courtyard House in *Suffolk, Archaeological Journal Vol 145*, pp. 272-289, published online 22 Dec 2014 https://www.tandfonline.com/doi/citedby/10.1080/00665983.1988.11077852?scroll=top&needAccess=true.

37 Anderson, S., Carr, R. D., Park, J., Holden, S., 2003, Architectural Terracotta from Westhorpe Hall, *Archaeological Journal 160*, pp. 125-159.

38 Henham Park history, see Historic England https://historicengland.org.uk/listing/the-list/list-entry/1000557.

39 Gift of Tattershall castle and elsewhere in Letters and Papers, Foreign and Domestic, Henry VIII, Volume 12 Part 1, January-May 1537, ed. James Gairdner (London, 1890), Henry VIII, April 1537, 26-30, pp 477-516. British History Online http://www.british-history.ac.uk/letters-papers-hen8/vol12/no1/pp477-516 [accessed 6 February 2020].

40 To the Crown, by Charles duke of Suffolk by indenture 30 Sept. 30 Hen. VIII. of the honor of Eye alias Eya, the manors and lordships of Eye ...and other lands, &c. in said cos.); Gairdner, J. and Brodie R.H. (eds), 1894, Letters and Papers: March 1539, pp. 26-31', in *Letters and Papers, Foreign and Domestic, Henry VIII, Volume 14 Part 1, January-July 1539*, London, pp. 239-264. British History Online http://www.british-history.ac.uk/letters-papers-hen8/vol14/no1/pp239-264 [accessed 25 January 2019].

41 Ibid.

42 Wingfield Frumbald's manor. 1538-1547. Minister's accounts, with other manors TNA SC 6/HENVIII/3372-3378.

43 Liddiard, R., 2015, Reconstructing Wingfield Castle, pp. 77-95 in Bloore P. and Martin, E. (eds), *Wingfield College and its Patrons*, Boydell Press, Woodbridge.

Wingfield Castle reborn, 1553–1624

The Jerningham Family

Jesus Christ both God and Man
Love they servant Jernegan[1]

The Tudor house that today surprises and delights the visitor to Wingfield Castle was built by Henry Jerningham in the mid-sixteenth century. Sometimes called 'Jerningham House', the new building replaced the original west range of the medieval castle, although some of the older building was incorporated. Keeping the curtain wall and building something modern inside was the perfect way for the new owner to stamp his mark on the place but retain that traditional Englishmen's castle for his home. Henry Jerningham was a courtier who became a man of action when required. His success brought him great rewards and the most significant early recognition of royal favour was the gift of Wingfield Castle and its estates.

64. Jerningham House, Wingfield Castle, the east façade.

Jerningham and his wife Frances were granted Wingfield Castle on 28 December 1553, by a grateful Queen Mary I.[2]

> Grant in fee to the queen's councilor Henry Jernyngham, knight, Vice-Chamberlain to the Household, in consideration of his service at Framhingham (sic) co. Suffolk, in the suppression of the rebellion of John, late Duke of Northumberland, and of other services daily rendered, and to Frances his wife of the manor, mansion and castle of Wingfield alias Olde Wingfield, co Suffolk, the park and the advowson of the rectory of the same, two crofts of land called 'Helwarde's croftes' in Wingfield late in the tenure of Henry Wingfield, and all the lands and liberties in Wingfield or elsewhere belonging to the said manor and

* Photograph from a series commissioned by Graham Baron Ash after restoration of Wingfield Castle in 1945.

castle.

Yearly value £35 2s 11d. besides the park.

To hold to the said Henry and Frances and the heirs and assigns of Henry in chief by service of one twentieth of a knight's fee.

Issues since Michaelmas last. These letters without fine or fee.

The antiquarian Walter Copinger's late Victorian eight volume 'bible', *The Manors of Suffolk*, gives the date of the grant as 1544, which has confused more recent historians and genealogists, not least because his references are incorrect.[3]

The Gap, 1538–1553. There is a troubling gap in the record of fifteen years between the Brandons leaving Suffolk in 1538 and the Jerningham family arriving. The Castle was in the possession of the Crown but we do not know whether the Crown was renting the estate to a tenant during these fifteen years. It would be usual for the Crown to do so, the tenant being supervised by the local Suffolk government receiver. There are receivers' accounts for the Suffolk estates exchanged by Brandon with the Crown for at least some of these years in the National Archive but they do not tell us who the tenants were or how the estates were being administered.[4] There are also some accounts (minister's accounts) for Wingfield Frumbalds Manor with other manors.[5] Steven Gunn has pointed out that following the dissolution of the monasteries, with the sudden acquisition by the Crown of dozens of valuable religious properties in every county, the administrative burden of local county and manorial receivers proved too much for the Crown's supervisory 'court of augmentations' and the accuracy of the records of the court and the preceding Court of General Surveyors is doubtful.[6]

Destruction of the east and north perimeter walls. Next there is the thorny question mentioned in the last chapter of exactly when the castle lost two of its perimeter walls. Liddiard suggests that the castle had been partly dismantled and asset-stripped in the period after the Brandons left.[7] This seems more likely than 1510 or 1525, both dates suggested by earlier observers. The easterly and northern walls of the castle may have been partly dismantled during the years between 1538 and 1553 or simply deteriorated from neglect. Certainly there is no evidence that the majority of easterly, western and northerly ranges survived after the mid-sixteenth century although there was a part of the southern range surviving until the mid-nineteenth century. The long fifteen year gap between Brandon leaving before Jerningham and his family made Wingfield Castle their home would allow ample time for deterioration of the fabric and plunder by local people. Buildings deteriorate very rapidly if their roofs are denuded of tiles, whether by storms or theft and good oak beams could readily be re-used.

No records of the transformation of Wingfield Castle from medieval fortified manor house into Tudor mansion have yet come to light although we can make some intelligent guesses about how and when the new Wingfield was constructed. The author had hoped that some of the voluminous records and papers of the Jerningham family in Norfolk Record Office and Staffordshire County Record Office would shed light on the rebuilding of Wingfield.[8] There are only some minor accounts and other bits and pieces referring to Wingfield, none pertaining to the creation of the new house.

Henry Jerningham, or Jernegan, (1509–1572). Jerningham was a man in his early forties when he acquired Wingfield, seventeen years married with five children. At the Dissolution of the religious houses, Henry and Frances Jerningham had purchased St Olave's Priory, Herringfleet by letters patent, dated 26th January, 1546 'in consideration of £92 8s. 6d.' Jerningham held the advowson of the church there and not long after his marriage, in 1537, he had taken a lease on the manor and rectory of Herringfleet.[9] The Jerninghams created a new home for themselves on the priory site. The remains of the three storey house lie just north of the ruins of the main priory buildings. We know the house survived to be later used by Jerningham's immediate descendants but now only a few ruins remain, although a splendid undercroft of the original priory is still visible.[10]

When Jerningham received the grant of Wingfield he had enough money to invest in something a little more showy than the house at St Olave's. I like to think of Henry Jerningham walking round the medieval Wingfield Castle, a little unloved perhaps since the Brandons left, ruminating about how splendid a new home he could create for his wife Frances and their children. He wanted a stylish but architecturally traditional new Tudor house. And that is what he built. But only four years later, in 1557, his fortunes had been enhanced yet again by the queen's generosity of a far superior, vast estate in Norfolk, the desirable Manor of Costessey (known sometimes as Cotesby but usually then as now, Cossey) with over twenty-five parishes and sub-manors. At Costessey, Jerningham built a Tudor mansion that was to become the family home for more than 360 years. Nevertheless Henry Jerningham kept Wingfield as one of his family homes and it became home to his oldest son, also named Henry, but called Harry, born about 1536. It is likely that Jerningham built the new Wingfield house some time between 1554 and 1557. We know that he did not finish his grander mansion house, Costessey Hall, until 1564 so he may have continued to live at Wingfield and to finish his ambitious project there over the ten years he was resident. Once he had embarked on the Costessey project, he may have lost interest in Wingfield but by then his heir Harry would have been twenty eight years old, possibly recently married and Wingfield would have been an ideal home for the new generation of Jerninghams.

Henry Jerningham became celebrated as one of the handful of Norfolk and Suffolk gentlemen who acted swiftly and effectively to implement Queen Mary I's claim to the throne and destroyed the short-lived reign of Lady Jane Grey. While Catholic Mary lived, Jerningham was the beneficiary of her generosity and gratitude and he and his family, like other Catholic gentry families in East Anglia, were safe from Protestant persecution. When Mary died in 1558 and her sister Elizabeth I came to the throne, Jerningham was dismissed and retired to his estates without fuss for the remainder of his days. His son and grandson continued to use Wingfield Castle as their home and though the third Henry Jerningham acquired a baronetcy, his financial fortunes declined and by the early 1620s he was in dire need of cash and was obliged to sell the castle.

The Jerningham or Jernegan Family. Some of the family called themselves Jerningham, some Jernegan. The consensus now is that the later form is merely a phonetic derivative of the former, used in an ad hoc fashion in some documents. The family finally settled on Jerningham in the late nineteenth century. Some branches of the family, and there were many, used one form, some the other. The family was one of Suffolk's older gentry dynasties. According to family tradition, repeated by the seventeenth-century antiquary John Weever, their ancestors arrived from Denmark in 1030.[11] A version of the story, thought to have been written about 1704, survives in the Norfolk Record Office.[12] Whatever the truth of this tale, the Jerninghams were certainly established in Suffolk by the late twelfth century. Sir Peter Jernegan inherited the manor of Somerleyton in Lothingland through his mother about 1310.[13] The manor covers Somerleyton, Ashby and Herringfleet. In 1314 Sir Peter was granted the patronage of the Augustinian priory of St Olave in the neighbouring parish of Herringfleet.[14] This longstanding connection with St Olave's was to prove useful to our Sir Henry at the Dissolution of the monasteries.

Henry Jerningham's upbringing and court service. Henry was born at the family manor of Somerleyton. The Jerninghams were prolific breeders and their family tree is too daunting to be recorded here. Suffice it to say that Henry's father was Edward Jerningham of Somerleyton, who died in 1515. His mother was Mary Scrope who died in 1548. Both parents had served in the household of Catherine of Aragon.[15] Mary's sister, Margaret Scrope, married Edmund de la Pole, the short-lived duke of Suffolk executed in 1513 who figured in Chapter 11, so Henry Jerningham was loosely connected to the de la Pole dynasty. Henry had three brothers and a sister but also half brothers and sisters through his mother's second marriage to Sir William Kingston, who became Constable of the Tower of London in 1524.

There are several references to Henry Jerningham coming from Huntingfield. His son, also Henry, is recorded in the Cambridge Alumni records as 'doubtless the son of Sir Henry Jernyngham of Huntingfield Hall, Suffolk and of Cossey, Norfolk, Knt.', repeating information from the Victorian antiquarian Alfred Suckling and from eighteenth century Francis Blomefield.[16] These seem to follow on from a reference in the mid-eighteenth century by Collins.[17] Huntingfield Hall, an old de la Pole manor, reverted to the Crown after the death of Edmund de la Pole's widow Margaret and was leased to one Nicholas Arrowsmith. It is possible that Jerningham was a tenant or guest of his aunt Margaret de la Pole in Huntingfield in his young adult days but it seems more likely that Huntingfield was written by mistake for Wingfield in Collins' history and then repeated by Blomefield.

Jerningham, the ambitious young courtier. In 1528, in his late teens, Henry was admitted to the Inner Temple and in the same year became constable of Gloucester Castle, a mainly honorary position as the castle had been largely demolished at the end of the fifteenth century. Round about the same time he entered the service of Henry VIII's older daughter Mary as a 'sewer'. This strange term means a person assisting at the royal table and arranging seating and so on, from the old French *'asseoir'*, to cause to sit, to seat. The royal households were full of young courtiers making their way in apparently humble jobs that were often combined with clerical and administrative positions. It had nothing to do with the other kind of sewer, which derives from the old French *'essouere'*, a drain or ditch.[18] Being a sewer was an honour. Princess Mary had a fairly modest household; the magnificence of her court waxed and waned as the king bestowed and removed royal favour on his elder daughter but her household provided good training ground for a young ambitious courtier.[19]

Jerningham became one of Henry VIII's Gentlemen Pensioners about 1540, an elite bodyguard of fifty men and five officers in constant attendance on the king, required to attend court at least nine months out of every year.[20] It was an honour for a young nobleman. He remained an official member of this elite until 1558, when he formally retired, although he is not listed in the roll call of 1553 as an active member, presumably because he was serving in Mary's household. He was present however at major state occasions and took part in the king's campaign in France in 1544 with his own contingent of five horsemen.

Jerningham's marriage is said to have been arranged by his stepfather, Sir William Kingston. In 1536 he married Kingston's granddaughter, Frances Baynham of Clearwell, in Gloucestershire. By Frances he had three sons, Henry, William and Francis, and two daughters, Mary, who married Sir Thomas Southwell (d.1568) of Woodrising, Norfolk and Jeronyma, who married Charles Waldegrave of Stanninghall. Henry founded the second of the two branches of the family descended from Edward Jerningham of Somerleyton. The other branch was headed by his older brother John. His half-kin included the influential families of Bedingfield, Blennerhasset and Drury, but Henry seems to have owed his early advancement, first in the service of Princess Mary and then at court, to his stepfather.

The Recusant Catholics of East Anglia. The Jerninghams were staunch adherents of the old religion but this did not prove too great a difficulty until after the death of Henry VIII. In 1539 Henry VIII's law of Six Articles put an end to the hopes of the more fanatical Protestant reformers, since it reaffirmed the main points of Catholic doctrine that Luther had criticised. Henry VIII persecuted radical Protestants who threatened his church or protested about his actions because he did not want a quite different sort of religion. In effect, on Henry VIII's death the Church of England was not a Protestant church but a Catholic church without a pope. The great families of Norfolk and Suffolk who thought of themselves as good Catholics loyal to Rome largely carried on as usual.

Princess Mary's younger half-brother Edward VI, Henry VIII's only male son, became king of England in 1547 at the age of nine but ruled only until he was fifteen. He was a boy with a well developed sense of his own importance and a self-righteous Protestant all too keen to implement his fanatically intolerant version of Protestantism. It may well be that Henry Jerningham, loyal to the Church of Rome, was careful not to make his presence felt too noisily at court during Edward's reign. He and his family almost certainly despaired of the direction that the king and his councillors were steering the religious life of the nation. After Edward VI's accession, Jerningham's activities are hazy save occasional references to him at court. It seems he was developing a strong loyalty to Henry VIII's rejected elder daughter, and became one of Mary's trusted advisors.

The Succession of Queen Mary I. The events surrounding the death of the young king, and the succession of a new monarch in 1553 brought Henry Jerningham honour and fame. He was a man who, faced with a serious threat to his employer, and also of course to his own position, swiftly intervened to ensure his mistress triumphed over her enemies. There were many other East Anglian gentry involved in her success, but Jerningham played a crucial role. He rode to Kenninghall Palace to steel Mary for a fight, supported her, rallied troops and took action locally. It was Jerningham who intervened at Yarmouth to dissuade the duke of Northumberland's fleet from taking offensive action. Henry Jerningham thus rose magnificently to the challenge posed by the succession and was rewarded with fame, fortune and a place in history.

Of course there are many even now who look back on the reign of 'Bloody Mary' and the bitter restitution of Catholic England during her short reign as nothing short of a disaster but at the time the majority of the country recognised Mary as rightful heir to the throne and supported her triumph over 'Queen' Jane and her father-in-law the duke of Northumberland. The background to the crisis and the story of Lady Jane Grey's nine days on the throne will be well-known to most readers so only the necessary background is given here. Since the story involves Charles Brandon's daughter and granddaughter it has relevance to the story of Wingfield.

The short-lived Queen Jane. In March 1533 Frances Brandon, elder daughter of Charles Brandon and Mary the French Queen, married Henry Grey, marquess of Dorset. Mary was in her final illness and rarely travelled from Suffolk but she came to London for her daughter's wedding, which took place at Suffolk Place, the Brandons' home in Southwark. Frances' first two pregnancies resulted in the births of a son and daughter but both died young. These were followed by three surviving daughters:

> Lady Jane Grey (1537 –1554) married Lord Guilford Dudley, son of the duke of Northumberland.
> Lady Katherine Grey (1540 –1568) married Edward Seymour, earl of Hertford.
> Lady Mary Grey (1545 –1578) married Thomas Keys.

Frances is said to have been a strong and energetic woman and in some ways took after her mother. After the death of her two young half brothers, Charles and Henry Brandon, the title duke of Suffolk reverted to the Crown, and was granted to Frances' husband as a new (third) creation. This new family of Suffolks lived at Bradgate in Leicestershire. Frances ensured her daughters were well educated. Henry Grey was best known for his zeal for the Protestant faith. In Parliament and on the Privy Council, Grey pushed for further Protestant reforms and was measure for measure every bit as fanatical as the young Edward VI. His daughter Jane was just as fervent in her Protestant faith.

As the niece of Henry VIII, Frances Grey was frequently at court. It was through her friendship with Henry's wife Katherine Parr that Frances's daughter Jane secured a place in the queen's household. There, Jane came into contact with Henry VIII's son by Katherine Parr and his future successor, Edward. When Edward VI succeeded to the throne in 1547, Jane followed Katherine Parr to her new royal residence and was soon established as a member of the inner circle of the nine year old king.

Although Frances Grey was Henry VIII's niece, she and Henry VIII's elder sister Margaret and Margaret's descendants had been removed from the royal line of succession by Henry's will, ratified by parliamentary act in 1543. Frances' descendants however remained in the line of succession but came after Edward's half-sisters Mary (later Queen Mary I) and Elizabeth (later Queen Elizabeth I).

Seriously ill, and fearing his own death, young Edward VI granted a request by his close advisor John Dudley, the duke of Northumberland, for the marriage of the Suffolks' daughter Lady Jane Grey to Northumberland's son, Lord Guildford Dudley, which went ahead on 25 May 1553. Edward subsequently altered his will to make Frances Grey's children his first heirs on the grounds of Mary and Elizabeth having been made illegitimate by their father. Jane Grey became his designated successor. The new succession plan was incorporated into Letters Patent by judges and it was intended to be ratified by parliament. Edward was persuaded that should Mary come to the throne, all the major reforms of the Protestant Reformation would be undone and she would most likely marry a foreign prince.[21] He was to be proved right in his fears of course. Edward died on 6 July 1553 before parliament had had a chance to pass a new Act of Succession and three days later Henry Grey, with Northumberland and other members of the Privy Council, proclaimed Jane Grey queen.

Subsequent events are recounted in a chronicle by Robert Wingfield, a descendant of the Wingfields of earlier chapters and a member of the extensive Wingfield family of Letheringham. He inherited lands in Brantham and Ipswich and wrote his *Vita Mariae Angliae reginae* [the life of England's Queen Mary] from the perspective of a fervent Catholic supporter. He played a role in the events of 1553 by playing host at his Ipswich home to Queen Mary during her journey to London from Framlingham Castle to claim the throne. Mary rewarded him with a £20 life annuity. His detailed account of Mary's *coup d'état*, written in Latin, covers the period from the death of Edward VI to summer 1554. It contains information on events in East Anglia not recorded anywhere else. It survived in a single manuscript, which was translated, edited and published by Diarmaid MacCulloch in 1984.[22] This account draws on the '*Vita Mariae*' but also on recent papers that have reconsidered the events from a modern perspective.[23]

MacCulloch points out that the unique interest of the *Vita Mariae* is the fact that it gives an East Anglian view of Mary's bloodless *coup* against the established government in Westminster. MacCulloch believes that it was primarily an East Anglian event. The significance of Mary's victory has seldom been sufficiently emphasised: it was the only time during the Tudor period when the provinces rose in rebellion against the central administration and won. Moreover, the victory was centred on an area of England where that same central government had successfully neutralised Kett's rebellion, a serious popular rising only some four years before. One feature of Mary's succession to emerge from all the accounts and which so puzzled the various spectator ambassadors in London, used as they were to the more aristocratic character of Continental civil strife, was the groundswell of popular support which carried Mary to victory. It was ordinary people who first flocked to Mary at Kenninghall, who demonstrated their discontent when conservative and Protestant gentry alike agreed to proclaim Jane at Ipswich and it was ordinary sailors who mutinied against their officers in the squadron sent to cut off Mary from the Continent. It was the common servants of the earl of Oxford who told him that he had to abandon Queen Jane and who threw into gaol the gentry who supported Northumberland. Nevertheless, without the help of the gentry and nobility, particularly those of East Anglia, her popular support would probably have been useless. Many of Mary's household before her *coup* were gentlemen of Suffolk, Norfolk and Essex, which may explain why she chose East Anglia for her stand against Northumberland. Robert Rochester, the comptroller of Mary's household, Rochester's deputy Henry Jerningham, and Edward Waldegrave were all local men. Another man, Ralph Chamberlain was still an active justice of the peace in the Liberty of St Edmund (the modern west Suffolk) despite his membership of Mary's entourage. No doubt in the weeks before the coup, as young Edward's health declined, these men had been making plans in their own neighbourhoods. The first gentlemen to join Mary's household at Kenninghall were Jerningham, Bedingfield, Shelton and Southwell, all from the same group of religiously conservative Catholic East Anglian gentry. Henry's nephew George Jerningham, his elder brother John's son, was also there.

The Lady Mary, who was living in Hunsdon in Hertfordshire, was tipped off by someone on the royal council that Edward had died and that there was an imminent plan to arrest her. She escaped and gathering supporters on the way, made for Kenninghall Palace, in south Norfolk, one of her favourite homes, (formerly the home of the duke of Norfolk), where she proclaimed herself queen on 9 July 1553, one day before Jane was proclaimed queen in London.[24] Mary and her personal council decided swiftly to send out messengers in all

65. Framlingham Castle today, very little changed from 1553.

directions to draw gentlemen of the surrounding countryside 'to do fealty and hasten to aid the queen'. Sir Henry Bedingfield hastened as asked, 'to which his timely and opportune arrival added further lustre, as did his two brothers, men of energy and good disposition. Sir John Shelton, a man of ancient and illustrious descent, was such a zealous partisan for the queen that he seemed to merit the greatest praise in this undertaking.' Sir Richard Southwell, possibly the wealthiest man in Norfolk, amply provided money, provisions and armed men towards the prosecution of a campaign against Northumberland.

Mary also solicited help elsewhere in the south and from Yarmouth. Support began to gather. Lord Hastings of Stoke Poges brought four thousand troops with him. Adherents came from all over southern England to join her in Norfolk. Norwich declared for her on 12 July and then the queen moved her headquarters to Framlingham Castle, having been persuaded that a more secure fortified base was necessary. Jerningham accompanied her there, then set out to discover where and how large Northumberland's army was.

Jerningham set out for Ipswich at dead of night, making his way to a crowded inn owned by Welshman Philip Williams, whom he knew to be sympathetic to Mary's cause. He found Philip drinking with a sailor, a man 'not inclined to hold his tongue', who claimed that a squadron of five ships of the late king Edward VI, laden with soldiers and weaponry, had been forced into the safety of Orwell haven by bad weather and was sheltering there. It was said that the crews were in a state of mutiny against their officers because of the disowning of Princess Mary. The officers therefore were obliged to stay put.

Jerningham was not a man easily taken in, and at first scarcely believed what the sailor had said but he and Williams discussed how they could strengthen Ipswich's defences, the richest town in Suffolk, against the approach of Northumberland, who was making speedily for Cambridge, in order to gather a greater force of reserves from Lincolnshire and other counties. Very early the next day Jerningham, accompanied by two other supporters Tyrrell and Glemham, rode out to inspect the ships in Orford Haven and ordered Sir Richard Brooke, the squadron's commander, to accompany them to Framlingham Castle.

Much of London supported Northumberland in these early days, it is thought because of extensive propaganda that Mary's Catholicism threatened her father's reforms and would leave England open to foreign influences. Northumberland was adept initially at raising support for Jane. But Jane's supporters had not reckoned on Mary's ability to summon huge forces of military strength. Even as Northumberland set off for Norfolk in his attempt to seize Mary, support for Jane was ebbing away and the royal council itself was divided about the legality of Jane's claim. The council finally reached the conclusion on 19 July that Mary was the rightful queen and proclaimed her so in Cheapside, London.

Meanwhile at Cambridge, the tide was turning against Northumberland. The duke quickly foresaw his coup was failing and desperately declared that he had changed his mind and now supported Mary. He was promptly arrested. The first priority was to send the queen word of what had happened and send the prisoners to London. The queen sent Lord Grey of Wilton and Henry Jerningham, whom she had already selected as vice-chamberlain and captain of the guard, which traditionally keeps watch over and protects the sovereign's person. Arundel, Grey and Jerningham found the duke in a dejected state, 'his spirit was entirely broken'.

The proclamation of Jane had failed not because of a large-scale rallying of forces in the country for Mary, but by a wavering Privy Council switching its allegiance to Mary during Northumberland's absence on campaign against her. The country continued to be divided in its loyalties to the two contenders for queen. Not everyone in East Anglia was happy about supporting Mary in the anxious weeks of July and August 1553; Kings Lynn burgers for example and the people in the marshes southwest of the Wash were opposed to a Catholic queen.

For a full week the burgers of Kings Lynn hesitated and deliberated. Robert Dudley, Northumberland's fourth son and future earl of Leicester, who had been waiting anxiously in Wisbech, stormed Kings Lynn and took it by force, declaring for Jane. Both Yarmouth and Boston declared for Dudley and his support of Jane in the early days but changed their minds as the wind blew the other way for Mary. Yarmouth sent a delegation to Norwich to find out which way the burgers there were going before finally supporting Mary, one guesses with misgivings. The story of Sir Henry Jerningham persuading the crew of a flotilla of six ships commissioned by Northumberland to change sides looks improbable but by then Yarmouth townsmen had already committed themselves to Mary so the sailors may not have taken much persuasion.

Mary's final Triumph—the Accession. Mary was persuaded by her household staff at Framlingham Castle and the rapidly growing number of supporters to ride into London in late July to claim the throne. An exhilarated Mary, who had been loved and scorned with seemingly equal fervor by her father, arrived in London on 3 August amid a jubilant crowd of supporters. Later that month Northumberland was tried for treason and beheaded, but not before he recanted his Protestant faith and proclaimed himself a Catholic once more, to the profound distaste of Jane Grey and her father.

One of Mary's early decisions was to make an emotional early pilgrimage to the Tower of London to free the 'martyrs' put there by her late father for persisting in their Catholic faith. One of the first prisoners to greet Mary at the Tower was the former duke of Norfolk, 79-year-old Thomas Howard, a survivor of six years imprisonment. Despite his reputation as a tough, resilient commander, Howard was physically small and had been suffering from rheumatism and troublesome stomach pains for years. Howard had been sent to the Tower in December 1546 for allegedly conspiring with his headstrong son, the earl of Surrey, to tamper with the succession during the waning days of the irascible Henry's reign. While both Howards had been found guilty on flimsy evidence, Norfolk had confessed, hoping for mercy. The king would have none of it and Surrey was beheaded on 19 January 1547, with his father scheduled soon to follow. However, Henry obligingly died nine days later, just six hours before the duke was scheduled to be executed. The Privy Council decided that keeping Norfolk in the Tower at such an advanced age would carry him away quite quickly anyway without them staining their hands with his blood. Among Mary Tudor's first official acts as queen was to restore Howard's dukedom and Order of the Garter. She also granted him moneys to buy back some of his personal property, including Kenninghall Palace.

The Wyatt Rebellion, 1554. Mary knew she needed a husband. Within a few months, she announced her intention to marry Philip of Spain, son of Charles V, emperor of Spain and the Low Countries, ten years her junior but who was nevertheless very keen to marry her. He was not attracted physically to her but saw the advantages of an alliance against France. If Mary picked up any rumblings of concern or antipathy to her marriage to a Catholic prince of a great foreign power she ignored them and disregarded the advice of her seldom-convened Great Council. She didn't like their advice so she simply did not assemble them again to discuss it. There was much lobbying and protest, which she ignored and sailed on heedlessly with her plans.

Virtually unnoticed at first, conspirators had begun meeting in London as early as November to plot a rebellion. One of their leaders was Sir Thomas Wyatt, who had voiced support for Mary in July but who utterly detested the idea of the country being dominated by Spain, as he perceived had happened to the Low Countries. Thus his enthusiasm for the new queen had rapidly soured. He gathered around him other equally disgruntled nobles. Conspiracies were hard to conceal in Tudor England, with informers everywhere, and Mary and her council were soon alert to what was afoot. Informants told the council specifically about Wyatt recruiting adherents. She asked the City Corporation for funds to raise an army against Wyatt but the corporation members scraped together only enough money to arm a paltry force of five hundred men-at-arms.

Somewhat improbably, Mary asked eighty year old Howard, duke of Norfolk to command her assembled troops. Norfolk himself had doubts about the adequacy of the small force against several thousand rebels in Kent. Mary offered her two hundred personal guards, under the command of Henry Jerningham, to serve under Norfolk. Though Norfolk continued to grouse about the number and quality of the men in his command and made the mistake of ignoring rumours that some of the men planned to go over to Wyatt's side, he planned as effectively as he could for the campaign. We do not know what Jerningham thought of this venture.

66. Sir Thomas Wyatt the Younger (1521–1554), painted circa 1540-42 and presumably commissioned by sitter's father, the poet Sir Thomas Wyatt Senior (1503–1542).

The Medway Bridge Fiasco. At the Medway Bridge, Norfolk was outnumbered at least fourteen to one, despite the late arrival of Lord Abergavenny with the several hundred troops he had raised for the queen. Sailors from ships riding at anchor below Gravesend had gone over to Wyatt. With only the faintest hope that more reinforcements might be found, Norfolk told his officers he was prepared to give battle if Wyatt decided to send his men across the bridge. Ordering his men to stay behind, Norfolk rode forward with Jerningham at his side to see where to place their guns for maximum effect, should artillery support become necessary. Satisfied that he knew what had to be done, Norfolk ordered forward his gunners and men-at-arms and gave the order to fire. As the first gun belched forth, Alexander Brett, one of Norfolk's captains, drew his sword and startled the duke and Jerningham by shouting as loudly as he could: 'We go about to fight against our native countrymen and friends in a quarrel unrightful and wicked! We are loyal Englishmen all, resisting the proud Spaniards who make the English slaves, spoil our goods, ravish our wives and deflower our daughters!'

Norfolk and Jerningham watched as their royal force broke ranks to join the other side, shouting: 'We are all Englishmen! A Wyatt! A Wyatt!' Nothing like this had happened since the Wars of the Roses a hundred years earlier. Norfolk sat motionless on his horse, still disbelieving the flight of the men over the bridge to the rebels' side. Norfolk's response to this mutiny was simply to pull his horse's head around and gallop away. One historian remarked later, 'Norfolk lived as long as he had because he never found anything worth dying for.' Jerningham must have been acutely embarrassed by the defeat and shame of this episode.

A bedraggled Norfolk, plus Jerningham and their handful of officers, straggled back into London without supporting forces or artillery. Mary turned to the Privy Council for advice and help. She found none and decided to call for public support. Within hours people assembled to hear the queen and miraculously she was able to stiffen the sinews of Londoners to oppose the rebels' arrival in London. As they approached Ludgate, to everyone's surprise and relief, Wyatt's resolve unraveled in the outermost streets of London. In a fitting reversal of fortunes, Jerningham took the rebel leader prisoner in a final skirmish at Charing Cross.

Norfolk withdrew to his beloved estate at Kenninghall. Jerningham had the responsibility for rounding up the men-at-arms who had gone over to Wyatt and his rebels. Arrested quickly, one hundred of them were tried within days, found guilty of treason, and hanged from the doors of their own homes in London. The rest were taken, bound and wearing nooses around their necks, to the tiltyard at Westminster to appear before Mary. Mary pardoned the deserters. The unfortunate Wyatt, however, was held in the Tower until April, when he was beheaded. After this rebellion, Mary decided that Jane Grey, her husband and her father must be executed too. Jane's mother Frances Grey *nee* Brandon was saved, mainly because of Mary's long-standing friendship with her. Jane was just sixteen when she was executed, an acquiescent but not entirely innocent pawn in a game her father engineered.

The consequences of Mary's accession for Henry Jerningham. After Mary's accession, Henry Jerningham, by now one of her most trusted servants, was appointed Vice-Chamberlain of the Household, Captain of the Yeomen of the Guard and a member of the Privy Council. He was created a Knight of the Bath at Mary's coronation. Henry's wife Frances also became one of the Queen's gentlewomen. It was at this point that he received the grant of Wingfield Castle and its domains.

Jerningham's decisive role in the suppression of Wyatt's rebellion in 1554 increased Mary's trust in him. In 1556 Jerningham sat on the special commission to investigate the Dudley conspiracy, and revisited the Continent on a mission to the Emperor. In April/May 1556 Mary sent Jerningham to see her by-then husband Philip in Spain to ask him to come and see her again, she was missing him and, although it doesn't say so in her letter to him, she needed him to sire an heir.[25] A year later Mary asked Jerningham, 'to make for the warres' (that is to the defence of Calais) with 'as many men as he can raise'.[26]

Jerningham became Master of the Horse, received an annuity of three hundred pounds and the gift of the manor of Costessey in December 1557. The Grant document, with the Great Seal of Mary I survives in the Norfolk Record Office.[27] Henry VIII's fourth wife, Anne of Cleves, had been given Costessey manor as part of a generous settlement on the annulment of their marriage in 1540. On Anne of Cleve's death in 1557, the manor reverted to the Crown so came into Mary's gift. The Manor of Costessey was one of the largest and most productive in Norfolk. Jerningham also received manors in Hereford and Gloucestershire.[28] For his new Norfolk house, he chose a site on the south side of the River Tud, which flowed through Costessey Park. This left the original Manor House on the north side of the river. Speculation still continues on whether the early Tudor building now standing in Costessey Park, is, in fact, the Tudor Manor granted to Anne of Cleves by Henry VIII.

Mary's Catholic reign led to huge changes in the Church of England in East Anglia. The Catholics were now in the ascendancy and some members of the Jerningham family were closely involved in the strict imposition of Catholic liturgy and traditions. John Noyes of Laxfield, an ardent Protestant shoemaker, who refused to believe in transubstantiation, the literal turning of communion bread and wine into the body and blood of Christ, was a tragic victim of the fanaticism of local men 'policing' the restitution of Catholic ideas. Sir John Jerningham's bailiff Robert Blomefield encouraged the chief Constable of Hoxne hundred and the under-constables of Laxfield, 'they being full of hatred and desirous to get to the truth' to institute an inquiry into the state of religious observance in Laxfield which led directly to the trial and execution by burning of John Noyes.[29] Laxfield Church even today bears witness to a Protestant religious fervour, devoid of images. Laxfield was the home of the Dowsing family into which iconoclast William Dowsing was born in 1596.

Altogether in Mary's reign there were thirty-one victims of Marian persecution in the diocese of Norwich, three from Suffolk in 1555, eight in 1556, nine in 1558. A hawkish bishop John Hopton dedicated to eradicating heresy had replaced a more sympathetic one, Thirlby, who was sent to Ely. Sympathy for the Catholics of Suffolk in this overwhelmingly Protestant leaning area of England, must have been thin.

67. Queen Mary I, c1554, by Antonis Mor*

Jerningham kept close connections to the Spanish court. Early in 1558 the count of Feria, one of Philip of Spain's diplomats, reported Jerningham's concern as to the defence of the kingdom. After the loss of Calais, Jerningham was one of the five Councillors recommended by Feria as most suited to membership of a conference about its recapture.[30] During the summer of that year Henry was also active in organising the defence of Kent against possible French invasion. When, in October 1558, the Queen made new arrangements for the use of her signet by her clerks, Jerningham was among the trusted councillors who were to be present at the stamping of all warrants. Jerningham became a Knight of the Shire (member of parliament) and served throughout Mary's reign, four times for Suffolk between 1553 and 1555 and once for Gloucestershire in 1558, where he presumably relied upon his Kingston connections for election.[31] The House of Commons Journal mentions him frequently as a bearer of bills to the Lords from December 1554 onwards. In 1558 the official record notes 'He has retired [as a gentleman pensioner]: a good man, a Christian, and a servant of your Majesty. Paid 1000 crowns 1558, 18 months owing.'[32]

Sir Henry Jerningham's later life. Queen Mary appointed Jerningham one of the six assistant executors of her will. She died in 1558 and Elizabeth her sister ascended to the throne. Little is known of Jerningham after the accession

* Several versions of this portrait were commissioned by Charles V Holy Roman Emperor and his son King Philip II of Spain from the artist Antonis Mor, from Utrecht, on the occasion of Philip's marriage to Mary I. This version was a gift from Mary to Sir Henry Jerningham about 1557, who later installed it in his new home, Costessey Hall, Norfolk, where it remained until it was sold in 1901. It now hangs in the Isabella Stewart Gardner Museum, Boston, Mass.

of Elizabeth, but we know she dismissed him from office and effectively put an end to his public career. He sued out a general pardon on 15 January 1559. It is said that he retired to Costessey Hall but other authorities say the Tudor house was not finished until 1564, a date that was said to be over the main door.[33] He would at last have had time to supervise more closely the final building works.

These later years at Costessey could not have been easy ones for the Catholic Jerninghams. In 1559, Elizabeth I outlawed the Mass and Catholics became recusants, 'refusers' who would not attend Protestant worship. Protestants were getting their own back. Until the 1570s, recusants were served by priests ordained under Queen Mary. These Catholic English priests were trained in Jesuit seminaries on the Continent. After Elizabeth's accession, a government clampdown led to the imprisonment of many of these priests in Wisbech Castle. This period of persecution gave the Church in East Anglia several of its martyrs, including the priests (St) Henry Walpole and (St) Robert Southwell. Costessey Hall included a Roman Catholic chapel that could be concealed from prying eyes.

Henry Jerningham made his will on 15 August 1572, and died on 6 September at the age of sixty-three. He was buried in the parish church of St Edmund at Costessey, survived by his wife, Frances, two of his sons, Harry and William, and one of his daughters, Jeronyma. Jerningham's will was proved 27 May 1573.[34]

Henry left Wingfield to his son 'Harry' and left the wherewithal to set him up in his household there. He also remembered the prisoners of the five prisons of London and Southwark and the inmates and warden of the almshouses founded from his lands in Herringfleet, making provision for the old church of St. Olave there to be rebuilt 'in such sort as I have determined'. To his sons Harry and William and his two daughters he left a large amount of plate. A nephew, Harry Jerningham, was to receive forty shillings yearly so long as he should remain at his books in Cambridge.[35] A marriage for his second surviving son William, who was still a minor, had been planned with Jerningham's ward Elizabeth Cornish. William was to have Old Wingfield Hall manor in Suffolk, Veales and Storers Fressingfield, some of it only after his mother's death, and an annuity of almost £120. He was still a minor when his father died. Henry's wife Frances received a life interest in his London property at Blackfriars with his two remaining sons dividing the remainder. His third son Francis appears to have died young.

Recusancy and lean times for the Jerninghams. The attitude of the Protestant Queen Elizabeth to the Catholic recusants was initially a fairly tolerant one. She wanted peace in England and her emphasis was on 'outward Conformity as opposed to Inward Conviction'. The strict Recusancy Laws imposed by the 1559 Act of Uniformity resulted in various punishments for Catholic recusants although there was considerable variation in their implementation. But the events of St. Bartholomew's Day, 24 August 1572, were not forgotten in England. On that day an estimated three thousand French Huguenot Protestants were massacred by French Catholics in Paris. The massacre was witnessed by Sir Philip Sidney, Sir Walter Raleigh and Sir Francis Walsingham. Similar atrocities elsewhere in France resulted in thousands more deaths and caused panic in England with fears of a Catholic invasion. An invasion did not materialise and the attitude of Elizabeth to English Catholics remained a moderate one. However, there were various Catholic plots that threatened the security of Queen Elizabeth and English Protestants. Mary Queen of Scots continued to present a focal point for such Catholic plots and conspiracies. The threat from English Catholics and Catholics from abroad eventually led to strengthening of the earlier Recusancy Laws and punishments were made harsher towards the end of Elizabeth's reign.

Additional Justices of the Peace were appointed in all areas of England. They produced Recusancy lists which supplied the government with details of Catholic recusants:

- People who held, or attended private masses, were to be punished by imprisonment
- Initially recusants were fined twelve shillings for non attendance of church
- The harsher Recusancy laws increased the fine to a massive twenty pounds a month.
- Non-payment of fines resulted in imprisonment.

After the expulsion of Jesuit priests in 1585 the first statute to address sectarian dissent from England's official Protestant religion was enacted in 1593. It specifically targeted Catholics, under the title 'An Act for restraining Popish recusants'. It defined 'Popish recusants' as 'those convicted for not repairing to some Church, Chapel, or usual place of Common Prayer to hear Divine Service there, but forbearing the same contrary to the tenor of the laws and statutes heretofore made and provided in that behalf.'

In the succeeding reign of James I (Mary Queen of Scots' son), the penalties and fines were increased by The Popish Recusants Act 1605 (3 Jac.1, c. 4) an Act that swiftly followed the Gunpowder Plot. This was an attempt by an English Roman Catholic group to assassinate the king and members of Parliament. The Act forbade Roman Catholics from practising the professions of law and medicine and from acting as a guardian or trustee; and it allowed magistrates to search their houses for arms. It also provided a new oath of allegiance, which denied the power of the Pope to depose monarchs. The recusant was to be fined £60 or was to forfeit two-thirds of his land if he did not receive the sacrament of the Lord's Supper at least once a year in his Church of England parish church.

The Jerninghams were in good company as recusants. The Howard dukes of Norfolk and other Howard family branches, the Bedingfields of Oxburgh, the Drury family of Hawkstead, the Tasburghs of Flixton, the Gages at Hengrave and the Huddlestones at Sawston all maintained the old faith when it was peculiarly disadvantageous to do so. The fines and prohibition impacted heavily on the Jerningham family fortunes.

Henry (Harry) Jerningham (often called Jernegan) c1536–15 June 1619, his first wife Eleanor (nee Dacres) and second wife, Frances Jerningham Bedingfield. Henry's older surviving son Harry lived at Wingfield Castle until his mother died at the end of 1583, when he moved to Costessey Hall. He retained the alternative spelling of his surname, Jernegan. In the Archives he is often referred to as Henry Jernegan the Elder to distinguish him from his elder son Henry, the first Henry's grandson. Father and son are often confused with each other in the record. Harry was not a knight. He was educated at Trinity College Cambridge and recorded as a fellow in 1566.[36] He married first Eleanor Dacres, from another staunch Catholic family, the third daughter of Lord Dacres of Gilsland. We know that after his mother Frances' death Harry inherited the family house at Blackfriars, London but sold it in lean times to George Carey, Lord Hunsdon, some time before 1603.[37] Eleanor died fairly young and Harry married his cousin, Frances Jerningham Bedingfield, the widow of Thomas Bedingfield. In 1570 her father John Jerningham was found guilty of abetting treasonable riots in Norwich, thought to have been a demonstration of support for Thomas Howard duke of Norfolk, then in prison. John Jerningham secured the Queen's pardon, but in the early 1590s Lord Burghley recorded in a note of Suffolk recusants that John Jerningham had fled the realm and was with the King of Spain.

Harry too was a staunch Catholic, but his two sons were removed to Westminster by Queen Elizabeth's court where they were brought up as Protestants. There is a touching entry in the Jerningham papers in 1593 when

Jernegan receives a letter from the Privy Council giving their consent to his request that his sons be allowed to spend 'some season' with him until 'the infection be more slacked in London'.[38] Plague was one of the hazards of life in Britain ever since its dramatic appearance in 1348 with the Black Death. In 1563, a thousand people were reportedly dying in London each week. In 1593, there were 15,003 deaths.[39] Young Henry and Thomas Jerningham came home and did indeed survive the plague. Their father Harry Jernegan made a will on 26 July 1596, but lived another 23 years.[40] He was buried at St Margaret's, Westminster.[41]

The Jerninghams lose Wingfield Castle Estate. It is impossible to be sure whether young Harry added to or improved Wingfield Castle buildings although we do know he lived there. It seems very unlikely that any substantial improvements were made at Wingfield after about 1580–90, when the family fortunes declined. Even before the turn of the sixteenth/seventeenth centuries, recusant fines and penalties imposed on the Jerninghams began to take their toll. The later years of the second Henry's life were marred by mounting debts and legal challenges to his property. When he died, his heir the third Henry spent years sorting out the debts and ensuing financial mess and eventually he was obliged to sell off the Wingfield estate bit by bit.

It was probably because of debts owing that inventories were taken during the years 1590–1599 at Costessey and Wingfield Castle of the contents of these houses 'together with a 'note of Stuff d(elive)d to St. Olaves', from Wingfield Castle.' Who commissioned the inventories and for what purpose is unclear.[42] The inventory is given in full at the end of this chapter. It provides a magically tangible insight into the way the rooms were used by the family. The list of goods transferred to St Olave's suggests that someone or possibly the whole family was planning to move there. Was that because Wingfield was becoming too expensive to maintain and they were retreating to a smaller home? We can only conjecture.

Elizabeth Forth, née Jerningham. The 1591 inventory tell us a good deal about how the rooms at Wingfield Castle were furnished and who traditionally occupied the bedchambers. One room was called 'Mistress Forthe's room', another was 'Miss Rookwoode's room'. Elizabeth Forth, née Jerningham, figured importantly in the family's lives in the late 1580s. She was the disgraced daughter of Henry's volatile and impoverished older brother John Jerningham of Somerleyton and sister of Henry's wife, Frances Jerningham Bedingfield. Henry and Frances supported young Elizabeth throughout her tribulations and gave her a home.

At some point in 1581 or 1582 Elizabeth, about 18 years old, had married clandestinely Charles Forth, the 16 year old son of Robert Forth of Butley Abbey, a staunchly Protestant family of clothiers, who were strongly opposed to the match. The marriage was a miserable failure and ended with the complete estrangement of the young couple. Robert Forth did not dispute the validity of the marriage and received the newly-weds into his home at Butley but he continued to disapprove. While an adequate marriage portion was evidently paid, Forth stubbornly refused to settle any jointure on his unwanted daughter-in-law or to make provision for her children. Elizabeth hated living with the Forths and did not much like her callow husband. After six years, during which she may or may not have engaged in secret trysts with an unnamed young gentleman in a wood, she left the Forths to come and visit her sister Frances at Wingfield and give birth to a daughter, then decided to stay. An attempted reconciliation was brokered by Lord Cobham and Lord Buckhurst, and Elizabeth returned to her husband and her father-in-law's home, but after seven weeks she left again, taking refuge again with Henry and Frances. She gave birth to a son, Francis, at the Bedingfield home at Oxbrugh, Frances' first marital home, about thirty-three weeks after her second departure from Butley.

This time the marital bond was frayed beyond repair. Elizabeth reportedly refused to sleep with her husband ever again, and her sisters allegedly caused depositions to be taken insinuating that Charles suffered from venereal disease. Meanwhile Charles denied that he was the father of Elizabeth's children, and lamented to many interlocutors that he was a dishonoured cuckold whose ignominy was such that he might be murdered as he walked the streets. He eccentrically prevailed on his father to disinherit him and fled the country, dying shortly after. There was no clear evidence that Elizabeth's son was illegitimate. Charles was undoubtedly mentally unstable, if not frankly deluded.

Immediately after Charles's flight, Elizabeth sued Robert Forth in the Court of Requests for the repayment of her dowry and for maintenance during the periods in which she had been living with her sisters. Henry Jerningham supported her and spoke in her defence but produced no evidence. Forth fought her with a countersuit, and amassed a number of depositions attesting to Elizabeth's undutiful and unloving behaviour. The Court however ruled in Elizabeth's favour and Forth was obliged to pay on both counts. Elizabeth and Charles' extraordinary story has been wonderfully told in a book by Ralph Houlbrooke, who chanced upon the Elizabethan Court of Request reports.[43] One cannot help but suspect that Elizabeth must have been a headstrong handful but Henry and Frances clearly did their best to help her.

'Mistress Rookwoode' cannot be identified for certain but was probably one of the Rookwood family of Coldham Hall in Stanningfield, a well established Catholic recusant gentry family who later achieved notoriety when Ambrose Rookwood took part in the Gunpowder Plot of 1606, for which he was hung, drawn and quartered. Mistress Rookwood could be one of his sisters or his half sisters of which there were several. Or perhaps she was related to Edward Rookwood at Euston who was to suffer bitterly for his Catholicism. We do not know whether Mistress Rookwood was a temporary or permanent resident with the Jerninghams but she was there often enough to have a room named for her.

Sir Henry Jerningham, Bt (c1570–1646) and his wife, Eleanor Throckmorton (1572–1646). The eldest of the second Harry Jernegan's sons (the third Henry) inherited Wingfield Castle in 1619. Young Henry and his brother Thomas went to Trinity College Cambridge in 1589. This third generation Henry, brought up at court to be Protestant, nevertheless married in 1598 into a well-known Catholic family, the Throckmortons of Coughton Court, Warwickshire, a centre of recusant activity throughout Elizabeth's reign. Henry Jerningham maintained the Protestant affiliation instilled at court long enough to be granted a baronetcy in 1621, the hereditary title of Knighthood created by James I in 1611.[44]

The Jerninghams were keeping their heads above water in 1589 when the Reeve's, Heyward's and Bailiff's accounts of manors owned by Jerningham, including Wingfield Frumbolds were collected.[45] But by 1592 Henry Jernegan the Younger, the third Henry and his wife Eleanor, had leased out the old family manor at Herringfleet. They later leased it back again for five years, suggesting a certain turmoil in their financial situation.[46] This arrangement did not hold for long and in 1604 Henry was granted an act to sell the manor of Dages in Raveningham and Herringfleet and also part of the site of the manor of Wingfield 'with capital messuage belonging, well-furnished' 'for the payment of his debts'.[47] On this occasion his marriage to Eleanor Throckmorton saved the day; her father came to the rescue, settled Henry's debt and the manor was re-settled on Henry and Eleanor. It was a temporary reprieve because in November 1610 the manor was sold again to Matthew Bedell.[48]

Thomas Howard had discovered how much money there was to be made out of the sale of oak from Wingfield Park and in 1597 Henry cut down a forest of four hundred oaks and fourteen elms in the park to sell for cash to three men called Raynor, Clare and Cressy.[49] This is a devastating destruction of a park, which for a time at least would no longer be available for hunting or indeed any other sporting activity. Times were clearly hard.

The manorial accounts were kept with precision during the 1590s.[50] But there followed a series of law suits against the Jernegans between 1608 and 1625 indicating their near bankruptcy and the need to raise money for Henry's father's debts. Cossey, Wingfield, Old Wingfield Hall, Syleham Comitis, Veales and Storars and the manors of Painswick, Haresfield, and Moreton Valence in Gloucestershire were all subject to challenge by those who were owed money.[51] In 1614 the manors of Old Wingfield Hall, Veales in Fressingfield and Storars, originally left to his uncle, William Jerningham, but then inherited by the third Henry, were sold, in 'an agreement for disposal of monies raised by sale to pay debts'.[52] Once again Henry managed to recoup these properties for a short time but in 1617 was obliged to grant a lease on the Manors of Costessey, Wingfield, Frumbalds, Old Wingfield Hall, Earls Syleham, Veales In Fressingfield and Storars co. Suffolk; Painswick, Haresfield and Moreton Valence in Gloucestershire to Sir Anthony Browne for the payment of his father's debts.[53] The complex leases and subleases on the various properties are painfully exposed in the archives.[54]

Henry and Eleanor retreated to Costessey and basically left Wingfield Castle and its demesne to rot. In 1618 a posse of local men, some of them gentlemen, tore across Wingfield park, pulling up railings and stealing any deer that they could lay their hands on. The men were led by Edward Copledicke gent, from a manor owning family in Horham. The others included John Goldsmith, John Parker, Robert Pride (possibly Prideaux) gent, William Owles, Hugh Butcher, John Offewood, John Thurstone (of Hoxne Abbey) and William Puller. These were not local ruffians or customary poachers but well-heeled local gentry and yeomen. They were surely trying angrily to compensate themselves for money lent to Henry that they realised they would never get back. They were prosecuted when Henry realised what was happening.[55]

The period between 1590 and 1625 was desperately sad for the owners of Wingfield Castle. Wingfield was abandoned and left unloved by proprietors no longer able to afford it. Was it around then that the physical destruction of the north and eastern medieval walls occurred, perhaps by both neglect and plunder? The question cannot be answered for certain and there were other times of crisis approaching but this seems one of the more likely times for Wingfield to be serially dilapidated if the walls had survived the neglect of the Crown's ownership in the 1540s. Local people may have helped themselves to whatever they wanted or felt was their due when there was no-one around to detect the desecration. Flint and stone were highly prized in an area where there was no natural stone and flint was saved for prestigious buildings.

Following the plunder of the park, Sir Anthony Browne, who now held the leases on the various Wingfield and Gloucester properties, having lent more money to the Jerninghams, agreed to the sale of the manors of Wingfield, 'Castle Frumbalds', Old Wingfield Hall and Earles Syleham to Thomas Bancroft. Bancroft then extended Browne's leases for a further sixty years with a schedule of debts to be paid off. A few years later eighty-eight acres of Wingfield Park, 'with messuages, woods and underwoods' was mortgaged to Thomas Wisse, the timber being reserved to the seller. But by 1624 the decision to sell Wingfield Castle estate was finalised.[56]

Copinger records that Wingfield Castle came into the hands of the Catelyn family, specifically Thomas Catelyn in 1625.[57] This ends the association of the Jerninghams with Wingfield. The Catelyns belong to a future chapter.

What happened to the Jerninghams after selling Wingfield? The family kept its Costessey estate until the Civil War, but then their lands were sequestrated, the park was abandoned, the deer destroyed, the mansion and the domain let to a farmer and a considerable part of the buildings fell into decay. The third Henry died in 1646 and his grandson inherited. The family fortunes revived however in the eighteenth century through fortunate marriages and in 1824 the Jerninghams (still mostly called Henry) acquired the title of Lord Stafford.

From 1826 Oxford architect John Chessell Buckler was employed, over a period of more than thirty years to produce at Costessey Hall a Gothic fantasy for Stafford which dwarfed the original Tudor manor. Costessey Hall was a superb folly with gables, turrets, pinnacles and chimneys, all dominated by a massive keep. After the death of Lord Stafford in 1913, the halls and the contents were auctioned. The hall stood empty until the outbreak of World War I, and then was commandeered by the War Office. Regiments of infantry, cavalry and artillery were stationed and trained at Costessey Hall. Shortly after the armistice the estate was broken up and sold at auction, with the unwanted hall being acquired by a demolition contractor. All that remains today is the belfry block by the eighteenth fairway of Costessey park golf course.

Inventory of Wingfield Castle, 5 November 1591[58]

Wingfeld Castell The inventory made 5 No: 1591

In the great chambre
6 hanginges: 4 wyndow peeces: 2 lyvery cupbordes, one long table with tresselles. A long grene carpitt

A square borde. 3 square turkye carpettes: 2 long form[es], A short forme. 9 buffet stooles. 2 great chayers one of satt[en?] the other of black velvet. A square grene velvet stoole imbrode[d] with gold: A square Cusshyn of yellow & Watchet vellet

A square Cusshyn of cloth of tyssow: ij olde Wyndow cuss[hyns] of the same, An other Cusshyn of cloth of gold which is at cosse[y] 2 foote stooles one of redd vellet, thother of tyssew 4 carrell Cusshinges, A payer of tables layed with bone ....?menn to them. 2 Andyrons garnished with latten A fire pann garnished, A payer of tonges: & a payer of bello[wes?] Item more 2 Drynking glasses of Christall: A play[ne?]glasse with a Cover, one Wyne bowll, 2 flat bowles for Cheries & strawberries, A paynted Dringing glasse A paynted glasse lyke a lyvery pott, A payer of snuffes

In the gallery
4 peeces of hanginges 2 of them sutable to the great cham[ber]

thother 2 of tapestrye. 2 Long formes: A buffet stoole

In my M[ast]ers chamber
5 peces of tapestrye hanginges. 2 Wyndowe peces. A bed, a woollbed, a trundlebedd. an other Wooll bedd: 2 do....beddes: a downe bolster, a fether bolster: 3 fustyn blanketes.

of lynsey woolsey. A twylt of redd sylk: one other counterpoynt of redd & grene saten of bridges lyned: 2 Wyndow Cusshins of yellow & Watchet vellet, A Chayre of tyssew A lyvery Cupborde. A nedlework Carpet. 2 buffetstoo[les] A payer of Andyrons garnished with latten. A fyre pan[n]A payer of tonges: A bedd tester of yellow 7 Whyte damas[k] 3 Curteyns of Whyte & yellow sarcenet: 2 downe pillow[es] 2 Wyndow Curteyns, A chamber pott, A low stoole of tyssew

In my M[ast]ers Closett
A lyvery Cupbord, A turky Carpet, A lowe stoole, A round table & a stoole in M[istre]ss Margetes closet

In the Nursery
A bedsted, A matt, 2 fetherbeddes. 2 bolsters. A Coverlet tapes[try] A red Coverlet lyned, a red blanket, an old redd velvet chayer 3 lyvery Cupbordes: An old turkye carpet, A bedd tester of redd clo.....layd with lace black & whyte, A Cofer, A buffet stoole, A fyre pann: 3 .....of hanginges one of Saye, one tapestry, the third turkye

In the next Chamber
A Chayer, A table, 2 necessaryes, A forme, & 2 tooles

In the Cookes chamber
A orded bedsted, A olde tester, A borde

In the chamber next the great chamber doore
5 peces of hanginges of Aris, A bedsted, A woollbed, a featherbed a bolster, 2 fusyn blanketes. A whute spannish blanket, A Coverlet of Imagerye, A tester of watchet satten of bridges...paned lyke nedlework: 3 Curteyns orengetawyny & purple A Counterpoynt sutable to the tester, An old red velvet chayer

2 Wyndow Cusshyns of dunnd? vellet; 2 olde wyndow curteyns 2 olde Wyndow Carpettes: a lyvery Cupbord: An old turkey Carpet, An old vellet stoole, A payer of yron doges. A fyre p[an?] a payer of tonges: a payer of bellowes: A Chamber pott An olde redd rugges:

In the next chamber
A bedsted, A matt, A fetherbed, a bolster, A blanket

A table, A olde turkye Carpet

In the voyd place between the chambers
A brusshing borde, A payer of tresselles

In Mistres Forthes Chamber
4 peces of Arrys, A bedstedd A woolbedd, A fetherbed & bolst[er] 2 stytched blanketes A Coverlet of Arrys lyned A livery Cupborde, A turkye Carpet, A old Wyndow Carpet, A Chayer layed with bone, A nedlework Cusshin, A low stoole covered with droppes, A wyndow Cusshin grene sattenA payer of yron

goddes: A fyre pan A chamber pott

In the ynner chamber to it

A bedsed, A matt, A fetherbed, A bolster, And blanket A tapestry Coverlett with the kingston Armes, A tester of Whyte lynnen, A brusshing borde, A necessarye

In the parlour at the halles ende

4 peeces of Arrys, A bedsted, A woll bedd, A tester of black vellet & Whyte satten stryped with golde, the Curte[yns?] to it of black & Whyte old sarcenet, A Chayer A stoole A forme A Cussyn, An other Cussyn of tapestrye, A payer of Andyrons, A fyrepann, A chamber pott

In the butlers chamber

A bedsted A matt A fetherbed & bolster A red Coverlet lyned

In the Stewardes chamber

A trundle bedsted, A matt, A table with tresselles. 2 peeces of stayned clothe, A Chayer. 2 buffet stooles.

In Master Henry Jernegans Chamber

5 peces of hanginges tatpestrye. A bedsted, A matt, A test[er]with the picture of Chryste, 3 Curteyns redd & tawney o[f]sarcenet, A Chayer A Cusshyn of cloth of gold: A for[me] A buffet stoole, A Cusshyn of tapestrye, 2 dogg yrons, A lyvery Cupbord A turkye Carpett, a Wyndowe peece

In the next chamber

A bedsted A matt A whyte tester

In Mistres Rookwoodes chamber

A bedsted, A matt, A tester yellow & black taffeta, O[ld?]paynted 2 peeces of stayned work A newe boxe

In the chamber over the gate house

A table with tressell, A Coffer supposed to be with thinges of Mistres Rookwoodes which is broken open: 2 empty Cofers A stylle. 2 Cofers Locked, to be carryed to Oxeburgh

The maydes chamber

An old bedsted A matt A forme A stoole

In Master Taylours Chamber
A borded bedsted: A Cupbord for grocery

The Butlers old Chamber
A borded bedsted

The Porters Chamber
A borded bedsted

The chamber over Owles his buttrye
A bedsted A matt A olde Tester

In the broad Chamber
A borded bedsted

In the Quenes chamber
A bedsted A matt a olde tester

In the Auditours chamber
4 peeces of hanginges A bedsted A woollbedd A fetherb[ed] a bolster, A pillowe, A fustyn blanket A Twylt, Another Twylt olde ymbrodered, A tester yellow damma[sk?] & black mockadow, 5 Curteyns yellow levyn taffetablack mockadow, A Chayer, 2 old Cusshinges A table A Chamber pott, Certeyn Cofers with evydences.

In the bakers chamber
A bedsted

In Messengers chamber
A bedsted, A Chayer, certeyn peeces of old turky carpe[tt]

In the hall
A pece of Arrys hangynge, A Cupbord A payer of Andyrons

In the Warderobe
A bedsted A matt. 2 fetherbeddes 2 bolsters, a flockbed a bolster, A Cussyn of leather without a case, A spruse Cofer, A Wyndow Cusshyn old tyssew without lyninge: 3 Cusshin[s] of cloth of golde. An other Cusshin of blewish cloth of golde A Cusshyn redd sylk stryped with greene: 2 Cusshins of cloth of tyssew: 2 Cases of olde tyssew Cussyns, one other Case of clothe of gold: An other Case with a pane of gold & letters

T & E. 2 other Cases cloth of gold wrought upon vellet A tester of grene tryped satten without Curteyns

A tester paned with cloth of gold & tawny vellet & liberdes heades 7 sondry letters upon it without Curteyns.

A Counterpoynt of Whyte satten with grene 7 redd flower[s] & braunches of golde. A longe Carpet pulham work 2 stooles of Crymsyn vellet for a lytter, A bottome for A lytter of redd satten stytched, A Cover for a lytter of black vellet paned with redde sylk & golde. 2 stoole glasses 10: olde Chayers of sondry fasshions, some of them broken 2 footestooles, An olde stoole covered with vellet, A presses A standerd barrel with yron, A case for A lytter of black lether lyned with redd buckeram. An other Case of blew

cloth lyned with black buckeram, 3 Cusshins needlework An olde Cusshyn with the Pollaxe, A olde turky Cusshyn 2 Cusshyns fustyan napes red & black olde, An yron Chest A Clock. A rable with tresselles, An old black vellet sadle layd with golde lase much therof torne awaye, A lytter lined with Crymsyn satten with the furnyture, An olde Covering lynded with tapestrye. 2 great Cusshins turkye Work at [?Com or lom]

An yron cofer A warming pann A fustyn blanke[t] A byble

Inventory Winfeld 23 Februar' 1595 Anno Regni Regine Eliz: xxxviij vo A note of Stuff d[elivere]d to St Olaves

Beddes 4: Bolsters 4: pillowes.1 Blankettes 2: Testers 4: Curteyns 2 sutes Coverlettes 3: Other peces of olde handinges to make Coverlettes 5.Hanginges of tapestrye & Arras 9. Cubbord clothes or carpettes 2: Windowe peces 2: Cussins of tapestry 2: of old cloth of tyssue 2: for Wyndowes of old cloth of tyssue 4: Quyltes [deleted: & Woolbeddes] 2: Woollbedd & Mattryce 1: Beddsteddes 9: Stooles 6: Fourmes 2: Cubbardes 2 square tables 2: whereof one with tresselles Chayres of waynscott 2: of tawney vellett 1:

Andyrons 2 payer: a fyer panne Platters 16: Disshes 18: sawcers 8: sallet disshes 6: porrengers 4: Plates 2:

Spetes 3 [?5] Brasse pottes 2: A payer of pothooks A fysshpane: Dripping pannes 2. A trevett, A hake

3 olde frames for chayers, & one lytle frame, A lowe stoole the back of an old velvet chayer A olde Cubberd to sett glasses in: Coffers 2

Notes

1 Inscription written on the brass memorial of Sir Thomas Jernegan of Somerleyton, died 1668, in St Mary's Church, Somerleyton, is now worn away.

2 Calendar of Patent Rolls, 1553–1554 I Mary part II, p. 57. Transcribed London: HM Stationery Office 1891, republished HMSO London 1937, online at University of Minnesota https://babel.hathitrust.org/cgi/pt?id=umn.31951001945221d&view=1up&seq=5.

3 Copinger, W. A., 1909, *The Manors of Suffolk; notes on their history and devolution, with some illustrations of the old manor houses, vol 4, The Hundreds of Hoxne, Lackford, and Loes*, Taylor, Garnett, Evans, Manchester, p. 109. Copinger's references are written O 1-2P and M1 Parl Rot 112.

4 Relevant papers: Receivers Accounts former Duke of Suffolk's lands 1539–1541 TNA SC 6/HENVIII/3377, 3376 and 3373, 1541–42 and 3378 1546–47; TNA SC 6/HENVIII/6924, 1540–1542 TNA SC 6/HENVIII/6923, 1544–46 SC 6/HENVIII/6927; Receiver General Crown Lands TNA SC 6/HENVIII/5977, 1540–42 TNA SC 6/HENVIII/6925, also 1543–1545, TNASC 6/HENVIII/6926.

5 Ministers Accounts for Wingfield Frumbalds Manor 1538–1547, TNA SC 6/HENVIII/3372-3378.

6 Gunn, S. J., 1995, *Early Tudor Government 1485–1538 The Crown Lands*, Palgrave MacMillan, New York, Chapter 3. The Crown Lands, pp. 113-121.

7 Liddiard, R., 2015, Reconstructing Wingfield Castle, in Bloore P. and Martin, E. (eds), *Wingfield College and its Patrons*, Boydell Press, Woodbridge, pp. 85.86.

8 Jerningham Collection, Norfolk Record Office. Donation by Sir Henry Jerningham, bt, 1922 Deeds and Grants, 16th century–1807; Manorial and Administrative, 1413–1821; Correspondence, mid 16th century–1778; and Original Document Folders, early 20th century, refs JER; and Family and Estate Collection of Lords Stafford (Stafford/Jerningham/Fitzherbert). Staffordshire Record Office, Series D641.

9 Smith W., Arnold, W, 1914, *St Olave's Priory and Bridge, Herringfleet*, online at http://www.gutenberg-e.org/mcintosh/chapter2.html and https://archive.org/stream/stolavespriorybr00wynnuoft/stolavespriorybr00wynnuoft_djvu.txt

10 English Heritage, *History of St Olave's Priory*, https://www.englishheritage.org.uk/visit/places/st-olaves-priory/history/

11 Weever, J., Tooke, W., 1767, *Ancient funeral monuments, of Great-Britain, Ireland, and the islands adjacent...*, printed by W. Tooke for the editor, London.

12 Account of the history of the Jerningham family from 1030 to c1704 written c1704, Jerningham Papers NRO JER 302a-b, 55X1.

13 The manor covers Somerleyton, Ashby and Herringfleet; there are several references to the Jerninghams origins in Ashby. See Venn, A Cambridge Alumni Database (ACAD), http://venn.lib.cam.ac.uk/Documents/acad/intro.html.

14 Houlbrooke, R., 2018, *Love and Dishonour in Elizabethan England: Two Families and a Failed Marriage* pp. 21–50, Boydell and Brewer, Woodbridge.

15 Weikel, A., 2004, Jerningham (Jernegan), Sir Henry (1509/10-1572), *Oxford Dictionary of National Biography*, online 2008 at https://doi.org.10.1093/ref:odnb/14785.

16 Suckling, A. I., 1847, *The History and Antiquities of the County of Suffolk:.., Volume 2,* p. 46, London, and Blomefield F. Vol 2, p. 415.

17 Collins, A., 1741, *The English Baronetage: Containing a Genealogical and Historical ..., Vol 1* p. 456.

18 Crowther, D., blog 2017, *The Early Tudor Court. Roles in the Royal Household,* https://thehistoryofengland.co.uk/resource/early-tudor-court/

19 MacIntosh, J. L., 2008, *From Heads of household to Heads of State: The Preaccession households of Mary and Elizabeth Tudor 1516 –1538*, Columbia University Press, New York, Chapter 2 online at http://www.gutenberg-e.org/mcintosh/chapter2.html.

20 Tighe, W. J., 1987, The Gentlemen Pensioners, the Duke of Northumberland, and the Attempted Coup of July 1553, Albion: *A Quarterly Journal Concerned with British Studies, vol. 19,* p. 1.

21 Loades, D., 1991, (2nd ed'n), *The Reign of Mary Tudor: politics, government and religion in England 1553-58*, p.

11-16.

22 MacCulloch, D., 1984, III The Vita Mariae Angliae Reginae of Robert Wingfield of Brantham 1594 *Camden Fourth Series Vol 29*, pp. 181-301, Cambridge University Press. Now online with new reference *Royal Historical Society Camden Fifth Series Vol 1* (1992) onwards ISSN: 0960-1163 (Print), 1478-5110 (Online). Downloaded from https://www.cambridge.org/core. IP address: 83.49.93.83, on 17 Feb 2020.

23 Hoak, D., 2015, *The succession crisis of 1553 and Mary's rise to power, in Catholic Renewal and Protestant Resistance in Marian England* ed. by Evenden, E. and Westbrook, V., Aldershot, pp. 17–42; Kewes, P., 2017, The 1553 succession crisis reconsidered. *Historical Research 2017* doi:10.1111/1468-2281.12178; Tittler, R. and Battley, S. L., 1984, The Local Community and the Crown in 1553: the Accession of Mary Tudor Revisited. *Historical Research Vol 57*, pp. 131-139.

24 Calendar of State Papers, Spain, Volume 11, 1553, ed. Tyler, R., 1916, pp. 82-3, London. British History Online http://www.british-history.ac.uk/cal-state-papers/spain/vol 11 [accessed 4 November 2020].

25 Calendar of State Papers, Spain, Volume 13, 1554-1558, Tyler, R. (ed), 1954, London, p. 267. Spain: May 1556. British History Online http://www.british-history.ac.uk/cal-state-papers/spain/vol13/p267 [accessed 14 February 2020].

26 Sir Henry Jernegan. Jerningham Papers NRO JER/335, 55 x 2

27 Grant by Philip and Mary of the manor and park of Costessey with its submanors NOR JER 244, 55X1...with Great Seal of Mary NOR JER 244, 55X, illustrated in Cassell, P., 1873, *Cassell's Illustrated History of England, Vol 2, Chapter XII.*

28 Ibid.

29 Wickins, P., 2012, *Victorian Protestantism and Bloody Mary: the legacy of religious persecution in Tudor England*, Arena Books, Bury St Edmunds, Chapter 3, John Foxe's martyrology and the Protestant martyrs of Suffolk, pp. 65-95.

30 Rodriguez-Salgado, M. J. and Adams, S. J., 1984, IV The Count of Feria's Dispatch to Philip II of 14 November 1558. *Camden Fourth Series Vol 29* pp. 302-344 online Cambridge University Press at https://www.cambridge.org/core/journals/camden-fourth-series/article/iv-the-count-of-ferias-dispatch-to-philip-ii-of-14-november-1558/95EE5BE6AFBAE51FEF8134ACF1F39714.

31 Dale, M. K., Jerningham, Sir Henry (1509/10-72), of Costessey, Norfolk; Herringfleet and Wingfield, Suffolk; Painswick, Gloucestershire, and London, History of Parliament online in Bindoff, S.T. (ed), 1982, *The History of Parliament: the House of Commons 1509-1558*, Boydell and Brewer, Woodbridge.

32 'Appendix: Miscellaneous 1558', in Calendar of State Papers, Spain, Volume 13, 1554-1558, ed. Tyler, R., 1954, London, pp. 450-456. British History Online http://www.british-history.ac.uk/cal-state-papers/spain/vol13/pp450-456 [accessed 15 February 2020].

33 Betham, W., 1801, The Baronetage of England, Ipswich, Burrell and Bransby, pp. 228-229; Kenworthy-Browne, J., Reid, P., Sayer, M., Watkin, D., 1981, *Burkes and Savills Guide to Country Houses, Vol III, East Anglia*, p. 101, Burke's Peerage.

34 Will of Henry Jerningham TNA PROB/11/55/240 dated 1619.

35 The nephew of Henry Jerningham's will is in the Norfolk Record Office, dated 1607, probably son of George Jerningham. NRO Jerningham papers. JER247.

36 Henry Jernyngham at Cambridge. See Venn, A Cambridge Alumni Database (ACAD), http://venn.lib.cam.ac.uk/Documents/acad/intro.html.

37 Green, N., 2010, Oxford Shakespeare, Henry Jernegan p1. http://www.oxfordshakespeare.com/Probate/PROB_11-55_ff_134-6.pdf.

38 Privy Council to Sir Henry Jernegan. Jerningham papers NRO JER341, 55X2.

39 Bell, W. G, 1951, Hollyer, B., (ed.) *The Great Plague in London* (Folio Society ed, original 1924.). Folio Society by arrangement with Random House, New York, pp. 3-5.

40 Will of Henry Jerningham died 15 June 1619. Jerningham papers NRO JER/246, 55X1.

41 Thornbury, W., 1878, 'St Margaret's Westminster', in *Old and New London: Volume 3*, London, pp. 567-576. British History Online http://www.british-history.ac.uk/old-new-london/vol3/pp567-576 [accessed 20

February 2020].

42 Inventories taken at Costessey and Wingfield Castle, 1590-1599. NRO Jerningham papers. JER/271, 55 x 1.

43 Houlbrooke, R. A., 2018, *Love and Dishonour in Elizabethan England: Two Families and a Failed Marriage*, Boydell Press, Woodbridge.

44 Grant of baronetcy to Henry Jerningham 1621 Jerningham Collection NRO JER 244a.

45 Reeve's, Heyward's, and Bailiff's accounts 1589 Jerningham Papers NRO JER/174, 622 x 3.

46 Manors of Dages in Raveningham and Heringeflete (Herringfleet) and site of manor of Wingfield... Jerningham papers NRO D641/3/E/1/2/1.

47 Private Acts 2 James I in Pickering, Danby, 1763 Statutes at large from the 39th year of Q Elizabeth to the 12th Year of K Charles II inclusive. Vol VII, Act 32.

48 Licence of alienation under the Great Seal was granted Henry Jernegan and Eleanor his wife for conveyance of the manor of Lothingland to Matthew Bedell, 1 September 1611. The history of Herringfleet and St Olave's priory, part VI 15th and 16th centuries online at http://www.lothingland.co.uk/hso6.

49 Wingfield Park. 400 oaks and 14 elms in the park. Bargain and sale, Henry Jernegan/Reynor, Clare, Crecye Henry...1597. Staffordshire County Record Office, D641/3/A/3/1/1.

50 Particular Receiver's accounts of revenues received from bailiffs of: Lothingland,... Staffordshire County Record Office D641/3/D/2/2 paper folios numbered 21-22, 24-31, 39-40, 45, 55-68.

51 Various law suits Henry Jernegan 1608-1625 TNA C 2/JasI/D6/25.

52 Manors of Old Wingfield Hall, Veales In Fressingfield and Storars. 1614 Staffordshire County Record Office D641/3/A/3/2/3.

53 Lease for 60 years Henry Jernegan, Henry Jernegan to Sir Anthony Browne et al. with schedule for payment of debts of Henry Jernegan the elder Staffordshire County Record Office D641/3/A/1/3.

54 1617 Manor of Old Wingfield Hall co. Suffolk with lands and tenements belonging in Wingfield and Stradbrooke; and Costessey Warren co. Norfolk; Assignment of leases Hyrne/Henry Jernegan/Mingay, Fawcett, Staffordshire County Record Office D641/3/A/1/4.

55 1618 October. Attorney General v Copledicke. Plaintiffs: Sir Henry Yelverton, Attorney General, at the relation of John Howard. Defendants: Edward Copledicke gent, John Goldsmith, John Parker, Robert Pridewe gent, William Owles, Hugh Butcher, John Offewood, John Thurstone, and William Puller. Subject: Deer stealing and destruction of palings in Wingfield park, belonging to Henry Jerningham the elder and Henry Jerningham the younger gentlemen of the Privy Chamber, October 1618 TNA STAC 8/27/14.

56 Wingfield Park with messuages, woods and underwoods. Mortgages by demise and in fee with agreements for extension of term and further borrowing to Sir Henry Jernegan/Holman and Sir Henry Jernegan/Wisse 1624-1632 SCRO D641/3/A/3/1/4-21. 1624 Manor of Wingfield, Wingfield Castle, park and lands belonging. Mortgage by demise, Sir Henry Jernegan/Holman. Staffordshire County Record Office D641/3/A/3/1/2-3

57 Ibid., 3, Vol IV Wingfield, p. 112.

58 Inventories taken at Costessey and Wingfield Castle, 1590-1599. Norfolk Record Office, Jerningham papers, JER/271, 55 x 1.

68. The western façade showing the exterior of Jerningham House, c1950.

Jerningham House

A new Tudor home at Wingfield Castle

Henry Jerningham's new Tudor house inside the castle walls takes first time visitors by surprise. Of course there is a hint from the pale rendered mortar of the massive west walls that some dramatic change has occurred since the original medieval fortified house was built. Even so one does not expect the long range of agreeably domestic and comfortable looking black and white extensions on the rendered, partly brick, partly timber-framed house. It is so different from the medieval walls traversed to arrive there.

The house stands at right angles to the gatehouse, built into the remains of the west curtain wall, probably on the site of the castle great hall and old residential wing. The house gives on to a pleasant courtyard area with gardens and other buildings. On the outer western façade the position and period of construction are indicated by two three-light mullioned and transomed windows. Crowning the ensemble are fine circular and polygonal brick chimneys with three-dimensional decoration. The flint footings of the western curtain wall remain but it is unclear how far up they survive because the whole façade has been rendered.

The Tudor 'Great Rebuilding'. In 1953, William George Hoskins, an influential historian of landscape and vernacular architecture defined the term 'The Great Rebuilding' in England as the period from the mid-sixteenth century until 1640.[1] Hoskins held that during this period improved economic conditions in England led to the expansion, rebuilding or architectural improvement of a large number of rural buildings and the creation of a different kind of home for people no longer satisfied with austere medieval interiors. They were now looking for greater comfort, sumptuous drapes and hangings and beautiful objects to make life both more convenient and pleasurable.

The precise time period, extent and impact of the Great Rebuilding is now contested. Brunskill agreed that in much of England it mainly spanned the period 1570–1640 but that there were variations both by region and by social class.[2] It was earliest in south-east England and East Anglia, later in the south west and Cornwall, was active from about 1670 to 1720 in Northern England and later still in Wales. In each region it was higher-income social classes that started the building enthusiasm and then the lower-income groups naturally aspired to do similarly.

The building boom was not simply due to improvements in the economy and disposable wealth but part of a cultural shift towards investment in the domestic environment and home in the lives of gentry families and merchants. Colin Platt has argued that the new family house, whether in town or country, owed almost nothing to the Middle Ages but had its origins in the increasingly sophisticated world of the Tudor and Jacobean courts, the refined taste of returning travellers and a growing popular demand for personal privacy, unobtainable in houses of medieval plan.[3] Another wealthy recusant Catholic, Sir Thomas Cornwallis, was busily engaged in re-building his house at nearby Brome at the same time as the rebuilding of Wingfield. Work went on at Brome from 1562 until 1569 and cost about £1,000.[4]

Henry Jerningham had been resident at Court and had seen the best, the costliest, the most ostentatious aspirational wealth of Princess Mary's father made bricks and mortar in the royal palaces. Indeed Jerningham was registered as resident at Court for tax purposes, although the Norfolk county authorities caught up with the family at Costessey in 1625.[5] Henry and Frances, or perhaps his son Harry, wanted a modern home with comfortable and grand rooms for their family, for entertaining and domestic pleasures. The most likely construction date for Jerningham House must have been between 1553 and 1557 but there is evidence of phases of construction or alteration in the later Stuart period.

In order to construct Jerningham House the western range of medieval buildings was deliberately removed. As we have noted previously it was possibly already in a state of dilapidation. Harrison in 1577 described well the aspirations of Tudor gentry.[6]

> Likewise in the houses of knights, gentlemen, merchantmen, and some other wealthy citizens, it is not geson [rare] to behold generally their great provision of tapestry, Turkey work, pewter, brass, fine linen, and thereto costly cupboards of plate, worth five or six hundred or a thousand pounds to be deemed by estimation. But, as herein all these sorts do far exceed their elders and predecessors, and in neatness and curiosity the merchant all other, so in times past the costly furniture stayed there, whereas now it is descended yet lower even unto the inferior artificers

> and many farmers, who, by virtue of their old and not of their new leases, have, for the most part, learned also to garnish their cupboards with plate, their joined beds with tapestry and silk hangings, and their tables with carpets and fine napery, whereby the wealth of our country (God be praised therefore, and give us grace to employ it well) doth infinitely appear.

Harrison's observations chime with Jerningham's aspirations, as seen from the 1591 inventory, where a rich selection of elaborate oak furniture, tapestry hangings and chairs and stools covered in rich velvets are carefully documented.[7]

There are remarkably few good descriptions however of Jerningham House in architectural reference works. Eric Sandon does not mention it at all except to give a map reference.[8] Pevsner's contribution is equally thin. The fact is that these two experts were never granted access. Emery was dedicated to the medieval and did not explore Jerningham House either. This author has been fortunate to have wonderful access to the buildings, also to have enjoyed one of the best descriptions of the detail provided by someone who grew up at the castle, Emily Lyndon-Stanford, who took the subject of the castle as the topic for her undergraduate thesis in 2007.[9] The listed building record below of 1955 is quite helpful too.[10]

> An impressive range some 40m long. Part rubblework, colour-washed or plastered, part timber framed to the upper floor, with good 16th century exposed close studding to the east. Roof plain-tiled to east, glazed black pantiled to west. Two storeys and attic. Various mullioned and mullion and transom windows: some original, others of later date and some 20th century copies of 16th century work. Fine diamond-leaded glazing with many stained glass panels, much of it old but all inserted 20th century from elsewhere. Two-storey rubblework entrance porch: Four centred arch, the hood mould supported on stops carved with falcons, the crest of the Jerningham family to whom the castle was granted in 1544[sic, should be 1553]. Above the entrance an oblong niche surrounded by guilloche work. Original doorframe and door. To north of porch a 3-storey stair tower: square, with splayed angles to ground and first floor. To the west a massive external stack with 4 octagonal shafts, 2 having moulded brick embellishment; star caps. 3 other external stacks, one with rebuilt octagonal shafts. Later axial stacks.

The Porch: The porch is original to the sixteenth century and is two storeys high. It is principally of brick with a four-centred arch, with the moulded hood supported on stops carved with falcons set in a coronet, the Jerningham crest shown above. The falcons are almost gone, weathered away now. The niche over the porch has ovolo mouldings, the term 'guilloche' used in the listed buildings description does not seem quite right for this early era. The head in the niche is modern. The inner door of the porch and its frame are original sixteenth century work. It seems likely that all the buildings on the west side of the old castle were refurbished or rebuilt, especially all the buildings north of the porch. The Great Hall south of the porch on the west side was probably the original site of the Great Hall in the medieval period but it has been extensively reconstructed.[11]

69. The Jerningham Crest, 'out of a ducal coronet or, a demi falcon, wings expanded'.*

70. The niche over the porch with modern stone head.

The roofing of the west range of buildings from the southwest corner tower to its northern end has clasped purlins and arched wind braces from the sixteenth century. (A clasped purlin is the joint held against the principal rafter by a collar, queen strut or raking strut.). Aitkens in his 2009 survey noted that assembly marks in the roof structure began at the south end with rafter number one and rose in sequence towards the north end, ending at the north end with assembly marks on collars and principal rafters going from one to four. The sequencing suggests that this roof was constructed all in

* Jerningham Crest, derived from book bindings, shown in Morris, John (edited Philip Oldfield) British Armorial Bindings, The Bibliographical Society of London © University of Toronto shown online at https://armorial.library.utoronto.ca/ordinaries/coronet-ducal-out?page=2. Described in Robson, T., 1830, *The British Herald, vol 2*, pp JER to JEW. Online at https://books.google.co.uk.

one phase. Inside, however, the north wall at bedroom chamber level is constructed with an open truss and arch brace which Aitkens suggests means that there was a pre-existing structure on the north which was subsequently demolished. This could have been part of the medieval ranges of course but we can no longer tell.[12]

71. Chimney stack on Jerningham House, 1934.

The Chimneys: Harrison made an interesting contemporary observation on the growth of chimneys in his 'Description of England' in 1577.[13] 'The multitude of chimneys latelie erected, whereas in their young daies each one made his fire against the reredos in the hall'. Wingfield Castle chimneys formed part of a study of Suffolk sixteenth century chimneys by Girling in 1934; he included some close-up photos of the chimneys.[14] These elaborately decorated stacks enabled the local brick craftsmen to show off their skill, their ingenious way of taking angular brick and manipulating the patterns of construction appear to be highly complicated but were achieved by simple means. In some cases all the bricks in the shaft were cast in the same mould, the pattern being obtained by correct placing of the bricks, one against another. The spiral and its variants such as zig-zags and lattice patterns were popular motifs.

The Staircase Wing: The porch, usually the dominant feature of a Tudor residence of this era, is completely overshadowed by a magnificent three-storey staircase wing to the north. This oak newel staircase winds up anti-clockwise to the top of Jerningham House, with a decorative oriel window at second floor level. The slight jettying of the second floor gives the wing its distinctive 'tipping forward' look that the author Dodie Smith noticed. In the early twentieth century the whole front façade was rendered to hide the oak timber frame but it was clearly meant to be seen and admired when constructed. Lyndon-Stanford records that before the present owner's time there was a carved lion's head incorporated in the newel post at second floor level. Alas, this was sawn off by a previous owner on leaving the castle.

The Interior: Inside the Tudor house there is a single range of rooms running north to south, the domestic offices and kitchen being on the north end, with the grander reception areas being sited further south. Throughout the building there are a number of good four-centre arched brick fireplaces classic to the late sixteenth century. Two staircases lead up to the chambers on the second and third floors.

72. Staircase wing, 2020.

In the south-east corner of the library there is a second spiral staircase housed in the south-east tower that leads to the upper chambers. This appears to be contemporary with Jerningham House and would have been the main access to the upper floors at the south end of the house. Now there is also an apparently mid-seventeenth century third staircase with carved balusters, of old oak but fitted together on a relatively recent, probably twentieth century oak structure, curiously lacking in newel post carvings. It is housed in the projecting wing at the south end of the house. This good quality oak staircase is constructed in a more sophisticated style than the newel stair, clearly designed for the family and their guests to ascend to the principal chambers above the Great Hall, leaving the newel stair for domestic and kitchen staff. It seems likely that this stair was put in in the mid-twentieth century but it does not quite have the perfectionist, finished style that Baron Ash was noted for. The author wonders if it was installed after his time. Certainly it was already there when the current owners arrived in 1987.

73. The 'seventeenth century staircase' constructed on twentieth century oak supports.

The Great Hall, south of the porch, is probably on the site of the original great hall of the medieval house. Indeed the original hall may have been in part incorporated into it.[15] The ceiling has ovolo-moulded ceiling beams of the Jerningham period. The next ground floor room north of the hall is the parlour, then north of that there is a small 'study' which may have been a serving area or a dining room for the family because a serving hatch still exists between parlour and kitchen, though now hidden by furniture. And next to the study is the magnificent Tudor kitchen with massive fireplaces. It is, as Emily Lyndon-Stanford remarks, a commanding room with a ceiling more than twelve and a half feet high and has two fireplaces. This kitchen was fashioned for serious cooking. The largest easterly fireplace has a span of fourteen feet, with a huge bressumer beam; the 'smaller' one a span of ten feet.

There is a small range of domestic storage rooms to the north of the kitchen which are modern but Lyndon-Stanford suggests that at one time, possibly in medieval days, there were some flint built larders and preparation rooms. An old photo taken in 1945 shows some residual flint ruins visible to the north side of the west wall, which could be the remains of these ancillary buildings. On the west wall of the kitchen there is a blocked late fourteenth century opening to the moat with a moulded arch, which suggests there was a service entrance to the castle over the west side of the moat. There is now later partitioning on the ground floor, much of it seventeenth century but inserted in a later period. There has been some reordering of arrangements inside the north end of the house in the modern era to enhance the comfort of residents.

On the first floor the grandeur of the thirty-five feet long great chamber suggests Jerningham was expecting important visitors. It has a plain barrel-vaulted ceiling, about nineteen feet high. The oak beams supporting this ceiling are long curved beams arranged at fourteen inch intervals over the length of the chamber. North of the great chamber is a further range of chambers, extending across the width of the house at the north end. At least two sixteenth century windows survive but, in the twentieth century, Baron Ash opened up or renewed most of the castle windows and it is difficult to identify originals.

74. The Great Chamber c1950.

Buildings on the east side of the courtyard: The workshop and storage building across the courtyard, running parallel to the east curtain wall, and mentioned on pages 40-41 (Buildings inside the Courtyard), has ancient timbers but early nineteenth century footings. This building long puzzled architectural historians. The timber framed building is not included in the Grade I listing of the castle, labelled on plans as 'a barn'. It serves as storage and workshop, with a nineteenth century gallery stair inside. It looks nondescript and utilitarian from the outside but it has a fine, ancient timber frame. The brick foundations however are nineteenth century. Aldwell says some stables were pulled down and this building inserted in 1826 at the same time the roof of the chapel wing was taken down but quotes no source for this account.[16] The timbers appear to have been moved here and re-erected or imported, but earlier than the nineteenth century, and probably in the seventeenth century. It seems entirely credible, as many observers have thought, that the 'new' buildings were constructed of re-used sixteenth century timbers, perhaps from the south-west range reassembled on new footings, although Liddiard concedes that the building could also have been imported from elsewhere and re-erected.[17] Aitkens points out that the distinctive queen post roof, typical of this part of Suffolk, is very similar to the roof of the barn at Wingfield College built in the 1520s by Charles Brandon. However, the earliest tree-ring dated queen post roof (c1478) known in Suffolk is in the very long barn range at Crows Hall near Debenham. There are other, earlier documented or tree ring dated queen post roofs quite nearby, for example at Bressingham (1401) and Wymondham (1423), and such plain roofs are hard to date without tree-ring dating. It is quite possible that when Brandon and his wife acquired the castle they made some alterations to the lay out of the buildings but it is also possible that Jerningham added this useful range. Without dendrochronology testing it isn't really possible to say exactly when it originated. The timbers include some massive in size and thickness, castle size perhaps, as well as these old queen posts. Certainly it was restored and renewed in the early nineteenth century but again it is not possible to say precisely how.

The Tudor Barn Complex:[18] Outside the modern curtilage of the castle on the east of the castle stand the long barns with fold yards and a cartshed/granary that now belong to Wingfield Castle Farm. These barns on the east side of the main driveway were sold off separately from the castle in the twentieth century. The barns were the subject of an Historic Buildings Project by Leigh Alston of Suffolk County Council Archeological service in 2010.[19] The castle and barns have a close visual relationship and historically the group makes up part of the early Tudor estate complex resuscitated after the Jerninghams took over the estate. The barn is almost certainly contemporary with Jerningham House, that is, just after 1553. It was highly fashionable to aggrandize the main house with a 'seigneurial landscape' of buildings in this way. This unusually long barn must have been the principal estate farm barn and the timber framing is of the high quality that one would associate with such a barn. The main barn with the survival of the whole first floor of fine framing of the main estate barn of the Jerninghams and the nineteenth century attached fold yards and adjacent cartshed/granary building also make up together a good example of a later nineteenth century farmstead. The buildings are of special architectural and historic interest and are considered a very significant group. The main barn of such an estate was normally sited just where the present building stands, that is, to one side of the base court. In the case of Wingfield Castle this was to the east away from the residential part of the castle on the west side. In size the barn compares with the examples at Framsden Hall, with twelve bays, and at Winston Hall Farm and Roydon Hall, which each have ten bays.

The barn is red brick and timber-framed with weatherboarding. The roofs are pantiled, over a much renewed nineteenth century roof structure, although with many ancient timbers reused. It is probable that the roof was originally peg-tiled, not thatched. The long barn was originally of ten bays, enlarged in the nineteenth century to twelve bays.[20] Part of the framing was replaced by brick in the 1860s. There are still however an unusual number of tie-beam surviving braces. Alston comments that the roof structure, originally with queen posts, is common for East Anglian barns built between the late sixteenth to the mid seventeenth centuries but the specific type of roof plates (edge-halved and bridled scarf joints) usually predate 1600, after which face-halved scarfs became the dominant form. The barn has three fold yards and ancillary buildings projecting southwards and a further outbuilding on the east end. These ancillary buildings do not appear on the tithe map of 1842 but are clearly visible on the first Ordnance Survey map of 1882. These brick rooms have detailed fretwork allowing for ventilation. The fold yards have been allowed to deteriorate in recent years and in places have lost their roof. The whole barn complex formed part of a model farm in the nineteenth century, created about 1860 by Sir Robert Adair. It would be sad to see it lost.

The mid-sixteenth century barn has a ground floor underbuilt in brick in the later nineteenth century when the main posts were probably cut, but retains the first floor of close-studded timber-frame with mid rail, jowled posts, wall plates and tie beams. Some curved and cranked wind-bracing remains. The end bays are floored and were originally probably for stabling on the ground floor. Most of the main frame is of chamfered timbers with ogee stops and is very similar to the framing in the residential range of Jerningham House. The roof is later twentieth century, as are the rest of the buildings. Standing south of the fold yards is the three-bay cart shed with granary above and a further single storey outbuilding attached to east. The early Tudor period appears to be one of expanding crop volumes leading to large barns being built. This one is also of interest in that part was floored, probably to provide stabling below.

Notes

1 Hoskins, W. G., 1953, *The Rebuilding of Rural England, 1570–1640 Past & Present, Volume 4*, pp. 44–59, https://doi.org/10.1093/past/4.1.44.

2 Brunskill, R. W., 1985, republished 2006 *Traditional Buildings of Britain: An Introduction to Vernacular Architecture*, Cassell's, London.

3 Platt, C., 1994, *The Great Rebuilding of Tudor and Stuart England, Revolutions in Architectural Taste*, Routledge (online edition 2013).

4 McGrath, Patrick and Rowe, J., 1960, The Recusancy of Thomas Cornwallis, *Proceedings of the Suffolk Institute for Archeology and History, vol 28,* pp. 226-271, online at http://suffolkinstitute.pdfsrv.co.uk.

5 Certificate of residence showing Sir Henry Jernegan to be liable for taxation in Norfolk and not in the Royal Household, the previous area of tax liability 1625 TNA E115/230/81.

6 Harrison, W., 1577, reissued 1587 by Holinshed, *The Description of England*, p. 32, http://public-library.uk/ebooks/43/52.pdf.

7 Inventories taken at Costessey and Wingfield Castle, 1590-1599, Norfolk Record Office Jerningham papers, JER/271, 55 x 1.

8 Sandon, E., 1977, *Suffolk Houses: a Study of Domestic Architecture*, Baron, Woodbridge, pp 340, 339.

9 Lyndon-Stanford, E., 2007, Wingfield Castle in the 14th and the 16th Centuries, dissertation submitted for BA Hons, University of Newcastle on Tyne.

10 Wingfield Castle Historic England Listing 29 July1955 Heritage Category: Grade 1 List Entry Number 1032894. Online at https://historicengland.org.uk/listing/the-list/list-entry/1032894.

11 Ibid. 9, p. 43.

12 Aitkens, P. G., 2009, Report on Wingfield Castle visit July 2009 undertaken for Virtual Past and University of East Anglia, unpublished.

13 Ibid. 6, p. 32.

14 Girling F.A., 1934, Suffolk Chimneys of the Sixteenth Century, *Proceedings of the Suffolk Institute of Archaeology & History volume XXII,* pp. 104-107.

15 Ibid. 9, p. 43

16 Aldwell, S W H 1933 Wingfield. SROI Gwen Dyke Collection HD1643/4/75, p4.

17 Liddiard, R., 2015, Reconstructing Wingfield Castle, in Bloore P. and Martin, E. (eds), *Wingfield College and its Patrons*, Boydell Press, Woodbridge, p. 85.

18 Long barn with fold yards and cartshed/granary with other outbuildings at Wingfield Castle Farm. Historic Buildings listing Grade II, List Entry Number 1390548, 04 August 2003.

19 Alston, L., 2010, Castle Farm, Wingfield, Suffolk WGD030. Historic Buildings Record, Oasis Ref: Suffolkc1-73597, Suffolk County Council.

20 Ibid., p. 309.

The Catelyn Family, 1624–1702

The Catelyn family owned and used Wingfield Castle as a residence from 1624. Through the turbulent religious times of the 1630s and the civil war of the 1640s they held on to their property by the skin of their teeth. They survived the Cromwellian Commonwealth under some difficulties but, with the Restoration of the Monarchy and the era of Charles II, the last Catelyn was rewarded for his unbending loyalty to the Crown. Sir Neville Catelyn and his third wife then led an apparently comfortable life up to the end of the Stuart era of William and Mary. Catelyn died just a few months after the accession of Queen Anne.

75. Sir Neville Catelyn (1634-1702) and his first wife, Lady Dorothea Catelyn, attributed to Robert Walker.

These portraits are thought to have originally hung in Wingfield Castle.

Identifying accurate dates for the Catelyn families' residence at Wingfield has proved difficult. Like many landed gentry they owned and used more than one property. There were tenants occupying Wingfield Castle for at least two periods during the seventeenth century, firstly during the Interregnum of the Cromwellian Commonwealth and secondly, at the latter end of the century when the Catelyns used Kirby Cane Hall as their primary home.

The Catelyns were lawyers, land-owners and back to Elizabethan times had served as members of parliament representing the City of Norwich or Norfolk, negotiating adeptly their personal survival through a combination of helpful alliances and silent non-participation. They did not shine on the political stage. In fact none of the Catelyns said very much in parliament or became visible leaders. Rather they were reliable and committed, and, more importantly, able to make compromises when necessary. Eventually the Wingfield Castle estate moved out of the family when Neville Catelyn's widow remarried after his death. The property was inherited by Neville Catelyn's eldest daughter's grandson and passed to another family dynasty, the Lemans.

The Catelyns lived through insecure, hazardous times at Wingfield. Civil War wracked the nation for some twenty-five years all told, if we include the years of growing animosity between political and religious factions in the late 1630s, the military conflict and the following interregnum up until the restoration of the monarchy in 1660. The Catelyns did not try, as many gentry did, to steer their way through the ideological minefields of religious enthusiasm for the established Church and for the new godly puritanism. They stuck to the traditional bishop-led episcopal church and were suspected of being Catholics, though they were not. From the outset they identified with the king's right to govern and not with the puritan parliamentary cause that very quickly assumed power in East Anglia.

Religious strife in East Anglia. Since Charles I's accession in 1625, the country had been gripped by an increasing anxiety about the form of worship adopted in the post reformation church and a fear of the influence of the Catholic queen and her circle. The king was attracted to Archbishop Laud's vision of conformity and formality in worship, including a rigid hierarchy of church management, which put the king at the top of the episcopacy.

In the 1620s and 30s the majority of the eastern counties' population was not 'puritanical', nor anti-episcopalian nor separatist. The word puritan has become so heavily laden with the opprobrium of later generations that the finer points of a simple, personal faith that rejects pomp, cant and authoritarian hypocrisy has been lost. 'Puritans' had embraced the notions of individual belief and 'Godliness', the importance of studying scripture as a means of understanding God's word and the urge to translate personal belief into an ethical way of conduct. Church ceremonies thus became simpler, excluding the bowing and bobbing; sermons became longer and more thoughtful and invited 'lecturers' gave additional sermons on Sunday afternoons. Altar rails were removed and the altar table moved to a central position in the nave so the congregation could break bread and sup wine together during eucharist. Choirs were disbanded and music banned. Images of Christ, of Mary and the Saints, devotional art, intricate carving and extravagantly decorated stained glass were unappreciated by those wanting a plainer worship.

Churches were already choosing to set the scene for later 'official' iconoclasts like William Dowsing to engage in what is now dismissed as vandalism but was symbolically important in linking individual men and their faith to a personal rather than an institutional deity. Most 'godly' folk in the 1630s, including Oliver Cromwell, did not want to leave the established church. They wanted to reform it, in particular to change the episcopacy, not abolish it. These changes were deeply disturbing to traditionalists, who watched the desecration and destruction of ancient treasures and tossing away of a much-loved liturgy with horror. It was not just that the established way of church and society was being threatened but the foundations of the state and England itself.

The first half of the seventeenth century was a time when Puritan influence was extending deep into Norfolk and Suffolk, permeating from towns into villages and engaging local gentry families as well as the labouring and tradesmen communities in rural areas.

There has been much debate about why the adoption of 'Godly beliefs' was so widespread in Suffolk, in contrast to Norfolk and Essex, where the landed gentry and prosperous yeomen were more split in their adherence to the traditional church and Puritan dissent was largely focused on towns.[1] It may have had to do with the high level of prosperity in the dairying regions of Suffolk and the widespread mercantile connection between the wool, linen and dairy areas of Suffolk and the Low Countries, where religious dissent was taking firm hold. Trade with London, where all kinds of dissenting ideas were being explored and citizens were overwhelmingly parliamentarian may have played a part. While the woollen cloth industry in south Suffolk was in serious decline, the north Suffolk agricultural areas around Wingfield were booming and gentry farming families were doing well, at least until the Civil War started.[2]

Thomas Catelyn, (died 1636). The first Catelyn purchaser of the Wingfield estate, Thomas Catelyn, was the second son of Richard Catelyn I, the head of a rising family in Norwich and Norfolk in the mid-sixteenth century. The family usually spelt their name Catelyn but many variations appear in documents, notable Catelin, Cateline and Catlin. Thomas' father was Sheriff of Norwich in 1531, an Alderman and later mayor who was also a Serjeant-at-Law, a member of the most senior cadre of lawyers created in the time of Henry VIII from whom all judges were chosen right up until the nineteenth century. They were superseded in the nineteenth century by King's (and now Queen's) Counsels, although Serjeants-at-Law had just that bit more grandeur and privilege.

The family lived at the Tower House in Bracondale, Norwich, a medieval house that is still extant in part. Fittingly, until very recently, it was part of the Judges' Lodgings. Richard Catelyn acquired property in Honingham, Norfolk and died at his manor house there in 1556.[3] Members of the Catelyn family had represented Norwich in several Tudor parliaments. Richard established himself as a country gentleman by buying Kirby Cane Hall in 1604, which remained the family's primary residence after the acquisition of the Wingfield Castle estate.

The Catelyn men were usually trained as lawyers at Lincoln's Inn and although there is no record of Thomas Catelyn there, the records are not complete for the period and it is likely that he studied at Cambridge and Lincoln's Inn just as his brother Richard did. The family is mentioned in the Heralds' Visitation of Norfolk, the family arms showing them as 'Catelyns of Wingfield Castle', described heraldically as '*Per chevron Azure and Or, three lions passant guardant in pale countercharged*'.[4] The arms appear in the later mature portrait of Neville Catelyn on page 271 (78).

When Thomas acquired Wingfield Castle in 1625, he was steadily acquiring property all over the counties of Norfolk and Suffolk.[5] He already owned property in Lakenham, Norfolk, and had negotiated the sale of previously acquired Norfolk manors to Sir Nathaniel Bacon of Stiffkey, including the manors of Hastingshall and Whitefooteshall as well as property in Saxthorpe, Heydon, Oulton, Itteringham, Mannington and Wickmere, a house in Irmingland, a pightle next to Corpusty common, and one rood in Irmingland.[6] His father had also dabbled in buying and selling property but had concentrated on the law. Thomas fell out with Bacon over one transaction, Bacon claiming he was owed money over a property deal, an assertion refuted by Catelyn.[7] Thomas' older brother, also called Richard, the heir to their father's property, bought Woolverstone Hall estate in Suffolk, siring another political Catelyn dynasty that included Sir Nathaniel Catelyn, who became Speaker of the Irish House of Commons in the Irish Parliament of 1634–5 and Recorder of Dublin.

Thomas married Judith Elrington (c1550-1615), the daughter of a gentleman in Theydon Bois, Essex but she died before Thomas bought Wingfield Castle. Thomas himself died in 1636, eleven years after the purchase of Wingfield, when the property passed to his only surviving son, Richard Catelyn II, who immediately set about confirming his right to various properties in Wingfield, Stockton and Kirby Cane.[8]

Richard Catelyn II (1583–1662). Catelyn was 53 years old when he inherited the properties at Lakenham, Kirby Cane and Wingfield. It is likely that he was usually resident at Kirby Cane Hall. It is where most of the family is buried. We know from the official record that Richard was living in Norfolk County when elected to parliament on 1640 and not in Norwich or Suffolk. There is reference to him 'of' both Kirby Cane and Wingfield in the official records. On inheriting Kirby Cane in 1636 he began to transform the old manor into a suitably grand house and although the hall now has a mainly Georgian façade, the house is essentially of seventeenth century construction with earlier sixteenth century elements.[9]

There is evidence too that there was a tenant at Lakenham Manor in the mid-seventeenth century and a later dispute over tithes cites Richard Catelyn's ownership of Wingfield.[10] He is also mentioned as owner in the Visitations of Suffolk in 1664 although he was already dead by then.[11]

76. Kirby Cane Hall, 2018.

Richard Catelyn II married first Mary, daughter of Sir Robert Houghton, one of the judges of the King's Bench; she died before he inherited his father's estates. They had one son Thomas. His second wife was Dorothy, daughter of Sir Henry Neville of Billingbere in Berkshire, who bore his second son, Neville Catelyn. A third son Richard III died young. Thomas, Neville's half brother, will figure again in this story. Richard's daughters included Anne, who married Thomas Leman, a 'gentleman' of Wenhaston in Suffolk, whom we will also encounter again. His second and third daughters married into Norfolk gentry families; their fourth daughter remained single.[12]

Richard Catelyn enters politics 1640. Since 1295, the Parliamentary County of Norfolk, along with all other English Counties regardless of size or population, had elected two members of parliament to the House of Commons, the electorate comprising only a small number of substantial freehold property owners. The county also included five parliamentary boroughs, Castle Rising, Great Yarmouth, Kings Lynn, Norwich and Thetford all returning two members each where voting could be by just a handful of people. When Catelyn decided to put himself forward for election he was ambivalent about it and no wonder. Declaring oneself for one party and one set of shifting gentry alliances was a decisive and public act. And it turned out his election was not strictly legal.

Disputes over religion were critical to the political meltdown that led later to the Civil War. As Richard Baxter, the Presbyterian divine, remarked 'The warre was begun in our streets before the king and parliament had any armie'.[13] And every parliamentary election amongst the burgesses eligible to vote in 1640 was a fraught choice, to elect either a solid supporter of the king or alternatively a fervent godly Puritan sympathizer. Richard Catelyn was elected as one of the two members for the city of Norwich in the general election of November 1640 that formed the Long Parliament. The second member was Richard Harman, a respected and moderate Alderman over whose nomination there was little dispute, being a compromise candidate. Catelyn though had to fight a contest with another man, John Tooley. The burgesses of Norwich were clearly looking for a traditionalist royalist supporter with conventional pro-church views on religion.[14] Catelyn, who had sat on the Norfolk Trustees for Religion in 1631 seemed superficially to fit the bill and won the local vote against Tooley 906 to 265.[15] Oddly though, it was Tooley's name that was submitted on the indenture to Westminster by sheriff John Dethick. Catelyn's displacement was quickly spotted by the other sheriff, John Osborne, who hastened to submit another indenture with Catelyn's name. But Dethick had spotted that Catelyn was not in fact eligible to stand since he was not a freeman of Norwich and lived in the County of Norfolk, presumably at Kirby Cane, not in the City.

Catelyn took his seat anyway but at the opening session his unconventional election was queried. With astonishing disregard for convention, the assembled members of parliament declared it was an honest mistake and therefore the election should stand and the sheriff filing the indenture should not be criticised.[16] The folk of Norwich however may have been disappointed by Catelyn's performance in parliament, which has been described as 'lacklustre'.[17] He sat on a few committees but made no significant contributions to debate. By May 1643 he had withdrawn. He did not sympathise with the way parliament was moving, particularly after the failed attempt by Charles I to seize five members opposed to him.

The county of Suffolk, along with Essex and Hertfordshire, submitted petitions to parliament early in 1642 indicating support for reformation of the church, punishment for religious 'delinquents' and Catholics, and aid for Ireland, and general support for parliament. Norfolk and the City of Norwich followed suit in March. Catelyn was isolated from his own communities' views and simply decided to stop attending parliament. He went to Westminster in February 1643 to join Harman in attempting to get a reduction on the levy imposed on the city of Norwich. But when he came home he complained to the Corporation of Norwich about the burden of his parliamentary duties and asked to be excused. The Corporation replied, with sympathetic words. They said, with understanding, 'it is likely to be painful, tedious and prejudicial to your own private affairs' but asked him to carry on notwithstanding.[18] He ceased attending parliament anyway and withdrew to Kirby Cane.

Civil War. So while the Long Parliament lasted twenty years, Richard Catelyn was in effect a member for only three. When the Civil War broke out later in 1642, he declared for the Royalist side against the Parliamentary side. Catelyn and six other members who had stopped attending were issued with a warning in May 1643 to 'be enjoined to attend the Service of the House within Ten Days, upon Pain of the Forfeiture of Two hundred Pounds a man to be levied on their lands and Estates'.[19] A month later the Deputy Lieutenant of Norfolk was ordered to impose the fine on Catelyn and Sir Charles Legros, a member for Norfolk.[20] By September neither of them had paid the fine, and an order in September doubled the fine to the huge £400 apiece.[21]

The fighting began in August 1642. Like many families the Catelyns were torn by divided loyalties. Richard's son Thomas had married Elizabeth Lewknor some time before 1618. The Lewknors were a strongly Puritan family from Denham, Suffolk. Elizabeth's father Sir Edward Lewknor had been an important puritan champion in East Anglia. Thomas however took his father's royalist position and joined the king's military forces. Richard's first father-in-law, Robert Houghton, was a strong supporter of parliament and also therefore at odds with his grandson Thomas's position. Richard's second son Neville, whose mother was Richard's second wife Dorothy, was ten years younger than his half brother and strongly identified with the royalist cause.

Suffolk gentry in general supported Parliament but when it came to fighting, most of the them seem to have done their best to remain neutral. The most active participants in Suffolk were a mixture of puritans and parliamentarians. Ipswich, Lavenham and Aldeburgh were strongly for Parliament. Ipswich fortified itself against the threat of the king's fleet. Other local families were divided over which side to support. Sir William Soame of Little Thurlow was an active parliamentarian, while his son, Stephen Soame sided with the king. At Little Bradley, Sir George Le Hunt and his sons were Royalists, all except one, Richard, who was a major in the parliamentarian Eastern Association. Close neighbours also fell out. The Blagges of Little Horringer Hall were Royalists and willing to fight for their cause. The Lucas Family of Horsecroft was equally strong in their support for parliament. In East Suffolk there were twice as many gentry supporting Parliament as supported the king.[22] In West Suffolk, however, their numbers were fairly even, with only a majority of two in favour of parliament. Neither did all Catholics fully support the king. Of thirty-four Suffolk Catholic families, only six supported Charles I. Of the sixty-four Royalist gentry families in Suffolk, these six Catholic families made up a mere nine per cent. Less than a hundred prominent men and their families were supporters of the king and of a non-puritan traditional religion. They would all be in peril as tension mounted. Riots broke out along the Stour Valley on the Suffolk/Essex border. Ostensibly rallying around the parliamentary cause, the protesters were fired by rising unemployment in the cloth trade and were also supporting the anti-enclosure movement that robbed commons' users of their access to land traditionally theirs.

The Catelyn family would not have felt comfortable or safe staying at Wingfield during the War. Their nearest gentry neighbours at Syleham Hall, the Barry family, were staunch parliamentarians. Few English shires played a more decisive or distinctive role in the Civil War than Suffolk. The County was wealthy and well organised, run by London merchants like Sir Nathaniel

Barnadiston from Kedington near Clare, who was energetic, and efficient as well as wealthy. At Lowestoft, Cromwellian soldiers overwhelmed the royalist sympathisers very quickly without bloodshed. Thomas Catelyn was among those who rapidly surrendered Lowestoft alongside Thomas Knyvett from Ashwellthorpe.[23] The War was then at an uncertain stage; full-blown battles had yet to be fought, so Catelyn and Knyvett did not remain prisoners. Norfolk began the Civil War in an equally ambivalent frame of mind to Suffolk but the Cromwellian forces made rapid inroads into Norfolk towns. Before long the county was totally under the control of the parliamentarians, controlled by the efficient Eastern Association, which rapidly established control of the administration of daily life in the eastern counties. Young men were being pressed into the parliamentary army and support for the royalist cause was effectively silenced.

Wingfield, Lakenham and Kirby Cane seized. Because of his continuing absence from Westminster, in 1644 Richard Catelyn was 'disabled' for 'deserting the service of the House' and his estate was sequestrated. We do not know where the Catelyn family went at that time but it is likely they stayed quietly at Kirby Cane. At the start of the Civil War, Parliament set up two committees, the Sequestration Committee, which confiscated the estates of Royalists who fought against Parliament, and the Committee for Compounding with Delinquents, which allowed Royalists whose estates had been sequestrated to 'compound' for their estates, that is pay a fine and recover their estates if they pledged not to take up arms against Parliament again. The size of the fine they had to pay depended on the worth of the estate and how great their support for the Royalist cause had been. The fine was frequently three times net annual income. The wheels of central administration turned slowly however and sequestration did not necessarily lead to immediate eviction. But it did result in a catastrophic lack of income from the estate.

1644 was a bad year for the Catelyn family. They lost their fortune and they lost Richard's older son, twenty three year old Thomas, a Captain in the Royalist army, who died in October at the second Battle of Newbury. Thomas had been a promising lawyer and was married with children. A year later Richard applied to compound for his estates. He asked to be allowed to do so by proxy instead of going to London, 'being very infirm and unable to travel'. He added that a further burden was that his wife had the care of eight small children. Some of the children must have been Thomas's.[24]

Richard Catelyn was eventually discharged without fine by order of the House in 1647. He was a signatory to the petition for a free parliament in

1660, his last formal political act. He died in 1662 and was buried in the church of All Saints at Kirby Cane. His heir was his eldest son by his second marriage, Neville Catelyn.

Was Wingfield Castle damaged in the Civil War? Numerous fortified manors and castles that could be used defensively were systematically 'slighted' during the Civil War by parliamentary forces, mainly to prevent them being garrisoned. Most of the known castle 'slightings' were in the Midlands, the North and Wales. There are no records of Suffolk castles or fortified houses being destroyed although many royalist houses were attacked and deer were stolen from unprotected parks. Much of the damage was by popular exploitation of opportunity.[25] Melford Hall was ransacked, plundered and a wing burnt down. In Norfolk, Sir Philip Knyvett, a lukewarm supporter of Parliament during the Civil War, demolished New Buckenham Castle, his own home, in 1649, probably at the request of Parliament. The Commonwealth authorities feared Royalist diehards might fortify the redundant castle. We have no evidence of Wingfield Castle being attacked. Lack of evidence does not mean of course that it was not. It was surely vulnerable to the predations of local parliamentarian enthusiasts, especially in the heady anti-papist pro-puritan riots of 1642.

The Civil War period may have been when the north and east curtain walls of Wingfield Castle were destroyed. The Catelyns were not living there and they could not have afforded to maintain it in pristine condition. At the time they were relatively impecunious. It is unlikely, however, that Wingfield Castle was slighted by any official parliamentary action. If it was damaged at this time it would have been the outcome of neglect and local unofficial mischief.

Thomas and Ann Caton, tenants at Wingfield Castle c1647–1658. Although Richard Catelyn had his property restored in 1647 he did not return to use Wingfield as a family home. The Wingfield Castle estate was rented out to Thomas Caton the elder (1597-1670) throughout the 1640s and early 1650s for an annual rent of between fifty and seventy five pounds.[26] The Catons were the prominent family in Thorpe Abbotts, Norfolk, settled at the hall there since medieval days.[27] They were intermarried with the Wythes of Brockdish, the Thurstons of Hoxne and many local minor gentry families in the Waveney Valley. Thomas and his wife Ann had a child, Henry, who died young and then a further child, Thomas the younger. Thomas and Ann died within a few days of each other in August 1670 and were buried in the Thorpe Abbotts family vault on his birthday.

The Catons had Puritan leanings; one of their nephews, Peter Caton became a Quaker.[28] We do not know how long the Catons were tenants at Wingfield, they were certainly paying rent from 1637 to the late 1650s. They continued at Wingfield after the restoration of Catelyn's property in 1647, when he was able to enter into a formal tenancy agreement and probably stayed until Neville Catelyn married in 1658 but this is speculation from the Kirby Cane Estate accounts. The Catons' son was educated by a Mr Ellis at Thorpe Abbotts between 1661 and 1665, before going up to Gonville and Caius College, Cambridge.[29] The younger Caton always lived at Thorpe Abbotts. The Catons were doing well in the mid-seventeenth century. Thomas had rebuilt the Thorpe Hall manor house in about 1620 and it remains essentially unchanged today.

Sir Neville Catelyn (1634–1702). Richard's only surviving son, Neville, used Wingfield as his main home from quite early on in his life, probably from before his first marriage. Neville was always referred to as 'of Wingfield Castle' until his death. Baptised on 3 March 1634 at Kirby Cane Church, Neville spent his childhood under the shadow of his father's stigmatising royalist affiliation. He adhered loyally to his father's royalist cause throughout the rest of his life. His only brother Thomas's death at Newbury occurred when Neville was ten. He attended Kings College, Cambridge, matriculating in 1650 and then probably returned home to Kirby Cane. In 1658 he married Dorothy, daughter of Sir Thomas Bedingfield of Darsham in Suffolk, at one time Member of Parliament for Eye.[30] It is believed the portrait on the first page of this chapter is of Dorothy. She died about 1665. Their two children, Thomas and Neville, born in 1662 and 1665, died in infancy and have their own memorial in Kirby Cane Church.

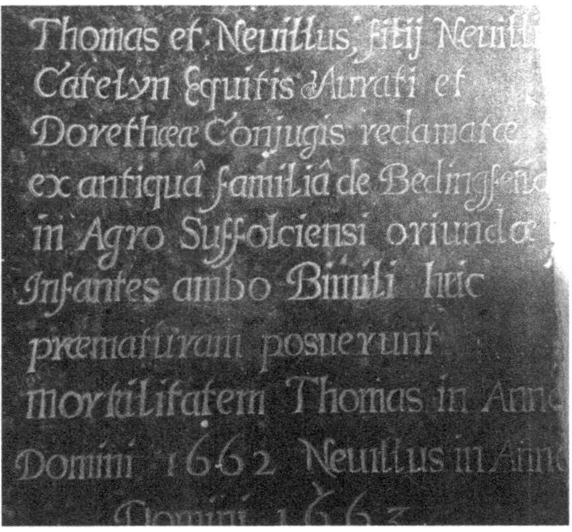

77. Memorial to Thomas and Neville Catelyn who died in infancy 1662 and 1665.

It is likely that Neville and Dorothy moved their household to Wingfield Castle after their marriage in about 1658, leaving Kirby Cane for his mother. Times were changing; the population was weary of the dour puritanical joylessness that the Cromwellian Protectorate imposed. Disaffection and popular resentment were rising, even in loyal East Anglia. Cromwell was sick and no-one could predict what would happen in national politics after his death. The exiled Charles II and his court were not forgotten by his supporters. The Catelyn family had managed to hold on to their property after paying the fines and the 'compound'. The Caton lease was terminated and a new era began for the castle. It was many years since a young couple had made the castle their primary home. Neville certainly used Kirby Cane Hall after his mother died but he used Wingfield as his own home through his personal griefs and shifting ambitions.

The Restoration of the Monarchy in 1660 was both a relief and a joy for the Catelyns. Catelyn immediately joined the royalist forces, becoming a major then a 'captain of militia horse' (the cavalry) for Norfolk. Unlike the parliamentary New Model Army under Thomas Fairfax, the royalist militias had the reputation of being somewhat undisciplined and unpredictable. We have no idea whether Catelyn had talent as a military man. He served for some years during the Anglo-Dutch wars. There is a report in parliamentary papers of five Swedish (enemy) vessels arriving at Yarmouth Harbour on 24 June 1667, when

> Sir Jacob Ashley [should read Astley] and Sir Knevitt (sic) Catelyne's troops of horse have come into town; also Sir John Holland's regiment of foot. A fly-boat is ready to be sunk at the entrance of the boom, to stop any fire-ship coming into the haven to destroy the shipping. Sir Henry Bacon's company, which was quartered at Lowestoft, has returned. None of the Dutch fleet are seen, but their guns are daily heard.[31]

Sir Jacob Astley, readily confused with his illustrious grandfather, a famous royalist commander, was a contemporary of Catelyn's at Cambridge. They served together in the militia and would later serve in parliament together. Catelyn was rather over-awed by the clever Astley and did not always share his more liberal views, on Catholic emancipation, for example. Where Astley grasped the bigger picture and had a vision of a better, more peaceable future, Catelyn could not get beyond his highly conservative traditional views. Astley was High Sheriff of Norfolk in 1664 and Commissioner of Trade between 1714 and 1717. He inherited various estates and built himself a new and very elegant house at Melton Constable during the post restoration period. Astley himself signed the Norfolk address for a free Parliament presented to George Monck in 1660, was created a baronet at the Restoration and given a post at Court. He was an ally of Catelyn during their parliamentary career but not a close one.

Neville was knighted for his loyalty by a grateful king at Somerset House in 1662. Life was looking up although he still had no heir. And then in 1665 Dorothy died. Neville married quite quickly a second time in 1666, to Elizabeth, daughter of Robert Houghton of Ranworth, a well-known parliamentary supporter. Neville had children by Elizabeth but they too all died young.[32]

Catelyn was given a number of other jobs after the Restoration. He was Commissioner for Assessment for taxes in Norfolk and Suffolk from 1661-80 and for Norfolk, Norwich and Suffolk from 1689-1690.[33] He became a JP in Norfolk from 1668-1688 and from 1689-1702, and for Suffolk from 1680-1685, Deputy Lieutenant of Norfolk from 1676 to February 1688, from November 1688 to 1702 and Deputy Lieutenant of Suffolk from 1680-1685. All these appointments carried income and were positions of modest influence. He must have discharged these duties with some fairness as he was clearly popular with gentry voters when it came to entering parliament. Neville's mother died in 1672 and at some time after that, before 1674, Neville and Elizabeth moved their primary residence from Wingfield to Kirby Cane. They rented out Wingfield Castle estate to a tenant, Thomas Catchpole and his wife Margaret and their children.

Thomas and Margaret Catchpole of Wingfield. There are very few sources of information about these Wingfield Castle tenants. The main source is the Hearth Tax Records of 1674, when Mr Catchpole is listed for the enormous number of twenty-five hearths.[34] This would have included the Castle, the accompanying farm, Old Wingfield Hall and various other estate houses. The next nearest tax burden in size was 'Mr Cornwallis' with twelve hearths at Brome Hall. Most taxed homes had one or two hearths. The tax was levied on occupiers, not always the owners. When he died in 1720 Catchpole left a very clear will and a probate inventory accompanied it.[35] He was referred to as a yeoman 'of Wingfield' but his main property was in Stradbroke and there is no mention of the castle in his will. The inventory refers to his Stradbroke property, which he leaves to his wife and then to his children. We do not know how long the tenants stayed but the lease would probably have been terminated when Neville Catelyn died in 1702.

Catelyn goes into politics. Catelyn entered Norfolk politics in 1675 as an adherent of the 1st earl of Yarmouth, (that is, Robert Paston of the Norfolk family who have already played a part in this narrative). His political adventures throw some light on his character. Paston was a monarchist who had sat out most of the Civil War in the Netherlands avoiding being identified with either side and paid large fines in 1644 to get back his estates at Oxnead and in London.[36] He was member for Thetford after the Restoration and an influential persuader. Catelyn was however defeated in a by-election in the county when he lost to Sir Robert Kemp. The election cost Catelyn an enormous six hundred pounds, about sixty-eight thousand pounds in today's money.[37]

Sir Robert Kemp was a churchman from a staunch royalist family, but who was nevertheless supported by 'all the godly party, whether Presbyterians, Independents, or Quakers', and by 'the greater part of the Roman Catholics.[38] This universal popularity was rare. Sir John Holland, a rational and moderate politician, mustered the duke of Norfolk's tenantry on Kemp's behalf. Holland was not a fan of Catelyn and successful in turning some clergy away from Catelyn to Kemp.[39],[40] The whole process was described in a letter to Holland from a friend who was a witness, clearly a somewhat partial one who did not like Catelyn either.[41] He believed that Catelyn stood against Kemp 'much against his own will and inclinations', observing that Catelyn's main support was 'most of those persons (whether of the clergy or laity) that are right for the Church of England', that is narrower in appeal than Kemp. If Catelyn had been able to read the series of letters of the period between Lord Yarmouth and other influential parties that now survive in the Yarmouth Letters in the Norfolk Record Office he may have been even less keen to put himself forward. Elections were fought and won by the machinations and plotting of the seriously landed gentry. [42]

On the day of the poll, Norwich was 'filled with a great number which the power and terrors, industry and art of the lord lieutenant, etc., had drawn and driven thither to vote for Sir Robert Kemp'. Catelyn's first setback was the seizure by his opponents of the *King's Head*, intended for his headquarters. His imposing cavalcade of 4,000 horse was thus 'necessitated to go to the *White Swan*, [near St Peter Mancroft] which is on the backside of the butchers' shambles ... very incommodiously situated' for Castle Hill, the usual venue for the county elections. After a view of the rival processions the sheriff, 'a soap-boiler of French origin', who acquitted himself well in the circumstances, decided that a poll would be necessary, and an agreement on procedure was reached orally and committed to paper by Kemp's man Hobart (the distinguished Whig politician Sir Henry Hobart, of Blickling). According to Catelyn's adherents, who did not sign the return, Hobart omitted a vital clause designed to eliminate double voting, and many of the electorate were left unpolled. Catelyn learnt an expensive lesson, that parliamentary elections in Norfolk were fraught with unexpected threats and reverses.

Political popularity waxes and wanes though and when a vacancy occurred in Norwich in February 1678, William Wyndham, brother-in-law of Yarmouth's rival Lord Townsend, thought it unwise to 'oppose so popular and notable a knight as Catelyn'. Before the poll, however, Wyndham unaccountably made way for Yarmouth's son, William Paston, to challenge Catelyn and poor Catelyn lost again. At the first general election of 1679 Catelyn was recommended to the county by Sir Joseph Williamson, who had lost his seat and was stepping down. Catelyn was also nominated by Yarmouth as a candidate 'devoted to the Crown'. By 1679 resignations and dismissals had removed the principal figures in the rival faction. 'A ferocious personal antagonism between the leaders', and the survival among the rank and file of the old enmities of the Interregnum, prepared the way for the exceptionally sharp political warfare that characterised Norfolk politics for the remainder of the period.

On the day of the by-election some eighteen or nineteen Cambridge scholars who were freeholders in Norfolk were brought in to vote and Sir Thomas Hare was said to have mustered four hundred votes for the court candidates. Browne commented. 'I never observed so great a number of people who came to give their voices', 'but all was civilly carried at the hill, and I do not hear of any rude or unhandsome carriage'. 'Only hock and sherry were on tap, the electorate abstaining on principle from heady French beverages.' 'With over 6,000 votes cast, and less than 500 separating the top of the poll from the foot, the result could not be declared until 11.00pm, when it was announced that the successful court candidate was Catelyn, not Calthorpe. The Members were carried on chairs about the Market Place after eleven o'clock with trumpets and torches, candles being lighted at windows,

78. Sir Neville Catelyn, 1688, oil on canvas, unknown artist.

and the Market Place full of people. ... There was a strange consumption of beer and bread and cakes, and abundance of people slept in the Market Place and lay like flocks of sheep in or about the Cross.'

One might have thought that this was the final decision and Catelyn had definitely won his seat but more shenanigans led to the vote being discounted, a bitter third disappointment. The candidates and tellers must do it all over again. On the day before the poll Catelyn's nerve broke, and he withdrew himself from the city because 'the rabble did asperse him with being popishly affected'.[43] His timorousness so disappointed his friends that they resolved not to support him again in the future. In spite of this luke-warm support, Catelyn was finally elected for Norwich unopposed in 1685 and was listed as a member of the opposition.

Elizabeth Catelyn dies in 1687. Neville's second wife Elizabeth died in 1687; their only son predeceased her. Perhaps her death allowed Catelyn a little more time for politics and he became a moderately active member of James II's parliament. He was not very vocal, indeed the author has not discovered a single speech in the Commons chamber but he sat on a few committees and voted when necessary.[44] In 1688 he told the Lord Lieutenant of Norfolk that he could not vote to support the repeal of the penal laws or the Test Acts (legislation that served as a religious test for public office and imposed various civil disabilities on Catholics and non-conformists).

Catelyn was a Church of England man through and through and was not about to change his mind to accommodate a shift in public perceptions that the threat from Catholics and Dissenters was diminishing. He was removed as requested from local office but restored in 1688 and followed the example of Sir John Holland in refusing to sit with the Roman Catholics during the months of James II's ousting and the Glorious Revolution that put Protestant William and Mary on the throne. Re-elected in 1689, Catelyn then became rather more active in committee, for example, hearing a petition from dealers in Norwich stuffs and also one to consider the establishment of a court of conscience for small claims in the city of Norwich.[45] He finally retired from Parliament in 1689.

Catelyn did not shine politically at any stage; he did his duty and no more. He never changed his mind when shifting times should perhaps have told him new approaches were worth considering. These days he would be disparagingly referred to as 'lobby-fodder'. Over the years Neville had grown corpulent and prosperous looking. A late portrait (78. p. 271) is sadly very damaged but worth inspecting, if only to contrast his florid appearance with the diffident thin young man of the earlier painting. Rotundity was a common enough state among politicians of the day. The poet Andrew Marvell, who was also an MP, commented that the corpulence of Robert Paston and Henry Hyde made them 'burdens of the earth'. Marvell couldn't resist a verse:-

> Hyde, whose transcendent paunch so swells of late
> That he the rupture seems of law and state;
> Paston, whose belly bears more millions
> Than Indian carracks, and contains more tuns.[46]

Neville was beginning to compete. Westminster then as now was full of places to drink, eat and gossip, the new London coffee houses even more enticing for men without wives to restrain their excesses.

Catelyn married a third time about 1695, to Mary Blois, the daughter of Sir William Blois of Grundisburgh. He was sixty-one years old; Mary was considerably younger at forty-one. Catelyn was a man of property and they were from similar social backgrounds. The marriage was short-lived. Neville Catelyn died in July 1702 and was buried in Kirby Cane church alongside so many of his family, in the vault he had built. When Neville died leaving no heirs, his property, including the Wingfield Castle estate, was left to his wife Mary in trust for her lifetime. But after her decease it was to go to Neville's oldest sister Anne, married to Thomas Leman of Wenhaston. Anne and Thomas Leman had in fact already died, many years before Neville.

Mary Catelyn remarries. Neville's widow Mary married again two years later in May 1704.[47] Her husband was Sir Charles Turner of Warham, MP for Kings Lynn from 1695-1738, an old associate of Neville's. Turner was exceptionally well connected politically, being a brother-in-law of Robert Walpole of Houghton. Charles and Mary made Kirby Cane their principal seat. It is not at all clear what happened to Wingfield Castle estate at that time. They may have used it as a third country house in addition to Warham Hall, Turner's family home, or it may have continued under the Catchpole tenancy or housed another tenant. There is one report of Richard Aldous (1685-1751) leasing the Castle from Warham.[48]

Turner died suddenly on 24 November 1738, at Robert Walpole's house at Houghton, 'as his gentleman was dressing him'.[49] He was buried at Warham. His will, dated 5 January 1738, charged the Warham estate with portions amounting to seven thousand pounds for the three daughters of his deceased son; otherwise his heir was his nephew John. Mary died the same year, possibly predeceasing Charles by a few months. She is buried with Neville Catelyn at Kirby Cane.

Neville Catelyn's will was challenged after Charles and Mary's death.[50] The question was whether the Turner heirs should inherit the properties that Mary had brought to her marriage to Turner or whether the heirs of Neville's niece Anne Leman should inherit. There were tricky codicils that were not easy to interpret. The legal opinion finally confirmed Anne's heirs' legitimate right to inherit the properties based on Neville's will. Wingfield therefore passed to Ann Leman's grandson Thomas.

Notes

1 Holmes, C., 1974, *The Eastern Association in the English Civil War*, Cambridge University Press, Cambridge, Chapter 1 Social Organization in East Anglia, pp. 7–15.

2 Dymond D. and Northeast, P., 1995, *A History of Suffolk*, Phillimore, Chapter 5 Reformation and Division 1530–1630, pp. 58–71.

3 Blomefield, F., 1808, Clavering Hundred: Kirkeby-Kam, in *An Essay Towards A Topographical History of the County of Norfolk, London, Volume 8* pp. 28-37, British History Online http://www.british-history.ac.uk/topographical-hist-norfolk/vol8/pp28-37 [accessed 20 December 2019].

4 Catelyn family tree and arms, in Bysshe, E., 1664, *The Visitation of Norfolk*, republished Norfolk Record Society, 1934 Vol 5, p. 49, published 1934 SROI HD2448/9/13/1. Online at Google Books.

5 Manor of Wingfield, Wingfield Castle, park and lands belonging 1624 Mortgage by demise Sir Henry Jernegan/Holman Staffordshire County Record Office Ref D641/3/A/3/1/2-3.

6 Bargain and Sale (copy) from Thomas Catelyn, gent to Sir Nathaniel Bacon and Dorothy his wife of the manors of Hastingshall and Whitefooteshall and property in Irmingland, Corpusty, Saxthorpe, Heydon, Oulton, Itteringham, Mannington and Wickmere, capital messuage in Irmingland, pightle next Corpusty common, and one rood in Irmingland 1605 Norfok Record Office, Townshend and other Papers BRA 926/60, 372X9.

7 Thomas Catelyn at Fakenham, to Sir Nathaniel Bacon, disputes money which Bacon claims he is owed, c1612, NRO Bradfer-Lawrence Collection, Bacon of Stiffkey, letter and papers BL/BC 8/20.

8 Catlyn v Calver, property in Stockton and Kirby Cane, Norfolk 1636 TNA C 3/398/65; Account of out-rents from the Kirby Cane estate 1610-1617, and of rents due to Richard Catlyn from Lakenham, Kirby Cane, and Wingfield (co. Suffolk) 1637. Also inventory of plate 1630 and rent and estate accounts 1630-1641, Knyvett-Wilson Family Collection NRO KNY 939 372 x 6.

9 Kirby Cane Hall Norfolk Historic Environment Record NHER Number 10690.

10 Gwillim, H., 1801, *A Collection of Acts and Records of Parliament: With Reports of Cases...respecting tithes etc, Volume 2* London p. 732.

11 Norfolk Visitation 1664–*Suffolk Extracts*, author: Bysshe, E. Sir; Norfolk Record Society 1934 SROI HD2448/9/13/1and; Visitations of Suffolk transcribed Metcalfe, W. C., 1882, by Hervey, Clarenceux, 1561, Cooke, Clarenceux, 1577, and Raven, *Richmond Herald*, 1612, with notes and an appendix of additional Suffolk pedigrees by Harvey, W. d 1567; British Museum, MSS Harleian1103; Cook, R. (d 1593) Raven, J. E.; Metcalfe.

12 Ibid. 3, pp. 28-37.

13 Baxter, R., 1658. *Of Justification: Four Disputations Clearing and Amicably Defending the Truth, Against the Unnecessary Oppositions of Divers Learned and Reverend Brethren*, Printed by R. White for N. Simmons and N. Elkins, London.

14 Holmes, C., 1974, *The Eastern Association in the Civil War*, Cambridge University Press, Cambridge, pp. 24-25.

15 Reynolds, M., 2005, *Godly Reformers and their Opponents in Early Modern England. Religion in Norwich c1560–*

1643, Boydell, Woodbridge. Chapter 11 The Puritan Revolution 1640-1643, pp. 236-252.

16 Jansson, M., Morrison, J. K., Plant A., Smith, A., 2000, *Proceedings in the Opening Session of the Long Parliament, House of Commons vol 1 November and December 1640*, Boydell, Woodbridge.

17 Ibid. 15, p. 247

18 Ketton-Cremer, R. W., 1969, *Norfolk in the Civil War*, Faber and Faber, London, reissued 1985 by Gliddon Books, Chapter 10 The Summer of 1643 pp. 187-223.

19 House of Commons Journal 19 Carl I. Vol 3, 9 May 1643 p. 77

20 House of Commons Journal 19 Carl I Vol 3, 22 June 1643.

21 House of Commons Journal 19 Carl I Vol 3, 16 September 1643.

22 Blackwood, G., 1989, The Gentry of Suffolk during the Civil War, Chapter 37 in Dymond, D. and Martin, E.(ed), *An Historical Atlas of Suffolk* 2nd edition,, Suffolk Institute for Archaeology and History p. 84.

23 Ibid. 18, p. 85.

24 Ibid., p. 288.

25 O'Riordan, C., 1993, *Popular Exploitation of Enemy Estates in the English Revolution. History, vol 78*, pp. 183-200.

26 Account of rent of Kirby Cane Estates and Wingfield 1630-1640. NRO KNY 939,372x6; Lease: Valentyne Saunders, late of Lyndon, co. Rutland, to Thomas Caton, the elder, of Wingfield Castle, co. Suffolk, gent and Thomas Caton of Thorpe Abbottes, co. Norfolk, his son and heir apparent. 16 June 1653. Leicestershire, Leicester and Rutland Record Office DG11/683; Quitclaim: Richard Watts releases to Thomas Caton of Wingfield Castle, co. Suffolk. 16 June 1653, Leicestershire, Leicester and Rutland Record Office DG11/682.

27 Burke, J., 1831, *A Genealogical and Heraldic History of the Landed Gentry; or Commoners of Great Britain and Ireland etc, vol 4*, p. 307, online at https://books.google.co.uk/books.

28 Ibid., p. 307

29 Venn, J., 1898 *Biographical History of Gonville and Caius College*, Record of Gonville and Caius College Alumni, p. 426.

30 'Neavill Catlin & Dorothea Bedingfield married ye 24th of May 1658 St Bride Fleet Street', London Metropolitan Archive, Composite register: baptisms 1653–Sep 1672 and Dec 1673–Apr 1674, marriages 1653–1666, burials 1653–Jun 1672, P69/BRI/A/005/MS06540, Item 001.

31 Calendar of State Papers Domestic: Charles II - volume 206: June 17-24, 1667 Charles II, 1667, ed. Green, M. A. E., 1866, London, pp. 198-229. British History Online http://www.british-history.ac.uk/cal-state-papers/domestic/chas2/1667/pp198-229 [accessed 20 March 2020].

32 Dates of marriages and births of children taken from Parish Registers of Kirby Cane and Ranworth quoted in entry in Cambridge Alumni Database (ACAD) Catelin N., p. 426. Online at https://venn.lib.cam.ac.uk.

33 Henning, B. D. (ed), 1983, Catelyn, Sir Neville (1634-1702), of Kirby Cane, Norfolk and Wingfield Castle, Suffolk. *The History of Parliament: the House of Commons 1660-1690*, Boydell and Brewer, Woodbridge.

34 Booth, G. (complier), 1905, Suffolk Hearth Tax Returns 1674, *Suffolk Green Books No XI, Vol 13*. Woodbridge.

35 Original Will of Thomas Catchpole of Wingfield Suffolk Record Office Ipswich (SROI) IC/AA1/149/95 and Probate Inventory SROI, FE1/13/84

36 Paston, Robert (1631-83), of Oxnead, Norfolk and Pall Mall, Westminster, published in Henning B.D. (ed), 1983, *The History of Parliament: the House of Commons 1660-1690*, Boydell and Brewer, Woodbridge, http://www.histparl.ac.uk/volume/1660-1690/member/paston-robert-1631-83

37 House of Commons Journal, Catelyn, Sir Neville. p. 32.

38 Ibid. 33.

39 Letter from Sir John Holland to Mr Barnard. 1 April 1675. He has heard That Sir Neville Catelyn may stand for election and urges Mr Barnard to use his influence among the clergy to vote for Kemp. NRO The Yarmouth Letters, BL/Y1/83.

40 Letter Rev'd John Gough, Oxnead to Lady Yarmouth. NRO Yarmouth Letters BL /Y1/89

41 Hayton, D. W., Cruickshanks, E., Handley, S. (eds), 2002, *The History of Parliament: the House of Commons 1690-1715,* Boydell and Brewer, Woodbridge, online http://www.histparl.ac.uk/volume/1690-1715/constituencies/

norfolk.

42 The Yarmouth Letters, 1660-1688. NRO. BL/Y.

43 Quoted by Cruikshank, E. in *The History of Parliament: the House of Commons, 1690-1715 volume 1*, 1983.

44 *Grey's Debates, 1667-1694* (originally published 1769) Debates of the House of Commons, From the Year 1667 to the Year 1694. Collected by Anchitell Grey. Online Volumes 8 and 9 at British History Online http://www.british-history.ac.uk/greys-debates. [accessed 30 March 2020].

45 Measures of Norwich Stuffs 1689 *House of Commons Journal Volume 10*: 11 May pp. 129-130, His Majesty's Stationery Office, London, 1802.

46 Quote from Paston, Robert (1631-83), of Oxnead, Norfolk and Pall Mall, Westminster in Henning, B.D. (ed), 1983, *The History of Parliament: the House of Commons 1660-1690,* Boydell and Brewer, Woodbridge.

47 Marriage of Sir Charles Turner and Dame Mary Catelyn 17 May 1704 The registers of All Hallows, Bread Street, and of St. John the Evangelist, Friday Street, London, published 1913, transcribed by Bannerman W. B.

48 Landed families of Britain and Ireland 23 Adair of Flixton and Ballymena. https://landedfamilies.blogspot.com/2013/04/23-adair-of-ballymena-castle-and.html

49 Turner, C. (1666-1738), of King's Lynn, Warham and Kirby Cane, Norfolk, published in *The History of Parliament: the House of Commons 1690-1715*, Hayton, D., Cruickshanks, E., Handley, S. (eds), 2002, http://www.histparl.ac.uk/volume/1690-1715/member/turner-charles-1666-1738.

50 The Will of Sir Neville Catelyn of Kirby Cane 1695 with codicil, 1700; quoted in full in a petition from Dame Mary Catelyn to Sir Nathaniel Wright, Lord Keeper, 1702 and Sir Neville Catelyn of Kirby Cane, 1695 and 1700; legal opinions re Catelyn's will from R. Britiffe (1737) and Robert Moreton (1741) Cambridge University Library and Department of Manuscripts and University Archives, box 43 The Buxton Papers, and box 97, folio number 8.

Wingfield Castle in the Eighteenth Century

The eighteenth century owners and occupiers of Wingfield Castle were East Anglian gentry folk who happened to have the good fortune to inherit property. Some lived at the castle for a time, many did not. For long periods the estate was leased out to tenants. Identifying these resident tenants is problematic since very few original leases or other documents have survived. The historian-in-a-fog must rely on newspaper accounts and the hard work of nineteenth century antiquarians, gentlemen who were not always reliable. Nevertheless, the eighteenth century was an interesting time for agricultural development on the estates of north Suffolk and while the individuals may not immediately strike the reader as leading gripping lives in quite the same way

79. Thomas Hearne, Watercolour of Wingfield Castle, Suffolk c1780.

as some characters from earlier chapters, we can learn a good deal from them about the development of high Suffolk and character of rural life in these heavy clay lands, where dairying was the main source of agricultural wealth. Another bonus is the wealth of handsome paintings and prints of the castle building that were created in the eighteenth century.

The watercolour on page 277 (79) by Thomas Hearne gave rise to multiple derivative prints and etchings, readily identified by the equestrian figure riding out across the bridge and lush foliage round the moat. In 1777, Hearne began work recording and illustrating the country's historic monuments for *The Antiquities of Great Britain.*[1] First Hearne produced drawings specifically for the project, then a collaborator, William Byrne, produced engravings after them. The works were issued in series for individual sale from 1778.

The Chain of Inheritance to the Leman Family of Wenhaston.[2] Neville Catelyn's sister Anne married Thomas Leman, a cavalry officer in the post-restoration army and gentleman of Wenhaston Hall, Suffolk, the son of Sir John Leman.[3] Sir John Leman of Charsfield, (1544–1632, Mayor of London in 1616) was a successful City merchant from whom the Wenhaston Lemans were directly descended. Sir John's father had been a prosperous tanner in Beccles. The family tannery and first home is now the much altered Waveney House Hotel in Beccles. Sir John Leman's later home, a beautiful flint building in Ballygate, was endowed as a School in his will and is now the Beccles and District Museum. The Leman coat of arms is displayed on a shield on the external end wall of the museum, shown on page 280 (81). The Sir John Leman High School continues to this day in Beccles.

Anne Leman died when she was just thirty-five years old, long before her brother, so the legacy inheritance of Wingfield Castle and other family estates passed first to Anne's son, Neville Leman, surely named after his uncle, but who also predeceased him in 1679. Anne's inheritance then passed to her grandson, yet another Thomas Leman of Wenhaston, who died in 1735, owning Wingfield Castle for a very short time. He left all his property to his unmarried sister Philippa Leman, who died in 1758.

We know that Philippa was living at Wenhaston Hall in 1748 because she suffered a serious burglary there. This traumatic night was described in the *Ipswich Journal*:

> ...the Dwelling House of Mrs Philippa Leman of Wenhaston in the County of Suffolk, was broke into, on the 5th instant, between the Hours of Ten and Eleven of the Clock in the night by Five Men armed and

80. Three Ladies of the Leman Family and their Dogs on a Terrace, by Benjamin Ferrers 1728, Tate Gallery. The three ladies in the painting are thought to be sisters Elizabeth, Philippa and Mary, the three daughters of Thomas Leman of Wenhaston, Suffolk, and his wife Ruth Suckling. The black and white dress may represent the loss and commemoration of a relative. The standing figure, wearing a half-mourning costume of black and white stripes, rests her hand consolingly on the shoulder of the lady next to her, in full mourning black.

> disguised, and a large Quantity of chased Plate was taken thereout; (Part of which was engraven with the following Coat of Arms in Lozenge, viz a fez between Three Dolphins, Or:) As also a considerable sum of money, together with a gold watch in a chased Case and a large Quantity of Household Linnen: .... [4]

Philippa offered a reward of £50 to anyone who would 'stop the Offender'. There is no report of anyone being apprehended, so Philippa probably lost her treasures.

When Philippa died in 1755, her estate was inherited by her cousin, twenty four year old Dr Robert Leman DD, (1734-1779). Probate was finally approved in 1757.[5] The fifteen page will is exceedingly long winded and complicated. A myriad small bequests and very detailed instructions suggest she must have been a popular, if pernickety, aunt. In her will she praised the manifold qualities of her brother Thomas and said how his death had distressed her. The chain of inheritance that Philippa put in place covered all eventualities should

Robert Leman and his heirs not survive. Robert Leman had the use of Wingfield Castle during his lifetime but after his death, the property would revert to another relative, Henry William Wilson. The total package of properties Leman and then Wilson would inherit included

81. The Arms of Sir John Leman on the wall of Beccles and District museum, formerly his endowed school. The Latin motto translates as "Learn or Leave".

> The manor of Kirby Hall with the members of Hales Hall and advowson of Kirby Cane, the manor of Sisland otherwise Charles, Kirby Hall, and appurtenances in Kirby Cane, Stockton, Ellingham, Hales, and Norton Subcourse, Geldeston, Thurlton, Haddiscoe, Sisland, Loddon, Heckingham, Chedgrave, Mundham, Thwaite, and Hardley (co. Norfolk) and Mettingham (co. Suffolk), the manors of Old Wingfield Hall and Wingfield Frumbalds, Wingfield Castle, and appurtenances in Wingfield, Syleham, Stradbroke, Hoxne, Weybread, Fressingfield, and Mettingham (co. Suffolk). [6]

Dr Robert Leman DD, 1734-1779. Robert came from a prosperous family based in Brampton Suffolk.[7] He took a keen interest in Wingfield Castle and did indeed live here, probably from 1758. First, a word of caution for genealogists and ancestor hunters; there was an almost contemporary cousin of Robert Leman, although longer lived, (1709-1799) with the same name, who also took Holy Orders and became the Rector of Ellough and Knodishall in Suffolk. The two are confused in many family trees on the web, giving highly inaccurate pedigrees. Another Robert Leman readily confused with our Wingfield resident was Robert Leman (1799-1869) a well known artist of the Norwich School, also called Robert Orgill Leman, whose father had assumed the name Leman on inheriting the Brampton estate.

Robert Leman of Wingfield Castle was born at Brampton Hall, Brampton with Stoven, Suffolk, the son of another Robert Leman (sometimes le Man, the place in France from where the family believed they originated). Robert's father was High Sheriff of Suffolk in 1744. His mother was Mary Prettyman, the daughter of Brampton Rector, Nunn Prettyman. The Prettyman (or often Pretyman) family were extensive in Suffolk, intermarried with other local gentry. Many Prettymans were clerics. Robert Leman was one of three children. His older brother Thomas would in the natural course of events have inherited his father's estate and the estates that accompanied Wingfield but he died before probate process was completed for Philippa's will in 1757.[8] Robert also had an older sister Mary.

Robert unexpectedly became a man of serious property on Philippa's death. The church was a respectable one for a second son with little expectation of an inheritance and indeed one of the few opportunities for the younger sons of gentry if they were not attracted to the military. Educated at Monk Soham with Mr Ray and then in Dedham, Essex with Mr Grimwood, he went up to Caius College, Cambridge age eighteen in 1751. He was a Scholar in 1752, took his BA in 1756, an MA in 1759 and became a Doctor of Divinity (DD) in 1778.[9] He remained a Fellow at Cambridge from 1759 to 1767, pursuing the conventional route for those intending to take Holy Orders. He completed his training after being ordained deacon at Ely in 1756, and became Curate of Waterbeach on the edge of the Fens.

Leman's interest in ancient buildings may have been kindled in the Fens, where his clerical senior, Robert Masters, the vicar of Waterbeach, was a keen antiquarian and wrote a history of the parish.[10] The curate who followed Robert Leman between 1767 and 1769 was also an antiquary, William Cole, who remarked that 'the dampness of the old vicarage house and Masters' condescension aroused a lasting antipathy.'[11] If Masters was a difficult colleague, Leman may well have found life in Waterbeach quite trying even after becoming a full priest in 1759.

Rector of Pakefield. Robert got his own living as rector of Pakefield, Suffolk in 1766, at the remarkably young age of 32.[12] Normally a young churchman could expect to do three or four curacies before the coveted rectory came his way. The Pakefield advowson, that is the right to recommend a member of the Anglican clergy for a vacant benefice, was in the ownership of his uncle William Leman of Charsfield, who had bought the advowson some years earlier. Robert's appointment was a classic example of eighteenth century nepotism.

The rectory of Pakefield had been 'in medieties', that is in the curious situation of having two rectors and two separate rectories, from medieval times until 1743, when Thomas Gooch of Benacre, one of the two advowson owners, managed to persuade the bishop, the second patron and the various 'churchwardens, overseers, and principal inhabitants of the parish' to consolidate the two rectories into one.[13] Curiously the final agreement was not signed until 1772. As a consequence of this ancient eccentricity, Pakefield Church was built for the equal accommodation of two congregations. Each half had its separate nave, chancel and altar, raised on a flight of steps, and beneath was a charnel-house, common to both medieties. A screen of elaborate workmanship extended through both parts of the church. Stairs in the north and south walls gave access to the respective rood lofts. The church even had two dedications, the south to 'All Saints' while the north aisle was simply 'Pakefield altera medietas' but may have been dedicated to St. Margaret.

Robert Leman inherited this curious double-aisled church and immediately set about improving it. The antiquarian Alfred Suckling commented 'The condition of the church is neat and reputable, and owes much of this to the liberality of Dr. Leman, a late incumbent, who new-floored and repaired it at his own expense, and erected the present pulpit, which is said to have superseded one of very ancient and elaborate workmanship.' Leman also gave the church a new communion cup and stand in 1769, still in use.[14]

Leman was a conscientious and popular priest. In the parish register Suckling noted an insert besides Robert's name, 'He was an admired preacher

82. The Church of All Saints and St Margaret, Pakefield.

and a strenuous assertor of the rites and ceremonies of the church of which he was so bright an ornament, and indefatigable in every part of the pastoral office'. Modern readers might interpret that to mean he was a fusspot and a stickler for convention but it was meant to be a compliment in an age of lax church habits. The quality of preaching was judged by the congregation. In the eighteenth century it was quite common for parishioners to move round from one church to another to see if the preaching was livelier. Samuel Johnson thought nothing of strolling in and out of several churches on Sunday mornings to assess the quality of the homily. Style and delivery were as important as content.[15] Leman seems to have been something of an orator and was invited by the Bishop of Norwich to preach in the cathedral.

The main feature of being employed in the Church of England in the eighteenth century was that successful clerics accumulated livings to keep up their income. Over-ambitious rectors and vicars took on so many livings at a time that they could not possibly have made much of a contribution to the work of the church. Absentee rectors were supposed to appoint curates to do the practical job of holding services and preaching but many held on to the stipends themselves. Robert was not only rector of Pakefield, but also vicar of Mendham and curate of Carlton Colville. Quite how he discharged his duties while living at Wingfield Castle we can only speculate. The carriage ride to Pakefield from Wingfield could have taken him through both Mendham and Carlton Colville but neither of these parishes was especially convenient.

Robert's attachment to the work of the Church was unusual in eighteenth century rural England where adherence to the Church was pretty thin among the population. The rural Church of England was characterised by lassitude and neglect. Churches were often left to rot. Church towers simply fell down from lack of maintenance. In his introduction to Parson Woodforde's diary Ronald Blythe memorably describes the Church of England of the late Georgian period as 'spiritually comatose'.[16] Dissenters had toned down their seventeenth-century puritanical ranting, the Unitarians were in an intellectual ascendancy in the thinking classes but without any troubling fervour of faith. Methodists had not quite yet roused their Wesleyan enthusiasm.

If the gentry were usually regular church-goers, the rest of the population was not. James Woodforde's three hundred or so flock in Weston Longville, a village eight miles west of Norwich, were only occasional worshippers. The relationship between the established church and the ordinary parishioner was not one of acquiescence and subservience. The church was there to baptise, marry and bury you; the rest was optional as far as the congregation were concerned. The only community occasions when the whole village attended church was to give thanks for the recovery of health of the monarch, the funeral of a popular villager or to pray for troops setting off to war. Most Sundays the parson was pleased to see 'two rails', about thirty communicants.[41] In Pakefield the usual number reported to the Bishop for the intermittent 'Visitation' was twenty and one suspects that was optimistic.[17] Being a parson however was not all about religion; he had many other roles to fulfill in the administration of the parish, although the churchwardens elected by the parishioners were possibly more crucial in this regard.

Robert Leman's work on the Castle. The castle may have been in quite poor shape when Robert inherited. John Kirby, who wrote a traveller's guide to the antiquities of Suffolk in 1735, remarked that the 'ruinous walls bespeak its former grandeur'.[18] Leman restored the foot drawbridge over the moat to the castle's former outer court, which was on the east side of the castle. His initials and the date 1768 can be seen carved on it. He also restored the inner two towers of the gatehouse and reroofed them.[19] At St Andrew's Church, Wingfield he painted over the wooden tomb effigies of Michael de la Pole, 2nd earl of Suffolk and his wife Katherine Stafford, possibly in an attempt to make them look more like stone.[20] The original figures were brightly polychrome but by the eighteenth century the colours would have been chipped away. Purists may tut-tut at Robert's 'improvement' but with the years the mellow 'stone' fits well with the other tombs.

83. Southeast corner of Wingfield Castle moat showing foot drawbridge restored by Robert Leman, 1768.

Life at Wingfield Castle. Robert Leman remained unmarried. Although he was proprietor of Wingfield until his death in 1779, at some point before then, the castle was also occupied by his maternal uncle, Robert Prettyman (1717-1801), and his wife Ann, his two sons and a daughter. It is not at all clear whether Robert Leman had moved out to be resident in the rectory at Pakefield or whether he was living with the Prettyman family. Robert Leman was only 46 when he died and he may have been ailing for some time. It is possible that his uncle and aunt came to care for him but so far no further clues have emerged. The Prettyman family used Wingfield Church for baptisms, marriages and burials up until the early nineteenth century, probably because, as a widow, Ann Prettyman continued in the village until her death in 1814.[21]

Life in Wingfield for Robert Leman and the Prettymans. In the late eighteenth century Wingfield was probably not an unpleasant place for landed gentry to live. The village was not as socially remote as we might imagine. Families worked hard at maintaining social contact. The well-to-do farmers, gentry and the established parson were in a perpetual state of 'rotation' between their homes, enjoying dinners, suppers and meetings. Rural society was a gregarious, gossipy, backgammon-playing, gambling, heavy-drinking and heavy-eating society. Church of England parsons and rectors were at the heart of the well-heeled classes. Dinner was taken about four in the afternoon so carriages could take guests home across unsatisfactory country roads at a respectable hour. Travel anywhere was hard going. Arthur Young, the Suffolk born agriculturalist, came through the dairying area of North Suffolk by coach in 1784. 'The roads grew bad, beyond all badness, the night dark, beyond all darkness, the guide frightened beyond all frightfulness'… 'I know not, in the whole range of language, terms sufficiently expressive to describe this infernal road'.[22]

Friends and relatives would arrive unannounced, which meant one needed to be in a constant state of readiness to entertain or accomodate, keeping victuals, wine and beer in quantities sufficient for people dropping in. This was also the era of wig wearing. Robert would have powdered his hair with starch or worn a wig on Sundays and special occasions, using the services of the village barber and peruke maker. The curate would have worn clerical dress and a wig even in the village. By 1770 the wig habit and hair powder were gradually dying out under the influence of powder tax.

Robert Leman's death; Wingfield Castle changes ownership and the Prettyman family continues as tenants. Robert died on 11 September 1779 at home at Wingfield Castle, though the papers reported incorrectly that he died at 'the residence of his father-in-law Mr Prettyman'.[23] Robert predeceased his own father by nine years. After Robert's death, ownership of the estate passed to a distant cousin, Henry William Wilson of Didlington and Ashwellthorpe and then to his heir Robert Wilson.

Robert Prettyman and his family however stayed on as resident tenants at Wingfield. We have a small glimpse into Prettyman's character from the diary of John Lincoln, a young indentured servant placed by the parish officers at Wingfield Castle when he was about twelve years old.[24] John was born in Wingfield in 1770, his father, a linen weaver, died young and his widow and ten children were left dependent on parish relief. John was placed at the age of ten to work for a hemp processor but his master's wife treated him cruelly so the parish officers removed him and found him a job as a general servant at the castle. He worked as a dairy hand every early morning helping five dairy maids, carrying heavy pails of milk to the dairy from the milking parlour, then moving on to general labouring in the afternoon. But he was also doing errands around the castle and one day picked up a book from the library. Fascinated he crept up to the library to read whenever he could and one day was surprised by Prettyman, who said 'John, you seem very fond of reading and as you are fond of books, come and read them and borrow them if you wish, but just keep your hands clean!' John stayed at Wingfield for three years until his mother moved to Lynn and he found a position in north Runcton. In adulthood he went on to work at the Royal Arsenal, Woolwich and the Royal Laboratory. His diary is testament to how well he managed to educate himself.

In November 1787 Robert and Ann Prettyman's daughter married 'Mr William Burcham of London' at Wingfield. Their son, also Robert, was married to a Miss Suggate from Wingfield too, in about 1788. In 1789 Prettyman ordered a book catalogue so presumably he also had time to read in his much appreciated library.[25] Prettyman was still on the Wingfield poll book in 1790.[26]

Prettyman and his family pursued the typical hunting, shooting lifestyle of the gentry. His name figures in the annual list of Suffolk Game licences.[27] The Prettyman family knew how to enjoy themselves. A ball at Redgrave Hall was prettily versified by George Betts of Wortham.

> Friend Gibbs was before us boxed up in his chaise,
> And ye Prettymans roll'd in a coach in their ease.
> The Lord of the Manor gave welcome to all
> But ye scheme we pursued was an elegant ball.[28]

At least two of Robert's brothers were clerics, another was a prosperous tenant farmer at Brockdish Hall. It is hard to know if Prettyman did anything for a living but there are advertisements in the local paper to indicate he was involved in some property transactions. Robert Prettyman died in 1801. His wife Anne lived on until 1814.[29]

Farming on the Wingfield Castle estate in the Eighteenth Century. The Georgian landscape of Suffolk was punctuated by a handful of grand estates and country houses that could well be described as stately homes. Nearby, the Cornwallis family, who controlled local politics in the borough of Eye, had their huge Tudor mansion at Brome. Hoxne Hall was also a substantial house even before it was transformed into the grandiose Oakley Park in the next century. The sprawling Syleham Hall in the next parish was extended in the eighteenth century to accommodate the social aspirations of the Barry family; the even grander Heveningham Hall was designed in 1788. There were more mansions created near Bury and Ipswich and a good deal of prettifying of old farmhouses to give them a modern Georgian façade. The great gardens and parks of the wealthier gentry and lesser aristocracy are shown in Hodskinson's 1783 map, more numerous in the west and attached to the greater houses near the towns.

But these larger estates were not typical of north Suffolk. The central and northeastern boulder clay lands were dominated by small farms and estates owned by prosperous yeomen and the lesser gentry. The Wingfield Castle estate was a modest 4-500 acres compared with the several thousand acres of the grand estates. Wingfield Castle must have looked decidedly old-fashioned and let us face it, small, when compared with the grander edifices of the wealthy.

Wingfield was at the heart of dairying country, which stretched twenty miles by twelve from Coddenham in the south to the Waveney in the north. There was plenty of arable land on the slopes of the river valleys along the Waveney and the Dove but crop cultivation was difficult on the heavy clay plateau until field drainage was put in, mainly in the mid to late eighteenth and early nineteenth centuries. Prior to this, the land became waterlogged in winter and only suitable for grazing. As winter drain digging became more widely adopted, arable farming became more popular, especially in the last decade of the eighteenth century when the price of home grown corn rose dramatically because of the naval blockade of foreign imports during the Napoleonic wars.

Arthur Young admired the local small polled cows. He wrote on his travels, 'Entering now the region of the true Suffolk polled cows, which are unexceptionably the finest in England for milking, we made enquires; dairies rise to 40 and 50; the points they attend to are these, a long body, large carcass, clean throat, snake-headed, thin tail, and short leg; they give six gallons a day in the height of the season.... We saw one very ill made cow, in respect to roundness of carcass, milked, and she gave a three-gallon pail quite full, which is not uncommon in this country; some few give four gallons twice a day.'[30]

Suffolk butter was famously good, the thin hard cheese famously bad but it was a profitable industry. On the low lying marshes, bullocks were fattened for beef, bought at the annual fairs in Hoxne and Halesworth from Scottish drovers and then sent on to Smithfield in London by another group of drovers.

The Land Tax Redemption Records are the most useful documents extant for showing the relative ownership of parish land and property at that time.[31] Land tax had been imposed on owners since the late seventeenth century but in 1798, the tax became a perpetual charge, which could be redeemed by the payment of a lump sum; landowners were thereby exonerated from future tax, although the redemption was optional. The lump sum equalled fifteen years' tax and purchased three per cent 'consols', a government stock investment without a maturity date, which would yield an annuity exceeding the tax by a fifth. So the records now in the National Archive list the sums to be paid by owners to escape tax in future. From the government's point of view this was a very attractive tax as it appeared to be optional. About a third of landowners paid the redemption charge.

The land tax list for Wingfield parish shows that the highest rate, over £36, was paid on land owned by Robert Wilson Esq., (Henry William Wilson's heir) of which £20 was allocated to Robert Prettyman Esq. as occupier. The next largest owners were Mark Butcher and John Cotton, who both paid £12 for land they farmed themselves. Stephen Cook, another farmer, paid £9. There were about two dozens or so other farmers with much smaller pieces of land and an equal number of tenant occupiers. The total tax redemption possible in Wingfield parish was £188, of which the Wingfield Castle estate owned nineteen per cent. This would correspond to an acreage of about four hundred and sixty four acres out of a total parish acreage of 2443 acres. Wilson did not own any land in the neighbouring parishes of either Syleham or Stradbroke. It was a decent sized estate, certainly enough to provide a comfortable living in the late eighteenth century.

The Wilson family. The connection of the Lemans and Wilsons was through common ancestry of the Knyvett and Suckling families, important gentry families in Norfolk. The Wilsons however had ancestry going back to the fourteenth century and aspirations to grandeur born of impeccable breeding far exceeding that of the Lemans. The acquisition and then holding on to their hereditary barony of Berners was a matter that greatly preoccupied them and their descendants up until the twentieth century. They were absentee landlords for Wingfield Castle estate until the middle of the next century. Ancient buildings often benefit from escaping the modernization that resident owners wreak on their homes but on the other hand are often left in a perilous condition by neglect. In the next chapter we will address the thorny question of what happened to the castle in the nineteenth century.

Notes

1 Monkhouse, William Cosmo Hearne, Thomas (1744-817) *Dictionary of National Biography 1885-1900, Vol 25.*
2 Inheritance documented in Copinger, W.A., 1905, *The Manors of Suffolk Wingfield vol IV* pp. 108-115 online at https://archive.org/details/manorsofsuffolkn01copiuoft/page/n4/mode/2up.
3 Lake, B., 2013, *The Story of Sir John Leman and the Leman Family of Warboys and Northaw* https://archive.org/details/STORYOFSIRJOHNLemanAndTheLemanFamilyOfWarboysAndNorthaw/page/n3/mode/2up.
4 *Ipswich Journal*, Saturday 4 February 1749.
5 Will of Phillipa Leman spinster of Wenhaston (co. Suffolk), dated 1755 and proved 1757. NRO Knyvett-Wilson Family Collection Title deeds Kirby Cane and elsewhere KNY 18, 369X3.
6 NRO Knyvett-Wilson Family Collection Title deeds Kirby Cane and elsewhere KNY 18, 369X3.
7 The Leman Family of Brampton; miscellaneous Leman family deeds and papers SROI, HD2434.
8 There is an extensive Leman family tree compiled by Suckling, A. I., 1847, *The History and Antiquities of the County of Suffolk, volume 2*, p. 184.
9 Venn, J. A., A Cambridge Alumni Database (ACAD) II, p. 67. Online at https://venn.lib.cam.ac.uk.
10 Masters, R., 1795, *A Short Account of the Parish of Waterbeach, British Library Archives and Manuscripts Collection*, ark:/81055/vdc_100000001301.0x00031f
11 Waterbeach Church in Wright , A. P. M. and Lewis, C. P. (eds), CP 1989 *A History of the County of Cambridge and the Isle of Ely, volume 9*, Chesterton, Northstowe and Papworth Hundreds, pp. 257-262. British History Online http://www.british-history.ac.uk/vch/cambs/vol9/pp257-262 [accessed 2 April 2020].
12 Robert Leman appointed Rector of Pakefield 1766, Church of England Database CCEd Record ID: 24707.
13 Suckling, A., 1846, Pakefield, in *The History and Antiquities of the County of Suffolk, Ipswich, volume 1*, pp. 279-287. British History Online at http://www.british-history.ac.uk/no-series/suffolk-history-antiquities/vol1/pp279-287 [accessed 31 March 2020].
14 Ibid. 13, p. 284.
15 Picard, L., 2000, *Dr Johnson's London: life in London 1740-1770*, Chapter 17 Childhood, Schooling and Religion. Phoenix Books.
16 Blythe, R., 1999, Foreword pp v-x to *James Woodforde 1758-1802, The Diary of a Country Parson*, edited by Beresford, J., Canterbury Press, Norwich.
17 Diocesan Records, Parish Visitations by the Archdeaconry of Suffolk. 18th century printed records for Deanery of Hoxne in Norfolk Record Office, see series DN/VIS.
18 Kirby, J., 1735, *The Suffolk Traveller, or A Journey through Suffolk*. Ipswich, p138. Online at https://books.google.co.uk/books [accessed 27.06.2020].
19 *Country Life*, 28 June 1913, p. 952.
20 Badham, S., 2015, Medieval Monuments to the de la Pole and Wingfield families, p. 166 Bloore and Martin 2015, quoting SROI The Corder Collection HD 2418-51, f 296.
21 The Will of Ann Prettyman. TNA Prerogative Court of Canterbury and Related Probate Jurisdictions: Will Registers; Class: PROB 11 Piece 1557.
22 Young, A., 1784, *A Tour through Suffolk, in Annals of Agriculture*, London, pp. 200-250
23 Robert Leman's death recorded in Venn. Advertisement for claims on the estate of Dr Robert Leman died 1779 Ipswich Journal Saturday 01 January 1780.
24 Lincoln, John b1777 Labourer and Footman NRO MC2669/29, 991x9
25 Rodd, T., 1789, Catalogue of twelve thousand tracts, pamphlets and unbound, volumes 1-6, List of Subscribers, p. 387.
26 1790 London, England, UK and London Poll Books. London, England: London Metropolitan Archives and Guildhall Library, online at Ancestry.co.uk.

27 Game duty paid by Robert Pretyman of Wingfield and Rev Nunn Pretyman of Cotton. *Bury and Norwich Post*—Wednesday 15 November 1786.

28 Doughty, K. F., 1912, *The Betts of Wortham in Suffolk, 1480-1905*, John Lane Co., 1912. Online at Ancestry.com. The Betts of Wortham in Suffolk : 1480-1905 [database on-line]. Chapter XIX. 1717-1734. Introduction of pheasant rearing, a grim wager, a spinsters calculation.

29 Death announcement, Anne Prettyman, Widow of Mr Prettyman of Wingfield Castle. *Oxford Journal*, Saturday, 29 January 1814.

30 Young, A., 1797, *General View of the Agriculture of the County of Suffolk, Drawn Up for the Consideration of the Board of Agriculture and Internal Improvement,* Macmillan, London.

31 Land Tax Redemption Office: Quotas and Assessments, 1798, Suffolk, Volume 2, p. 452. Records of the Boards of Stamps, Taxes, Excise, Stamps and Taxes, and Inland Revenue. The National Archives. Series IR23.

The Early Nineteenth Century at Wingfield Castle

Absentee Landlords and Resident Tenants

Life in agricultural north Suffolk in the early Nineteeth Century. Throughout the nineteenth century, Wingfield Castle estate was owned by wealthy proprietors who lived elsewhere. Both the Wilson/Berners family and the Adairs who followed them were very grand families indeed and collected

84. View of Wingfield Castle, Wingfield, Suffolk by Edward Dayes, 1791 (London 1763–1804) pencil and watercolour. Much of Dayes' topographical work depicted ruins, painted in a palette dominated by blues and greens, which had an influence on the early work of J M W Turner.* He laid out detailed rules for the correct method of laying down the colours in landscape. His work is said to illustrate the transition from the eighteenth to the nineteenth century style of topographical watercolour.

* Reynolds, Graham 1998 Watercolours: A Concise History. London: Thames and Hudson, p. 72.

property and land across East Anglia and further afield in Britain and abroad. They were absentee landlords to the tenants who lived at Wingfield and farmed the land. For the owners, the castle estate was simply a generator of income that enabled them to pursue a lifestyle far removed from the gentry farmer and the agricultural labourers who toiled on the land. Land was still the main source of wealth for the aristocracy and gentry but the wealthier echelon of landowners also had lives in London, frequently travelled abroad for the sheer enjoyment of it and engaged in other diversionary pursuits, for example, the new mania for science, especially natural history, and the arts and sport.

The archives contain relatively few records relating to Wingfield Castle during these years except some rather dry manorial accounts and lists of tenants. What emerges is that the castle was quite neglected after the 1830s until it was appreciated once again as a historical treasure in the mid-twentieth century. Tudor Jerningham House, so charming when it was built, was by the early nineteenth century old-fashioned and perhaps not especially desirable. Wealthy families were beginning to disguise their old Elizabethan and Stuart seats in Palladian style or add Georgian façades. Wingfield Castle remained largely untouched, though some of the old medieval castle range of buildings were removed, probably as a consequence of increasing dilapidation. There was no wholesale modernisation or improvement.

Landlord absenteeism was prevalent in England at the end of the eighteenth century and steadily increased.[1] Large tracts of the north of England were devoid of resident landowners, and in parts of Lincolnshire in the mid-nineteenth century only seven per cent of parishes had permanently resident substantial landowners.[2] If a man owned several estates, by definition if he was living on one of them he was an absentee on all the others. As the nineteenth century progressed, increasing amounts of property in land were acquired by the landed elite until, by 1861, there were only thirty thousand landowners of any kind among a population of thirty million. By 1873 four fifths of the acreage was in the possession of fewer than seven thousand proprietors.[3] The law of primogeniture and complex family settlement arrangements fostered the accumulation of property in one line of descent.

Absenteeism did not necessarily bring about inefficient estate management or rack-renting but modernisation and the introduction of agricultural innovation tended to be slower than it might otherwise have been.[4] Most substantial proprietors employed land agents to supervise accounts and many also had land stewards to manage individual properties. Alternatively, as at Wingfield, the proprietor was very careful to appoint resident tenants who were well-qualified to look after proprietors' interests. The Wilsons appointed gentry relatives from Cambridgeshire as resident tenants in the first instance after the Prettymans departed.

Absentee landlords were usually deeply unpopular in Suffolk, where it was complained they were apathetic to improving their land, for example by investing in drainage and that there was no visible personal leadership of agricultural improvement in the county as was evident in Norfolk by the earl of Leicester and others. Furthermore, tenants grumbled that leases were drafted in overly confining terms, dictating types of crop rotation, for example, reducing the ability of farming innovators to experiment. Another regular cavil was that land was managed too much for the gentlemanly sports of hunting and shooting of game, which increased incentives for poaching but diminished agricultural labouring opportunities in honest arable farming and husbandry.[5]

Between 1750 and 1840, the population of England and Wales more than doubled. Cereal output also nearly doubled, but demand kept pace with or ran ahead of supply for the whole of the period. Average wheat prices remained reasonably low during the period 1770-1795, but rose dramatically through the Napoleonic wartime period from 1796 to a peak in 1811-1815. Prices then declined post-war again, although not to the levels before 1795. Later in the century, from 1846-50, wheat prices fell even further. A rising wheat price was good for farmers but very hard on the labouring population of rural Suffolk who had to buy bread at higher prices.

After the enclosures of rural land by agreements between farmers, which had occurred largely informally in Wingfield in earlier centuries, it became more common for labourers to be paid by the day or week or by results, and to be employed for short periods for harvesting, hedging, ditching, threshing and so on. Hiring was on a casual basis and no payment was given if no work was done. 'Living in' with the farmer's family, quite common in earlier times, largely disappeared.

The local village population was, however, increasing rapidly across Norfolk and Suffolk. Stradbroke increased from 1,215 in 1801 to 1,637 in 1841 and Diss from 2,540 in 1801 to 2,934 in 1831.[6] Wingfield parish had 69 inhabited houses in 1801 with 521 inhabitants, rising to 133 houses by 1851 with 654 inhabitants. This is double what it is now in 2020, when the parish population of Wingfield is estimated to be about 350. Partly, the higher numbers of people two centuries ago was a reflection of the manpower necessary for agricultural activities and the downturn in opportunities in the industrial towns.[7] Pay declined in part because of the surplus of rural labour. The boom during the Napoleonic wars was not sustained and deflation after 1815 led to stagnation of agricultural employment, an inability of surplus population to migrate to towns for work and the slow but insidious threat created by the development of agricultural technology and machinery. The prolonged recession was made worse by the rural labour market being swamped by half a million men and their followers being demobilised from the victorious army and navy.

The social and financial gulf between farmer and labourer widened. Hiring for less than a year meant the unemployed could not claim on the poor rates. In 1795 one village in Berkshire, Speenhamland, invented a well-meaning relief scheme to support poor labourers that was adopted over much of England following a decision by local magistrates. Instead of fixing minimum wages for poor labourers, the practice was to raise working men's income to an agreed level, the money to come out of the parish rates. This allowance was designated as the price of three gallon loaves a week for each man. A gallon loaf was 8½ pounds, (about four kilograms). A wife and children received the value of an extra 1½ loaves each. The money was to cover all expenses. This allowance system lasted until the new poor law enactment of 1834.

It was intended to be a safety net in hard times but when widely adopted across much of England the extra pay became part of the framework of the labourer's life. Landlords complained the system encouraged idleness because labourers got the same whether they worked hard or not. These days we call it the benefit trap. The system also provided an opportunity for unscrupulous employers and landlords to reduce wages and raise rents, knowing their greed would be redressed from the public purse. Productivity fell, so poor relief was cut as a deterrent, which caused further hardship, one of the trigger causes of the ensuing protests and riots.

Rural Unrest. Low wages, harsh laws and the introduction of agricultural machinery on an increasing scale created unrest and resentment. Machine-wrecking became widespread. The first 'wrecking' in the area was at Hockham in the Breckland of southwest Norfolk in 1816, after which four ringleaders of a group of a hundred were convicted for riotous assembly, two being sentenced to twelve months in Norwich Castle jail. There were more disturbances at Downham the following day, following the refusal of local farmers to increase wages. Two of those apprehended were hanged.

Unrest came to a head in south Norfolk in February 1822. There were episodes of rick-burning and machine breaking in villages as near to Wingfield as Dickleburgh, Denton, Scole and Alburgh between 1821 and 1830. Hatcher Nunn Prettyman, the farmer at Brockdish Hall, a relative of Robert Prettyman at Wingfield, suffered rick burning one night in 1792, one of the earliest episodes recorded locally, that must have caused some anxiety among other larger farmers.[8] The parish clerk of Syleham, Charles Souter made a special note in his diary and also commented on a threatening note being dropped in the street. It turned out to have been dropped by rebellious John Stannard, an unemployed pauper who had often been in receipt of poor relief in Brockdish and regularly in trouble with the law.[9]

Then the 'wrecking' of newly invented wooden threshing machines began in Suffolk in earnest. There were riots across Suffolk in 1822, largely focused on the hated machines. Threshing machines were also the targets of incendiary attacks at Cockfield and Clare. The same year, farmworkers dragged a thresher from Shimpling to Burston and dumped it on the Green. Fifty men made a road-block, unhitched the horses and smashed the machine with hatchets, hooks and crowbars. Soldiers took six men, followed by two hundred angry protesters, to the Saracen's Head in Diss to face the Justice. All six were jailed. But protests continued. The later protests and riots were often referred to as 'Swing Riots' because loosely organised groups, when writing anonymous threatening letters to landowners, magistrates and farmers, would sign themselves 'Captain Swing'.

Those most likely to be involved in dissidence were young unmarried men, who in many ways suffered most from becoming paupers dependent on relief, since they received least from the parish and were most likely to be obliged to undertake the most physically demanding and most degrading of parish labour, working, for example, on road gangs. They were in a sense the 'natural rebels', least educated and with least to lose. John Stannard, mentioned above, was typical. Others who were likely to revolt were those who lived on the margins of the local community, on the almost inevitable edge of legality, such as poachers and smugglers, both notoriously active in the uprisings of 1816 and 1830.

Robert Harvey, a local farmer witness before the 1821 Select Committee on Agricultural Distress, owned land on the Norfolk-Suffolk border.[10] According to Harvey, 'In four parishes in which I am concerned, take nine out of ten occupiers of land, they have very much reduced their number of labourers'. He preferred taking on extra men to paying higher rates, but he paid them only 1/9d a day, 3d less than the average for 1800-1814. The custom of providing beer had been ended 'in conformity with the general practice of the neighbourhood'.

There was a fierce gleaning dispute in 1820 between the poor of Hoxne and Eye hundreds, both areas much involved in the 1822 troubles, and in Loddon there was a riot directed against the overseers and churchwardens.[11] This happened soon after the introduction of new scales of relief for men working on the roads, which gave married men with three children 1/4d a day and single men 1/2d. The total crime figures were rising steeply: committals for Suffolk rose by 73.3 per cent in the five years 1815-20, and the increase for Norfolk was 106.5 per cent over the same period.[12]

Agricultural workers on the Wingfield Castle estate and the farm bailiffs would have been talking about the unrest and increased lawlessness the same as everyone else. They would have been wondering whether to support the protesters or censure them. We do not know how the estate workers regarded their employers or were treated by the wealthy people who held the Wingfield tenancies. The troubles were not remote but talked about openly and were worrying enough for the government to produce some highly repressive legislation against protests and rioting. So, as we describe the leisured lives of the proprietors of Wingfield Castle, we should have in the back of our minds the social conditions of those who served them.

The Proprietors

The Berners Barony. Henry William Wilson was a commoner, a very wealthy one who had inherited through the Knyvett, Suckling and Wilson families a portfolio of estates all over East Anglia. His son Robert managed, with some negotiation, to add lustre to the estate by a revival of his inheritance of the ancient Berners barony. The barony had been created in 1455 for Sir John Bourchier, who became constable of Windsor Castle. The Berners barony is so ancient that it was established by writ of summons, signifying that it can descend through both male and female lines, although there is no straightforward default to a female heir and in practice it proved rather difficult in later centuries for women to establish their hereditary right to the title.

It was only in 1711, after a gap of near two hundred years, that the barony's continuing existence was established by the claim of one of the women of the Knyvett family. It took her nine years to be confirmed by the House of Lords as eighth Baroness Berners. On her death in 1743 the barony again fell into abeyance, for a further eighty nine years, until the abeyance was terminated in 1832 in favour of Elizabeth Knyvett's grandson Robert Wilson (1761-1838), who became the ninth Baron Berners. It was largely through the tenacity of this somewhat eccentric but popular man that the barony was not lost.

Robert Wilson was a bachelor and was succeeded by his younger brother, the tenth Lord Berners. When he died the title passed to his son, the eleventh Lord. The inheritance became progressively more complicated but the Berners sold their ownership of Wingfield Castle in 1856 so we are spared the intricacies of the later barony inheritance. In some ways this is a shame because the best known Lord Berners, Gerald Hugh Tyrwhitt-Wilson, (1883 –1950), also known as Gerald Tyrwhitt, was a talented composer, novelist, painter, exquisite aesthete and gay icon who makes the earlier Lords Berners look decidedly monochrome. He and his 'Mad Boy' partner Robert Heber-Percy sprayed their resident doves bright pink, blue, yellow and green and stuffed their home at Faringdon House, Oxfordshire with the treasures of generations of Berners. The portraits of Neville and Dorothy Catelyn on page 257 (75) emerged at the Faringdon House sale after Berners' death.[13]

Colonel Robert Wilson, 9th Baron Berners (1761–1838).[14] Robert was the eldest of Henry William Wilson's four children, born at the large estate of Ashwellthorpe, Norfolk. In 1781, presumably to establish title to their inheritance from Robert Leman and their right to do with it as they wished, Wilson and his oldest son, Robert Wilson, had engaged in a legal procedure, 'to suffer a common recovery' to their use.[15] This ancient convoluted process looks impressive and important on parchment in the Norfolk Record Office, confirms title to the estate. Common recoveries were used to break entails (conditions stipulated in wills or settlements which limited the descent of freehold land to certain individuals) and transfer land. Once the common recovery had been achieved ('suffered' in legal language), the land and property could be sold to somebody else, mortgaged or settled in a new way.[16] The outcome was a very clear route for inheritance of a property.

Robert regarded Didlington, another family estate in the Brecks near Thetford, as his main home. Before being granted the peerage in 1832 he was known as 'Sporting Colonel Wilson', the rank he held when discharged from the army at the cessation of the Napoleonic war hostilities in 1815.[17] When his father inherited Wingfield Castle, Kirby Cane Hall and a myriad associated estates in 1779, he was already in possession of a large property portfolio. So, when his father died in 1796, he inherited the vast majority of his huge estate holdings. His brother Henry, a cleric, went to live at Ashwellthorpe,

85. Wingfield Castle, etching by Henry Davy, 1827.

another family owned estate. There were also estates in Leicestershire, at Allexton, Tugby, Goadby and Keyworth used by descendants of his brothers. Occasionally some of the family used Kirby Cane Hall but for at least a part of the time that estate was rented out. Wingfield Castle estate was one of the smaller holdings.

Robert Wilson dedicated himself to hunting, horse racing and falconry; he was exceptionally skilled at all three. He owned and bred racehorses at his stud near Brandon for the races at Newmarket and further afield. He trained the horses himself and over the course of forty years bred May-Day, Camarine, Juniper, Erebus, Spotlight, Lamplighter and the most famous, Phosphorus, which won the 1837 Derby at odds of 40 to 1.[18] The author, not being a racing devotee, was surprised to find these horses now have their own Wikipedia pages, so renowned are they.

Wilson was a keen fox-hunter, riding with the West Norfolk Hunt and later becoming Master of Foxhounds. Another early enthusiasm was for the revival of the sport of falconry. In 1814 he became President of the Confederated Hawks of Great Britain, later the Falconry Club. The new Lord Berners, having fought hard for his title, did not make a significant contribution to the House of Lords. He voted twice, once in 1833 and again in 1834 but was never sufficiently moved to hazard a speech.[19] He never married. He enjoyed his sporting life and spent the fashionable season at Bath.[20] When he died in 1838, the title and the majority of his estates were inherited by his brother the Rev. Henry Wilson, tenth Lord Berners.[21] His brother Henry was altogether a more sober minded chap and did not go in for either horse racing or hawking. There is one small legacy of Robert Wilson visible at Wingfield, a plaque on the eastern curtain wall with the initials RW and the date 1820. We must assume he visited at least once.

Reverend Henry Wilson, 10th Lord Berners (1762–1851). The tenth Lord Berners had the conventional education for an eighteenth century churchman. Educated at Harrow, he went up to Cambridge in 1780, took a BA in 1784, an MA in 1789 and was later ordained deacon at Norwich. He then took advantage of the numerous family owned advowsons to become firstly rector of Alexton in Leicestershire, where he was officially resident from 1789-1845, and then rector of Kirby Cane from 1820-1851, where he settled at the hall in later life. In 1788 he married Elizabeth Sumpter, daughter of Thomas Sumpter of Histon Hall, Histon, Cambridgeshire, whose singular will led to Wingfield Castle being occupied for many years by her brother William, of whom more later.

The only intervention in the Wingfield Castle Estate I can find for the tenth Lord Berners was a grant he and his son gave of a small parcel of land, or 'croft', to be annexed to the glebe.[22] This Lord Berners was not a great contributor to the House of Lords either; 'his mental constitution was not fitted for the anxieties or excitement of a political life', although he did manage to get in to Westminster to vote in favour of the Reform Bill.[23] In those days it was possible to vote by proxy without the trouble of going into London and he consistently voted with the Whigs, 'a firm and constant supporter', his obituary noted.[24]

Berners was involved in a curious legal case in 1844. A former butler, William Norris, 'brought an action to recover damages for slander' against Lord Berners.[25] Norris had entertained a young man called Worr one night in his room at Kirby Cane Hall 'because of a tempest coming on', the weather being too bad, he said, for him to go home. The following morning Berners summarily sacked Norris without notice and without wages. Young Worr's father, a shoemaker in Kirby Cane, whom it appears was a good friend of Norris, visited Berners to collect money owed to young Worr. 'In conversation', that is Worr asking why Norris had been summarily dismissed, Lord Berners declared 'Norris was a b----r'. Buggery was a capital offence until 1861 and it was only five years since the last English hanging of two offenders. Accusing someone of buggery was no small matter. The older Worr said under cross-examination that Berners was an aged man and had an 'impediment in his speech' but there was no mistaking what he said.

Norris had admitted to Worr that he had been discharged for improper conduct with two boys in a stable 'but it was merely a game of tickling'. Norris did however admit to Worr that one of the 'tickled' boys had slept with him at the Bird in Hand at Wreningham and that Norris had paid the boy the morning after to keep quiet. Worr further said that he had 'run into' the Honorable Robert Wilson (Lord Berners' second son and also a cleric) who had heard something of the story from his father. Wilson allegedly told Norris that he should leave without fuss 'as it would not be pleasant for him to stay' but commented that his father should not have sacked Norris without warning or wages.

Berners had sufficient wealth to engage one of the foremost barristers of his day, Sergeant at Law John Barnard Byles, who had achieved legal fame

86. Rev. Henry Wilson, 10th Lord Berners (1761-1851) and his wife Elizabeth, nee Sumpter (1763- 1845), portraits by Robert Scott Tait.

with a popular textbook on Bills of Exchange called 'Byles on Bills'. It is said that Byles called his horse 'Bills' and would shout out as he approached 'Here comes Byles on Bills'. The flamboyant Byles told the judge that Berners denied using the 'b' word 'in the sense imputed' but rather the noble lord was simply trying to warn Worr about his son's association with Norris. The judge rather laconically pointed out that in any case the jury should decide whether Norris' history suggested that there was no slander in the first place, given Norris' admitted behaviour with boys. The jury, in a mood not to subject the gabby Norris to further risk of prosecution and yet not wanting to cast a poor light on the elderly Berners, decided the 'word' had never actually been spoken, against all evidence. The case was dismissed. Another triumph for Byles and another Victorian fudge about illegal but popularly acknowledged relationships. The author wonders what Henry thought about his elder bachelor brother Robert and how he would have reacted to his wildly eccentric twentieth century descendant, the very publically queer fifteenth Baron.

Henry William Wilson, 11th Lord Berners (1797–1871). The tenth Baron Berners died age 90 and his eldest son, another Henry, inherited the fortune. An altogether more driven character than his father and with ambition to get things done, Henry, educated at Eton and Emmanuel College, Cambridge, was active particularly in Leicestershire, where he rebuilt Keythorpe Hall and mainly lived there during his lifetime, although he also lived at Ashwellthorpe, Norfolk. He married Maria Crump from Alexton Hall in Leicestershire. He was a Justice of the Peace for Norfolk, Rutland and Leicestershire. Interested in improving agriculture, he became President of the Royal Agricultural Society in 1858. He also held the mainly ceremonial offices of Constable of Leicester Castle and Deputy Lieutenant of Leicestershire.

Henry took his role in the House of Lords seriously, speaking on a number of liberal Whig causes and often supporting the evangelical social reformer Lord Shaftesbury. Berners vigorously supported the campaign to abolish the 'removal' provisions in the Poor Law that forcibly removed destitute paupers back to the parish where they had a 'settlement', to prevent them becoming a charge on the parish. It was a heedless and cruel process that took up far too much parish overseers' time. The campaign failed but Henry continued to contribute to parliament for the rest of his life.

Lord Berners disposed of several properties during the early nineteenth century. By 1856 he had decided that it was time to sell the Wingfield Castle estate. It was a favourable time to get a good price and Berners was a canny investor. Until then, the Berners family had tenants at Wingfield, managing

87. Henry William Wilson, 11th Lord Berners, 1797–1871. Engraved by D. J. Pound from a photograph by Mayall.

the land and at first living in a style similar to previous gentry owners. Matters subsequently deteriorated.

William and Sophia Sumpter, Tenants at Wingfield Castle, c1801/2–1834. During the Berners' ownership of the castle, the main tenant to follow Prettyman was William Sumpter (1771-1848), his uncle by marriage. He was the second surviving son of Thomas Sumpter of Histon Hall, Histon in Cambridgeshire, (1735-1806) a gentry family farming in the vegetable and fruit growing area of the Fens. William was one of twelve siblings but many died of consumption when young. William's older sister Elizabeth married 10th Lord Berners in 1788. William had no expectation of inheriting the Histon estate, which was due to pass to his surviving elder brother Richard. He needed to find somewhere to set up home for his family. The Wingfield Castle Estate became vacant after Robert Prettyman's death and William must have seemed an ideal tenant, of the right 'quality' and a close relative.

William Sumpter moved into Wingfield Castle about 1802 and looked for a wife. In 1805 at Redenhall Church he married Sophia Cotton from a large prosperous yeoman farming family based in Weybread who farmed land in Brockdish, Weybread and Wingfield.[26] William and Sophia had six children while living at Wingfield: James 1806, Sophia 1808, Lydia 1809, Harriet 1811,

Charlotte 1814 and William Richard 1819. An earlier William born in 1815 died soon after birth.

The Sumpters had their fair share of family grief and joy. Their eldest daughter Sophia married Charles Marris, a solicitor in Cambridge in 1830.[27] A year later their daughter Lydia died at Wingfield 'after a few days illness, aged 21. Her early loss is deeply lamented by friends and regretted by the poor.'[28] Then in 1833 their third daughter Charlotte married Revd Charles Bohun Smith, vicar of Alfriston in Sussex.[29] One would normally expect to see a gentleman like William Sumpter recorded in local newspapers as belonging to various associations, subscribing to worthy books and participating in local affairs. Sumpter is noticeably absent from local newspapers apart from his children's birth and deaths. We really have very little notion of his character or activities.

William's oldest brother Thomas was gifted academically but had died young suddenly in his rooms at Kings College, Cambridge 'in the prime of life, after a few days illness'.[30] The second older brother, Richard, stayed in Histon and went into fruit and vegetables at Histon with his father, becoming part of the relatively new local market gardening industry.[31] The proximity of the city of Cambridge encouraged the development of this fertile flat land in the early nineteenth century. For efficiency's sake Richard needed to consolidate the disparate strips of family land holdings there and neighbouring Impington. He was keen to inclose land in the parish that his father Thomas Sumpter owned. His father may not have been so keen but acquiesced in Richard's ambitions. The inclosure of Histon and Impington was deeply unpopular locally, although the numerous smallholders and commoners were never sufficiently organised to prevent it. The final outcome, a private inclosure Act, required a great many exchanges of small plots of land and a huge number of displaced commoners.[32] Thomas Sumpter was one of three principal allottees in Histon.

The Sumpters' aggressive bid for land clearly caused ructions between Thomas and his son Richard. When Thomas Sumpter and his wife both died in 1806, Richard and William were the only surviving sons; the five daughters were married and settled elsewhere. It was naturally expected that the four hundred acre Histon estate and the market gardening business would go to Richard. To everyone's astonishment, Thomas's will appointed two of his grandsons as executors, Henry Wilson, his daughter Elizabeth's oldest son and future eleventh Lord Berners, and John Hibbert, the son of Thomas' daughter Charlotte and her husband. These two executors were directed to sell the estate and all Thomas' effects and the resulting cash was to be 'divided among all my children equally, except my son Richard.'[33] Richard was to inherit nothing.

88. Watercoloured print of Wingfield Castle c1820, with lake and mountains added for artistic effect.

The executors, however, perhaps mindful of the fact that Richard was running the market gardening business and already selling produce successfully, decided to ignore the will and conveyed to Richard the manor house, twenty-five acre park and one hundred and eight acres of land in Histon parish used as market garden. The rest of the land was distributed between the surviving daughters and William. Whether this was to keep the family peace, a sense of fair play to Richard or because of family pressure we do not know but the executors' judgment was not formally objected to. It is the author's suspicion that Thomas did not trust Richard to look after the estate or the family's interests and he was right. Though Richard Sumpter got his market garden and his house, Histon Hall, he quite quickly sold a large part of the land for commercial gain to the growing number of keen market gardeners locally. He retired young to enjoy his small estate and spent his cash.[34] Richard died at the relatively young age of fifty-four in 1817. His brother William of Wingfield Castle then inherited this much reduced manorial estate and Histon Hall.[35]

William and Sophia Sumpter give up the tenancy of Wingfield Castle estate. The Sumpters did not move from Wingfield Castle to Histon Hall until after Michaelmas 1834. While they were tenants at Wingfield, William and Sophia probably had quite a good income and there was therefore little incentive to move to Histon after his brother died in 1817. There was little land left to farm in the Cambridgeshire estate. Sophia's family were nearby in Harleston, Weybread and Wingfield; their children all grew up at Wingfield. The castle had become home. But by 1834, William was sixty-three years old and he and Sophia wanted to retire. Their oldest son James French Sumpter had gone up to Cambridge to pursue a clerical career, all his daughters except Harriet were married and she was soon to be. Their youngest son William was not ready at fifteen to take on a tenancy of this size. William accordingly gave notice to his brother-in-law that they wished to give up the tenancy. The auction advertisement by Elvis and Sons, Auctioneers, read:-

Wingfield Castle and Hall sale

Near Harleston.

All the entire superior stock &c., on the above farms, The Property of Wm SUMPTER Esq.. declining the occupation at Michaelmas next

By AUCTION

By Mr BLOMFIELD

On Thursday 11 September, and following days.[36]

Wingfield Castle Estate in 1834. For much of the Sumpters' tenancy, agriculture was still in depression after the Napoleonic Wars. Investment in farm machinery extended to Ransome's of Ipswich new iron plough introduced in 1795 but not very often to the new threshing machines. There was a local abundance of labour, which provided little incentive for the landlord to invest in any practice likely to increase unemployment and hence dependency on the local poor rate. The workers were virulently antipathetic to these new machines and however productive they might be the farmers generally did not want to make matters worse. After the riots of 1822, machines were dangerous to own, required complex negotiation between workers, farmers and landlords, and turned out not all that much cheaper than using manual labour.

Dairying in north Suffolk had been gradually declining over these years but arable agriculture was increasingly taking over the clay lands of the estate. But there was little profit to be had for farmers in 1834. The recession was ending and relatively good times lay ahead but it may not have been easy to find new tenants to take on farms of this size.

The man who took up the tenancy was from a large farming family in Suffolk who probably knew no other way of life. Joseph Tacon would probably not have identified with the gentry but with the prosperous farmers in the locality.

Joseph Tacon and his family (1786–1872), tenants at Wingfield Castle 1834–1862). The Suffolk Tacon family was mainly comprised of middling farmers but Joseph was related to a branch who established a successful brewery in Eye and another smaller brewing venture in Beccles. The earliest reference to Joseph Tacon as a farmer at Wingfield Castle is in 1837, when he is cited in an advertisement praising 'Owen's Copenhagen animalized carbon' as the cheapest and best manure for turnips and mangel wurzel.[37] He did not take on the whole estate but only 350 acres of it. In 1825 some fifty-one acres of the estate had been sold separately, of which half was freehold, half copyhold.[38] It is likely Joseph and his wife Susannah, usually called Susan, had taken on the tenancy shortly after it was advertised in 1834. Joseph was already forty-eight years old, Susan the same age, when they came to Wingfield, an experienced and reliable couple.

Joseph was named in the Wingfield parish polling list of 1841, and he and Susan were listed in the 1841 census as resident at the 'Castle Farm'. Increasingly the castle was referred to as a farmhouse, which suggests that the castle had lost some of its polished gentry appearance. In 1844, White's Directory listed Joseph as a farmer at the 'Castle'.[39] The farming community in Wingfield was already dominated by the large landholding of Sir William Adair of Flixton Hall but there was also proprietor Robert Butcher at Wingfield College and his tenant George Fenn Pretty at College Farm, John Crisp at Wingfield Old Hall, Lionel Kerry at Chickering Hall and a dozen or so smaller farmers, including Bilby Farrow, Isaac Filby, Robert and Hannah Gowing, Jonathan Hart and the eccentric Absalom Feavearyear.

Feavearyear was also the village carpenter, who is still remembered today for constructing in 1840 his own brick mausoleum in his garden on Wingfield Green, now a listed building. It is said that Absalom, a non-conformist, had a violent disagreement with the parish priest, during which he swore he would never enter the church again. 'Oh yes you will' replied the parson 'You'll have to die sometime'. To thwart the priest Absalom built his own burial place. The three tombstones inside the mausoleum are dedicated to Absalom, his wife and son although when it came to their turn, his wife and son preferred the more conventional parish churchyard.

The village in the 1840s. Wingfield was a remarkably self-sufficient village in 1844 considering its small size.[40] It had a National School with both a master and a schoolmistress, a grocery store run by Maria Burrows, two blacksmiths, William Davis and William Precious, and a tailor, David Fisk. There were two beer houses, one run by Absalom's wife Fanny and one owned by John Spall. There was also a public house, the Kings Head. The church was under the direction of the Reverend Edward D Bolton MA, who had a modest but adequate stipend of one hundred and fifty pounds a year.

The Tithe map of 1840 shows Joseph Tacon farming 374 acres of Lord Berners' land in Wingfield, 290 arable acres and 84 pastures of grazing land.[41] Other larger tenants of Lord Berners were John Crisp with 124 acres, Bilby Farrow with 67 acres and a small hempland farmed by Jonathan Mobbs, who had a cottage and garden nearby. In the 1851 census Tacon declared he was farming 350 acres in Wingfield and employing sixteen labourers. Later that year, Susan Tacon died age 65 and was buried at Wingfield. Less than a year later Joseph married a woman forty years his junior, Betsey Simpson, who was just twenty-two years old. She had been living with her mother in Lowestoft and working as a schoolmistress, according to the 1851 census. It was an unusual marriage but it lasted. Betsey had a daughter three years later. By the 1861 census, when Joseph was 70 years old, he had added some land to his holding and it then stood at 366 acres. He was also renting two grazing marshes in Norton Subcourse from the Kirby Cane Estate.[42]

When Joseph Tacon's lease ran out in 1862, the new owner of the estate, Sir Robert Adair, did not offer him an extension. Perhaps Adair wanted a younger man who would farm in a new way. Joseph was clearly proud of his stock, it must have been a wrench to leave after thirty years in Wingfield.[43] Tacon and his wife did not give up the farming life however. In 1871, at the age of 85 he was tenanting a 140 acre farm in Ubbeston. Betsey was 42 and their daughter 17. He died in 1872 and left less than £2000, all to his wife.[44] He was buried with his first wife Susan at Wingfield. Betsey died in 1885.

The Sale of Wingfield Castle Estate. In 1856, Lord Berners decided to sell Wingfield Castle Estate.[45] It was to be sold at auction on 1 August at the Kings Head, Diss.

> An extremely compact and well-cultivated estate, tithe rent charge and Manors, with the picturesque ruins of Wingfield Castle replete with historical and antiquarian interest and situate in SUFFOLK, at a short distance from the Railway and Market towns of Harleston, Eye and

> Diss. Howlett and Lenny are honoured with instructions ....
>
> 616 ACRES of fine deep-soil Arable and highly productive Pasture Land, with a due proportion of ornamental Plantations and Woods. With the principal Lot will be included the valuable Manors of Wingfield Castle and Wingfield Frumbals, which, with the Farm Residences, Buildings, and Land, are of the fair estimated annual value of nearly £1000. This property is in part tithe free and except for 4 acres entirely freehold and land tax redeemed. Also the entire Tithes of the Parish, extending to 2150 Acres, and commuted into an appropriate Rent charge of £700 per annum, and leased from the Bishop of Norwich for a term of 21 years years from the 13th day of June, 1843. Particulars and conditions of sale of this important Property, with a view of the Castle and Plans of the Estate, are in course of preparation, and may be obtained, days previous the Auction, at Garraway's Coffeehouse, London; the principal Inns at Ipswich, Bury, and Norwich; of Philip Wilson, Esq., solicitor, Lynn; and of the Auctioneers, Wissett, near Halesworth, Suffolk.

The fact the castle is described as 'picturesque ruins' suggests that it had a dilapidated appearance and the estate may not have been maintained in a good state. The castle was described in a trade directory of 1858 as 'handsomely mantled in ivy', a sure indication that the walls were being neglected.[46] Berners sold Wingfield Castle to the most obvious local prominent person who already held substantial land in the parish, Sir Robert Shafto Adair of Flixton Hall. It seems likely that the deal was negotiated before the auction. Adair had inherited the vast Adair estates from his father William in 1844 and was rapidly expanding his holdings and bringing new ideas to local agriculture, including the concept of a model farm.

Changes to Wingfield Castle in the early to mid-Nineteenth Century. John Wodderspoon, who wrote a diverting but fanciful guide to 'Historic Sites and Other Remarkable Places in Suffolk' published in 1839, noted that at Wingfield Castle

> 'the visitor can ascend by a winding stair to the upper story of the gateway, which contains a noble apartment...The turrets from which we step into the space above the gate are turned into dove cotes and here instead of the belligerent sounds giving earnest of war and danger, may be heard the cooing of the feathery inhabitants, whose happy voices denoting peace and security to themselves and owner, echo through the vaulted space'.. 'The court yard is divided between the usual homestead

of a farmhouse and a well arranged peaceful garden.'[47]

There were no roofs on the towers, the house was a simple farmhouse.

In 1844 White's directory described the south front as 'still tolerably entire' but whether that included the internal range of medieval buildings along the southwest front is difficult to say. Emery confidently says that the medieval southwest range was in place 'until the mid 19th century'. [48] The roof of the old southwest range can be clearly seen in the etching by Davy completed in 1827 (85, p. 291) and is even more clearly prominent in Edward Dayes' watercolour from the late eighteenth century (84, p. 291). The roof of the west range is however certainly absent in an undated pencil sketch from the late nineteenth century shown on page 312 (89). Aldwell says the stables that were sited in the eighteenth century inside the medieval southwest range to the west of the gatehouse, which are thought to have been where the chapel was originally, were pulled down in 1826 but if that is the case, the shell of the medieval building along the inside of the south west curtain wall was still standing at that time.[49]

Wingfield Castle estate became part of the huge Adair family estate in 1856 and remained in their ownership for near on 130 years. The family's rather sad decline from Victorian prosperity to struggling postwar landowners mirrors that of so many great estates in England. We'll meet the Adairs in the next chapter.

Notes

1 Roebuck, R., 1973, Absentee Landownership in the Late Seventeenth and Early Eighteenth Centuries: A Neglected Factor in English Agrarian History. *Agricultural History Review, Vol. 21*, pp. 1-17.

2 Rawding, C., 1992, Society and Place in Nineteenth Century North Lincolnshire. *Rural History Vol 3*, pp. 59-85.

3 Beckett, J. V., 1984, The Pattern of Land Ownership in England and Wales, 1660-1880, *Economic History Review 37*, pp. 1-22.

4 Theobald J., 2001, 'Distant Lands': The Management of Absentee Estates in Woodland High Suffolk, 1660–1800. *Rural History, Vol 12*, pp. 1-18.

5 Caird, J., 1852, *English Agriculture in 1850-51*, Longman Brown Green and Longmans, London, pp. 145-146, online at https://books.google.co.uk.

6 Pursehouse, E., 1966, 'Hard times in Brockdish', *Waveney Valley Studies*, Diss Publishing Co (reprinted 1983).

7 Suffolk Observatory Population Report Parish of Wingfield, 2018 https://www.suffolkobservatory.info/population/report/view/62646f73d23e489098a5cdad7a116eed/E04009278.

8 Anonymous diary dated 1784-1824 called the Brockdish diary now thought to be written by Charles Souter, Parish Clerk of Syleham NRO MC 2329/2.958x4. "Sept 1792 Mr Prettymans corn stacks willfully set on fire damage".

9 *Ipswich Journal*, Saturday 7 February 1789 and Anonymous Diary NRO MC 2329/2.958x4. 23 November 1793.

10 Select Committee on Agricultural Distress. Parliamentary Papers 1821 (668) Vol IX, 9-13.

11 Muskett, P., 1984, The East Anglian Agrarian Riots of 1822. *The Agricultural History Review Vol. 32*, pp. 1-13.

12 Gordon, B., 1976, 1822: The Causes of Agricultural Distress. *Political Economy in Parliament 1819–1823* pp. 122-134, Palgrave Macmillan, London.

13 Zinovieff, S., 2014, *The Mad Boy, Lord Berners, My Grandmother And Me.* Jonathan Cape, London.

14 Cokayne, G. E., with Gibbs V., Doubleday, H.A., White, G. H., Warrand, D. and Lord Howard de Walden (eds), 2000, *The Complete Peerage of England, Scotland, Ireland, Great Britain and the United Kingdom, Extant, Extinct or Dormant, 1st ed'n 1910 vol II*, p. 158, Alan Sutton Publishing, Gloucester, 2000.

15 Knyvett-Wilson Family Collection Title deeds Kirby Cane and elsewhere NRO KNY 18, 369X3.

16 Ibid.

17 Claim of Robert Wilson to barony of Berners: House of Lords, TNA TS11/762/2388. Statement of the claim of Robert Wilson of Didlington and Ashwellthorpe to the Barony of Berners with his pedigree. NRO PD 19/38.

18 *New Sporting Magazine 1838 Vol 14*, p. 359.

19 Lords Hansard, Relations with Portugal. HL Deb 03 June 1833 vol 18 cc238-99.

20 *Bath Chronicle and Weekly Gazette*, Thursday 25 February 1836

21 The Will of Robert Wilson, 9th Lord Berners, NA PROB 11/1894/416.

22 Grant of croft to be held jointly by the Bishop of Norwich and the perpetual curate of Wingfield, Rev. John Edge Daniel 1 February 1847 Ref SROI FC84/C1/1

23 Obituary 10th Lord Berners. *Gentleman's Magazine 1851 Volume 189*, p. 430.

24 Ibid.

25 Slander. Norris v Lord Berners. Court report *Norfolk Chronicle* Saturday 3 August 1844, p3 and Assize Intelligence, Norwich. *Globe* 2 August 1844.

26 The story of the Cotton family of Weybread is told in Chapter 8. The Cotton Family, pp. 168-192 in Murphy, E., *The Moated Grange, A history of south Norfolk through the story of one family home 1300-2000.* Book Guild, Sussex. The marriage of William and Sophia reported *Ipswich Journal,* 7 Decmber 1805.

27 *Ipswich Journal,* Saturday 23 January 1830.

28 *Bury and Norwich Post,* Wednesday 1 June 1831.

29 *The Suffolk Chronicle,* Saturday 29 June 1833.

30 Cambridge Alumni Database (ACAD), online at http://venn.lib.cam.ac.uk.

31 Histon: Economic history, in *A History of the County of Cambridge and the Isle of Ely: Volume 9, Chesterton, Northstowe, and Papworth Hundreds*, pp. 97-101, Wright, A. P. M. and Lewis, C. P. (eds), London, 1989. British History Online http://www.british-history.ac.uk/vch/cambs/vol9/pp. 97-101 [accessed 21 April 2020].

32 Ibid.

33 The Will of Thomas Sumpter of Histon, Cambrideshire, copy. TNA PROB-11/2072/99/1, IR 26/332/200.

34 Histon: Manors and other estates, in *A History of the County of Cambridge and the Isle of Ely: Volume 9, Chesterton, Northstowe, and Papworth Hundreds*, pp. 94-97, Wright, A. P. M. and Lewis, C. P. (eds), London, 1989. British History Online http://www.british-history.ac.uk/vch/cambs/vol9/pp94-97 [accessed 21 April 2020].

35 Will of Richard Sumpter of Histon, Cambridgeshire TNA PROB 11/1597/311.

36 *Suffolk Chronicle or Weekly Advertiser and County Express,* Saturday 23 August 1834.

37 Thomas Bunn Advertisement. *Norwich Mercury,* Saturday September 1837.

38 Advertisement *Bury and Norwich Post* 8 June 1825.

39 White, W. *History, Gazetteer, and Directory, of Suffolk*, Sheffield, R. Leader, 1844. pp. 475-477.

40 Ibid. p. 475.

41 Tithe Commission and successors: Tithe Apportionments, Wingfield Parish, Suffolk 1836-1929. TNA IR 29/33/173.

42 Plans, elevation and particulars of sale of the Kirby Hall Estate, Norfolk. Two freehold grazing marshes in Norton Subcourse, Norfolk, containing 13a, 2r, 10p in the occupation of Joseph Tacon, 1869 SRO (Lowestoft) 1039/12/4.

43 Advertisement George Durrant. *The Suffolk Chronicle; or Weekly General Advertiser & County Express*, Saturday

27 September 1862.

44 Joseph Tacon 1872. National Probate Calendar (Index of Wills and Administrations), 1858-1966, 1973-1995. Probate to Widow Betsey, executors Robert Gowing from Wingfield College, farmer and John Clarke, bank agent Beccles.

45 Advertisement for sale of Wingfield Castle Estate in the *Bury and Norwich Press* 9 July 1856, p. 1.

46 White, W. *History, Gazetteer, and Directory, of Suffolk and the towns near its borders,* p. 727, 1858.

47 Wodderspoon, J., 1839, *Historic Sites and Other Remarkable and Interesting Places in the County of Suffolk*, pp. 269-277, Longman, Orme, Brown, Green and Longmans, Ipswich.

48 Emery, A., 2000, *Greater Medieval Houses of England and Wales Volume II*, p. 16.

49 Aldwell, S. W. H., 1933, Wingfield, its Church, Castle and College p. 34, republished 1994, Wingfield Family Society, Athens, Georgia, 2007, Lyndon-Stanford p. 37.

89. Sketch of South Façade Wingfield Castle, late nineteenth century.

Wingfield Castle, An Ordinary Farmhouse, 1856–1939

The late nineteenth and early twentieth centuries were not kind to Wingfield Castle. The new proprietors became even more detached from their land than the Berners and the tenants less appreciative of the architectural treasure they lived in. A gentleman's residence became an ordinary farmhouse.

The sale of the Wingfield Castle Estate in 1856 to Sir Robert Shafto Adair expanded his already extensive Suffolk estate by a further five hundred acres or so. Based around Flixton Hall, near Bungay, his property stretched from south west of Bury St Edmunds north along the Waveney Valley beyond Beccles. The estate encompassed about twenty-five manors across Suffolk and Norfolk. It was said that the Adairs owned all the land between Wingfield Castle and Flixton Hall and it is true that many of the manors in north east Suffolk came under Adair ownership in the mid Victorian period, although there were many landholdings not contiguous with the main estate that the Adairs also garnered. The Berners were wealthy but the Adairs vastly more so. And, like many of the Victorian landed elite without obvious aristocratic forebears, the Adairs had made their fortune in the eighteenth century engaging in government business, which moved them up an echelon from Anglo-Irish landowners to plutocrats.[1] The family name of the Adairs of Flixton died out in 1988 with the death of Sir Allan Adair but he had already given Wingfield Castle to his eldest daughter Bridget, Lady Darrell. When the Flixton estate was sold off after the Second World War, she retained the castle until her long term tenant Graham Baron Ash died in 1980.

The Adair Family of Flixton Hall and Ballymena Castle. The Adair family roots lie in the ferociously protestant heart of County Antrim in Northern Ireland, at Ballymena, where fanatic Orange Ireland continues to harbour 'troubles' even today.[2] In 1626 a prosperous Scot from Galloway, William Adair, acquired newly-settled lands at Ballymena in exchange for part of his patrimony in Wigtownshire; his son, Sir Robert, built Ballymena Castle at the centre of the new estate. The Adairs are regarded as the founding fathers of Ballymena town.

A century later Sir Robert's descendant, another William Adair (1700-1783) made a fortune as an army agent, a curious but lucrative role in the civil department of the British Army. The agent hovered between the paymaster-general and the paymaster of the regiment, through whom every regimental concern of a pecuniary nature was transacted. Agents acted in part as bankers to the army but they had the administration and accountability of the public emoluments and personal incomes of some five thousand officers scattered over all parts of the rapidly growing empire. They acted as official brokers for the sale and purchase of Military Commissions and were the recognised intermediaries for effecting regimental exchanges and transfers. They were also the executive agents for the onerous and responsible work involved in clothing and equipping the army. The role required business experience and capacity, and a mastery of the regulations and practice governing the army. They lent money to impecunious officers and made a packet from government, regimental commanders and officers alike. The Adairs continued this role through the Napoleonic wars when there were quarter of a million men and 10,000 officers recruited. No wonder the Adairs got rich.

It was William Adair who purchased the Flixton Hall estate in Suffolk from the heirs of the last of the Tasburgh family and moved in to the stylish Jacobean manor that Tasburgh had built.[3] The Flixton and Ballymena estates were inherited by William's descendant Sir Robert Shafto Adair, first baronet (1786-1869). He acquired yet more land and property in 1846.

Sir Robert Shafto Adair, 1st baronet (1786–1869). The moated Jacobean house at Flixton was severely damaged by fire in 1846, so Sir Robert employed Anthony Salvin, an enthusiast for pastiche castles, to carry out a reconstruction, turning an elegant seventeenth century house into a bolder Victorian creation with more grandiose castellations, extensions and chimneys. It did not entirely obliterate the old form of the house but the moat and setting was destroyed.

The castle at Ballymena was let at this period; the first baronet seems to have been more interested in his Suffolk estate than his Irish one. But his son, **Robert Alexander Shafto Adair, 2nd baronet and later Lord Waveney,** usually called by his third name 'Shafto', made a number of visits to Ballymena from 1840 on and he moved there in 1846 to administer the estate on behalf of his father. He had married Theodosia Meade in 1836 but they had no children. He arrived therefore just as the effects of the Irish potato famine were about to reach catastrophic proportions. A Whig, he was elected to a constituency in Cambridge at the general election in 1847, the year he wrote a pamphlet on the famine.[4]

90. The first Flixton Hall, built c1615.

Adair's pamphlet gives his personal narrative of the famine as it affected the tenants on his estate, explaining how the policies put in place by the Government were translated into concrete action on the ground and how the local community was responding to the crisis. The aim was to better address how the famine might be tackled in the future. Although the famine had a less devastating impact in Ulster than in other parts of Ireland, between fifteen and twenty per cent of the Antrim population died of starvation and thousands migrated to Canada and America. Adair does not play down the devastation that he witnessed but his confidant response to the tragedy is written in an unfortunate, self-satisfied tone.

From 1865 onwards, Shafto Adair employed the famous Belfast architects, Lanyon & Lynn, to rebuild Ballymena Castle in the Scots baronial style as his main residence. It rivalled Balmoral as a grandiose parody of a Scottish castle but in an Irish setting of course. It may not have matched Wingfield in medieval class but as fantasy it did well enough. The Irish castle was not completed until 1887, and though greatly loved by Shafto Adair, was neglected by his descendants and eventually demolished in 1957 after having lain empty for some years and been vandalised. The site is now a car park. Adair land in

County Antrim then extended to some six to seven thousand acres. In 1870, Adair donated a People's Park to Ballymena, engaging fifty labourers to work for six months landscaping it.

Shafto Adair was a prodigious builder on his estate around Flixton too, replacing old cottages and farm buildings on the tenanted farms in Suffolk. Like many landlords he was trying to provide better incentives for farmers to take up vacant tenancies during the darkening recession after 1870.[5] He also provided schools in St Cross and Flixton. In Homersfield he restored St Mary's Church, rebuilt the Black Swan public house, reconstructed the bridge over the Waveney and rebuilt the estate cottages. The first Sir Robert Adair bought the Wingfield Castle estate in 1856 but he died in 1869. Shafto, the second baronet, was preoccupied with building his Irish home and angling for a parliamentary seat. For much of the late 1850s and 1860s it is unlikely that the Adairs took any particular interest in Wingfield Castle. Their estate in Suffolk extended to about fourteen thousand acres by the end of the century; Wingfield was a small fragment.

Sir Shafto Adair was often called 'Colonel Adair' after he became lieutenant-colonel of the East Suffolk militia artillery (1853–81) and was appointed one of several military ADCs to Queen Victoria in 1857, a ceremonial honour. He wrote on militias and national defence. One of his pamphlets, 'The Militias of the United Kingdom', appeared in four editions from 1855 to 1860. He was a leading Liberal and president of the Ulster Reform Club. He conscientiously participated in many aspects of public life in Ulster, especially in Ballymena, where it is said that 'he gave regular entertainments to all classes of society; those of the poorer classes, who smuggled away as much food as they ate, perhaps enjoyed these occasions the most.'[6] In the 1860s and 1870s he published a number of pamphlets on the Church of Ireland and regarded himself as an expert on Italy. His pamphlet of 1847 on emigration and outdoor relief went into three editions. On 5 June 1845 he was elected a Fellow of the Royal Society; in those days a clubbable presence was more pertinent to election than expertise in science.

Sir Shafto Adair was created Lord Waveney of South Elmham in 1873 on Gladstone's recommendation. Perhaps his position as Provincial Grand Master of the Suffolk Freemasons was a factor in his elevation or, as is so often the case, the peerage was a consolation prize for the many Liberal parliamentary seats he had fought but failed to win. He served with a notable lack of distinction as Liberal Party Member of Parliament for Cambridge for seven years from 1847–52 and 1854–7. Before winning Cambridge he twice contested East Suffolk unsuccessfully and was mercilessly pilloried in the press in conservative Ipswich.

Later in life he threw his hat into the ring for parliamentary seats in Canterbury and then for Antrim but was ignominiously defeated on both occasions. Perhaps with all his other interests he simply did not have time to engage in the necessary negotiation that a successful political career demanded. However he found his voice in the House of Lords and contributed regularly to debate, particularly on Irish matters, on which he was moderately supportive of more devolved government but predictably vehemently against moves towards Home Rule, swimming against the tide of his own party.[7] He lived mainly in his grand castle at Ballymena from 1884 until his death in 1886, aged 74, when the peerage became extinct. His younger brother Hugh succeeded to the baronetcy.

Sir Hugh Edward Adair (1815–1902). Flixton became the home of Shafto's younger brother, Hugh Edward Adair (1815–1902). Not to be outdone in architectural ambition by his brother, he remodelled and extended Flixton Hall in 1888-92 to the design of Fairfax B. Wade, taking Victorian excess to new heights of extravagance, or 'fruitiness' as one website has it.[8] His additions and alterations resulted in a house of sixty rooms. Where Salvin's work had been relatively restrained, Wade gave full rein to the Victorian free style at its most exuberant.

Hugh was educated at Harrow and St John's College, Oxford and before becoming an MP was a practising barrister. He married a cousin in 1856. A Liberal Party MP for Ipswich from 1847-1874, parliamentary Hansard records twenty-six speeches in all. Compared with some of his contemporaries this is not a bad batting average. The urge to be seen performing in parliament was less pressing on MPs in pre-television days. A later Suffolk MP Harry Foster recalled going 'to Flixton, and seeing that splendid specimen of fine old English gentleman Sir Hugh Adair.' Sir Hugh told him, 'Your work is very different from what mine was when I was in Parliament.' 'He said that when he sat in Parliament his constituency was a very contented one; they were always satisfied and only expected to see him once a year.' It was a comfortable life.

Adair was a supporter of extending publicly funded education for Catholics and Dissenters but balked at supporting more radical ideas to support the Roman Catholic church. It would surprise modern politicians how much parliamentary time was taken up then by nuances of religious practice and education.[9] Hugh Adair died at Tunbridge Wells in 1902, aged 86.

Sir Frederick Edward Shafto Adair (1860–1915), 4th baronet was Hugh Adair's son. Frederick Adair was not particularly fond of Flixton or Ballymena. A bachelor, his interests were more singular. He went to Sandhurst and took a commission as Captain of the Third Battalion Rifle Brigade but preferred shooting game to regular army life and did not pursue an army career. He spent five months in 1894 on a long hunting trip to Baltistan (northern Pakistan) and Ladakh (India), submitting regular letters to '*The Field*' that were later published as a book.[10] He took a personal interest in farming and managed two of the Flixton farms himself, breeding prize-winning show cattle and sheep.[11] He took part in and designed costumes for pantomimes and painted in watercolour, exhibiting at the Suffolk Art and Aid Association on 28 October 1908, winning a highly commended card, thus achieving a listing in '*Suffolk Artists*'.[12]

Times were changing for the landed property elite. The middle decades of the nineteenth century had seen a revolution in farming in East Anglia. This period of High Farming, 'high input, high output' suited larger farms with secure tenants and access to landlord capital. These years had been prosperous ones and we will look at the impact of this new prosperity on the Wingfield Castle tenants later in this chapter.

The Adairs had not perhaps invested as much in farm buildings during the good years as one might expect given their other philanthropic investments. A farm survey undertaken on the Flixton estate about 1870 found farm buildings in a rather poor condition. One of the farms at St Cross South Elmham had farm buildings 'deficient of proper shedding, inferior farmsteads and yards exposed to cold winds'.[13] The total cost of the repairs would be six thousand pounds. The annual income of the estate was just under twenty thousand pounds a year but little had been invested in improving buildings at this point. Tenants could still readily be found though rents were high because profits were still to be made, so there had seemed no pressing need to invest.[14] This survey however prompted Shafto Adair to apply to the new government sponsored Lands Improvement Company for loans towards new buildings and cottages, which led to substantial improvements on most of the Adair farms and the creation of model farm buildings at Wingfield.

Farming incomes were not sustained as the century ended. The Great Depression of British Agriculture that occurred during the late nineteenth century is usually dated from 1873 to 1896.[15] The turndown was caused by the dramatic fall in grain prices that followed the opening up of the American prairies to cultivation in the 1870s and the advent of cheap transportation on the new steamships. British agriculture did not really recover from this depression until the Second World War.

By 1881 the census showed a decline of over 92,000 agricultural labourers in the previous decade, with an increase of more than 53,000 urban labourers. Many men had migrated to the cities to find employment. Between 1871 and 1901 the population of England and Wales increased by forty-three percent but the proportion of male agricultural labourers decreased by over one-third. A Royal Commission on the Depression in Trade and Industry in 1886 heard from Sir James Caird that the annual income of landlords, tenants and labourers had fallen by £42,800,000 since 1876.[16] No other country witnessed such a social transformation. British policy contrasted with those adopted on the Continent. Every wheat-growing country imposed tariffs in the wake of the explosion of American prairie wheat except Britain and Belgium. Subsequently, Britain became the most industrialised major country with the smallest proportion of its resources devoted to agriculture.[17] Britain's dependence on imported grain during the 1830s was two per cent; during the 1860s it was twenty four per cent; during the 1880s it was forty-five per cent. By the outset of the First World War, Britain was dependent on imports for four-fifths of her wheat and forty percent of her meat.

The impact on landowners like the Adairs was astonishing. During the first three-quarters of the nineteenth century, the British landed aristocracy were the wealthiest class in the world's richest country. But by the 1880s the new global elite were American businessmen, who made their wealth from industry rather than land and British manufacturers eclipsed the aristocracy as the richest class in the nation.

And then came Chancellor of the Exchequer David Lloyd George's land tax reform, actively supported by the young Winston Churchill, still in his idealistic phase. The 1909/1910 People's Budget was a proposal of the Liberal government that introduced unprecedented taxes on the lands and incomes of Britain's wealthy to fund new social welfare programmes, notably old age pensions. It passed the House of Commons in 1909 but was blocked by the House of Lords for a year. The Lords was stuffed full of hereditary Tory landowners, but the law was eventually passed in spite of them in April 1910. The budget also included a proposal for the introduction of complete land valuation and a twenty per cent tax on increases in value when land changed hands. This was the first budget in British history with the expressed intent of redistributing wealth amongst the British population. It was a key issue of contention between the Liberal government and the Conservative-dominated House of Lords, leading to two general elections in 1910 and the enactment of the Parliament Act in 1911 to prevent the Lords ever again blocking legislation completely, a constitutional shift that gave the Commons absolute supremacy. It is no surprise to find that Frederick Adair abandoned his family's traditional Liberal sympathies and became a Conservative.

A further problem for huge landowners was the introduction of Estate duty, a death duty tax and tax on lifetime transfers that was introduced in 1894 to replace probate duty. Estate duty was eventually replaced by capital transfer tax in 1974/1975 and, subsequently, by inheritance tax. It was a bid to raise money to pay off a four million pound government deficit. And, over the course of the early twentieth century, the tax burden began to break up some large estates. The vast Victorian country houses became too expensive to staff and increasingly unfashionable. Flixton Hall was beginning to feel like a white elephant.

Frederick Adair sold most of the family properties in Ulster to estate tenants and then donated a huge drinking fountain to the people of Ballymena, constructed inside his uncle's People's Park. Frederick himself lived mainly in quite a modest, remodelled house in Aldeburgh, Adair Lodge.[18] In 1904 most of the Flixton estate land was sold off but not the Wingfield Castle estate. It seems quite likely however that Frederick was giving some serious consideration to selling Wingfield. In June 1913, *Country Life* magazine ran a feature on the Castle, 'the property of Sir Frederick Adair, Bart', describing it as 'a quiet and busy farm', and 'a frontispiece of a castle'.[19] The photos show Jerningham House totally covered in render, the common late Victorian way of disguising Tudor black and white in East Anglia at that time. The gatehouse, shown on page 37 (16), was covered in ivy. *Country Life* was the perfect showcase for a property about to be advertised for sale. The First World War ensued and the castle was not sold. Frederick died in 1915 at the young age of fifty-four. His funeral was made all the more imposing because some eight hundred members of the Shropshire Yeomanry, who were then encamped at Flixton Hall, participated in the ceremonial.[20]

Frederick's brother, another **Sir Robert Shafto Adair (1862–1949), 5th baronet**, inherited the estate in 1915. He lived at Flixton on occasion but stayed mainly in London. He was a patron of the arts and a director of the Royal Academy of Music. Deputy-Lieutenant of County Antrim, he held the unique office of 'King's Clog', a right to receive a small annuity from the

Crown created by Charles II in 1636 from shares he sold in the New River Company, the water company formed to bring water to the City of London. How the recipient of this small grant is chosen is a mystery. Robert Adair decided after the retirement of William Groom, the tenant at Wingfield at the beginning of the Second World War, to rent out Wingfield Castle. A happy choice was made, as we shall see.

The fifth baronet was too old to serve in the two World Wars but his heir **Sir Allan Adair, 6th baronet (1897–1988)** served in both as a career officer. He joined the Grenadier Guards in 1916, went to France just after the Battle of the Somme and was at the front until the end of the war, awarded the Military Cross in 1918 and bar in 1919. Between the wars he was a regimental

91. Jerningham House, Wingfield Castle.

commander. He became Major General during the Second World War, commanding the Guards Armoured Division, which advanced one hundred miles in one day to liberate Brussels, one of the more dramatic feats of the war. Described as 'diffident, light-hearted in manner, sometimes a little vague' he was a formidably talented commander, professionally competent and possessed inflexible determination.[21] After the war he became Colonel of the Grenadier Guards. Like his father and grandfather he was a prominent Freemason. He wrote his memoirs, which were readable enough to be reprinted several times. [22] He married Enid Dudley Ward, whose photographs appeared regularly in the society pages of the *Sketch* and *Illustrated London News* in the 1920s. They had three daughters and one son Desmond, who was killed age 23 in the fighting at Monte Cassino, Italy in late 1943, so the baronetcy became extinct when Allan died.

92. Portrait of Enid Shafto Adair and baby Desmond in 1922.

Allan never liked Flixton Hall. In his memoirs he said it was 'a vast, uncomfortable mausoleum, still with no proper central heating. In winter the children had to wear their overcoats when moving from room to room'. The mansion deteriorated badly during the Second World War, and after his father died, facing the demands of death duties and a dwindling estate income, Allan first sold the contents and then Flixton Hall itself and the estate. Despite efforts by both the East and West Suffolk County Councils to buy Flixton Hall and two hundred and fifty acres of the land for use as a joint farm institute, the Ministry of Agriculture vetoed the scheme so it was sold privately to a speculator, R G Lawrence. Two years after the purchaser had removed and sold all the protective lead from the roof, water was causing serious problems to the interior so he applied and gained permission to demolish the building in June 1952. As a result, one of the most magnificent Victorian buildings in East Anglia was lost. One small floor area survives today and is used for farm storage.

Allan and his wife lived at Anmer Hall on the Sandringham estate until he retired, when he returned to the Waveney Valley to live at Harleston and then Raveningham, Norfolk. Enid died in 1984; he died on 4 August 1988 at the age of ninety. When the Flixton estate was sold, Allan gave Wingfield Castle to his daughter Bridget, who subsequently married one of Adair's junior officers, Jeffrey Darrell. Lady Darrell held on to the estate while the tenant Graham Baron Ash was alive but sold it after his death in 1981.

The Wingfield Castle Tenants, 1862-1938. The Adairs had the reputation of being fair and generous landlords to their tenants, according to George Durrant, the retired land and estate agent whose family had dealt with the

Adairs over a century. In an interview with the author in 2012 Durrant contrasted the just and thoughtful style of the Adairs with some other local large landowners he and his father had observed at work in pre-war days, 'They were decent people to do business with'. The day-to-day supervision of contracts and tenancies was delegated to land agents but the chain of Adair proprietors took an interest in who was to be appointed when a tenancy came up for re-letting. It seems to have been Robert Adair's choice to terminate James Tacon's tenancy in 1862, although it is not clear why, nor why he agreed to the eccentric appointment of an individual with no farming experience whatsoever.

93. Major-General Sir Allan Shafto Adair Bt KCVO CB DSO MC.

Henry Sharp (1801–1881), tenant Wingfield Castle estate 1862–1866. Henry grew up in Deptford, south London, where his father kept a tallow chandlery on the High Street. In the mid Victorian period gas lamps were rapidly making tallow and wax candles obsolete so his father added a more lucrative enterprise, pawnbroking.[23] By the time Henry took over the shop the pawnbroking side of the business was dominant. Pawnbroking made Henry rich. He seems to have been a responsible person, donating regularly to funds 'for sick and decayed pawnbrokers'.[24] It wouldn't have been a hugely popular cause! Henry married Charlotte and four children Charlotte, James, Elizabeth and Alfred followed. His wife died some time before the census of 1861. By then Henry had also purchased property in Greenwich but clearly he was hankering after a different sort of life. He had made a packet; he fancied himself as a gentleman farmer, so why not take on a real castle to live in?

It was surely every Victorian gentleman's dream, harking back to knights of old and the English myth of a glorious Arthurian bygone age of chivalry that infused the Victorian art of Pre-Raphaelite painting, the poetry of Tennyson and gothic revival architecture. When Henry read Durrants' advertisement for a farm with 366 acres and a castle to live in, he decided to follow his dream. If he visited Wingfield to take a look, he must have noticed that the castle could probably do with some restoration but like others before and since, his first gaze seduced him. Sharp must have had sufficient persuasive powers to convince Robert Adair and his bailiff that he had the wherewithal to manage the workforce and somehow all would be fine.

But the tenancy did not work out well and in May 1866 the position was re-advertised in The Times, alongside several other Flixton Hall estate farms. It seems that Shafto Adair decided to have a clear out of inefficient farmers. The following farms to be let with new tenancies:[25]

Burgh St Peter. Farm with 169 acres
Loddon. Farm with 154 acres
Wingfield castle. 'A very superior farm' with 366 acres with gardens and pleasure grounds
St Margaret's Ilketshall. Shadow Barn Farm with 289 acres
Flixton. A farm with 194 acres
Flixton. A farm with 134 acres
St Margaret Ilketshall, a farm with 129 acres
Fressingfield and Stradbroke. A Capital farm 127 acres
Flixton. A good farm with 112 acres
St Cross, South Elmham, a farm with 73 acres.

Adair was changing the tenancies on 1747 acres of mainly arable land. The reason is not difficult to fathom. It seems likely that he was dissatisfied with the productivity and profitability of the farms, the current tenants being the least competent of the many on the estate. 1866 was the first year the national Parish Summaries of Agricultural Returns were collected.[26] These annual surveys of agricultural land and livestock were completed voluntarily by landlords and submitted to the Board of Trade (the forerunner of the Ministry of Agriculture, Fisheries and Foods) from which statistics about farming were derived. The very act of collecting this material would have brought home to Shafto Adair which of his farms were performing well and which were not. The material from this early survey has not survived in the National Archive so we cannot be sure whether this was the stimulus for the change of tenancies but it seems at least possible. Wingfield Castle farm was the largest of the tenancies to be advertised.

Though he lost his castle, Henry Sharp did not give up his dream of becoming a gentleman farmer. He moved to a farm in Badingham, Suffolk, of about 185 acres, ending his days at Bridge Place, Badingham. His children married and lived elsewhere. The 1881 census finds him living alone with a housekeeper and three other servants. He died later that year, leaving a tidy sum of £21,104, about £1.4 million today.[27]

James Hall (1833-1888), tenant farmer at Wingfield Castle 1866–1888. James Hall put in a bid for the advertised castle estate tenancy and was accepted. The new lease was signed on 14 May 1866.[28] James was a much safer pair of hands than Sharp. He had grown up on Chickering Hall farm, Hoxne, where his parents John and Mary Hall were respected tenant farmers, part of the local farming community of north Suffolk. He was the last of eight children, his parents well into their forties when James was born. James would have understood from a young age the character of the land and the most suitable livestock. And though he was in his early thirties when he took on the Wingfield Castle tenancy, he had his father, a near neighbour, to consult and advise.

James' mother died in 1862 and his father retired from his own tenancy and moved in with him. James was farming 477 acres with fifteen men and some boys. They had a housekeeper, Mary Alban, and her 'assistant', Mary Fisk, who was actually James' sister, plus another general servant, Mary Aldous,and two young boys, acting as groom and servant. James' sister Mary had married Henry Fisk from Great Glemham, who joined the London police in Kensington. Ten years later however Henry was living in the shady district of Saffron Hill near Holborn working as a private security guard and living with a woman called Charlotte. Mary returned to Suffolk and henceforth lived with her brother, where she remained as a housekeeper.

James Hall played his part in village life. In 1879 he hosted a two day bazaar in aid of the church restoration fund.[29] 'The visitors were free to roam at will into the courtyard of the old castle. The tower above the gateway was taken advantage of to obtain a shilling from each visitor. An interesting museum was arranged on one of the floors.' The museum 'curiosities' were mainly provided by the vicar, a former missionary, Reverend Price, with other objects lent by Lady Walker, Lord Waveney and various other local clerics. The occasion had managed, with the generosity of Lord Waveney and other local gentry, to generate the sum required for the completion of works on the church. The same year, Lord Waveney, President for 1879 of the British Archaeological Association, hosted an ambitious four day visit to Suffolk, arranging a tour of the castle and hosting a reception there on 14 August.[30]

A less happy event was the near drowning of a young woman and the loss of a valuable pony in the moat in 1875. John Davy, the Inspector of Nuisances (a public health official) at the Hoxne Union, had gone to see James Hall on business and left his trap, with his daughter sitting inside, a few yards outside the castle gate. The pony suddenly started backing towards the moat 'into which it finally turned a somersault' with Miss Davy inside. 'Miss Davy rose to the surface and her father by wading in managed to rescue her but the pony entangled in harness and vehicle, was unable to regain its footing and was drowned.'[31]

James died in 1888 and was buried in Wingfield churchyard. He never married. Probate yielded just under seven thousand pounds. One of his two executors was his nephew William Groom, the son of his sister Elizabeth. William Groom appears to have slipped effortlessly into a new tenancy at Wingfield Castle.[32]

William Groom (1845-1938) Tenant farmer at Wingfield Castle Farm, 1889-1926. Like James Hall, Groom was a farmer through and through. Born in Woodbridge, his father Roger Groom was a farmer and innkeeper/brewer at the Sun Inn in Martlesham who later took on a farm tenancy at Beacon Hill Farm, Martlesham. William won his own sixty six acre farming tenancy at Framsden when he was in his late twenties and in 1875 married another farmer's daughter, Emily Ann Freeman from Ringsfield. William and Emily moved into Wingfield Castle with his three children, William Roger then eight, Ernest John four and baby Elizabeth Dorothy, with two general servants. William's elder, son William Roger, grew up to take on a tenancy at St Martin's farm in Wingfield.

William and Emily Groom were both public-spirited sort of people. William became a Suffolk JP, serving on the Eye bench.[33] He was churchwarden, Chairman of the Parish Council and overseer, serving as vice-chairman for the Hoxne Poor Law Union and chairman of the Rural District Council from 1894, the newly created locally elected body. In short he had his finger in every Wingfield pie. In later years he chaired the local branch of the Conservative party.[34] The couple threw open the castle and the grounds for fund raising events for the church, with 'boating on the moat and tennis on the court'.[35] One year they entertained 'a large tour of Yarmouth Archaeologists', followed by a good lunch at the Fox and Goose in Fressingfield, dodging some heavy showers to hear a historical paper given by Rev Dr Raven before tea with the Reverend and Mrs Raven at Fressingfield Rectory.[36] One memorable Sunday in 1911, the Grooms hosted an outing for eighty old people living in the Hartismere Union Workhouse, driven over from Eye in brakes.[37] They were given a tour of the castle, a tea and after, plenty of 'rural sports', with 'an ample supply of tobacco for the old men'. Before leaving, all were given a home brewed pint of beer. It is a reminder that workhouses had long ceased to function as anything other than homes for the sick and frail elderly although it would be another forty years before their role was officially recognised and workhouses turned into 'caring' institutions.

William sold his lambs through Gaze's Auctions Diss and his 'prime fat oxen, heifers and bulls' through George Durrant's auctions in Harleston.[38] William was proud of his prize winning cattle, coming first in the Suffolk Show in 1904 with 'a choice over-year black Scottish heifer' which he sold the same day for £19 10s (about £1,500 today).[39] He organised ploughing matches for the villages of Wingfield, Syleham and Brockdish with his neighbour James Read at Monks Hall in Syleham. The men of Syleham beat everyone else and the fifteen ploughmen and organisers had 'a capital tea' at the White Horse in Syleham.[40]

In 1906 William Groom had a nasty accident driving back over Stuston Common from Diss station in a pony and trap with a lady visitor. The horse fell, the straps of the harness snapped and the occupants were pitched out onto the road. The lady was 'much bruised but not broken' but was laid up at the castle with the family for some time. William was not so badly hurt.[41]

The Great War and the Post-War Years. The Government largely neglected agriculture after the 1870s during the long years of depression. The development of refrigeration and the advent of steam engines and railways impacted heavily on British farmers because other countries were suddenly able to transport produce across huge distances to UK ports. Meat, eggs, grain and other goods were carried on ships from Australia, South Africa and Brazil. Britain also depended heavily on Germany for wheat, flour and sugar beet. By the outbreak of the First World War in 1914, Britain was sixty per cent reliant on imports for food supplies and other commodities such as fuel and fertilisers.

The question of domestic food production was raised in a report in 1905 from the Royal Commission on the Supply of Food and Raw Materials in Time of War. It recommended that 'it may be prudent to take some minor practical steps to secure food supplies for Britain'. The Government believed at the beginning of the war that overseas imports of food would be uninterrupted and focused on the carrying capacity of the merchant fleet and the Royal Navy to keep the shipping lanes open and did not heed early warnings. Lord Lucas, the President of the Board of Agriculture confidently told the House of Lords on 4 August 1914 'there was no occasion whatever for public alarm over food supplies'.[42] This was true at first; in 1914 and 1915 the yield of cereals was increased and prices were buoyant but the improved productivity was gained by omitting the traditional root crop break in the old rotation system, impoverishing crop yields. Then in 1916 imports from North America were hit by poor harvests and the closure of the Dardanelles halted imports from the Black Sea area. By 1916-7 the German U-boat campaign was effectively interrupting supplies. Eventually as imports were threatened by blockade the need to strengthen domestic production was finally accepted. Arable land was expanded to replace pasture wherever possible and that required better drainage in boggy clay lands like north Suffolk.

By 1917 the case for government intervention in food production policy was compelling. Rowland Prothero, Lord Ernle, the President of the Board of Agriculture, a member of the Cabinet, who was both an agriculturist and a historian, believed that the state must first provide incentives to plough up grassland and plant cereals and then to guarantee the prices of wheat and oats. The Corn Production Act of 1917 was successful in maintaining bread supplies, or was considered so at the time, and an Agricultural Act also established a minimum wage for farm workers and by which local agricultural boards set fair wages. The new national minimum wage of twenty-five shillings a week for agricultural labourers was set in London. This represented a substantial increase for farm workers in north Suffolk but was affordable for farmers as a result of the new guaranteed prices the government were funding. These Acts created the resented but largely unchallenged culture of subsidised farming that we still have today. Another legacy from these years is British Summer Time, introduced in May 1916 to maximise daylight hours for farm workers and factories. The clocks went forward an hour for the very first time that summer. It was a 'temporary wartime measure'.

During the first year of the war the Suffolk countryside was virtually emptied of horses, from the heavy draft horses such as the Shire and Suffolk Punch to riding ponies. Crucial to agriculture at the time, the impact was immense on farming families of having their finest and most beloved horses requisitioned for essential war duties, mainly in Flanders. But it did serve to hasten the introduction of early tractors and machinery. The horses were transported to the ports where they were hoisted onto ships to cross the Channel. On arrival in France they would soon be confronted by the horrors of the front line, either as cavalry horses or beasts of burden.

As a result of government support, the First World War brought prosperity to the farms of north Suffolk but there was a desperate shortage of younger men to fill new jobs. Increasingly landlords were turning to older men and also women to solve their labour problems. Farming was a bleak prospect for many landlords before the war although the Adairs were wealthy enough to be able to ride the storm. It was tenant farmers like William Groom whose incomes were marginal in the first years of the twentieth century. But the outlook changed quickly and dramatically with the outbreak of the Great War in 1914. The tension between the need to expand production of food and yet to raise a volunteer army of young men for the army was most keenly felt in the countryside and patriotic Suffolk had a high rate of volunteers in 1914 and 1915.[43] Landowners encouraged their workers to join up in what was believed at the outset likely to be a short-term loss to the land.

Many Wingfield men volunteered but from 1916 many more were conscripted to fight on the front as losses mounted. At first only single men aged eighteen to forty-one were taken; quite quickly this was raised to include married men and by 1918 all men from eighteen to fifty-one were called up, if fit enough to go, unless they were exempted by occupation. Farmers were exempt but their dwindling workforce had to be supplemented by older men, teenage boys, often illegally kept away from school, and in the early years of the war some reluctant local women were persuaded to work the fields. Farm workers were eventually recruited from a new cadre of lower middle class girls in the Women's Land Army. These women proved to be better workers than the men designated unfit for military service who were optimistically sent to farms but who turned out to be unfit for agricultural labour too.[44] From 1917 there were also some German prisoners of war available. The local War Agricultural Subcommittee accepted one hundred and fifty POWs and housed them in the old Kenninghall Workhouse and at Geldeston Mills. The committee decided the prisoners would be best employed in drainage of the Waveney, an unpopular and back-breaking job, rather than on farms.

It is sometimes thought that the Great War was remote to the ordinary people who stayed at home in England. This was certainly not true in north Suffolk. German Zeppelin raids over Britain started in Norfolk first and bombs also fell on Bury St Edmunds and Sudbury during an attack by Zeppelin airships on the night of 31 March to 1 April 1916 killing twelve. Zeppelin airships were capable of travelling at about 85 mph and carried up to two tons of bombs. Twenty-four fifty kilogram high explosive bombs and ineffective three kilogram incendiaries were dropped. There was enough damage to have a terrorising effect on the local population. Throughout the war Zeppelin airships floated high over the Norfolk and Suffolk skies to reach London. The Groom family would have seen them overhead many a time. New pilots in early warplanes were also practising their skills; the death rate was shocking. One pilot died on crashing near Harleston.

So close was Suffolk to Germany and the northern reaches of the Western Front that it was said that in certain weather conditions you could hear the roar of guns from the battlefields of Flanders from as far north as Southwold. Indeed, Southwold suffered its first Zeppelin raids in April 1915 and was shelled by four German destroyers and a submarine in January 1917. With no sirens to warn of impending attacks, the church bells were 'jangled', and later tolled when the coast was clear. Lowestoft also came under attack, from four German battle cruisers in April 1916, killing three people and damaging more than two hundred homes. The official advice from the County of Suffolk to civilians was to stay in their cellars.

One Lowestoft man wrote of watching the local effort by nineteen fishing vessels to quell the attack 'from the Hun dreadnought, it was magnificent but not war; it was a case of a wasp stinging a tiger.' 'It was suicide to attack the enemy, but in doing so they drew the fire from the town and the Huns put their 12-inch guns on them and failed to hit them except once that I saw. The columns of water were going up where the shells went into the sea exactly like very high church steeples all round our boats. I would not have missed seeing it for fifty pounds.'[45] Invasion was a very real threat along the East Coast, hence the lines of concrete and stone pillboxes, fortified round or hexagonal bunkers built in 1916.

The last years of the Great War were profitable ones for farmers as long as the subsidy and tariff system stayed in place. But the end of the Great War brought other social and economic changes that must have had a gloomy impact on the Grooms and other villagers. The government was in massive debt as a result of the war effort, inflation more than doubled between 1914 and its peak in 1920, while the value of the pound fell by 61.2%. Those who fought in the war either never returned or in many cases, never fully recovered from their experiences. One in five Suffolk combatants were dead; a quarter of the survivors had serious disabilities. Wingfield erected a memorial in 1921 to the twelve men who never came home. These twelve were lost out of a total village population of 390, that is higher by 50% than the average loss in Britain. The Suffolk Regiment on the front in France suffered greatly. For many village girls their chances of marriage and children were much diminished. In the 1921 census there was a twenty per cent excess of women over men in the 25-29 age group and by 1931, a half of these women were still single, and over a third never married while still able to bear children.[46]

Post war rural recession. Canny landowners wondered for how long the halcyon days of war-time subsidy would continue. Many farms in England were sold to tenants between 1918 and 1922, partly because of the fear of a return to the bad old prewar days. The increase to a historically high level of Schedule Tax on income from land, which encouraged landowners to convert a highly taxed income into zero-tax capital gain provided a further strong incentive to sell farmland. Sir Frederick Adair had died in the early part of the war; the new owner of the estate, Sir Robert Shafto Adair, was occupied in London. He moved from 9 Lower Berkeley Street, Mayfair to fashionable York House, Kensington in 1917, then and now described by estate agents as 'one of the most desirable residential locations in the world.' Adair wrote letters to *The Times* in 1918 protesting about the Government's hike in income tax and death duties to raise money for the war effort. No doubt he had experienced these personally when Frederick left the estate to him in 1915.[47]

Sure enough, the Agriculture Act that protected farm wages and corn prices was repealed in 1921. The government was facing a potential £20 million subsidy bill for the agricultural sector, when other parts of the economy had no such protection and high food prices were resented by a predominantly urban electorate. The result of repeal was a rapid reduction in agricultural wages by as much as forty per cent in one year, and the increased indebtedness of arable farmers. Nearly a quarter of agricultural land was sold by the end of 1922.

It would have been a struggle for the Groom family to make ends meet. It is not surprising that the castle was neglected during these harsh post-war years. Canadian grain flooded in to Britain once more and yet again the government proved reluctant to intervene in the agricultural sector. A catastrophic depression hit rural England. The speed of the postwar changes was bewildering for farmers; the price of barley and oats was halved between 1920 and 1922. Wages for labourers dropped first to 30 shillings a week for a 54 hour week then after a poor harvest in 1922, farmers wanted to drop it further to 25s.

Henry Mutimer for the Diss branch of the National Farmers Union appealed to labourers to make common cause with farmers to change the Government's mind, to reinstate subsidy, 'our interests are his interests'.[48] Labourers felt differently. In 1923, serious agricultural unrest exploded in Norfolk and then spread to Suffolk, culminating in violent strikes in north Norfolk. In Suffolk there was a very mixed response to the strike, partly perhaps because under Henry Mutimer's leadership the farmers of Diss and district NFU took a conciliatory attitude to their labourers' difficulties and did not reduce wages

94. South East Corner of walls and Gatehouse early 1940s.

in spite of the poor earnings.[49] But farmers let many workers go when they couldn't afford to pay them and many farm tenants got into serious debt.[50]

The agricultural dislocation of depressed postwar rural Suffolk led to a palpable sense of community lost.

> It had died away - the old bluff, hospitable life of the countryside - like a summer's day. I saw it fade from the top of my stacks as I worked, or from the window of my barn…it died slowly, like a cloudless afternoon, splendid to the last. Fewer grew the company..the countryside around us became lonely, thinly populated. The old community I had known on coming here ten years ago was now almost gone.

Adrian Bell [51]

By 1925 William Groom had had enough of farming. He was eighty years old, surely time to let a younger man continue the struggle. William and Emily officially retired from farming in 1926.[52] There was a sale of some of their furniture and other effects from the castle and they moved to 98 Christchurch Street, Ipswich.[53] William Groom died in 1938, Emily lived on to great old age.

Their son **William Roger Groom (1881–1968), his wife Ethel and their son Roger,** who had been tenants at St Martin's Farm in Wingfield since 1908, then moved to the castle and took on the farm tenancy until 1937.[54] Their son Roger (1914-2003) recalled spending a good deal of his boyhood at the castle first with his grandparents and then with his parents. He remembered them 'digging a flower bed inside the moat', and finding some rather disturbing medieval leg irons that now hang in the castle gateway. He heard tales of Henry VIII knocking down some of the walls and other half remembered stories that impressed him as a boy.[55]

The Grooms put in some creature comforts. The castle was one of the first places in Wingfield to get electricity, which most of the village did not have before the Second World War.[56] The larger Suffolk towns like Bury and Ipswich got connected early but villages were overlooked and it was an expensive luxury. The Eastern Electricity Board promised in 1948 that everyone would be connected 'soon'.[57] Farmers in Eye were still complaining about the slow rate of development of supply in 1955.[58]

The younger Grooms stayed on as tenants of the castle until September 1937, when they put their household furniture and poultry into an auction sale at Thomas Gaze in Diss and moved out, the 'last of the last' yeoman farming family to use the castle as the heart of a farm.[59] Henceforth the castle would be a residence for people with incomes from ventures far removed from agriculture.

The land that had once supported the castle was taken on by Mr and Mrs Alfred Gordon Askew at Castle Farm and became quite separate from the castle property. It remained with the Adair estate until 1949, since when it has changed hands with the farm.

By the mid 1930s the castle was a sad shadow of its former splendour, as can be seen in a grainy old snap from that time (94. p. 332). The crenellations were in need of repair; the towers were choked with ivy. The gatehouse had a gaping doorway. It was possible for visitors to walk in to the courtyard to explore as they wished. It looks as if nothing much had been done to conserve the walls for many years. But even a dilapidated castle attracts sightseers. During the 1930s Wingfield Castle became a 'destination' beauty spot for parties of enthusiastic cyclists from clubs who toured East Anglia every weekend.[60] It provided the perfect backdrop for a photo opportunity. The castle featured on a poster produced for London & North Eastern Railway (LNER) to promote rail travel on the mid Suffolk Light Railway. Few ventured the tedious journey from Ipswich to Brockford, to Stradbroke and then via Eastern Counties bus. Stradbroke Station opened in 1908, and closed in 1952 after forty spectacularly unsuccessful years.

Sir Shafto Adair had no use for a rundown farmhouse inside a ruin. In April 1938 Knight Frank Rutley advertised the castle in *The Times* with 6¼ acres of garden 'to let unfurnished on a lease of £150 rising to £200', together with the possibility of renting anything from four hundred acres to four thousand acres for 'excellent shooting'. Electric light, a kitchen garden and a tennis court were other attractions. There were no takers. Another war was already in the air; no one wanted to commit to such a potentially costly rental property.

95. Wingfield Castle, LNER poster, 1923-1947.

Notes

1 Thompson, M., 1988, The Landed Aristocracy and Business Elites in Victorian Britain. Actes du Colloque de Rome 21-23 November 1985 in *Publications de l'Ecole Francaise de Rome. Vol 107*, pp. 267-179.

2 In 2015 after many years of intimidating Catholics attending their church and arson attacks, loyalist fanatics picketed the church to prevent admission by the congregation. The population is largely Protestant. The town was the home of Ian Paisley, leader of the Democratic Unionist Party. *Belfast Telegraph* 4 October 2013

3 Flixton Hall was built in 1615 by John Tasburgh. In 1753, the direct male line of the Tasburgh family became extinct and the Estate passed to the Wyborne family who sold it to William Adair. Ian Hancock, Flixton, Waveney and the Adairs. Aviation Museum History online at https://www.aviationmuseum.net/Adairfamily.htm. Accessed 13 May 2020.

4 Adair, A. S., 1847, *The Winter of 1846-7 in Antrim, with Remarks on Out-door Relief and Colonisation*, London, James Ridgway, 70 pp. The text, with a foreword by Brian Logan, was re-edited by Eull Dunlop in 1997 and published by the Mid-Antrim Historical Group. Published online by Hutchinson, Wesley 2014 'And this in thriving and prosperous Antrim!': An Anglo-Irish landlord's perspective on the Famine. *Revue Francaise de Civilisation Britannique* pp. 89-105 https://doi.org/10.4000/rfcb.263

5 East Suffolk Council 2020 Homersfield Conservation Area Appraisal. On line at https://www.eastsuffolk.gov.uk/assets/Planning/Design-and-Conservation/Conservation-Area-Appraisals/Homersfield-CAA-Feb-20.pdf

6 Lunney, L. A., Sir Robert Alexander Shafto. *Dictionary of Irish Biography*, Royal Irish Academy https://dib.cambridge.org.
7 Ball, S. (ed.) 2008 Dublin Castle and the First Home Rule Crisis: The Political Journal of Sir George Fottrell 1884-1887 *Camden 5th Series, Volume 33*, pp. 60-63, Cambridge University Press, Cambridge.
8 Landed Families of Britain and Ireland (23) Adair of Ballymena Castle and Flixton Hall, baronets. http://landedfamilies.blogspot.com/2013/04/23-adair-of-ballymena-castle-and.html.
9 Floyd, R. D., 2008, Church, *Chapel and Party: Religious Dissent and Political Modernization in Nineteenth Century England*, Palgrave Macmillan, London, Chapter 5 Religion and Politics in an East Anglian Port City: the case of Ipswich pp 68-89.
10 Adair, F. E. S., 1895, *Sport in Ladakh. Five letters from "The Field"*, Horace Cox,London. Republished in 1899 as *The Big Game of Baltistan and Ladakh: A Summer in High Asia, Being a Record of Sport and Travel in Baltisan and Ladakh.*
11 Report of Sir Frederick Adair's funeral *Diss Express*, Friday 16 April 1915.
12 Suffolk Artists, online at https://suffolkartists.co.uk/index.cgi?choice=painter&pid=4759.
13 Adair Family Papers, SROL HA12/D4/26.
14 Wade Martins, S. and Williamson, T., 1999, *Roots of Change: Farming and the Landscape in East Anglia c1700-1870*, Chapter IV High Farming, c1830-1870, pp. 131-153.
15 Fletcher, T. W., 1973, The Great Depression of English Agriculture 1873-1896, in P. J. Perry (ed.), *British Agriculture 1875-1914,* Methuen, London, p. 31.
16 Sir James Caird quoted in Final Report of the Royal Commission appointed to inquire into the Depression in Trade and industry 1886, p xix online at https://archive.org/details/finalreportroya00indugoog/page/n20/mode/2up/search/Caird.
17 Perren, R., 1995, *Agriculture in Depression, 1870-1940,* Cambridge University Press, Cambridge, Introduction pp. 2-5.
18 Landed Families. http://landedfamilies.blogspot.com/2013/04/23-adair-of-ballymena-castle-and.html.
19 Wingfield Castle, Suffolk, *Country Life,* 28th June 1913, pp. 952-956.
20 Hancock, I., *Flixton, Waveney and the Adairs*, Aviation Museum History https://www.aviationmuseum.net/Adairfamily.htm.
21 Obituary, Major General Sir Allan Adair. *The Times*, Saturday 6 August 1988, p. 10.
22 Adair, A., 1986, *A Guards' general: The memoirs of Major General Sir Allan Adair*, Hamilton.
23 James Sharp pawnbroker advertisement, High St Deptford, *South Eastern Gazette*, Tuesday 11 January 1848.
24 The First Annual Report of the Committee to the Governors 1848 Volume 9. Pawnbrokers' Society for the relief of their sick and decayed Journeymen, afterwards called the Pawnbrokers' Society for the relief of their sick and decayed Members, and afterwards the Pawnbrokers' Charitable Institution, London.
25 Farms to be let. *The Times,* 3 May 1866, p. 19.
26 Ministry of Agriculture, Fisheries and Food and predecessors: Statistics Divisions: Parish Summaries of Agricultural Returns, TNA MAF 68.
27 Death of Henry Sharp 11 September, 1881, reported *Norfolk Chronicle,* Saturday 18 February 1882. Probate Calendar 1881 England & Wales, National Probate Calendar (Index of Wills and Administrations), 1858-1995 Original data: Principal Probate Registry. Calendar of the Grants of Probate and Letters of Administration made in the Probate Registries of the High Court of Justice in England. London.
28 Wingfield Castle Farm to James Hall 14 May 1866, Adair Family Archives SROL 741/HA12/D8/4/45.
29 Wingfield Church Restoration Bazaar. *Diss Express,* Friday 19 September 1879.
30 BAS meeting *Morning Post,* 4 August 1879.
31 Wingfield. A Pony Drowned. *Ipswich Journal,* 28 November 1875.
32 Death Announcement William Groom. *Diss Express,* Friday 21 January 1938. Tenancy Agreement Wingfield and Syleham 27 September 1889. SROL 741/HA12/D8/8/85
33 New Suffolk JPs, *Diss Express,* Friday 3 December 1920.
34 *Diss Express* ,Friday 1 February 1929.

35 Wingfield Sale of Work, *Diss Express,* Friday, 12 August 1898.
36 Fressingfield. Archeologists on Tour. *Diss Express,* Friday, 30 June 1893.
37 *Diss Express,* Friday, 1 September 1911.
38 *Norfolk Chronicle,* Saturday, 24 June 1893; *East Anglian Daily Times,* Wednesday 9 December 1896.
39 *Norfolk News,* Saturday, 17 December 1904.
40 *Diss Express,* Friday, 22 May 1891.
41 *Diss Express,* Friday, 27 July 1906.
42 Hansard, 4 August 1914, quoted in *The Agrarian History of England and Wales. Vol VIII, 1914-39*, p. 70. Whetham, E., 1978, Cambridge.
43 A good overview of recruitment in East Anglia is given in Meeres F. *Norfolk in the First World War*, 2004, Phillimore. Sussex, Chapter 1, pp. 1-24.
44 Ibid. pp. 106-111.
45 Remark by Thomson, A.J., in Wrathall C., 2018, Great war stories and the role East Anglia played during the First World War. Abellio Greater Anglia blog at https://www.greateranglia.co.uk/about-us/news-desk/blog-post/great-war-stories-and-role-east-anglia-played-during-first-world-war. 27 September 2018.
46 Nicholson, V., 2008, *Singled Out: How Two Million British Women Survived Without Men After the First World War*, Oxford University Press, Oxford.
47 High Prices at Sales. Letter, Sir Shafto Adair, *The Times,* Thursday 4 April 1918.
48 *Norfolk News,* 25 Feb 1922, p. 2.
49 Howkins, A., *Poor Labouring Men. Rural Radical in Norfolk 1870-1923*, Routledge, London, pp. 160-165.
50 Depwade Union Board of Guardians Minutes for 1920-23 describe a rising tide of unemployed applying for relief or Council sponsored work. There was no increase in workhouse inmates from Brockdish in these years but it was estimated that by November 21 one third of agricultural labourers were unemployed. They were set to labouring in gravel pits at Roydon, Needham and Boyland, paid at 2s less per week than the going rate for employed men. Other unions in Norfolk awarded additional relief to men with large families but not Depwade, where the tone remained tough throughout. NRO ref C/GP/45-50. The Depwade Union Guardians minutes are dry as dust. The Eastern Daily Press however published a wonderful blow-by-blow account of meetings which makes more entertaining reading, cuttings carefully pasted into scrap books by the Union themselves. NRO DC2/12/2-5.
51 Chapter 8 Adrian Bell and The East Anglian Farming Community pp. 191-212 in Snell, K. D. M., 2016, *Spirits of Community: English Senses of Belonging and Loss*, Bloomsbury, London.
52 *Diss Express,* Friday, 21 January 1938.
53 Moore Garrard and Sons, Auctions, *Framlingham Weekly News,* Saturday, 1 September 1928.
54 Wedding William Roger Groom and Ethel Marguerite Riches. *Evening Star,* Thursday, 1 October 1908.
55 Personal recollection of Roger Groom to Michael Lyndon-Stanford, c2000 and information from David Groom, William Groom's great, great grandson to author 13 May 2020 via Ancestry.co.uk message board.
56 Knight, Frank and Rutley advertisement for Wingfield Castle to let. *The Times,* 14 April 1938 p. 26.
57 *Suffolk and Essex Free Press,* Thursday, 27 May 1948.
58 *Bury Free Press,* Friday, 16 December 1955.
59 Thos Wm Gaze and Sons. *Diss Express*, Friday, 20 August 1937.
60 *Yarmouth Independent,* Saturday, 16 May 1936.

96. Two of the 2nd Battalion Gordon Highlanders Regiment billeted at Wingfield Castle, c1940, with companions.

The Renaissance of Wingfield Castle, 1938–1980

Wingfield Castle lay empty after the Grooms moved out in 1938. A new tenant, Graham Baron Ash, who had had his eye on the castle since his first visit in 1913, was hovering in the wings waiting for the aging Sir Robert Adair to agree the terms of a lease. It is quite possible that he had seen the castle featured in *Country Life* in 1913 and was taken with it. Ash wanted to get started on 'saving the castle' to fulfill his ambition to create the perfect ancient backdrop for his exquisite taste in antique furniture, paintings and objet d'art.[1] Adair would not sell it in 1938 and matters were inevitably soon delayed further because, like so many other large houses, Wingfield Castle was requisitioned early on in the Second World War for War Office purposes. The army arrived in 1939-40 to take part in the extensive East Anglian defence installations created to combat the threatened invasion from sea and air. The soldiers were followed by Land Girls, who used the castle as a hostel while working on local farms.

However, Ash, with canny negotiating skill, managed to persuade Adair in 1943 to give him a forty-year lease on the property, even though he would not be able to take possession until after the army departed. Ash continued to live at his home, Packwood House, in Warwickshire until the castle was de-commissioned by the War Office in 1945. Then he started his two-year programme of restoration and renovation.

Suffolk in World War Two. Suffolk was on the front line of anti-invasion defences between 1940 and 1943. In 1944 it became an assembly and training ground for troops preparing for the invasion of France. By 1940 the beaches of Suffolk had become inaccessible, covered with barbed wire and gun emplacements to slow any invasion. Further back from the coast trenches or 'stop-lines' scarred the landscape. At the same time, sixty-two ugly concrete airfields were rapidly constructed on the plains of north Suffolk; country lanes were suddenly full of USAAF and British military personnel. The conflict abruptly ended the long pre-war agricultural recession that had left Suffolk poor and backward.

There were British troops all over Suffolk in any billet to be had but in 1942 the numbers of military personnel suddenly swelled even further with the arrival of the United States 8th Air Force. Between then and 1945 more than 350,000 US personnel arrived and travelled through East Anglia heading to destinations in Britain. But 50,000 stayed, mostly crews and support ground staff of the heavy bombers, which made daytime raids on occupied Europe. By 1944, Wingfield villagers were accustomed to the roar of B24 Liberators and B17 Flying Fortresses as huge aerial armadas took to the skies from the local airfields at Eye, Metfield, Thorpe Abbotts, Tibenham, Bungay, Flixton, Ellough, Horham, Holton, Mendlesham and Great Ashfield. However it was British army troops, not Americans, who were billeted at Wingfield Castle, members of a Searchlight Battalion manning anti-aircraft stations nearby, from the Second Battalion of the Gordon Highlanders.[2]

97. The Gordon Highlanders billeted on Wingfield Castle 1940.

2nd Lt Kenneth W Waller in front row centre.

Sizeable country houses like Wingfield Castle were requisitioned to serve as hospitals, storage areas, billets for troops, headquarters for senior staff, prisoner of war camps and indeed any military or civilian function that was necessary to the war effort. Lucky owners found themselves displaced by girls' schools from urban areas, unlucky ones got the army. By 1941, more than two million troops were stationed in the UK from the United States and the Commonwealth as well as Great Britain and were accommodated wherever a bed could be found, in private homes, rapidly converted halls and larger houses.[3]

Framlingham Castle was used to billet troops in the war and was prepared to become a siege base for troops in the event of an invasion on the east coast. Redgrave Park in Suffolk was turned into the 65th General Hospital US Army, the largest military hospital in Europe with 1450 beds.[4] The occupying troops did a great deal of damage to the house, and after the War, the owner John Holt Wilson decided to demolish the Hall to raise money to invest in the estate. The interior features, fireplaces, ceilings and staircases were sold. A huge prisoner of war camp occupied Redgrave Hall Park south of the Capability Brown lake. German, Italian and later Ukrainian prisoners were sent out to work on local farms. By 1945 over a quarter of all farm workers were POWs.

In quite a few cases the war destroyed the house altogether. Troops saw a billet, a bunk bed and a mess; they were largely uninterested in the history. At Egginton Hall in Derbyshire departing troops left all the taps on and the resultant flooding brought the ceilings down and rotted the woodwork, forcing its demolition. Both Shillinglee in Sussex and Appeldurcombe on the Isle of Wight were burnt out by the Canadian and Australian troops billeted there.

98. The Gordon Highlanders billeted on Wingfield Castle 1940-1944 in front of Jerningham House.

The extensive defences put along the coast of Suffolk from Lowestoft down to Harwich and Felixstowe were designed to slow up any invasion force. Though they were extensive, they were not realistically able to stop an enemy force, they were more likely to confuse and delay progress if an invasion occurred.[5] The war in the air however was a constant battle against incursions by the Luftwaffe stationed just a short distance away across the Channel. From 1939 to 1944, Suffolk was on the flight path for raids on the industrial Midlands. The air defences included radar stations, anti-aircraft gun batteries, barrage balloons and searchlight sites. Anti-Aircraft Command had overall control of this new kind of warfare directed at the skies.

Radar was being pioneered at Orford and Bawdsey. Batteries of searchlights were placed across Suffolk in order to illuminate targets for AA Batteries and night fighters. The reality of much searchlight duty was hours of monotony, interspersed with sudden confrontations with enemy aircraft and immediate action to support anti-aircraft guns. The activity was on the coast, but there were searchlight batteries based in north Suffolk near Wingfield at Horham, Metfield, Flixton, Earl Soham and Halesworth.[6] It seems likely that the young men in the photographs (97. p. 340 and 98. p. 341) were manning these local batteries.

Searchlights were at first deployed in a grid layout with six thousand yard intervals between searchlight sites. The idea was that this spacing would sufficiently concentrate beams so at least one searchlight would be able to pick up and illuminate a target. When one searchlight picked up an enemy aircraft, two others from neighbouring detachments would also concentrate on it (the so called 'three beam rule'). The pyramid of light formed would signal the position of the enemy aircraft to the anti-aircraft guns or to the interceptor fighters. The actual illumination of the target was not essential for fighters as long as a beam was close enough to the target to act as a 'pointer'. An intersection of two beams, preferably three, was considered as an adequate 'pointer'. Later these sites were amalgamated into clusters.

The AA brigades were made up of men from many battalions and regiments and were constantly being split up and re-formed as AA command changed strategy. But members of platoons and companies stayed with their comrades and continued to wear their distinctive regimental uniforms. The men who served in East Anglia were mainly territorials who were automatically mobilised at the outset of war. Regulars with combat experience were needed at the front. The history of these territorial volunteers serving at home is poorly documented compared with those who served abroad. Inevitably the surviving war diaries in the National Archive concentrate on the dramatic challenges of the theatre of war. Being posted to a searchlight battery was tedious but far less dangerous than serving at the front and most of these men would have considered themselves to have a lucky posting, particularly when the expected invasion of Europe was being planned in early 1944. They would be aware that thousands of troops were massing in Suffolk for the second and third follow-up waves of sea-borne invasion to be launched from Harwich heading for the beaches of Normandy.

Young men who volunteered in the early days of the war chose regiments on the basis of personal connection or sometimes simply whim. The Suffolk author Julian Tennyson plumped for the London Irish because their HQ was in the Kings Road a few steps from his flat. He was then transferred to the Oxford and Bucks Light Infantry when he got a commission because they had an officer vacancy.[7] The Gordon Highlanders regulars were mainly Scots but the territorials' home towns were widely dispersed across Britain. Lowlanders adopted the Highland battalions' Tam O' Shanters, 'diced glengarry' caps and dress kilts with pride. The date of the photographs shown in this chapter is unknown but on a piece of paper accompanying them, which may not be contemporary, is a note that the person in the centre of the front row with arms crossed may be 'Ken Waller'. Forces war records confirm that Kenneth W Waller of the Second Gordon Highlanders was promoted Second Lieutenant in 1940 and transferred to the Royal Artillery in February 1942.[8] He seems to be the Platoon Commander in the group photo. Waller's transfer was one of a large group around this time from infantry regiments to the RA, when infantry battalions were converted into Anti-Tank and Anti-Aircraft Regiments of the Royal Artillery.[9] Ken Waller (1917-1999) was born in Sidcup, Kent, the son of an accountant. He survived the war and returned to civilian life in Bexleyheath, marrying in 1946 and fathering five children.

The Land Girls of Suffolk. When the Gordon Highlanders moved out of the castle, the Women's Land Army (WLA) moved in. We know nothing of these women, how many there were or how long they stayed. The Women's Land Army made a significant contribution to boosting Britain's food production during the Second World War. Since many male agricultural workers joined the armed forces, women were needed to provide a new rural workforce. The WLA had originally been set up in 1917 but disbanded at the end of the First World War. It was revived in June 1939. Women were initially asked to volunteer and more than twenty thousand city and town dwelling girls and young women saw the opportunity to work out in the open air, perhaps harbouring a rather idyllic view of life in the countryside. One third came from London. But from December 1941, women could also be conscripted into land work. At its peak in 1944, there were more than eighty thousand women in the WLA. Land girls did anything ordinary agricultural labourers did, in all weathers and conditions and could be directed to work anywhere in the country.

99. Suffolk Land Girls at Culford.

Conditions could be very basic, living in dormitory hostels, many purpose built, some run by the YWCA. Later group billets in large houses like the castle were used. The

Women's Timber Corps established in 1942 was also working locally. There was a large training camp for these 'Lumber Jills' at Culford near Bury St Edmunds, one hundred and fifty women would be rapidly trained for a month and then dispatched to forestry work anywhere they were needed. They were paid far less than male agricultural workers and at the end of the war received no plaudits or commemorative medals though the work continued until the early 1950s. After fifty years, surviving women veterans were finally allowed to join the armed forces at the Cenotaph commemorations in November 2000 and in 2008 a medal was donated to survivors. Most were long dead.

Hostels were built at Lakenheath for a hundred and twenty girls, Leavenheath for seventy, Risby for twenty five. Other large houses taken over as billets were Peasenhall Hall, Alpheton Rectory, the Moat House Ipswich, The Old Rectory in Halesworth, Tranmer House at Sutton Hoo and Hope House, an old orphanage in Foxhall Road, Ipswich. Irene Grimwood, eighty-one years old when interviewed by the *Ipswich Star* in 2003, said 'We did hoeing, harvesting, hedging and pulling up sugar beet...and muck spreading' 'One time we had to lead a horse around a field, which I didn't like much as I am terrified of animals. It was nice to work outdoors but it was extremely hard work and we didn't get paid much. Everything was old fashioned; we didn't have any of the machines, such as combine harvesters, we were working with huge horses.'[10] The girls were carted round the countryside in buses and lorries to wherever farmers needed them, organised by the local 'War Ag'. Milking and dairy work was the most sought after, digging up beet and lumber work was much less popular. The Land Girls moved out of Wingfield Castle in 1945 and Graham Baron Ash took possession.

The Castle at the end of the War. One of the wartime photographs shows that the exterior render visible on the Jerningham House photographs in *Country Life* in 1913 and in a photograph taken in 1925 had been removed by 1940 to expose the timber frame. Presumably this was done by William and Emily Groom. If so, then it suggests that the 1920s/30s mania for all things 'Tudor', whether mock or authentic, had influenced the decision to expose the frame some time before they departed in 1938. Interestingly the property restorer of nearby Monks Hall, in Syleham, which would be well known to the Grooms, also decided in the mid 1930s to remove the render on that timber-framed hall. The Grooms would certainly have noted the improved, or at least more modish appearance of that neighbouring house.[11]

Graham Baron Ash (1889-1981) The first word that comes to mind to describe Baron Ash is grand, perhaps grandiose. A hyper-sensitive bachelor of exquisite taste, he adopted from a very young age the manner of a fastidious aristocrat but while he had the money, indeed a great deal of it, and inspired devotion in a handful of close friends and those who worked for him, he was rather condescended to by the upper middle class to which he aspired to belong. He was a ferocious snob and yet also generous to a fault as a host. He was overtly charming, correct, concerned for his guests' comforts, ever so slightly fussy, even obsessive. His wartime record speaks of a courageous, decent, caring man. He worked hard to make his mark as a collector of fine antique furniture and art and left a legacy at his first home Packwood House in Warwickshire and then at Wingfield Castle that has ensured the survival of two treasured buildings.

In both his homes Ash created a private world where only a chosen few came to enjoy his carefully orchestrated version of country house hospitality. James Lees-Milne, the discreetly bisexual architectural historian and luminary of the National Trust in the mid-twentieth century, thought the 'Baron' 'ridiculous', although he too was fussy, fastidious and a terrible snob and also haled from a family that had acquired wealth relatively recently.[12] Lees-Milne admitted Baron was 'a very good host...so long as his guests did not stay too long and were at least half as tidy as he was himself....' In the ferociously cold winter of 1947, when England was in the depths of post-war austerity, Lees-Milne writes in his diary 'Then to Packwood and lunched with Baron. We had sherry and *pate de foie gras*, as good as it used to be; omelette with quince jam and rum blazing; port wine…'[13].

Ash always kept himself slightly at a distance from his guests and most of his neighbours under a veneer of apparent bonhomie. Few, it seems, ever got very close to the man except perhaps his friend Johnny Leader at Monks Hall and his brother-in-law John Mellor. His main concern was to be seen to be doing things 'right'. His social nervousness was not calculated to put people at their ease and that may be why he never formed any enduring close relationship, or at least this is what his butler Horace Stanley thought.[14] The impression he and his house gave had to be perfect, and that perfection had to be in the terms of his perception of what a country house and its owner should be. But as others have pointed out, this is not what real upper class country houses are like, being usually stuffed full of old boots, messy dogs and fraying furniture.

His pursuit of perfection would brook no untidiness; Lees-Milne again: '... he hated disorder. If one stayed a night at Packwood and left a book lying on a downstairs table it would be removed a minute after one quitted the room...'[15] Such was the perfection sought by Baron Ash; nothing ever out of place in his house, nor in his life. This social anxiety pervaded every corner of his dealings with the outside world. Lees-Milne records being driven by Baron Ash in a pony cart where Ash flourished a whip over the pony and cried, 'Now then laddie! Whoa, little laddie!' nervously, without admitting it. 'He continually expressed the hope that I was not nervous. I was not in the very least'.

The apotheosis of Ash's social ambitions was a visit to Packwood House by Queen Mary in August 1927, when she was entertained very formally to tea in the Great Hall, orchestrated in every detail of ceremonial procedure, table decoration, flower displays and refreshments by Ash himself. He even accommodated Queen Mary's famous acquisitiveness for small *objets de vertu* in homes she visited by setting out a covetable grey Rockingham porcelain tea service, which she duly admired. He was able to wrap up a cup and saucer for her to take away, in addition to the official silver dish gift. Queen Mary is said to have remarked afterwards to Lady Bradford, 'Really these bachelors seem to live very comfortably'.[16]

Baron Ash's Early Life. Graham Baron Ash, known always as Baron and often as 'The Baron', which he encouraged, was the only son of Alfred Ash and his wife Emily, *née* Barker. Alfred J. Ash was a successful Birmingham industrialist whose grandfather and then later his father had established a huge zinc and galvanised iron manufacturing plant that had grown by supplying the railways, thus making the family rich. When Baron was born on 18 August 1889 the family was living in leafy suburban Birmingham in a comfortable large house in Acocks Green, a prosperous area of detached Victorian villas. The villas have since become multi-occupancy flats in a deprived run-down-looking neighbourhood and Rougemont, the Ash family home, is long gone. Alfred had a number of directorships but was principally chairman of Ash and Lacy, which then specialised in perforated zinc sheeting and still thrives today as a group of specialist building materials companies with a group annual turnover in excess of fifty million pounds.

This prosperous household, into which Baron's sister Beryl (known as Betty) was born two years later, had two live in maids and carried on very comfortably. Baron was indulged by devoted parents, who perhaps from his earliest childhood, recognised the unusual qualities in their son. For his fifth birthday Alfred and Emily bought him a miniature pony carriage built for the famous dwarf Tom Thumb and a Shetland pony to pull it. Baron was sent off to Radley College, Oxfordshire for a typical public school education but declined to go to university afterwards, instead returning to his father's world to learn the business. He claimed afterwards to have been put to selling dustbins door to door 'but I had to get home to change for dinner'. It might be suspected that his claim was created for the purposes of dinner party repartee.

The Purchase of Packwood House. In 1904, when Baron was fifteen, Alfred bought at auction Packwood House, a somewhat old-fashioned large country house with a spectacular topiary garden. It was for generations the home of the Fetherstons but had recently had other owners. Alfred said he bought it because 'the Boy wanted it' but like many other middle class families, the Ash family was abandoning deteriorating Acocks Green in favour of a country residence in leafy Warwickshire, south of Solihull. The family moved in in 1905 and immediately began a programme of renovations. Alfred appears to have been a keen restorer, and perhaps this was where Baron got his 'restoration fever'. Alfred is said to have been a confident, extroverted, cheerful person, enjoying all his good fortune, who loved nothing more than breezing around in his sumptuous Rolls Royce. He was a gregarious and generous host, the new house being regularly filled with guests, especially at Christmas.

The World Tour. In 1910, age twenty-one, Baron set off on a world tour, a present from his parents. He went alone, taking eight months to circumnavigate the globe by a total of fourteen steamships, plus many trains and cars, stopping in Ireland, America, Canada, Korea, China, Hong Kong, India, Aden, Egypt and finally Italy, taking souvenir photographs of every building of note, which he later mounted in two volumes of his memoirs of the trip. This adventure was no gap year, it was the eighteenth century grand tour recreated for the twentieth. He later said he chose this year abroad in preference to going to Oxford or Cambridge but one cannot but wonder whether a spell of university life would have eased his social diffidence. Baron returned to the galvanised zinc industry with his head stuffed full of the treasures he had seen. Perforated zinc sheeting was not his cup of tea. He was soon rescued from industry by the outbreak of World War One in 1914.

The Baron's War. Following the outbreak of war, the British Red Cross Society and the order of St John pooled resources to set up an ancillary medical service. Some members of the prestigious Royal Automobile Club (RAC) volunteered to lend and/or drive their own cars to supplement the available ambulances.[17] Graham Baron Ash, who kept rooms at the RAC Club for his trips to London, is listed as one of these volunteer owner/drivers, one of 1250 individuals who served in France alongside the ambulances. It is clear he also drove ambulances and his medal citation refers to him as a chauffeur. When he applied to join the new Royal Flying Corps in 1917, his application enlistment papers refer to him as 'driving an ambulance for the BRCS for past

13½ months'. His address was 'BRCS Convoy AP6S11, British Expeditionary Force'.[18] Perhaps like many others, his own car did not survive. He was based at Étaples, a port in the Pas de Calais where a huge training base, sprawling ordnance and general supplies depot and vast hospital were sited alongside an army base for British, Australian and Canadian forces heading for the front. There was also a Prisoner of War camp. At its height there were 100,000 men there. The hospital could treat huge numbers of patients and these were not in short supply.

Étaples did not impress the British women who volunteered to work at the base. In the words of Lady Olave Baden-Powell, 'Étaples was a dirty, loathsome, smelly little town'.[19] On the other side of the river was the smart beach resort of Le Touquet but that was officer territory and there was no mixing. Étaples was a particularly notorious base camp for those on their way to the front. The officers and NCOs in charge of the training, the 'canaries', had a reputation for not having served at the front, which created a certain amount of tension and contempt. Both raw recruits and battle-weary veterans were subjected to intensive training in gas warfare and bayonet drill and long sessions of marching at the double across the dunes for two weeks.[20] It was a miserable place to be stationed. The poet Wilfred Owen, passing through on his way to the front, wrote 'I thought of the very strange look on all the faces in that camp; an incomprehensible look, which a man will never see in England; nor can it be seen in any battle but only in Etaples. It was not despair, or terror, it was more terrible than terror, for it was a blindfold look and without expression, like a dead rabbit's.'[21]

In September 1917 after almost a year of troubling incidents of insubordination as well as obvious contempt of the officers by the infantrymen, there was a full-scale mutiny at Etaples, way beyond the capacity of local Military Police to quell. It took more than four hundred reinforcements from the Honourable Artillery Company to put down the rioting and threats to use guns on the troops. The report of the board of inquiry set up immediately after the mutiny to investigate the causes was destroyed ten years later.[22] We can hardly be surprised at Baron Ash's decision in late 1916, when trouble was already brewing, to get out of this base as fast as he could. He volunteered for the newly expanding Royal Flying Corps in April 1917 and returned to England to train as a pilot at the airbase in Scampton, Lincolnshire.

Ash received his pilot's licence in June 1917 and was sent back to France to active service. Flying planes was fine by him; it was landing them that seemed to have been something of a challenge. After four crashes on landing solo flights, he was transferred, probably by mutual agreement, to become a Balloon Artillery Officer, flying tethered observation balloons to spot enemy targets for guns and then phoning their location for action by British guns.

Hanging fifty feet below a huge hydrogen balloon in a wicker basket four thousand feet in the air, an attractive target for enemy fire, was no picnic. Yes, he had a parachute and he had made at least one parachute jump over foggy Hyde Park. He carried on this life with comrades, who referred to themselves as 'balloonatics', until the war was near its end. He was not lacking in courage and had no fear of heights apparently. Typically, at Tournai, he had the chance to go and see the cathedral and admire its wonderful Gobelin tapestries, carefully put away for safety. He commented on their huge worth and went into rhapsodies of praise for the collection of gold and silver embroidered copes. 'I never saw such superb things'. The following day, the Kaiser abdicated, and the armistice was signed. Baron duly commented on these events in an off-hand kind of way but it hardly ranked with the thrill of gazing on fine things.[23] His wartime diaries end shortly after the armistice in November 1918. 'I would not have missed these last few months for anything'. He came home with a Gobelin tapestry fragment purchased at great cost and with some difficulty.

100. Photo of Graham Baron Ash Royal Flying Corps, 1917, Packwood House, Warwickshire.

101. Photo of Graham Baron Ash about to take off in an observation balloon on the Western Front, 1917.

Baron's sister Betty married

Colonel John Lesley Mellor in 1917. Mellor joined Ash and Lacy in 1922 and eventually became a successful managing director and chairman. Baron was close to John for the rest of his life, one of his few real friends. Baron's mother Emily died in early 1918 so it was to a rather quiet Packwood that Baron returned to live with his father. Not surprisingly he was obliged to re-join the company, but this time as a director.

The Transformation of Packwood House. Alfred and Baron soon began the metamorphosis of Packwood House from eighteenth/nineteenth century country house to the Tudor mansion they thought it should be. For three years, however, they let out the house and rented the home of an antiquarian dealer, Oliver Baker, in Stratford-upon-Avon. Why they did this is not clear but they acquired from Baker suitable stuff for Packwood. So began Baron's attachment to Stratford, Shakespeare and local Warwickshire heritage. Alfred's pleasures were a little less high-brow. He bought a string of twenty racehorses that he kept at Newmarket. He was quite a successful owner but while Baron dutifully accompanied his father on trips to the races, it was not a sport Baron enjoyed. Baron sold the racehorses the day his father died.

Alfred's death in 1925 left Baron a wealthy man. He inherited over £80,000 plus Packwood House, a sum today worth over five million pounds. His sister's inheritance was about twenty thousand pound. Having found himself appointed Chairman of Ash and Lacy, he discharged his role competently but ten years later resigned his position to devote himself entirely to his restoration project at Packwood. He acquired even more wealth by selling his shares in the increasingly successful company. He indulged himself with his own custom built Rolls Royce convertible, with its specially made blue glass Spirit of Ecstasy that lit up at night 'to make it easy to find outside a theatre at night'. He gave parties and receptions as his father had done, welcoming groups to witness progress and enjoy the now apparently Tudor house with medieval flourishes. The City Temperance Cycling Club, the Garden Club of America, the British Dental Association, the Birmingham Archaeological Society, a party from the Junior Imperial League, all were welcomed and duly admired the apparently ancient house and given tea. He gave other parties for more influential members of local society. All were suitably dazzled by this handsome, charming bachelor. But most of his energy was invested in collecting suitable furniture, tapestries, objects and pictures. He frequented the best salerooms and auction houses in the country. He also bought a huge number of items from Baddesley Clinton, the nearby medieval manor house owned by Cecil Ferrers, who could no longer afford the upkeep and who became a friend. Dining at Baddesley Clinton with Cecil and Undine was a model of how he wanted his dinners to be. He hosted concerts in the Great Hall of Packwood, newly built out of an old barn but ancient-looking when kitted out with fine panelling, tapestries and old oak. It was at a concert here in 1931 that he met a young James Lees-Milne. He was to become a friend, in a waspish kind of way but his crucial role in the National Trust was clearly important in Baron's later decision to give Packwood to the Trust.

A large house and garden, plus a penchant for entertaining and a hectic schedule, needed staff. Ash had eleven. His housekeeper and cook Dorothy Eden, a succession of butlers, including the devoted Horace Stanley from 1936 to 1939, were the key employees but they were assisted by parlour maids, a kitchen maid, footmen, a head gardener with four assistants and a chauffeur. Ash lived a formal, regular sort of life, drank abstemiously, dressed every night for dinner whether there were guests or not, as did the butler. Guests were often there for superb food and conversation. He liked gossip so long as it was not scurrilous. His weekend guests however found no sports on the agenda; although Baron was a fair shot he did not host shooting parties.

A country gentleman of decent lineage needs a coat of arms and a motto, so

102. Packwood House, Warwickshire.

Baron duly acquired a highly respectable pedigree from the College of Arms tracing the Ash ancestors back to 1539. Baron had established that he was related to Dr John Ash (1723–1798) an eminent physician who built up a successful medical practice in Birmingham and co-founded the Birmingham General Hospital, one of the most generous philanthropists to the city. His portrait by Joshua Reynolds had been commissioned by the governors of the hospital and hangs today in Birmingham City Art Gallery. Later research confirmed that Baron was a direct descendant of the doctor.

Baron Ash's arms are strikingly simple. His motto '*Non nobis sed omnibus*', (Not for us alone but for everyone) was carefully chosen to reflect his stated aim. 'I am rescuing whatever I can from other places and preserving it here. I do this as an antidote to the decay and demolition of so many old houses all over the country'.

Perhaps the high point of Baron's social ambitions was his appointment as High Sheriff of Warwickshire for 1938 to 1939. It was then and remains now a ceremonial dressing-up role whose main function was to host dinners in Judges' Lodgings for High Court Circuit Judges and to be present with the Lord Lieutenant of the county for royal visits. He found the Judges' Lodgings in a shabby state and characteristically set about equipping the crucial dining room with better quality tableware. The role suited his talents down to the ground. He was able to dress up in velvet coat, lace jabot and knee breeches, wear his medals from the war and he made friends with several members of the legal profession. The position also put him at the heart of the Birmingham and Warwickshire social scene. He chose to be drawn in pastels in his High Sheriff's outfit by Dennis Dring RA.

103. The Arms of Graham Baron Ash.

Not long after relinquishing the High Sheriff role, the country again went to war. Ash signed on with the RAF and was sent to do an administrative job at RAF Abingdon. He seems to have had plenty of leave to indulge in antique hunting and it was during the war that he conceived a plan to acquire Wingfield Castle. Baron had spent thirty-five years beautifying Packwood House and garden but it was now finished. It had become a masterpiece to show off his skill at recreating a grand Tudor house. He wanted a *bonafide* medieval or ancient home to attack next, a building that would be his home rather than a museum to engage others. A man in his early fifties perhaps does not feel the same urge to show off as a man in his twenties.

Not everyone admired Baron's changes to Packwood as much as he would have wished. The writer and architectural historian Nikolaus Pevsner, a stickler for authenticity, wrote about Packwood in his magisterial multi-volume tour of England:

> The long gallery and great hall to the N. were only made c1925-30. Their brick exterior looks rather like part of a grammar school and the provision of new period exteriors and interiors in this way is something more appropriate to America, where real houses don't exist, than in England. On the whole, the stables are more rewarding than the house.

Oh dear! Curiously Pevsner was not half so sniffy about Anglesey Abbey in Cambridgeshire, which had received the same kind of treatment in the 1920s from Lord Fairhaven, another fastidious bachelor with a passion for fine antiques. Anglesey Abbey is also a pastiche of a medieval house. Baron Ash later punished Pevsner by refusing him access to Wingfield Castle, an inconvenience for us future historians. He was not going to risk another slight. And his 'friend' James Lees-Milne, who was working for the National Trust, commented in his later memoirs that 'Packwood House was a sixteenth century house 'mutilated' by its twentieth century owners' and that 'it would probably have been refused after the war'.[24] Both Packwood and Anglesey are tributes to the men who created them, who wanted comfortable show homes for entertaining that reflected the enthusiasms of wealthy men of taste at the time. They are wonderful places to visit for their contents alone and to appreciate what they were trying to achieve.

Sometime around 1940 Ash accepted a role as lifetime Trustee of the Shakespeare Birthplace Trust and served on the executive committee from 1941. He donated to them his collection of ancient deeds and documents relating to Packwood that went back to 1407. The same year he negotiated with the National Trust to donate Packwood House, most of its contents and 133 acres of land providing a capital sum of thirty thousand pounds for its continuing upkeep. Lees-Milne claims Ash was to prove a difficult and interfering donor, insisting that the Trust follow his conditions to the letter; fresh flowers in every room, no furniture or pictures to be moved. He continued to live there until the move to Wingfield Castle in 1945 but he never forgave the Trust for holding a fashion show in the great hall, reputedly using the refectory table in the hall as a catwalk, just one among many disrespectful events as far as he was concerned.

Baron Ash comes to Wingfield Castle. Ash took a forty year lease on Wingfield Castle in 1943.[25] He predicted no doubt that it would probably see him out and it did. The Land Army was still using the castle as a hostel so it was not until 1945 that he gained possession. Then he seems to have commuted from Packwood to oversee the restoration, which was sorely needed, staying at the Scole Inn for his visits to see progress.

By 1945 the roof needed replacing, ivy covered the walls, brambles grew around the base of the ancient walls, jackdaws were nesting in the chimneys and fireplaces were unusable. The barrel-vaulted great chamber was completely hidden, having been sealed off from the rest of the house and was only rediscovered when the restorers tore down the ceiling of a small bedroom at the top of the staircase. But even before he was able to move in to the Castle, Baron Ash had been collecting suitably grand furniture and artwork. Before he had signed the lease he had acquired a seventeen feet tall Queen Anne tester bed reputedly made by Francis Lapiere (1653-1714), a rare treasure that would fit perfectly into this grandest of bedrooms.

There was a basic electricity supply by this time but totally inadequate for Baron's vision of how the castle should look. He paid for a better supply to be brought from Brockdish, enabling Wingfield village to benefit at his expense, a generous gift much appreciated locally.[26] Ash appointed a building company, Reades of Aldeburgh, which had considerable experience of renovating Suffolk buildings in a sympathetic way and the site foreman Charles Rouse was to prove a sympathetic and enthusiastic ally.

104. Portrait of Baron Ash, by Dennis Dring RA 1943.

An army of workman descended on the castle. They resurfaced the driveway, replaced the roof, restored the flint walls to pristine condition,

105. The Great Chamber with Queen Anne period bed reputedly by Francis Lapiere (photgraph 1950)

plastered and painted inside and out. Scaffolding was constructed inside the moat to reach the outer west walls. The Victorian casements were replaced by sashed and mullioned Tudor reproduction windows of Austrian oak distressed to look four hundred years old. The moat was dredged of several hundred years worth of detritus and discarded household waste. Wartime shortages of materials meant that Ash had to get permits to buy building materials. These were in very short supply, even paint and plaster were difficult to find so he acquired what was available and made it look authentic. But with a little help from his friends, possibly using Ash and Lacy and their connections, he was able to put in a central heating system. A steel stack for the burner was artfully run up an existing Tudor chimney. The fuel tank came from a company that had been building submarines.

Baron fashioned a suite of domestic rooms, turning the old Tudor kitchen into a dining room and creating a butler's pantry to store porcelain and crystal for the table. Every room was furnished with the highest quality of antique furniture, oak and walnut, never later than eighteenth century; later furniture he considered inferior. Lees-Milne had sneered at his purchases for Packwood; those at Wingfield were to be the finest available and as he gained experience, the quality of his art collection dramatically improved too.

One of the first visitors in 1947 was James Lees-Milne, who characteristically wrote in his diary:

> 21 November 1947. Arrived at Wingfield Castle to stay the night. A lovely place it is. From 1.00pm to 12.30 after midnight I was with Baron, who did not once stop talking, fishing for compliments for his generous gift of Packwood to the Trust and praising himself. But his food was good….' 'We walked in the dusk to Wingfield church to see the de la Pole tomb made of wood.[27] Baron is allowed no petrol for his car [government post war austerity measures] and is very isolated. But he does not mind. He sees himself as a medieval baron marooned

106. Wingfield Castle west wall, south west tower and part of south wall: above 1945 before restoration, and right after restoration, 1950.

> and defensive within his castle, a happy isolationist.' The next day he continues, 'The East Anglian wind kept me awake last night. It delighted Baron in making him feel ever more marooned as though on board ship, himself the captain, nice Miss Eden his faithful crew and very efficient and solicitous cook-housekeeper'.

Dorothy Eden came with Baron from Packwood. He sent her off to a Cordon Bleu cookery course in London and the results were spectacular. She created miracles in her somewhat basic kitchen, without any help, then orchestrated the glamorous dinners to perfection. She made the butter swans for each place setting, putting a tiny piece of parsley in each beak and made an ice cream swan to float over ice blue chopped gelatine 'waves' for desert. One Christmas she made a remarkably accurate Wingfield Castle cake with a marzipan Michael de la Pole riding over the drawbridge. Would not the first Michael and Katherine have enjoyed that? There was always a spectacular centre piece, another for dessert and always Dorothy Eden standing demurely by the

107. The dining room, Wingfield Castle, 1950.

serving table in her black uniform and white cap and apron, self effacing but totally indispensable. Miss Eden took command of the small suite of rooms on the ground floor north side of the house and cultivated a small garden here. Baron Ash called it appropriately enough 'The Garden of Eden'.

Miss Eden retired in 1960 to a little house in Bury St Edmunds. Baron wrote, 'I miss her very much/ I now have a manservant (my steward), who has taken on her work, Housekeeping, Cooking and Waiting on me and my guests which as you may well imagine keeps him busy'. In fact Miss Eden was not quite gone, he re-engaged her to organise a party in 1962 in the newly restored guardroom to commemorate the restoration of the gatehouse. He also invited her to join him for Christmas lunch throughout the early 1970s.

Baron moved in to Wingfield Castle when restoration was only half complete in 1947. He embarked on the Great Hall soon afterwards. He found a vast Flemish tapestry, a mid-sixteenth century 'fleur de choux' design woven in Enghien, to cover the north wall of the newly revealed enlarged hall. A smaller, similar one sold at Christies in London for £8,000 in 2000.

New friends. In late 1947 Baron met Lt. Colonel Johnny Leader and his American wife Amoret (always called Weeny) who lived at Monks Hall, down on the River Waveney in Syleham, just two miles from the Castle.[28] Johnny had just returned from service in India but for most of the war he had remained in Suffolk as the liaison officer between the British and American military forces stationed there.

The Leaders brought a glamour to the locality quite distinct from the usual upper class country set. They were young, uncommonly good-looking, with the loud confidence born of two families of impeccable heritage of American and Anglo-Irish descent. Their noisy charm, gift for entertaining and endearing devotion to English country living shaped local social life and the lives of their many friends for seventy years. They had bought Monks Hall in 1936 after a property restoration enthusiast had done basic renovations. Like Baron Ash they wanted their home to look ancient, suitably furnished with good stuff and comfortable. They were well off on Weeny's inherited wealth but did not have the income at Baron's disposal.

Baron and Johnny liked nothing better than careering round the countryside in Baron's car, going to auctions and country house sales, which were all too common as the post-war tax regime bore down on the propertied classes. They picked up architectural salvage and various decorative treasures and pictures for both their homes. The ebullient, loquacious Johnny had all the self-possession

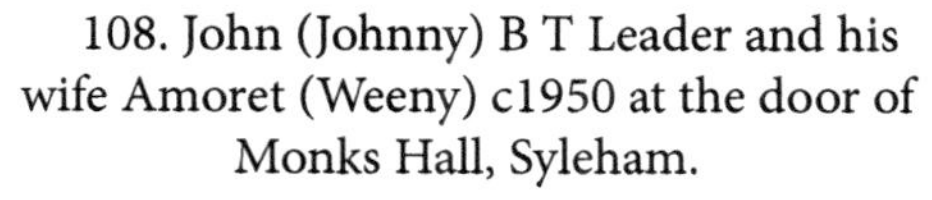

108. John (Johnny) B T Leader and his wife Amoret (Weeny) c1950 at the door of Monks Hall, Syleham.

109. Monks Hall, Syleham, 1950s.

and lack of social self-consciousness that eluded Baron. They formed an enduring friendship that lasted until Baron's death. Another wealthy couple, Alfred Henry Michell, a property developer and his wife and son Charles moved into the Depperhaugh, a sprawling Victorian country house in Hoxne parish and also became part of Baron's social circle.

Baron was proud of his creation and was becoming, although rather detached and private, part of the local community. He would never plunge in, as he had at Packwood, but, very occasionally, he opened Wingfield Castle for a local good cause. In 1948 he hosted a party in the courtyard, with tea in the Great Hall, in aid of St Andrew's church restoration fund. He slowly formed friendships with local grandees, his landlord Sir Allan Adair at Flixton, the Tollemaches at Helmingham Hall and the author Ryder Haggard at Ditchingham Hall, from whom both he and Johnny Leader bought unwanted architectural salvage and antiques.

Baron's eye for valuable antiques and pictures improved over the years. In 1948, he bought at Woodbridge Abbey sale a 'Victorian' painting of figures clustered round the virgin, darkened by dirt, layers of varnish and tar. Cleaning revealed a lost centre panel of the triptych The Adoration of the Magi by Martin Schwartz, circa 1500. It hung in his drawing room for many years but was later donated to Norwich Cathedral, where it can be seen as an altar-piece in The Jesus Chapel.

He always kept in touch with his former staff at Packwood. While he seems not to have missed the house, he missed the famous topiary garden, which was never quite recreated at Wingfield though he planted some yews to fashion some topiary hedges. The yew hedges served to make a type of 'walled garden', which they do to this day. He also erected a row of antique statues alongside the northern part of the moat. He was fascinated by the stories of those who had lived at the castle before him. He was particularly taken with the sojourn of the prisoner poet Charles of Orléans and the possibility that he may have introduced tennis to England. He could not find a reference for this, and neither can this author, although Charles used tennis as a metaphor for life in one poem.

Over the years he ditched his Rolls Royce and chauffeur in favour of a Rover 100 and took to using a Raleigh bicycle around the narrow Wingfield lanes, always impeccably dressed in a Savile Row tweed suit but topped off with a green pork-pie hat.

The Gatehouse and Guardroom. One of Baron's last projects, between 1960 and 1962, was the restoration of the gatehouse and guardroom on the first floor. In addition to the total restoration of the four towers and installation of the new lead roof, a new but authentic wooden roof was made, and he also bought a fourteenth century hooded fireplace from Ryder Haggard at Ditchingham Hall. The work was again undertaken by Wm. C. Reade of Aldeburgh. All the sheet glass was replaced with leaded lights; some fine medieval stained glass was purchased as a lot from dealers. The glass excess to his requirements was donated to Norwich cathedral.

110. Graham Baron Ash in his 50s, photograph date unknown.

He found an impressive eighteenth century church clock to add to the internal east tower of the gatehouse to face the courtyard. The restored guardroom proved to be a perfect reception space, where up to eighty people or so can be accommodated.

It is clear from Reade's accounts that the restoration works on the castle, especially to the curtain walls, were extensive.[29] The missing crenellations were restored and the windows in the southern curtain wall were refashioned and tidied up. The surviving walls were made safe, secured from bad weather and neatly finished.

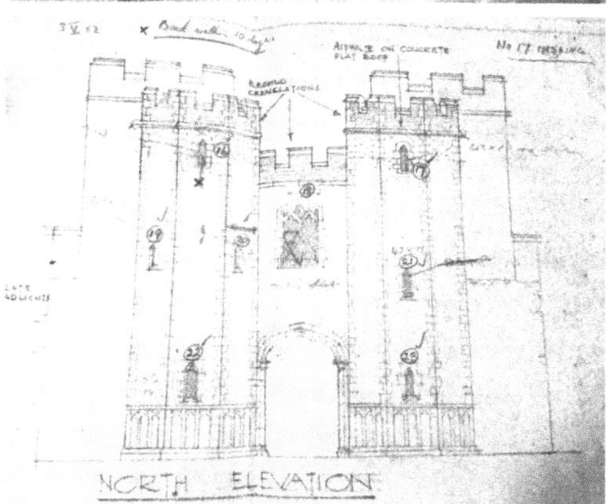

111. Building elevation plans for the restoration of the Gatehouse, Wingfield Castle.

Ash had become an important collector of fine art by the mid 1970s, especially of fine seventeenth century Dutch paintings and still life. He loaned out several of his pictures to exhibitions. But by the late 1960s looking after Wingfield Castle was becoming difficult for him. He wrote to Professor Alastair Smart in New York in 1967:[30]

> For many reasons, largely difficulties in obtaining ANY STAFF at all here at the Castle [I have been ALONE for one year out of fifteen months, I am selling 61 pictures at Christies on October 4. Furniture in the morning of that day [and somewhat unusually] my 61 pictures in the afternoon. The day's sale will be of my things only. I am therefore shutting up FIVE ROOMS here and shall remain in the rest of the house without [I hope] so much difficulty and responsibility. I am now 78 and have found it very difficult to do everything!

The capital letters for emphasis were typical of Baron's letters. The sale at Christies generated £80,000. Ash gave numerous substantial gifts of money to Norwich cathedral. His generosity is recorded in a plaque in the nave. And like so many residents of Wingfield Castle before him, he gave generously and anonymously to St Andrew's Church, Wingfield, paying for the refurbishment of the Lady Chapel, carpet and kneelers, a brocade and silk hanging for behind the altar to mark the coronation in 1953, silver candlesticks and crucifix and numerous other items.

Until the end of his life he corresponded with Dennis Lindup, the gardener at Packwood, and visited occasionally, always impressed with the gardens there, as he well might be. His old butler, Stanley and his wife, sent Baron flowers every birthday; they knew exactly what he would most appreciate.

Although he repeated his offer to buy Wingfield castle three times, Sir Allan Adair refused, so Ash was obliged to continue as tenant. He rarely entertained in later life. His last recorded visitors were in 1975. As time went on he spent more and more time alone, endured a broken hip at the age of eighty-seven, which necessitated a stay in the Norfolk and Norwich Hospital, which he detested, and later suffered a small stroke. He came home with 'two medical orderlies', male nurses who cared for him and engaged some male servants. One drank his cellar dry, one he sacked for serving tinned carrots after being repeatedly asked not to. Then he found Jennifer Pipe, who lived just on the Green. 'If you treated him right, he treated you right. Everything had to be done perfectly but he paid very well. He was a very generous man'.[31] She remembered that he paid in brand new consecutive numbered pound notes, some of which she has kept to this day as a memory of him.

Baron Ash died, aged ninety-one, at 9.15pm on Wednesday 20 February 1980 in his cot bed in a small first floor room at Wingfield Castle. It remains largely unchanged today. He directed that his effects should be sold through Christie, Manson and Woods; the arrangements had been made years earlier. The auction at the castle on 30 May included 337 lots and fetched over £200,000 including £24,000 for the Feuille de Choux tapestry. A rare painting on copper by Breughel the Younger fetched £16,000, a scene on the Grand Canal by Edward Seago, £11,000. The magnificent bed was sold to the National Trust and can now be seen in the Blue Bedroom at Beningbrough Hall, North Yorkshire. Porcelain, silver, plate, books, clocks, furniture and precious objects, all went. His life's work was dispersed for the next generation to enjoy.

With three years to run, the lease on Wingfield Castle expired on Baron's death and ownership reverted to Bridget, Lady Darrell, the eldest daughter of Sir Allan Adair. She decided to sell. Wingfield Castle was bought by a succession of owners and then, in 1987, was fortunate to fall into the hands of the current owners, who have loved and cherished this place, made it their own and brought family life once more to this historic building. So let us leave sleepy Wingfield here, with Michael de la Pole's proud crenellations standing for over six hundred years next to the unchanging Green.

Notes

1 Miles, M., 2004, *The Baron of Packwood*, published by Mike Miles, Birmingham, p. 29.
2 Reference to Wingfield Castle troops belonging to a searchlight battalion was mentioned by G.B. Ash in Miles, M., 2004, *The Baron of Packwood*, published by Mike Miles, Birmingham, p. 29.
3 Robinson, J. M., 2014, *Requisitioned: The British Country House in the Second World War*, Aurum Books, London.
4 Redgrave Park. http://www.redgravepark.co.uk
5 Liddiard R. and Sims, D., 2018, *A Very Dangerous Locality. The landscape of the Sufolk Sandlings in the Second World War*, University of Hertfordshire Press. Chapter 4 The Landscape of Air Defences 1939-45, pp. 129-166.
6 Maps of the locations of searchlight batteries, Figures 4.9-4.11, in 1940, 41 and 42 are shown on pp. 146-148, Liddiard and Sims 2018.
7 Tennyson, J., 2019 edition, *Suffolk Scene*, Lowestoft, Poppyland Publishing, Lowestoft, Biographical Introduction by Murphy E. pp. 7-22. (original edition 1939, published by Blackie.)
8 *London Gazette,* 6 February 1942 2nd Lt K. W. Waller 130682 transfer from the Gordon Highlanders the Royal Artillery.
9 Much of the research on these photos was undertaken by Ian Riley and Dennis Reeves of the Liverpool Scottish Regimental Museum Trust.
10 Land Girls Reunion *Ipswich Star,* 22 August 2003. https://www.ipswichstar.co.uk/news/land-girls-reunion-1-134832
11 Murphy, E., 2018, *Monks Hall, The History of a Waveney Valley Manor*, Lowestoft, Poppyland Publishing. Chapter 14, Richard Horry Winn, 1900-1942, owner of Monks Hall 1935-1936, pp. 200-208.
12 Bloch, M. 2009 Lees-Milne J., *The Life,* John Murray, London, p. 8 and Lees-Milne, J., *Diaries 1946-1947 Caves of Ice*, 27 October 1946.
13 Lees-Milne, J., 2006, Diaries, (ed. Michael Bloch) 1942-54, John Murray, London, p. 270.
14 Horace Stanley, butler at Packwood House 1936-39, Recorded memories, Packwood House archive, The National Trust.
15 Ibid. 12, p. 376.
16 Ibid. 1, p. 16
17 Reports of the Joint War Committee and the Joint War Finance Committee of the British Red Cross Society and the order of St John of Jerusalem in England on Voluntary Aid rendered to the Sick and Wounded at home and Abroad and to British Prisoners of War 1914-1919, HMSO 1921 Ambulance Section pp167-189.
18 Enrolment papers Graham Baron Ash, Royal Flying Corps 1917. TNA WO1914-22, 339/102417.
19 Baden-Powell, O., 1987, *Window on My Heart*, Hodder & Stoughton, London, quoted in The Etaples Mutiny, Wikipedia. https://en.wikipedia.org/wiki/Étaples_mutiny.
20 Baker, K., 2006, *Mutiny, Terrorism, Riots and Murder: a history of sedition in Australia and New Zealand; Dural NSW*, Rosenberg Publishing, quoted in The Etaples Mutiny, Wikipedia. https://en.wikipedia.org/wiki/Étaples_mutiny.
21 Owen, W., 1967, *Collected Letters*, Oxford University Press, Oxford, quoted in The Etaples Mutiny, Wikipedia. https://en.wikipedia.org/wiki/Étaples_mutiny.
22 Hansard. Etaples Mutiny Question by Eric Moonman MP. HC Deb 05 April 1978 vol 947 c152W https://api.parliament.uk/historic-hansard/written-answers/1978/apr/05/etaples-mutiny
23 *Ash wartime diaries*, Packwood House, National Trust.
24 Lees-Milne, J., 2003, *Beneath a Waning Moon, Diaries 1985-1987*, John Murray, London.
25 Lease 1943 referred to in Miles 2004 p. 29
26 Information supplied by Gwyn Turrell, personal communication 24 September 2020.
27 The tomb made of wood is that of Michael de la Pole, 2nd Earl of Suffolk and his wife Katherine Stafford, see Chapter 5.
28 Murphy, E., 2018, *Monks Hall: The History of a Waveney Valley Manor*. Poppyland Publishing, Lowestoft. The story of the Leaders is told in Chapter 16 The Leader Family at Monks Hall, 1937–2016, pp. 209–236.
29 The Accounts of Wm. C. Reade Ltd are now held by their successor M. S. Oakes Ltd, Lowestoft, uncatalogued.

30 Letter Graham Baron Ash to Professor Alastair Smart, 24 August 1967, quote from Miles, 2004 p35. Alastair Smart (1922-1992) Head of the Fine Art Department at the University of Nottingham was an expert on Allan Ramsay. Ash and Smart became acquainted when Ash was researching his purchase of Ramsay's portrait of James Adam, architect. The picture now hangs in the Laing Art Gallery in Newcastle upon Tyne.

31 Ibid. 1, p. 36.

The Changing Castle

Wingfield Castle's Place in History

'It's not a real castle is it?' asked a Suffolk neighbour, dismissing Wingfield rather airily as 'a house that looks like a castle'. 'So name me a proper castle near here then', I challenged, admittedly already knowing that the answer would be one of the great Norman castles of the eleventh or twelfth century. A 'real castle' has a keep (donjon) on a motte (mound) surrounded by a bailey wall enclosure of watchtowers, an impregnable military fortress constructed to withstand siege and invasion, the sort of castle English Heritage souvenir shops sell in cardboard kits so you can build your own.

In Suffolk, Framlingham Castle looks the part, especially when approached from the north, although it never had a tower keep, and Orford Castle, while retaining an impressively polygonal tower keep, has lost its ring of towers and bailey walls. Other early 'proper' castles like Eye and Bungay are merely evocative ruins. Indeed, Suffolk is a little short of surviving Norman castles because not many stone ones were constructed, there being a shortage of stone and flint locally. Most early castles in Suffolk were made of wood atop earth mounds.[1] We need to look further afield for 'real castles'.

112. Orford Castle Keep, Suffolk.

The great castles of Wales, albeit mainly thirteenth century, are emblematic of these manifestations of lordship and conquering power, indeed the apotheosis of imperial domination of the landscape. I spent many happy childhood holidays scrambling over the walls of the castles of Pembrokeshire, absorbing my father's tales of the Middle Ages. Manorbier, Pembroke, Carew and Cilgerran Castles were the perfect setting for my brothers to re-enact Norman warriors attempting to subdue the rebellious Welsh. But I was a girl not much interested in warfare. All I could see were grand mansions, fabulous palaces with great views where I could create my own future dream home. Curiously the historical discourse about the purpose and meaning of castles may, at last, be catching up a little with my childhood imagination.

The historical narrative for the development of castles, from the Norman Conquest to the fourteenth century, has been traditionally couched in terms of their having a predominantly military function. The entrenchment of Norman sovereignty over the rebellious English was the primary purpose. Priority later shifted towards the new military function of combatting treacherous behaviour of Norman barons disputing local lordship and the king's requirement to keep them in check. By the late twelfth and early thirteenth centuries, according to this narrative, the changing nature of warfare, away from sieges towards open battles and the shifting focus from internal domestic strife to war abroad, reduced the need for private castles of the early Norman sort. So gradually the castle went into decline and over the thirteenth and fourteenth centuries lords chose to build grand 'fortified' manor houses with only the appearance of military might. The largely domestic functions becoming pre-eminent as the threat of invasion and local insurrection receded. In other words, 'real castles' outlived their usefulness and only the architectural trappings of defence were left by the fourteenth century. And yet this will not do. Some of Britain's favourite castles, such as Bodiam discussed below, Bolton Castle in Wensleydale, Maxstoke Castle, Warwickshire, Amberley Castle, Sussex are undoubtedly 'real castles' but they were constructed primarily as grand residences in the late fourteenth century. So it is with Wingfield.

In a relatively short space of time, perhaps the last twenty years, a new generation of 'castleographers', as Liddiard has called them, has queried the military historians' orthodoxy.[2] Liddiard has provided an excellent synthesis of the new thinking in his blessedly concise and readable book, *Castles in Context*, which sums up the developmental shifts in the appreciation of the castle's purpose.[3] Charles Coulson first suggested that the military symbolism of solid towers, battlements, crenellations, arrow slits, gun loops and moats may not have been purely, or even primarily, military, but rather a statement of lordly status, a nostalgic emblem of what a lord's palace should look like.[4] Functionalism was important but at times subservient to status.

Other authors have explored the practical 'HQ' functions of a castle, pointing out that early castles were akin to 'office blocks'.[5] The administrative machinery required for running multiple dispersed manors, holding on to territory while imposing a watchful lordship over the productivity of well dispersed land, while keeping rivals at bay, was at least as complex as the task of regional business managers today. The business of the de la Poles was largely administered for over a hundred years from Wingfield Castle. People in charge want others to know that they are; a prestigious building is an easy way to convey the message to underlings. It is no accident that multinational enterprises, even today, choose castle-like structures as emblems of their financial power. Recently Danish-Icelandic artist Olafur Eliasson has completed a fortress-like contemporary style 'castle' as headquarter offices in the Vejle Fjord in Denmark for Kirk Capital, a huge holding and investment company.

And castles were highly popular in Victorian times as themes for local territorial military offices and parade grounds. A prime example is the Gibraltar Barracks in Bury St Edmunds, headquarters of the Anglian regiment built in 1878, although perhaps owing more to an Andalusian Moorish citadel than Norman castle for its architectural provenance. Finsbury Barracks, the home of the Honourable Artillery Company in the City of London, and the Cecily Hill Barracks standing at the entrance to Cirencester Park are others, both built in 1857 for local militias.

McNeill has stressed how the early medieval castle further served the purpose of solidifying the relationship of one lord and his family to his superior lord, establishing a loyalty link and forging both friendship and the continued willing subjection to the king and his immediate family.[6] McNeill explored this theme further in the early medieval castles of Ireland but his ideas could be said to be still relevant in later centuries at Wingfield, for example, in the gift from Henry VIII of the castle and the de la Pole estates to Charles and Mary Brandon. Mary I's subsequent gift of Wingfield to Henry and Frances Jerningham secured the loyalty of the Jerningham family in a similar way. Their dogmatic support of the Catholic church was encouraged by the queen's generosity and then, forever imprinted, on the family.

The aesthetics, the sheer beauty of a castle in its landscape, is increasingly regarded as crucial to our understanding of these monuments. Coulson used Bodiam Castle, Sussex, built contemporaneously with Wingfield, as a case study to illustrate that apparently military buildings were not always constructed with effective military defences, nor built for obvious defensive purposes and their setting was meant to be admired in a striking view.[7] Others came to the same conclusions.[8] For most visitors today, Bodiam is simply the

113. Bodiam Castle, East Sussex.

most perfectly beautiful castle, a suitable setting for Camelot. The National Trust have cleverly engineered an approach to Bodiam that takes the breath away, and the man who built it, Sir Edward Dallingridge (c1346-1393), surely planned it that way.

So I come back to the question 'what is a castle'? I referred, in the second chapter, to John Goodall's definition in his compendium of English castles that 'a castle is the residence of a lord made imposing through the architectural trappings of fortification, be they functional or decorative'.[9] Shifting the focus to the castle's role as residence provides Goodall's readers with a more flexible and convincing narrative of its long history and also allows the author to add no fewer than two hundred years to the life span of 'castles', jettisoning the notion that there are 'real castles' and chronologically later 'others'. If it looks like a castle, well it is a castle! This will serve us well at Wingfield, where the defences are not impregnable, the militaristic appearance seems largely to have been adopted for style reasons. What we have now, in any case, is a wonderful Tudor house inside a ring of older fortifications.

The adoption of a military architectural style in the fourteenth century reflected an aspiration to be seen as part of the ruling class. There are late fourteenth century houses in Suffolk that were not built as castles. Columbine Hall near Stowupland, for example, is of a similar period to Wingfield Castle but is not castle-like. Robert Hotot, the probable builder, was a justice of the peace, but not a member of the nobility. A fourteenth century castle is evidence of high aspiration and a declamatory statement of status. Whether Michael de la Pole and his family gave any thought to such meanings is impossible to know. When a twenty-first century billionaire builds his 'Mcmansion' in the gated enclaves of Surrey, he is primarily thinking of advertising his financial power, not ruminating over architectural niceties.

Wingfield Castle has survived, though in much altered form, for over six hundred years, one of only a handful of similar local survivals from over fifty fortified houses and castles identified in the historic county of Suffolk.[10] Survival of great houses over several hundred years depends a great deal on location, primarily because modern urban development has not destroyed their value as private homes, or, they have remained so large and dominant that they have been transformed into museums, offices and tourist attractions. Smaller fortified houses, like Wingfield, are safer in rural locations. The pattern of villages in mid-Suffolk has changed little since Wingfield Castle was constructed. Remote from the county towns of Ipswich, Lowestoft and Bury St Edmunds, there has been no urban encroachment on Wingfield. Michael de la Pole and his successors would, even today, instantly recognise the triad of St Andrew's church, Wingfield College and his castle.

In Michael's day however, castles were a very familiar part of the landscape. Suffolk was a populous county, near the coast and, of course, the need to control the ambitious Bigod family in Norman times produced Henry II's string of castles, built specifically to rival the Bigods'.[11] Eye, Bungay, Clare, Framlingham and Haughley castles were still extant in the fourteenth century.[12] There remained residual earthworks at Bramfield, Ilketshall St John, Ipswich, Weeting, Freckenham, Thetford and Walton, a fort of the Saxon Shore built by Romans and reused by Normans, still visible until the mid-eighteenth century but now, like so much of the medieval east coast, beneath the waves. There were at least twenty-seven castles in the Suffolk of the late fourteenth century although, it must be admitted, that many were wooded overgrown earthworks left behind from earth and timber originals.[13] Nevertheless, everyone was familiar with the dominant position of castles, if only because they were in contrast to the relatively modest dwellings of even quite wealthy landowners. When William Langland, a contemporary of the first Michael de la Pole, searched for an inspirational metaphor theme for faith for his narrative Piers

Plowman, castles were an obvious choice.

> So you shall come to a court as clear as sunshine
> The moat is as mercy, round that mansion
> And the walls are of Wisdom, against Wicked Will,
> And crenellated with Christendom to save mankind
> Buttressed with Believe if you would see salvation
> The bridge is built of prayer the better to proper you,
> The gates hang him on the hinges of charity
> But the tower of truth is in the set above the sun,

William Langland

Visions concerning Piers the Ploughman, translated by Nevill Coghill 1959.[14]

It was surely the same ubiquity of castles that inspired Charles of Orléans to use the castle metaphor in the poem quoted on page 132.

Much of course has been lost at Wingfield, not least the east and north curtain walls and the majority of the medieval building ranges inside the walls. Now the story of its ownership and successive residents has been told, we can begin to make a tentative suggestion about when these walls were removed. The first likely period is the years between 1538 and 1553 when simple neglect may have led to its deterioration (see pp. 185–209). The process of administration of Henry's Dissolution of the monasteries tied up court and regional officials across the nation, the usual band of administrators who would have supervised vacant royal property were simply preoccupied with the mammoth task of getting control of the assets of religious establishments and disposing of them. The long fifteen year gap, after Brandon left and before Jerningham and his family made Wingfield Castle their home, would allow ample time for deterioration of the fabric and plunder by local people; buildings deteriorate very rapidly if their roofs are denuded of tiles, whether by storms or theft and good oak beams could readily be re-used. We simply do not know when the two curtain walls were dismantled, but the years 1539 to 1553 seem likely, and accords with local oral tradition. We have no recorded evidence of this at all.

The second period when dilapidations may have occurred is the period towards the end of the Jerningham family's ownership between 1610 and 1625, when Wingfield and its park were at the mercy of local people helping themselves to whatever they could lay their hands on. The Jerninghams deep in debt and unable to fight back effectively. The following Catelyn era, though it included the Civil War, seems to have left Wingfield Castle largely unharmed, a result of the deals Richard Catelyn did with the Committee for Compounding with Delinquents, but for three years, between 1644 and 1647, the house was unoccupied.

From the Commonwealth period to the present day the house has been more or less continuously occupied or, if unoccupied, almost always reasonably well maintained by absent owners. Owners and tenants had enough money to maintain the surviving fabric, although, in the twentieth century period between the wars, probably insufficient was spent on maintenance. Baron Ash was obliged to invest a sizeable fortune in restoration after the Second World War and it is to his credit that later owners have been able to build on his legacy to create the comfortable home Wingfield Castle is today.

Notes

1 Higham, R. and Barker P., 1992, *Timber Castles. Exeter Studies in Medieval Europe*, Liverpool University Press, Liverpool.

2 Liddiard, R., 2016, *Late Medieval Castles*, Boydell Press, Woodbridge, Introduction p. 2.

3 Liddiard, R., 2005, *Castles in Context*, Windgather Press, Barnsley.

4 Coulson, C., 1979, Structural Symbolism in Medieval Castle Architecture. *Journal of the British Archaeological Association* p. 132.

5 Gormley, S. and McNeill, T., 2001, Castle or office block? *Archaeology Ireland, Vol 15*, pp. 1-5.

6 McNeill, T., 1992, *English Heritage Book of Castles*, Batsford, London.

7 Coulson, C., 1992, Some Analysis of Bodiam Castle East Sussex, revised in Liddiard R. (ed) 2016 *Late Medieval Castles*, Boydell and Brewer, Woodbridge.

8 Taylor, C., Everson, P. and Wilson-North R., 1990, Bodiam Castle, Sussex, *Medieval Archaeology* p. 34.

9 Goodall J., 2011, *The English Castle: 1066–1650,* Yale University Press, New Haven, Introduction pp. 1-11.

10 List of the medieval fortified sites of the historic county of Suffolk. Gatehouse Gazetteer and bibliography of the medieval castles, fortifications and palaces of England Wales and the islands, http://www.gatehouse-gazetteer.info/Indexs/EngCounty/Suffolk.html.

11 Bates, M., 1974, *Regional Military Histories: East Anglia*, Osprey Publishing, Oxford, Chapter 4 The Middle Ages, pp. 61-90.

12 Redstone, V. B., 1903, Notes on Suffolk Castles. Haughley castle and its Park, *Proceedings of the Suffolk Institute for Archaeology and History, Vol XI*, p. 301 online at http://suffolkinstitute.pdfsrv.co.uk, [accessed 5 June 2020].

13 McAndrew, D., 2008, PhD thesis, University of London, *Catalysts and Constraints of castle-building in Suffolk c1066-1200, Vol 1*, Chapter 1 Introduction pp. 33-39.

14 Langland W., c1377, *Visions concerning Piers the Ploughman*, translated by Coghill, N., Phoenix House, London, 3rd edn 1959, p. 47.

Appendix: de la Pole Family Tree

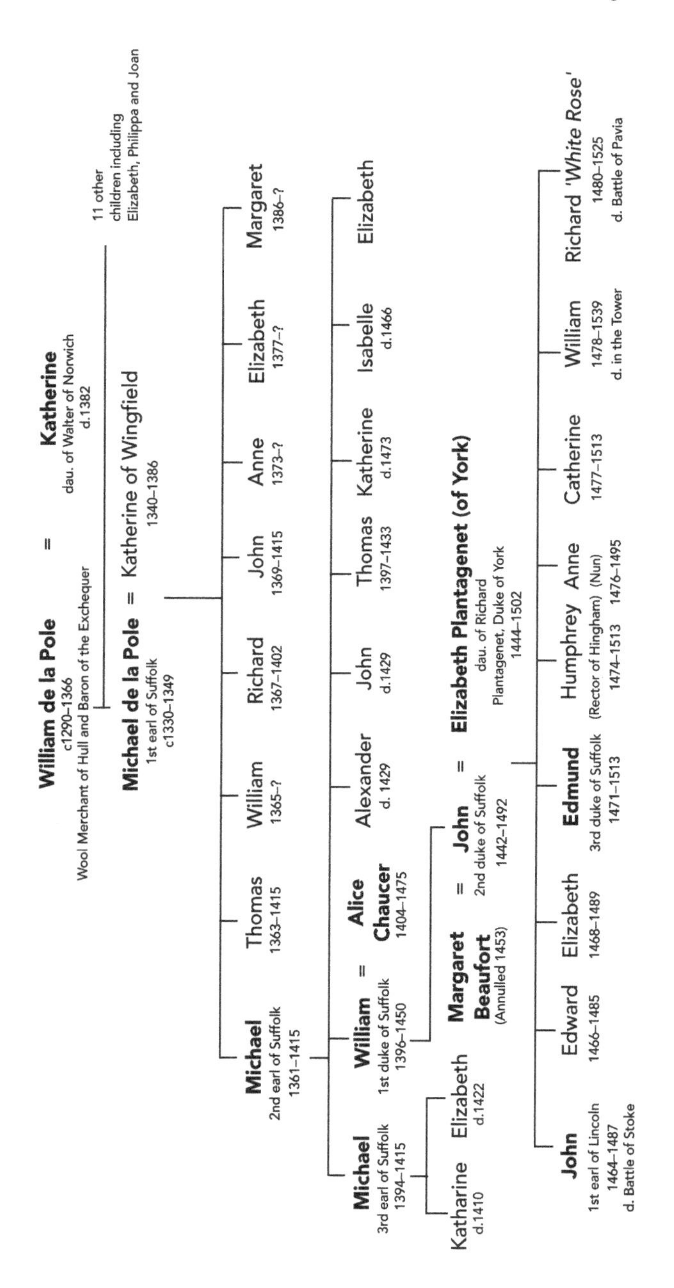

Illustrations with credits

Acknowledgements

1. Map of Suffolk showing places in the book, credit: Poppyland Ltd collection, contains Ordnance Survey data © Crown copyright and database right 2010–19

Chapter: Introduction

2. Illustration from *I Capture the Castle*, by Dodie Smith, drawing by Ruth Steed from a sketch by Dodie Smith, 1948.
3. Gatehouse and south curtain wall, Wingfield Castle, etching by William Byrne 1780 after a watercolour by Thomas Hearne, public domain.
4. Jerningham House, within Wingfield Castle, photo c1950, credit: Michael Lyndon-Stanford.

Chapter: A Castle Takes Shape, 1385

5. Wingfield Castle Gatehouse, 2019, credit: author.
6. Early eighteenth century print of Huntingfield Old Hall, credit: plate 185 p.189, Sandon, E., 1977, *Suffolk Houses*, Baron Publishing, Woodbridge (company dissolved in 1980s). Sandon's Papers deposited in Suffolk Record Office do not include this old print. Copyright on published photo of sketch may be owned by Sandon's son and or descendants, who cannot be traced at the time of publication.
7. Mettingham Castle. Mettingham Castle, from an 18th century print, c1735 Unidentified sketch after Buck, credit: author's collection.
8. Suggested map of Wingfield Castle and deer park, credit: Robert Liddiard.
9. Petition by William Frombold, c1326, the National Archives Petitions to the King and Council, credit: National Archives 1326/7, TNA Ref SC 8/1/14/680.

Chapter: The First Building

10. Aerial view of Wingfield Castle c2000, credit: Michael Lyndon-Stanford.
11. A 16th century drawing of Suffolk Palace, the de la Pole mansion in Hull, by John Rogers c1542, now demolished, public domain licence, credit: British Library Shelfmark: Cotton MS Augustus I ii 13

Chapter: The Origins of the de la Pole Family

Chapter: The Rise of Michael de la Pole

Chapter: The Later Career of Michael de la Pole

altered early portrait c1390, public domain, Wikimedia Commons user CharlieRCD.

28. The Coronation of Anne of Bohemia as Queen of England, illustration from Liber Regalis, illuminated manuscript 14th century, credit: Westminster Abbey Library MS 38.
29. Robert de Vere fleeing Radcot Bridge after the 1387 battle; taken from the Gruthuse manuscript of Froissart's Chroniques (c1475), public domain.
30. Charterhouse seen in a woodcut from Thomas Gent's 1735 *History of Hull*, a facsimile published in 1869 by MC Peck & Son of Hull, credit: Hull City Archive.
31. Wingfield College, credit: author.

Chapter: The de la Poles Recover Their Home, 1387–1415

32. Michael de la Pole, 2nd earl of Suffolk and Katherine Stafford, his wife, tomb monument in St. Andrew's Church Wingfield c 1415, Creative Commons 4.0 licence, Wikimedia Commons user Eebahgum.
33. The murder of Thomas of Woodstock from Froissart's Chroniques, public domain.

Chapter: The Most Despised Man in England

34. Foliate initial 'S' with the heraldic arms of William de la Pole at the beginning of John Lydgate's Siege of Thebes, 1425-50, credit: British Library, MS Arundel 119, f 4.
35. Ewelme Manor or Palace, extended after 1430 by William and Alice de la Pole. 18th century print later coloured, by Nathaniel and Samuel Buck 1789, credit: author.
36. The Siege of Rouen 1419, from Vigiles du roi Charles VII, 1490s manuscript, Martial d'Auvergne's History of the Hundred Years, Paris, BnF, département des Manuscrits, Français 5054, public domain.
37. William de la Pole's personal heraldic emblem, an ape's clog. From Fox Davies, A. C., 1909, *A Complete Guide to Heraldry*, figure 682, public domain.
38. Thomas Montagu, 4th earl of Salisbury is fatally injured at the siege of Orléans in 1428. Illustration from Les Vigiles de Charles VII, manuscrit de Martial d'Auvergne, c1484, BnF, Manuscrit Français 5054, folio 54 verso, public domain.

Chapter: William de la Pole's Rise and Fall 1430–1450

39. Alice, duchess of Suffolk, alabaster tomb effigy St Mary's Church, Ewelme, Oxfordshire, Creative Commons 3.0 licence, Wikimedia Commons user Sciencebloke.

40. Portrait of Charles duke of Orléans 1472 from Statutes, Ordonnances and armorial of the Order of the Golden Fleece, National Library of the Netherlands, Gérard collection no. A 27, public domain.
41. Margaret of Anjou. A detail from the Talbot Shrewsbury Book, British Library Royal 15 E vi , 1430-60, public domain, credit: wikimedia Commons https://commons.wikimedia.org/wiki/File:MargaretAnjou.jpg
42. Murder of the duke of Suffolk', from Doyle, J. W. E., 1864, *A Chronicle of England B.C. 55–A.D. 1485*, p. 396, Longman, Roberts & Green, London, artist: James William Edmund Doyle, public domain.

Chapter: Surviving William

43. Sketch of Wingfield Castle from southwest, *Church leaflet St Andrew's Wingfield*, by Graham Redelsperger, credit: Graham Redelsperger.
44. Scything hay 15th century England, public domain, credit: British Library MS Royal 14 E VIf.
45. The arms of John de la Pole, 2nd duke of Suffolk (1442–1491/2), KG in a 15th century stained glass window at the Church of St Mary the Virgin, Iffley, Oxfordshire, John donated the gothic windows to the church after becoming owner of nearby Donington manor, public domain, wikimedia commons user Motacilla.
46. Tomb of Alice de la Pole, duchess of Suffolk, St Mary's Church, Ewelme. Public domain, credit: Alastair Rae.

Chapter: The Last of the de la Poles at Wingfield Castle

47. Arms of John de la Pole, earl of Lincoln, Creative Commons 4.0 licence, wikimedia commons user Thom.lanaud + elements from Sodacan.
48. Tudor Rose Emblem, Creative Commons 4,0 licence, wikimedia commons user Sodacan.
49. Margaret of York, duchess of Burgundy, wife of Charles the Bold, Netherlandish portrait unknown artist c 1468, credit: Musee de Louvre, Paris.
50. The alabaster tomb effigies of John 2nd duke of Suffolk (d1492) and Elizabeth, duchess of Suffolk (d 1503), credit: unknown.
51. Richard de la Pole, wearing French clothing. A portrait once thought to be a French nobleman, but the hat badge is of a white hart, the emblem of Richard II. Portrait sold at Christie's 2013, credit: unknown.

Chapter: Glamorous New Tenants for Wingfield Castle, 1514–1544

52. Charles Brandon, duke of Suffolk, engraving by Bartolozzi after a chalk drawing by Hans Holbein the Younger c.1535. Black and coloured chalks,

Chapter: Wingfield Castle reborn, 1553–1624

Chapter: Jerningham House

68. The western façade showing the exterior of Jerningham House, photo c1950, credit: Michael Lyndon-Stanford.
69. The Jerningham Crest, 'out of a ducal coronet or, a demi falcon, wings expanded', redrawn, credit: The Bibliographical Society of London. British Armorial Bindings and University of Toronto
70. The niche over the porch with modern stone head: credit: author.
71. Chimney Stack on Jerningham House, photo from F A Girling 1934, credit: Suffolk Institute of Archaeology and History.
72. Photo of Staircase Wing, credit: author.
73. The '17th century staircase' constructed on 20th century oak supports, credit author.
74. The Great Chamber c1950, credit: Michael Lyndon-Stanford.

Chapter: The Catelyn Family, 1624–1702

75. Sir Neville Catelyn (1634-1702) and his first wife, Lady Dorothea Catelyn, attributed to Robert Walker. These portraits are thought to have originally hung in Wingfield Castle. credit: unknown.
76. Kirby Cane Hall today, credit: Hermione Crisp.
77. Memorial to Thomas and Neville Catelyn who died in infancy 1662 and 1665, All Saints Church, Kirby Cane, credit: author
78. Portrait of the older Neville Catelyn, credit: Norfolk Museums Service.

Chapter: Wingfield Castle in the Eighteenth Century

79. Thomas Hearne, watercolour of Wingfield Castle c1780, copy print, credit: Michael Lyndon-Stanford.
80. Three Ladies of the Leman Family and their Dogs on a Terrace, by Benjamin Ferrers 1728, credit: Tate Gallery.
81. The Arms of Sir John Leman on the wall of Beccles and District Museum, formerly his endowed school, credit: author.
82. The Church of All Saints and St Margaret, Pakefield, credit: author.
83. Southeast corner of Wingfield Castle moat showing foot drawbridge restored by Robert Leman 1768. Drawing by G E Chambers 1930. P 87 in M R James 1930 Suffolk and Norfolk: A Perambulation of the Two Counties with Notices of their History and their Ancient Buildings, Dent and Sons, public domain.

Chapter: The Early Nineteenth Century at Wingfield Castle

84. Print of view of Wingfield Castle, Wingfield, Suffolk by Edward Dayes, 1791 (London 1763-1804), original pencil and watercolour, credit: MLS.

Chapter: Wingfield Castle, An Ordinary Farmhouse, 1856–1939

Chapter: The Renaissance of Wingfield Castle, 1938–1980

National Trust.

102. Photo Packwood House, public domain, wikimedia commons user Bs0u10e01
103. The Arms of Graham Baron Ash, derived from Landed Families of Britain and Ireland, redrawn, credit: Nicholas Kingsley.
104. *Portrait of* Portrait of Baron Ash, by Dennis Dring RA, 1943, hangs at Packwood House, National Trust, credit: Bridgeman Images & The Estate of Dennis William Dring.
105. The Great Chamber with Queen Anne period bed reputedly by Francis Lapiere (photograph 1950), credit: Michael Lyndon-Stanford.
106. Wingfield Castle west wall, south-west tower and part of south wall, left 1945 before restoration and right 1950, credit: Michael Lyndon-Stanford.
107. The dining room, Wingfield Castle 1950, credit: Michael Lyndon-Stanford.
108. John (Johnny) B. T. Leader and his wife Amoret (Weeny) c 1950 at the door of Monks Hall, Syleham, credit: Monks Hall Archive.
109. Monks Hall, Syleham, credit: Monks Hall Archive.
110. Graham Baron Ash in his 50s, photograph date unknown, credit: National Trust.
111. Packwood House, National Trust Collection NT 557552.1.2., credit: National Trust.
112. Building elevation plans for the restoration of the Gatehouse, Wingfield Castle, Reade of Aldeburgh, November 1960. Original plans by M. S. Oakes Ltd, credit: author.

Chapter: The Changing Castle

113. Orford Castle Keep, credit: author.
114. Bodiam Castle East Sussex, Creative Commons 2.0 licence, wikimedia commons, photo user Allen Watkin.

Further Reading

Castles and other buildings

Brunskill R. W., 1985 republished 2006, *Traditional Buildings of Britain: An Introduction to Vernacular Architecture*, Cassells, London.
Emery, A., 2000, *Greater Medieval Houses of England and Wales Vol II East Anglia, Central England and Wales*, Cambridge University Press.
Goodall, John 2011 *The English Castle: 1066-1650,* Yale University Press.
Liddiard, R. (ed), 2016, *Late Medieval Castles*, Boydell, Woodbridge.
Liddiard, R., 2005, *Castles in Context*, Windgather Press.
McNeill, T., 1992, *English Heritage Book of Castles*, Batsford.
Sandon, E., 1977, *Suffolk Houses: a Study of Domestic Architecture*, Baron, Woodbridge.

Suffolk history

Amor, N., 2016, *From Wool to Cloth, the Triumph of the Suffolk Clothier*, Bungay.
Bailey, M., 2015, *Medieval Suffolk*, Boydell, Woodbridge.
Bloore, P. and Martin, E. (eds), 2015, *Wingfield College and its Patrons*, Boydell, Woodbridge.
Dymond D and Northeast, P., 1995, A History of Suffolk, Phillimore, Sussex.
Holmes, C., 1974, *The Eastern Association in the English Civil War*, Cambridge, Cambridge University Press.
Howkins, A., 1985, *Poor Labouring Men. Rural Radicalism in Norfolk 1870-1923*, Routledge, Kegan Paul.
Liddiard R., and Sims, D., 2018, *A Very Dangerous Locality. The landscape of the Suffolk Sandlings in the Second World War*, University of Hertfordshire Press.
MacCulloch, D., 1986, *Suffolk and the Tudors, Politics and Religion in an English County, 1500-1600,* Oxford University Press, Oxford.
Murphy, E., 2018, *Monks Hall, The History of a Waveney Valley Manor*, Poppyland Publishing, Lowestoft.
Robinson, J. M., 2014, *Requisitioned: The British Country House in the Second World War*, Aurum Books.

Characters in the book

Borman, T., 2018, *Henry VIII and the Men who Made Him*, Hodder and Stoughton, London.
Bryson, S., 2018, *La Reine Blanche: Mary Tudor, a life in letters*, Amberley, Stroud.
Castor, H., 2014, *Joan of Arc, a History*, Faber and Faber, London.
Castor, H., 2005, *Blood & Roses: The Paston Family and the Wars of the Roses*, Faber and Faber, London.
Curran, S., 2011, *The English Friend: A Life of William de la Pole, first duke of Suffolk*, Lasse Press, Norwich.
Gunn, S. J., 1988, *Charles Brandon, Duke of Suffolk: c.1484-1545*, Blackwell.
Head, D. M., 1995, *The Ebbs and Flow of Fortune, the Life of Thomas Howard, 3rd duke of Norfolk*, University of Georgia Press, Athens.
Horrox, R., 1983, *The de la Poles of Hull*, East Yorkshire Local History Society, East Yorkshire.
http://www.bbc.co.uk/history/british/middle_ages/birth_of_parliament_01.shtml.
Jones, M., 2018, *The Black Prince, England's Greatest Medieval Warrior*, Pegasus books, New York.
Saul, N., 1997, *Richard I*, Yale University Press, New Haven.

Battles and Wars

Baldwin, D., 2006, *Stoke Field, the Last Battle of the Wars of the Roses*, Pen & Sword Books Ltd, Barnsley.
Barker, J., 2005 (new edition 2015), *Agincourt: the King, the Campaign and the Battle Little*, Brown, London.
Curry, A., 2005, *Agincourt: a New History*, Tempus, Stroud.

General History

BBC History Online, Dodd, G., 2011, *The Birth of Parliament*—http://www.bbc.co.uk/history/british/middle_ages/birth_of_parliament_01.shtml.
Kelly, J., 2006, *The Great Mortality: An Intimate History of the Black Death, the Most Devastating Plague of All Time*, Harper Collins, New York.
Loades, D., 1991 (2nd ed'n), *The Reign of Mary Tudor: politics, government and religion in England 1553-58*, Routledge.
Porter, S., 2000, *The Great Plague*, Sutton Publishing.
Roskell J. S., Clark L., Rawcliffe, C., 1993, *The History of Parliament: the House of Commons 1386-1421*, ed. Boydell and Brewer, Woodbridge.
Rubin, M., 2005, *The Hollow Crown: A History of Britain in the Late Middle Ages*, Penguin Books.

Index

A

B

C

D

I

J

K

L

M

N

O

P

R

S

T

U

Y